social deviance

Edited by

Ronald A. Farrell
State University of New York at Albany

and

Victoria Lynn Swigert
College of the Holy Cross

J. B. Lippincott Company
New York / Hagerstown / Philadelphia / San Francisco

SOCIAL DEVIANCE, Second Edition

Distributed in Great Britain by Blackwell Scientific Publications
London   Oxford   Edinburgh

Library of Congress Cataloging in Publication Data

Farrell, Ronald A, comp.
  Social deviance.

  Includes bibliographical references and index.
  1. Deviant behavior—Addresses, essays, lectures.
2. Conformity—Addresses, essays, lectures.
I. Swigert, Victoria Lynn, joint comp. II. Title.
HM291.F27 1978   301.6'2   78-6566
ISBN 0-397-47385-0

social deviance

To Judi

contents

part four

part five

preface

The first edition of *Social Deviance* was guided by three organizational objectives: to present a comprehensive coverage of the major sociological theories of deviance; to show how these different perspectives might be brought together to obtain a more complete understanding of deviance causation; and to emphasize that the social processes that produce and maintain deviance are essentially the same ones that produce and maintain conformity.

These parallel themes have been retained in the second volume. At the same time, the intent has been to incorporate current developments in deviance causation. Thus, in addition to the selections contained in the original work, this edition presents a number of theoretical efforts that have emerged in recent years. These contributions both elaborate the more general theoretical perspectives and significantly expand the integrative theme of the book.

It should be made clear that the work does not include critiques of the several theories nor does it deal with related research. Rather, in order first to familiarize students with the range of possible explanations of deviance, attention is focused exclusively on the presentation of assumptions central to the classical and contemporary statements of the discipline.

Deviance literature is characterized by one of the more extensive, yet fragmented bodies of theory in the field of sociology. In addition, while much of this theory explains deviance in terms of the same social processes used to explain conformity, deviance continues to be regarded as abnormal or pathological behavior. *Social Deviance* addresses these issues by examining the possibilities for an integration of the different theories through a general sociological approach to behavior. In this manner, non-conformity is conceptualized as a multifaceted outcome of normal, rather than aberrant, social processes.

The theories presented have been organized under the following headings: *The Functionalist Approach, Theories Focusing on Societal Definitions, The Interactionist Perspective, Anomie Theory, Social and Cultural Support Theory, Theories of Social and Cultural Conflict,* and *Integrative and Processual Theories of Deviance.* These perspectives deal with factors that provide the fundamental guidelines within which deviance may be understood. While they traditionally have been treated as alternative and often competing explanations of deviance, each may be viewed as contributing to a more thorough understanding of the phenomenon. That is, each perspective may be construed as focusing on a particular aspect of the more total process of deviance creation.

The theories are presented in an order that reflects the processual nature of behavior. Each perspective is prefaced with a synopsis of the articles included in the section as well as a statement of the points at which the particular approach merges with preceding ones. The first part of the book focuses on the structural origins of non-conformity by dealing with the functions of deviance for the maintenance of the social system; Part Two attends to the nature of social definitions and their influence on the creation of deviance categories; Part Three focuses on the interpersonal processes occurring between the deviant and reacting others and the effects that this interaction has on the definition of self; Part Four examines the strain toward adaptation that the rejected non-conform- ist experiences and the modes of adaptation that are available to him; Part Five deals with the learning process through which the deviant takes on the normative patterns of a supportive subculture in an attempt to adapt to societal rejection; and Part Six deals with the inevitable conflict that exists between subcultures and the larger society and suggests that this conflict serves to reinforce the original definitions and reactions. Finally, the last section of the book contains several works which illustrate more explicitly a num- ber of alternative methods by which the major theories may be integrated toward the development of a general theory of social deviance.

The selections presented in this volume represent theories that are central to the discipline. By exploring the several conceptual frameworks and pointing to the possibilities for their integration, we have intended not only to familiarize students with the basic perspectives on deviance but to emphasize their potential for ex- planation. The study of non-conformity, if it is to be cumulative, must rely upon a sound theoretical base. All too often, however, research is without reference to theory or establishes that link in the most cursory and, frequently, *ex post facto* manner. Through a comprehensive and integrative treatment of the wide spectrum of approaches to deviance, we have hoped to equip the student with the richness and flexibility of a theoretical tradition so critical to the scientific study of deviant behavior.

Ronald A. Farrell
Albany, New York

Victoria Lynn Swigert
Worcester, Massachusetts

January, 1978

acknowledgments

Several persons have offered suggestions and comments which have been helpful in the development of this work. For their contributions, we are particularly grateful to Professors Leslie T. Wilkins of the State University of New York at Albany, John A. Winget of the University of Cincinnati, Frank F. Furstenberg of the University of Pennsylvania, and Charles H. Logan of the University of Connecticut.

We also wish to thank Senior Editor A. Richard Heffron and the editorial staff of J. B. Lippincott Company for their thoroughness and tact in all matters affecting our manuscript.

General Introduction

Theories of Personal and Social Disorganization

Earliest developments in deviance theory attributed non-conforming behavior to various forms of personal and social disorganization. That is to say that pathological conditions within the individual and, later, within the social environment were seen as the primary causes of such behavior. The *psychosoma* theorists sought the origins of déviance in abnormal physical and mental characteristics. For example, unusual variations in height, weight, skull size, intelligence, and most recently, chromosome structure, have been taken as signs of criminal potential. Similar in approach were the *social disorganization* theorists. This perspective maintained that criminal behavior was not a product of inherent physical or psychological properties, but rather a manifestation of the breakdown of social organization. Factors associated with urban-industrialized society, such as rapid social change, cultural diversity, and impersonality, were seen as major contributors to the problem of crime. The secondary relations that characterized the city, for example, meant the erosion of primary ties and consequently, an erosion of the traditional norms and behavioral definitions that are transmitted through primary groups such as the family, neighborhood, and small community.

The premises contained in these and other variations of disorganization theory required that deviant behavior be considered a unique phenomenon to be studied apart from other phenomena that occurred in society. It was thought that the non-conformer, by virtue of his physical, mental, or social deviation, had escaped the more universal processes that shape everyday life. Supportive research for these views was, however, disappointing. Predictions of criminality from physical and personality profiles proved to be erroneous. At the same time, theories of social disorganization failed to account for the persistence of conforming behavior among "disorganized" groups as well as for the relative stability of rates of deviance over time.

The theories presented in this work represent major departures from the premises of disorganization theory. Rather than viewing the deviant as a product of personal or social pathologies, each of these perspectives contributes to the notion that deviance results from the same processes that shape conformity. A major significance of this theme lies in its implications for the development of a general theory of human behavior.

The Functionalist Approach

The first perspective to be dealt with is *functionalism.* A major premise of the functionalist approach is that personal or social disorganization *does not* underlie deviant behavior. Rather, deviance is seen as a major factor in the very organization of a social system. The question is raised, in fact, of whether or not society could exist at all without such behavioral polarities. Non-conformity calls attention to the entire range of behavior for which a society has developed normative definitions. As such, it serves to demarcate acceptable limits as well as to ratify the value of conformity. This primary assumption within functionalism makes a crucial contribution toward a generalized theory of behavior. The recognition that both conformity and deviance represent varying degrees of the same dimension demands that we examine both behaviors in terms of the same general social processes.

Theories Focusing on Societal Definitions

Another important contribution to this approach comes from the *theories focusing on societal definitions.* The definitional approach has its roots in social disorganization theory. W. I. Thomas, a major contributor to both perspectives, posited, for example, that modernization and industrialization led to a breakdown of common behavioral definitions. The legacy of Thomas and his successors, however, has been to contribute substantially to a theory of both deviance and conformity.

The concept of societal definition contains several important elements. First, the *definition of the situation* represents the medium through which behavioral norms are communicated. The generality of this proposition easily lends itself to an application to the previous comments on functionalism. Norms limiting behavior patterns must, of course, be communicated. This communication of norms occurs through the positive and negative sanction of human acts as they occur in society. Through the repeated application of these definitions of the situation, behavioral boundaries become established for conformer and deviant alike.

Also within this theoretical tradition is contained the concept of *diversity of definitions*. This is a notion that will become especially important in the discussion of cultural diversity and conflict. It suffices here to note that behaviors, and the norms that make them salient, are group specific. In a complex society, normative and behavioral uniformity is therefore an unrealistic expectation. Rather, there exists a plurality of codes for living that are positively or negatively evaluated by differing groups. It is the subsequent clash of these definitional frameworks which has important consequences for deviance and conformity.

The definition of the situation is also a tool for defining *individuals* as conformers or deviants, as well as for communicating general behavioral categories. Thus, as with the functionalist argument, an emphasis of societal definition theorists is to examine processes that act on individuals and their behavior. From this perspective, acceptable and unacceptable behavior, conformity and deviance, or normality and abnormality occur independent of the mental, physical, or moral characteristics of the individuals involved. They are a matter of social definition.

The Interactionist Perspective

This concern with the impact of the social definition on the individual leads to a discussion of a third theoretical framework, the *interactionist perspective*. This approach has developed out of the more general social psychological theory of *symbolic interactionism*. The fundamental assumption of symbolic interactionism is that participation in a social system is a function of shared symbols. Individuals rely on these symbols for the expression of needs, values, and expectations, as well as for the development of a personal identity. It is through the internalization of the definitions of the social system that we become capable of interaction within it; similarly, it is through the interactive process that self definitions become formulated. In a very real sense, according to this perspective, by means of the acquisition of symbols society becomes represented in the individual.

As the social definition is the medium by which behavior categories are determined, then, the symbolic communication of these definitions is the medium by which behavior comes to have personal meaning for the members of a social system. A significant aspect of this interaction that occurs between the individual and society is the confirmation of status and role. Beliefs and behaviors appropriate to age, sex, class, and other socially important positions are acquired through symbolic participation within the individual's most significant groups. The process is essentially the same for all members of society. This is the theme that has characterized the several contributions to symbolic interaction theory since the early works of Charles Horton Cooley.

Developing out of this general social psychological approach is the *interactionist perspective* on deviance, often refered to as *labeling theory*. As with symbolic interactionism, the interactionist perspective on deviance emphasizes that social definitions are powerful forces in the formation of individual behavior. The social definition, these theorists maintain, is particularly important because of its impact on the individual's definition of self. Once a person's behavior becomes defined as deviant, the definitional pressures that are leveled against him have implications for his personal identity. If the community reacts toward him as though he were deviant, he comes to identify himself as such. The major importance of this perspective, then, is in its intensified focus on the creation of deviant identities through the process of symbolic interaction.

Anomie Theory

Anomie theory presents still further dimensions toward the development of a general theory of behavior. The theoretical perspectives thus far discussed emphasize the social functions of deviance and the processes by which such behavioral categories become established within a social system and within the personal identities of its members. Related to these approaches, anomie theorists treat the social structural properties that generate the behavioral differences that come to be defined as appropriate or inappropriate.

A major point of emphasis in anomie theory is its proposition that opportunities for approved behavior are differentially distributed in society. The primary criterion for this distribution is social class.

When individuals have acquired a committment to the norms that define behavior but, at the same time, are denied access to the modes of expressing that committment, the problem of alternatives arises. The development of adaptive behavior that varies from social acceptance is often the outcome.

A related contribution of anomie theory is in its explanation of the emergence of *deviant subcultures*. The concept of subculture takes on a clearer meaning when it is viewed in light of the previous discussion of the impact of culture on behavior. For it is principally in terms of the theory of subcultures that the contributions of anomie theorists merge with these other perspectives.

Once a social system systematically induces the need for alternative behavior, it also generates the need for those thus affected to develop a system of roles and definitions which supports that behavior. The resultant culture (subordinate to the larger culture of which it is a part) becomes a system of shared symbols, communicated through the process of interaction, and out of which subculturally sanctioned roles, definitions, and personal identities emerge. It is within this circle of significant others, then, that the individual learns the identity and behavior appropriate to his role in society. The subculture, therefore, performs the same function as any other reference group. The same process of interaction and shared meaning operate within the cultures of both deviant and non-deviant groups.

Social and Cultural Support Theory

This is also the theme of *social and cultural support theory,* with an important difference. The theoretical conclusions arrived at by anomie theorists are founded on the assumption of an imperfect integration of certain culturally defined goals and the institutionalized means for their attainment. The notion of an imperfectly integrated social system reveals the social disorganization origins of this approach. Social and cultural support theory, on the other hand, makes no such assumption of normative monolithism. Rather, the concept of normative heterogeneity is an integral part of the theory. In order to understand criminal behavior, states this perspective, the theorist must recognize that within cultural pluralism are also found varying ratios of definitions that are favorable or unfavorable to the commission of crime. These definitions are transmitted to the members of different subcultures through the same general processes of interaction discussed above. Once again, the conclusion arrived at is that behavior is a product of participation in a cultural (or subcultural) system. These learning processes are uniformly applicable to all behavior forms, criminal or non-criminal.

Theories of Social and Cultural Conflict

The final theoretical approach we have called *theories of social and cultural conflict*. The title was intended to convey the fact that while, in general, these theories treat deviant behavior as a product of conflicting culture systems, the origins of the approaches are distinct. The culture conflict tradition has its roots in the study of the patterns of behavior that emerged when immigrant groups settled in the United States. The problem of conformity, these theorists argued, is in the problem of the contact of disparate culture systems whose members have been socialized to different and sometimes mutually exclusive behavioral definitions. The second, and more recent, trend in the development of conflict theory focuses around the political implications of value pluralism. The concept of a conflict between opposing cultural systems was generalized to include the notion of interest group competition. In a politically organized society, such as our own, it is inevitable that groups will compete for the right to impose a single set of norms and values on all other groups. This is the reward of political victory. Political and legal subordination, on the other hand, is the price of defeat.

Toward an Integrative-Processual Theory

The theories included in this work cover a range of approaches to what we feel is a common theme. Each perspective adds to the development of a general theory of behavior. The contribution of the *functionalist approach* lies in the proposition that both conforming and non-conforming behavior are intimately related in society. Without the boundary maintenance function of the deviant these theorists question whether or not social organization is possible at all. *Theories focusing on societal definitions* examine the medium by which behavior becomes recognized as conforming or deviating. The definition makes visible those areas that lie beyond acceptable limits. In addition to this structural arguement, this perspective states that the definition is also the vehicle by which individuals are identified as occupying acceptable or unacceptable roles in society. Approaching this issue from a more social psychological level, the effort of the *interactionist perspective* is to identify those processes by which the definitions become represented in the individual. The focus shifts somewhat with the contributions of *anomie theory*. For the concern here is with the discovery of the sources of non-conforming behavior. In that effort, these theorists call our attention to cultural diversity. Groups of people who do not have full access to the dominant cultural system, band together in an effort to cope with their exclusion. The result of such problem solving behavior is the rise of subcultures. *Social and cultural support theory* also treats the problem of diversity. It maintains that while the behavior patterns within cultures and subcultures may differ, and in fact, be antagonistic, the process of acquiring these patterns is similar across all groups. Finally, *conflict theory* adds that cultural diversity means political competition. The right of imposition of normative standards and behavioral definitions becomes the right of those groups who are successful competitors.

All these theories, regardless of their particular approach to the problem of non-conforming behavior, share the assumption that the deviant is a product of the same learning and interaction processes that act upon the conformist. Implied in the commonality of this theme that has characterized so much of the literature on deviance, is a call for systematic integration of these theoretical perspectives. Several theorists have made promising beginnings toward that end, and their work is included in the final section. It is hoped that the organization of this book, as well as the suggestions included for theoretical integration, will not only encourage others to explore alternative strategies for the study of deviant behavior, but will also constitute a necessary step toward the development of a general theory of behavior.

part One

The Functionalist Approach

It is commonly thought that deviant behavior implies a condition that is pathological and disorganizing to society. But the very fact that deviance has been a persistent feature of all societies has led a number of sociologists to question this assumption and to reexamine the nature of deviance and its implications for the benefit of the system. Thus, the theorists presented in this section suggest that deviance is an outcome of normal social processes and serves to maintain social systems.

Emile Durkheim held that deviance is not an intrinsic quality of behavior as such, but is rather the definition accorded that behavior by the *collective conscience*. The collective conscience maintains both a cause and effect relationship with deviance. Because the *collective type* (that is, the total representation of social norms and values) exists in no one individual, there is a tendency toward non-conforming behavior. If the collective conscience is sensitive and exacting, much of this behavior is likely to be defined as deviant. The defining process and the persons so defined then come to serve the function of maintaining the boundaries for the rest of society. Thus deviance, itself a product of collective definition, provides the social system with a vivid demarcation between acceptable and unacceptable behavior.

An additional dimension of the boundary-maintaining function of deviance is provided by George Herbert Mead. Like Durkheim, Mead saw that the visibility of the deviant serves to reinforce the solidarity of the members of society by distinguishing between the virtuous and the transgressor. This solidarity depends upon the activity of defending the social system from the threat of the deviant. Mead argues, for example, that it is only in terms of the protection of property and property relations against the deviant that property assumes a value. Thus, there is no intrinsic valuation of social relationships except in their defense from encroachment. Mead terms this phenomenon the *sacrificial value of social relationships*. It is also a phenomenon that precludes reintegration of the nonconformist into the social system. For, if what is valuable in a society is defined in terms of the threat to those values, the visibility and isolation of the deviant become mandatory.

While Durkheim and Mead used these ideas to explain deviance at the societal level, they may also be applied to the small group situation as well. In this regard, Robert Dentler and Kai Erikson suggest that groups induce the development of deviance in the same way that they induce leadership. The function of both role occupants is to establish the identity of the group by defining the range of collective performance. In addition to boundary maintenance, the deviant also functions to validate the reward system. Reflecting Mead's argument on the sacrificial value of relationships, Dentler and Erikson suggest that rewards for conformity become desirable only insofar as the punitive treatment of the deviant is established as a comparison. They explain that the functions served by the deviant are so important to the group that such persons are alienated only when their behavior becomes a serious threat to group solidarity.

The notion of the boundary-maintaining function of deviance is utilized by Kai Erikson in his analysis of the formation of the New England Puritan community. The selection presented here raises the question implicit in earlier functionalist arguments. If a social system uses its non-conformists to demarcate behavioral boundaries and to reinforce internal solidarity, is it not possible that communities might organize in such a way as to produce and maintain the required amount of deviance? Erikson cites the activity of institutions that deal with the deviant and the permanent nature of the deviant role itself as evidence suggestive of this possibility.

Finally, Anthony Harris argues that the distribution of behavioral boundaries is determined by the interests of the more powerful groups in society. That is, the range of behaviors and the kinds of persons assigned to deviant roles must be assessed in terms of the functions performed for white, male, middle class dominance. Removal of portions of the black male and blue collar populations from their legitimate statuses does not threaten the socio-political order. The functional dispensability of such groups is reflected in the abundance of deviant *type-scripts*, expectations regarding non-conformity, with which they are defined. Assignment of other groups to deviant roles, however, is more problematic. Male hegemony, for example, depends upon the maintenance of women in the home.

Their removal to illegitimate statuses would seriously threaten the ability of males to maintain their institutional control, given the need to replace incarcerated females with members of their own ranks. Since women are functionally indispensable to male dominance, deviant type-scripts are noticeably absent. Women are not expected to deviate nor do they anticipate their own involvement in illegitimate behavior. In this manner, dominant interests are maintained.

The functionalist approach, then, leads us to examine the role of the non-conformist as instrumental in a social system. In much the same way that individuals in the occupational structure contribute to the economic stability of society, the deviant functions to maintain behavioral stability. Punitive reactions against the transgressor reinforce societal values and make visible socially established boundaries of behavior. Such responses also unite conforming group members and call out in them feelings of moral righteousness. This notion of the functional utility of deviance requires that we consider the role of the non-conformist as an instrument of definition, carving out the properties of a group as it distinguishes itself from others. Viewing the non-conformist as necessary to the maintenance of social systems, this approach raises the question of the creation of deviance as a class, a class promoted through institutions designed to *manage* the deviant.

The Normal
and the
Pathological
Emile Durkheim

If there is any fact whose pathological character appears incontestable, that fact is crime. All
criminologists are agreed on this point. Although
they explain this pathology differently, they are
unanimous in recognizing it. But let us see if this
problem does not demand a more extended consideration.

We shall apply the foregoing rules. Crime is
present not only in the majority of societies of one
particular species but in all societies of all types.
There is no society that is not confronted with the
problem of criminality. Its form changes; the acts
thus characterized are not the same everywhere;
but, everywhere and always, there have been men
who have behaved in such a way as to draw upon
themselves penal repression. If, in proportion as
societies pass from the lower to the higher types, the
rate of criminality, i.e., the relation between the
yearly number of crimes and the population, tended
to decline, it might be believed that crime, while still
normal, is tending to lose this character of normality. But we have no reason to believe that such a
regression is substantiated. Many facts would seem
rather to indicate a movement in the opposite direction. From the beginning of the [nineteenth] century, statistics enable us to follow the course of
criminality. It has everywhere increased. In France

the increase is nearly 300 per cent. There is, then, no phenomenon that presents more indisputably all the symptoms of normality, since it appears closely connected with the conditions of all collective life. To make of crime a form of social morbidity would be to admit that morbidity is not something accidental, but, on the contrary, that in certain cases it grows out of the fundamental constitution of the living organism; it would result in wiping out all distinction between the physiological and the pathological. No doubt it is possible that crime itself will have abnormal forms, as, for example, when its rate is unusually high. This excess is, indeed, undoubtedly morbid in nature. What is normal, simply, is the existence of criminality, provided that it attains and does not exceed, for each social type, a certain level, which it is perhaps not impossible to fix in conformity with the preceding rules.[1]

Here we are, then, in the presence of a conclusion in appearance quite paradoxical. Let us make no mistake. To classify crime among the phenomena of normal sociology is not to say merely that it is an inevitable, although regrettable phenomenon, due to the incorrigible wickedness of men; it is to affirm that it is a factor in public health, an integral part of all healthy societies. This result is, at first glance, surprising enough to have puzzled even ourselves for a long time. Once this first surprise has been overcome, however, it is not difficult to find reasons explaining this normality and at the same time confirming it.

In the first place crime is normal because a society exempt from it is utterly impossible. Crime . . . consists of an act that offends certain very strong collective sentiments. In a society in which criminal acts are no longer committed, the sentiments they offend would have to be found without exception in all individual consciousnesses, and they must be found to exist with the same degree as sentiments contrary to them. Assuming that this condition could actually be realized, crime would not thereby disappear; it would only change its form, for the very cause which would thus dry up the sources of criminality would immediately open up new ones.

Indeed, for the collective sentiments which are protected by the penal law of a people at a specified moment of its history to take possession of the public conscience or for them to acquire a stronger

---

[1]From the fact that crime is a phenomenon of normal sociology, it does not follow that the criminal is an individual normally constituted from the biological and psychological points of view. The two questions are independent of each other. This independence will be better understood when we have shown, later on, the difference between psychological and sociological facts.

hold where they have an insufficient grip, they must acquire an intensity greater than that which they had hitherto had. The community as a whole must experience them more vividly, for it can acquire from no other source the greater force necessary to control these individuals who formerly were the most refractory. For murderers to disappear, the horror of bloodshed must become greater in those social strata from which murderers are recruited; but, first it must become greater throughout the entire society. Moreover, the very absence of crime would directly contribute to produce this horror; because any sentiment seems much more respectable when it is always and uniformly respected.

One easily overlooks the consideration that these strong states of the common consciousness cannot be thus reinforced without reinforcing at the same time the more feeble states, whose violation previously gave birth to mere infraction of convention—since the weaker ones are only the prolongation, the attenuated form, of the stronger. Thus robbery and simple bad taste injure the same single altruistic sentiment, the respect for that which is another's. However, this same sentiment is less grievously offended by bad taste than by robbery; and since, in addition, the average consciousness has not sufficient intensity to react keenly to the bad taste, it is treated with greater tolerance. That is why the person guilty of bad taste is merely blamed, whereas the thief is punished. But, if this sentiment grows stronger, to the point of silencing in all consciousnesses the inclination which disposes man to steal, he will become more sensitive to the offenses which, until then, touched him but lightly. He will react against them, then, with more energy; they will be the object of greater opprobrium, which will transform certain of them from the simple moral faults that they were and give them the quality of crimes. For example, improper contracts, or contracts improperly executed, which only incur public blame or civil damages, will become offenses in law.

Imagine a society of saints, a perfect cloister of exemplary individuals. Crimes, properly so called, will there be unknown; but faults which appear venial to the layman will create there the same scandal that the ordinary offense does in ordinary consciousnesses. If, then, this society has the power to judge and punish, it will define these acts as criminal and will treat them as such. For the same reason, the perfect and upright man judges his smallest failings with a severity that the majority reserve for acts more truly in the nature of an offense. Formerly, acts of violence against persons were more frequent than they are today, because respect for individual dignity was less strong. As this has increased, these crimes have become more rare; and also, many acts violating this sentiment have been introduced into the penal law which were not included there in primitive times.[2]

In order to exhaust all the hypotheses logically possible, it will perhaps be asked why this unanimity does not extend to all collective sentiments without exception. Why should not even the most feeble sentiment gather enough energy to prevent all dissent? The moral consciousness of the society would be present in its entirety in all the individuals, with a vitality sufficient to prevent all acts offending it—the purely conventional faults as well as the crimes. But a uniformity so universal and absolute is utterly impossible; for the immediate physical milieu in which each one of us is placed, the hereditary antecedents, and the social influences vary from one individual to the next, and consequently diversify consciousnesses. It is impossible for all to be alike, if only because each one has his own organism and that these organisms occupy different areas in space. That is why, even among the lower peoples, where individual originality is very little developed, it nevertheless does exist.

Thus, since there cannot be a society in which the individuals do not differ more or less from the collective type, it is also inevitable that, among these divergences, there are some with a criminal character. What confers this character upon them is not the intrinsic quality of a given act but that definition which the collective conscience lends them. If the collective conscience is stronger, if it has enough authority practically to suppress these divergences, it will also be more sensitive, more exacting; and, reacting against the slightest deviations with the energy it otherwise displays only against more considerable infractions, it will attribute to them the same gravity as formerly to crimes. In other words, it will designate them as criminal.

Crime is, then, necessary; it is bound up with the fundamental conditions of all social life, and by that very fact it is useful, because these conditions of which it is a part are themselves indispensable to the normal evolution of morality and law.

Indeed, it is no longer possible today to dispute the fact that law and morality vary from one social type to the next, nor that they change within the same type if the conditions of life are modified. But, in order that these transformations may be possible, the collective sentiments at the basis of morality must not be hostile to

[2]Calumny, insults, slander, fraud, etc.

change, and consequently must have but moderate energy. If they were too strong, they would no longer be plastic. Every pattern is an obstacle to new patterns, to the extent that the first pattern is inflexible. The better a structure is articulated, the more it offers a healthy resistance to all modification; and this is equally true of functional, as of anatomical, organization. If there were no crimes, this condition could not have been fulfilled; for such a hypothesis presupposes that collective sentiments have arrived at a degree of intensity unexampled in history. Nothing is good indefinitely and to an unlimited extent. The authority which the moral conscience enjoys must not be excessive; otherwise no one would dare criticize it, and it would too easily congeal into an immutable form. To make progress, individual originality must be able to express itself. In order that the originality of the idealist whose dreams transcend his century may find expression, it is necessary that the originality of the criminal, who is below the level of his time, shall also be possible. One does not occur without the other.

Nor is this all. Aside from this indirect utility, it happens that crime itself plays a useful role in this evolution. Crime implies not only that the way remains open to necessary changes but that in certain cases it directly prepares these changes. Where crime exists, collective sentiments are sufficiently flexible to take on a new form, and crime sometimes helps to determine the form they will take. How many times, indeed, it is only an anticipation of future morality—a step toward what will be! According to Athenian law, Socrates was a criminal, and his condemnation was no more than just. However, his crime, namely, the independence of his thought, rendered a service not only to humanity but to his country. It served to prepare a new morality and faith which the Athenians needed, since the traditions by which they had lived until then were no longer in harmony with the current conditions of life. Nor is the case of Socrates unique; it is reproduced periodically in history. It would never have been possible to establish the freedom of thought we now enjoy if the regulations prohibiting it had not been violated before being solemnly abrogated. At that time, however, the violation was a crime, since it was an offense against sentiments still very keen in the average conscience. And yet this crime was useful as a prelude to reforms which daily became more necessary. Liberal philosophy had as its precursors the heretics of all kinds who were justly punished by secular authorities during the entire course of the Middle Ages and until the eve of modern times.

From this point of view the fundamental facts of criminality present themselves to us in an entirely new light. Contrary to current ideas, the criminal no longer seems a totally unsociable being, a sort of parasitic element, a strange and unassimilable body, introduced into the midst of society.[3] On the contrary, he plays a definite role in social life. Crime, for its part, must no longer be conceived as an evil that cannot be too much suppressed. There is no occasion for self-congratulation when the crime rate drops noticeably below the average level, for we may be certain that this apparent progress is associated with some social disorder. Thus, the number of assault cases never falls so low as in times of want.[4] With the drop in crime rate, and as a reaction to it, comes a revision, or the need of a revision in the theory of punishment. If, indeed, crime is a disease, its punishment is its remedy and cannot be otherwise conceived; thus, all the discussions it arouses bear on the point of determining what the punishment must be in order to fulfil this role of remedy. If crime is not pathological at all, the object of punishment cannot be to cure it, and its true function must be sought elsewhere. . . .

[3]We have ourselves committed the error of speaking thus of the criminal, because of a failure to apply our rule (*Division du travail social*, pp. 395–96).

[4]Although crime is a fact of normal sociology, it does not follow that we must not abhor it. Pain itself has nothing desirable about it; the individual dislikes it as society does crime, and yet it is a function of normal physiology. Not only is it necessarily derived from the very constitution of every living organism, but it plays a useful role in life, for which reason it cannot be replaced. It would, then, be a singular distortion of our thought to present it as an apology for crime. We would not even think of protesting against such an interpretation, did we not know to what strange accusations and misunderstandings one exposes oneself when one undertakes to study moral facts objectively and to speak of them in a different language from that of the layman.

The Psychology of Punitive Justice

George Herbert Mead

The revulsions against criminality reveal themselves in a sense of solidarity with the group, a sense of being a citizen which on the one hand excludes those who have transgressed the laws of the group and on the other inhibits tendencies to criminal acts in the citizen himself. It is this emotional reaction against conduct which excludes from society that gives to the moral taboos of the group such impressiveness. The majesty of the law is that of the angel with the fiery sword at the gate who can cut one off from the world to which he belongs. The majesty of the law is the dominance of the group over the individual, and the paraphernalia of criminal law serves not only to exile the rebellious individual from the group, but also to awaken in law-abiding members of society the inhibitions which make rebellion impossible to them. The formulation of these inhibitions is the basis of criminal law. The emotional content that accompanies them is a large part of the respect for law as law. In both these elements of our respect for law as law, in the respect for the common instrument of defense from and attack upon the enemy of ourselves and of society, and in the respect for that body of formulated custom which at once identifies us with the whole community and excludes those who break its commandments, we recognize concrete impulses—those of attack upon the enemy of ourselves and at the same time of the community,

From "The Psychology of Punitive Justice" by George Herbert Mead in The American Journal of Sociology, Vol. 23, 1918, pp. 586–92. Copyright 1918. By permission of The University of Chicago Press.

and those of inhibition and restraint through which we feel the common will, in the identity of prohibition and of exclusion. They are concrete impulses which at once identify us with the predominant whole and at the same time place us on the level of every other member of the group, and thus set up that theoretical impartiality and evenhandedness of punitive justice which calls out in no small degree our sense of loyalty and respect. And it is out of the universality that belongs to the sense of common action springing out of these impulses that the institutions of law and of regulative and repressive justice arise. While these impulses are concrete in respect of their immediate object, i.e., the criminal, the values which this hostile attitude toward the criminal protects either in society or in ourselves are negatively and abstractly conceived. Instinctively we estimate the worth of the goods protected by the procedure against the criminal and in terms of this hostile procedure. These goods are not simply the physical articles but include the more precious values of self-respect, in not allowing one's self to be overridden, in downing the enemy of the group, in affirming the maxims of the group and its institutions against invasions. Now in all of this we have our backs toward that which we protect and our faces toward the actual or potential enemy. These goods are regarded as valuable because we are willing to fight and even die for them in certain exigencies, but their intrinsic value is neither affirmed nor considered in the legal proceeding. The values thus obtained are not their values in use but sacrifice values. To many a man his country has become infinitely valuable because he finds himself willing to fight and die for it when the common impulse of attack upon the common enemy has been aroused, and yet he may have been, in his daily life, a traitor to the social values he is dying to protect because there was no emotional situation within which these values appeared in his consciousness. It is difficult to bring into commensurable relationship to each other a man's willingness to cheat his country out of its legitimate taxes and his willingness to fight and die for the same country. The reactions spring from different sets of impulses and lead to evaluations which seem to have nothing in common with each other. The type of valuation of social goods that arises out of the hostile attitude toward the criminal is negative, because it does not present the positive social function of the goods that the hostile procedure protects. From the standpoint of protection one thing behind the wall has the same import as anything else that lies behind the same defense. The respect for law as law thus is found to be a respect for a social organization of defense against the enemy of the group and a legal and judicial procedure that are oriented with reference to the criminal. The attempt to utilize these social attitudes and procedures to remove the causes of crime, to assess the kind and amount of punishment which the criminal should suffer in the interest of society, or to reinstate the criminal as a law-abiding citizen has failed utterly. For while the institutions which inspire our respect are concrete institutions with a definite function, they are responsible for a quite abstract and inadequate evaluation of society and its goods. These legal and political institutions organized with reference to the enemy or at least the outsider give a statement of social goods which is based upon defense and not upon function. The aim of the criminal proceeding is to determine whether the accused is innocent, i.e., still belongs to the group or whether he is guilty, i.e., is put under the ban which criminal punishment carries with it. The technical statement of this is found in the loss of the privileges of a citizen, in sentences of any severity, but the more serious ban is found in the fixed attitude of hostility on the part of the community toward a jailbird. One effect of this is to define the goods and privileges of the members of the community as theirs in virtue of their being law-abiding, and their responsibilities as exhausted by the statutes which determine the nature of criminal conduct. This effect is not due alone to the logical tendency to maintain the same definition of the institution of property over against the conduct of the thief and that of the law-abiding citizen. It is due in far greater degree to the feeling that we all stand together in the protection of property. In the positive definition of property, that is in terms of its social uses and functions, we are met by wide diversity of opinion, especially where the theoretically wide freedom of control over private property, asserted over against the thief, is restrained in the interest of problematic public goods. Out of this attitude toward the goods which the criminal law protects arises that fundamental difficulty in social reform which is due, not to mere difference in opinion nor to conscious selfishness, but to the fact that what we term opinions are profound social attitudes which, once assumed, fuse all conflicting tendencies over against the enemy of the people. The respect for law as law in its positive use in defense of social goods becomes unwittingly a respect for the conceptions of these goods which the attitude of defense has fashioned. Property becomes sacred not because of its social uses but because all the community is as one in its defense, and this conception of property, taken over into the social struggle to make property serve its functions in the community, becomes the bulwark of these in possession, *beati possidentes.*

Beside property other institutions have arisen, that of the person with its rights, that of the family with its rights, and that of the government with its rights. Wherever rights exist, invasion of those rights may be punished, and a definition of these institutions is formulated in protecting the right against trespass. The definition is again the voice of the community as a whole proclaiming and penalizing the one whose conduct has placed him under the ban. There is the same unfortunate circumstance that the law speaking against the criminal gives the sanction of the sovereign authority of the community to the negative definition of the right. It is defined in terms of its contemplated invasion. The individual who is defending his own rights against the trespasser is led to state even his family and more general social interests in abstract individualistic terms. Abstract individualism and a negative conception of liberty in terms of the freedom from restraints become the working ideas in the community. They have the prestige of battle cries in the fight for freedom against privilege. They are still the countersigns of the descendants of those who cast off the bonds of political and social restraint in their defense and assertion of the rights their forefathers won. Wherever criminal justice, the modern elaborate development of the taboo, the ban, and their consequences in a primitive society, organizes and formulates public sentiment in defense of social goods and institutions against actual or prospective enemies, there we find that the definition of the enemies, in other words the criminals, carries with it the definition of the goods and institutions. It is the revenge of the criminal upon the society which crushes him. The concentration of public sentiment upon the criminal which mobilizes the institution of justice, paralyzes the undertaking to conceive our common goods in terms of their uses. The majesty of the law is that of the sword drawn against a common enemy. The evenhandedness of justice is that of universal conscription against a common enemy, and that of the abstract definition of rights which places the ban upon anyone who falls outside of its rigid terms.

Thus we see society almost helpless in the grip of the hostile attitude it has taken toward those who break its laws and contravene its institutions. Hostility toward the lawbreaker inevitably brings with it the attitudes of retribution, repression, and exclusion. These provide no principles for the eradication of crime, for returning the delinquent to normal social relations, nor for stating the transgressed rights and institutions in terms of their positive social functions.

On the other side of the ledger stands the fact that the attitude of hostility toward the lawbreaker has the unique advantage of uniting all members of the community in the emotional solidarity of aggression. While the most admirable of humanitarian efforts are sure to run counter to the individual interests of very many in the community, or fail to touch the interest and imagination of the multitude and to leave the community divided or indifferent, the cry of thief or murder is attuned to profound complexes, lying below the surface of competing individual effort, and citizens who have separated by divergent interests stand together against the common enemy. Furthermore, the attitude reveals common, universal values which underlie like a bedrock the divergent structures of individual ends that are mutually closed and hostile to each other. Seemingly without the criminal the cohesiveness of society would disappear and the universal goods of the community would crumble into mutually repellent individual particles. The criminal does not seriously endanger the structure of society by his destructive activities, and on the other hand he is responsible for a sense of solidarity, aroused among those whose attention would be otherwise centered upon interests quite divergent from those of each other. Thus courts of criminal justice may be essential to the preservation of society even when we take account of the impotence of the criminal over against society, and the clumsy failure of criminal law in the repression and suppression of crime. I am willing to admit that this statement is distorted, not however in its analysis of the efficacy of the procedure against the criminal, but in its failure to recognize the growing consciousness of the many common interests which is slowly changing our institutional conception of society, and its consequent exaggerated estimate upon the import of the criminal. But it is important that we should realize what the implications of this attitude of hostility are within our society. We should especially recognize the inevitable limitations which the attitude carries with it. Social organization which arises out of hostility at once emphasizes the character which is the basis of the opposition and tends to suppress all other characters in the members of the group. The cry of "stop thief" unites us all as property owners against the robber. We all stand shoulder to shoulder as Americans against a possible invader. Just in proportion as we organize by hostility do we suppress individuality. In a political campaign that is fought on party lines the members of the party surrender themselves to the party. They become simply members of the party whose conscious aim is to defeat the rival organization. For this purpose the party member becomes merely a republican or a democrat. The party symbol expresses everything. Where simple social aggression or defense with the purpose of eliminating or encysting an enemy is the purpose of the community, organization through the common attitude of hostility is normal and effective. But as long as the social organization is dominated by the attitude of hostility the individuals or groups who are the objectives of this organization will remain enemies. It is quite impossible psychologically to hate the sin and love the sinner. We are very much given to cheating ourselves in this regard. We assume that we can detect, pursue, indict, prosecute, and punish the criminal and still retain toward him the attitude of reinstating him in the community as soon as he indicates a change in social attitude himself, that we can at the same time watch for the definite transgression of the statute to catch and overwhelm the offender, and comprehend the situation out of which the offense grows. But the two attitudes, that of control of crime by the hostile procedure of the law and that of control through comprehension of social and psychological conditions, cannot be combined. To understand is to forgive and the social procedure seems to deny the very responsibility which the law affirms, and on the other hand the pursuit by criminal justice inevitably awakens the hostile attitude in the offender and renders the attitude of mutual comprehension practically impossible.

The Functions
of Deviance
in Groups

Robert A. Dentler / Kai T. Erikson

Although sociologists have repeatedly noted that close similarities exist between various forms of social marginality, research directed at these forms has only begun to mark the path toward a social theory of deviance. This slow pace may in part result from the fact that deviant behavior is too frequently visualized as a product of organizational failure rather than as a facet of organization itself.

Albert Cohen has recently attempted to specify some of the assumptions and definitions necessary for a sociology of deviant behavior (2). He has urged the importance of erecting clearly defined concepts, devising a homogeneous class of phenomena explainable by a unified system of theory, and developing a sociological rather than a psychological framework—as would be the case, for example, in a central problem which was stated: "What is it about the structure of social systems that determines the kinds of criminal acts that occur in these systems and the way in which such acts are distributed within the systems?" (2, p. 462). Cohen has also suggested that a theory of deviant behavior should account simultaneously for deviance and conformity; that is, the explanation of one should serve as the explanation of the other.

In this paper we hope to contribute to these objectives by presenting some propositions about the sources and functions of deviant behavior in

From "The Functions of Deviance in Groups" by Robert A. Dentler and Kai T. Erikson in *Social Problems*, Vol. 7, No. 2, pp. 98-102. By permission of the authors and The Society for the Study of Social Problems.

small groups. Although we suspect that the same general processes may well characterize larger social systems,* this paper will be limited to small groups, and more particularly to enduring task and primary groups. Any set of propositions about the functions of deviance would have to be shaped to fit the scope of the social unit chosen for analysis, and we have elected to use the small group unit in this exploratory paper primarily because a large body of empirical material dealing with deviance in groups has accumulated which offers important leads into the study of deviance in general.

With Cohen, we define deviance as "behavior which violates institutionalized expectations, that is, expectations which are shared and recognized as legitimate within a social system" (2, p. 462). Our guiding assumption is that deviant behavior is a reflection not only of the personality of the actor, but the structure of the group in which the behavior was enacted. The violations of expectation which the group experiences, as well as the norms which it observes, express both cultural and structural aspects of the group. While we shall attend to cultural elements in later illustrations, our propositions are addressed primarily to the structure of groups and the functions that deviant behavior serves in maintaining this structure.

Proposition One

Our first proposition is that *groups tend to induce, sustain, and permit deviant behavior.* To say that a group *induces* deviant behavior, here, is to say that as it goes through the early stages of development and structures the range of behavior among its members, a group will tend to define the behavior of certain members as deviant. A group *sustains* or *permits* this newly defined deviance in the sense that it tends to institutionalize and absorb this behavior into its structure rather than eliminating it. As group structure emerges and role specialization takes place, one or more role categories will be differentiated to accommodate individuals whose behavior is occasionally or regularly expected to be deviant. It is essential to the argument that this process be viewed not only as a simple group adjustment to individual differences, but also as a requirement of group formation, analogous to the requirement of leadership.

The process of role differentiation and specialization which

*One of the authors (Erikson) is currently preparing a paper which deals with the broader implications of the problems discussed here.

takes place in groups has been illuminated by studies which use concepts of sociometric rank. Riecken and Homans conclude from this evidence: "The higher the rank of a member the closer his activities come to realizing the norms of the group . . . and there is a tendency toward 'equilibration of rank'" (8, p. 794). Thus the rankings that take place on a scale of social preference serve to identify the activities that members are expected to carry out: each general rank represents or contains an equivalent role which defines that member's special relationship to the group and its norms. To the extent that a group ranks its members preferentially, it distributes functions differentially. The proposition, then, simply notes that group members who violate norms will be given low sociometric rank; that this designation carries with it an appropriate differentiation of the functions that such members are expected to perform in respect to the group; and that the roles contained in these low-rank positions become institutionalized and are retained in the structure of the group.

The most difficult aspect of this proposition is the concept of *induction* of deviance. We do not mean to suggest that the group creates the motives for an individual's deviant behavior or compels it from persons not otherwise disposed toward this form of expression. When a person encounters a new group, two different historical continuities meet. The individual brings to the group a background of private experience which disposes him to certain patterns of conduct; the group, on the other hand, is organized around a network of role priorities to which each member is required to conform. While the individual brings new resources into the group and alters its potential for change and innovation, the group certainly operates to rephrase each member's private experience into a new self-formula, a new sense of his own needs.

Thus any encounter between a group and a new member is an event which is novel to the experience of both. In the trial-and-error behavior which issues, both the functional requirements of the group and the individual needs of the person will undergo certain revisions, and in the process the group plays an important part in determining whether those already disposed toward deviant behavior will actually express it overtly, or whether those who are lightly disposed toward deviating styles will be encouraged to develop that potential. *Inducing* deviance, then, is meant to be a process by which the group channels and organizes the deviant possibilities contained in its membership.

The proposition argues that groups induce deviant behavior in the same sense that they induce other group qualities like leadership, fellowship, and so on. These qualities emerge early and clearly in the formation of new groups, even in traditionless laboratory groups, and while they may be diffusely distributed among the membership initially they tend toward specificity and equilibrium over time. In giving definition to the end points in the range of behavior which is brought to a group by its membership, the group establishes its boundaries and gives dimension to its structure. In this process, the designation of low-ranking deviants emerges as surely as the designation of high-ranking task leaders.

Proposition Two

Bales has written:

> The displacement of hostilities on a scapegoat at the bottom of the status structure is one mechanism, apparently, by which the ambivalent attitudes toward the . . . 'top man' . . . can be diverted and drained off. These patterns, culturally elaborated and various in form, can be viewed as particular cases of mechanisms relevant to the much more general problem of equilibrium (1, p. 454).

This comment provides a bridge between our first and second propositions by suggesting that deviant behavior may serve important functions for groups—thereby contributing to, rather than disrupting, equilibrium in the group. Our second proposition, accordingly, is that *deviant behavior functions in enduring groups to help maintain group equilibrium.* In the following discussion we would like to consider some of the ways this function operates.

GROUP PERFORMANCE

The proposition implies that deviant behavior contributes to the maintenance of optimum levels of performance, and we add at this point that this will particularly obtain where a group's achievement depends upon the contributions of all its members.

McCurdy and Lambert devised a laboratory task which required full group participation in finding a solution to a given problem (5). They found that the performance of their groups compared unfavorably with that of individual problem-solvers, and explained this by noting the high likelihood that a group would contain at least one member who failed to attend to instructions. The group, they observed, may prove no stronger than its weakest member. The implication here, as in the old adage, seems to be that the group would have become correspondingly stronger if its weakest link were removed. Yet this implication requires some consideration: to what extent can we say that the inattentive member was acting in the name of the group, performing a function which is valuable to the group over time? To what extent can we call this behavior a product of group structure rather than a product of individual eccentricity?

As roles and their equivalent ranks become differentiated in a group, some members will be expected to perform more capably than others; and in turn the structure of the group will certainly be organized to take advantage of the relative capabilities of its members—as it demonstrably does in leadership choice. These differentials require testing and experimentation: the norms about performance in a group cannot emerge until clues appear as to how much the present membership can accomplish, how wide the range of variation in performance is likely to be, and so on. To the extent that group structure becomes an elaboration and organization of these differentials, certainly the "weak link" becomes as essential to this process as the high-producer. Both are outside links in the communication system which feeds back information about the range of group performance and the limits of the differentiated structure.

As this basis for differentiation becomes established, then, the group moves from a state in which pressure is exerted equally on all members to conform to performance norms, and moves toward a state in which these norms become a kind of anchor which locates the center of wide variations in behavior. The performance 'mean' of a group is of course expected to be set at a level dictated by 'norms'; and this mean is not only achieved by the most conforming members but by a balance of high and low producers as well. It is a simple calculation that the loss of a weak-link, the low producer, would raise the mean output of the group to a point where it no longer corresponded to original norms unless the entire structure of the group shifted as compensation. In this sense we can argue that neither role differentiation nor norm formation could occur and be maintained without the "aid" of regular deviations.

REWARDS

Stated briefly, we would argue that the process of distributing incentives to members of the group is similarly dependent upon the recurrence of deviant behavior. This is an instance where, as Cohen has urged, an explanation of conformity may lead to an explanation of deviance. Customarily, conformance is rewarded while deviance is either unrewarded or actively punished. The rewards of conformity, however, are seen as "rewarding" in comparison to other possible outcomes, and obviously the presence of a deviant in the group would provide the continual contrast without which the reward structure would have little meaning. The problem, then, becomes complex: the reward structure is set up as an incentive for conformity, but depends upon the outcome that differentials in conformity will occur. As shall be pointed out later, the deviant is rewarded in another sense for his role in the group, which makes it "profitable" for him to serve as a contrast in the conventional reward structure. Generally speaking, comparison is as essential in the maintenance of norms as is conformity: a norm becomes most evident in its occasional violation, and in this sense a group maintains "equilibrium" by a controlled balance of the relations which provide comparison and those which assure conformity.

BOUNDARIES

Implicit in the foregoing is the argument that the presence of deviance in a group is a boundary maintaining function. The comparisons which deviance makes possible help establish the range in which the group operates, the extent of its jurisdiction over behavior, the variety of styles it contains, and these are among the essential dimensions which give a group identity and distinctiveness. In Quaker work camps, Riecken found that members prided themselves on their acceptance of deviations, and rejected such controls as ridicule and rejection (7, pp. 57–67). Homans has noted that men in the Bank Wiring Group employed certain sanctions against deviant behavior which were felt to be peculiar to the structure of the group (3). A group is distinguished in part by the norms it creates for handling deviance and by the forms of deviance it is able to absorb and contain. In helping, then, to give members a sense of their group's distinctiveness, deviant behavior on the group's margins provides an important boundary-maintaining function.

Proposition Three

Kelley and Thibault have asserted:

> It is common knowledge that when a member deviates markedly from a group standard, the remaining mem-

bers of the group bring pressures to bear on the deviate to return to conformity. If pressure is of no avail, the deviate is rejected and cast out of the group. The research on this point is consistent with common sense (4, p. 768).

Apparently a deviating member who was *not* rejected after repeated violations would be defined as one who did not deviate markedly enough. While there is considerable justification to support this common-sense notion, we suggest that it overattends to rejection and neglects the range of alternatives short of rejection. The same focus is evident in the following statement by Rossi and Merton:

What the individual experiences as estrangement from a group tends to be experienced by his associates as repudiation of the group, and this ordinarily evokes a hostile response. As social relations between the individual and the rest of the group deteriorate, the norms of the group become less binding for him. For since he is progressively seceding from the group and being penalized by it, he is the less likely to experience rewards for adherence to . . . norms. Once initiated, this process seems to move toward a cumulative detachment from the group (6, p. 270).

While both of the above quotations reflect current research concerns in their attention to the group's rejection of the individual and his alienation from the group, our third proposition focuses on the common situation in which the group works to prevent elimination of a deviant member. *Groups will resist any trend toward alienation of a member whose behavior is deviant.* From the point of view of the group majority, deviants will be retained in the group up to a point where the deviant expression becomes critically dangerous to group solidarity. This accords with Kelley and Thibault's general statement, if not with its implication; but we would add that the point at which deviation becomes "markedly" extreme—and dangerous to the group—cannot be well defined in advance. This point is located by the group as a result of recurrent interaction between conforming members who respect the central norms of the group and deviating members who test its boundaries. This is the context from which the group derives a conception of what constitutes "danger," or what variations from the norm shall be viewed as "marked."

From the point of view of the deviant, then, the testing of limits is an exercise of his role in the group; from the point of view of the group, pressures are set into motion which secure the deviant in his "testing" role, yet try to assure that his deviation will not become pronounced enough to make rejection necessary. Obviously this is a delicate balance to maintain, and failures are continually visible. Yet there are a great many conditions under which it is worth while for the group to retain its deviant members and resist any trend which might lead the majority membership and other deviant members to progressive estrangement.

References

1. Bales, Robert F., "The Equilibrium Problem in Small Groups," in *Small Groups*, A. Paul Hare, et al., eds. (New York: Knopf, 1955), 424-456.
2. Cohen, Albert K., "The Study of Social Disorganization and Deviant Behavior," in *Sociology Today*, Robert K. Merton, et al., eds. (New York: Basic Books, 1959), 461-484.
3. Homans, George W., *The Human Group* (New York: Harcourt, Brace, 1950).
4. Kelley, Harold H., and John W. Thibault, "Experimental Studies of Group Problem Solving and Process," in *Handbook of Social Psychology*, Vol. II, Gardner Lindzey, ed. (Cambridge: Addison-Wesley, 1954), 759-768.
5. McCurdy, Harold G., and Wallace E. Lambert, "The Efficiency of Small Human Groups in the Solution of Problems Requiring Genuine Cooperation," *Journal of Personality*, 20 (June, 1952), 478-494.
6. Merton, Robert K., *Social Theory and Social Structure*, rev. ed. (Glencoe: Free Press, 1957).
7. Riecken, Henry, *Volunteer Work Camp* (Cambridge: Addison-Wesley, 1952). 57-67.
8. Riecken, Henry, and George W. Homans, "Psychological Aspects of Social Structure," in *Handbook of Social Psychology*, Vol. II, Gardner Lindzey, ed. (Cambridge: Addison-Wesley, 1954), 786-832.

On the Sociology of Deviance

Kai T. Erikson

Human actors are sorted into various kinds of collectivity, ranging from relatively small units such as the nuclear family to relatively large ones such as a nation or culture. One of the most stubborn difficulties in the study of deviation is that the problem is defined differently at each one of these levels: behavior that is considered unseemly within the context of a single family may be entirely acceptable to the community in general, while behavior that attracts severe censure from the members of the community may go altogether unnoticed elsewhere in the culture. People in society, then, must learn to deal separately with deviance at each one of these levels and to distinguish among them in his own daily activity. A man may disinherit his son for conduct that violates old family traditions or ostracize a neighbor for conduct that violates some local custom, but he is not expected to employ either of these standards when he serves as a juror in a court of law. In each of the three situations he is required to use a different set of criteria to decide whether or not the behavior in question exceeds tolerable limits.

In the next few pages we shall be talking about deviant behavior in social units called "communities," but the use of this term does not mean that the argument applies only at that level of organization. In theory, at least, the argument being made here should fit all kinds of human collectivity—families as

From *Wayward Puritans: A Study in the Sociology of Deviance* by Kai T. Erikson. pp.8-19. Copyright © 1966 by John Wiley and Sons, Inc. Reprinted by permission of John Wiley and Sons, Inc.

well as whole cultures, small groups as well as nations—and the term "community" is only being used in this context because it seems particularly convenient.[1]

The people of a community spend most of their lives in close contact with one another, sharing a common sphere of experience which makes them feel that they belong to a special "kind" and live in a special "place." In the formal language of sociology, this means that communities are boundary maintaining: each has a specific territory in the world as a whole, not only in the sense that it occupies a defined region of geographical space but also in the sense that it takes over a particular niche in what might be called cultural space and develops its own "ethos" or "way" within that compass. Both of these dimensions of group space, the geographical and the cultural, set the community apart as a special place and provide an important point of reference for its members.

When one describes any system as boundary maintaining, one is saying that it controls the fluctuation of its constituent parts so that the whole retains a limited range of activity, a given pattern of constancy and stability, within the larger environment. A human community can be said to maintain boundaries, then, in the sense that its members tend to confine themselves to a particular radius of activity and to regard any conduct which drifts outside that radius as somehow inappropriate or immoral. Thus the group retains a kind of cultural integrity, a voluntary restriction on its own potential for expansion, beyond that which is strictly required for accommodation to the environment. Human behavior can vary over an enormous range, but each community draws a symbolic set of parentheses around a certain segment of that range and limits its own activities within that narrower zone. These parentheses, so to speak, are the community's boundaries.

Now people who live together in communities cannot relate to one another in any coherent way or even acquire a sense of their own stature as group members unless they learn something about the boundaries of the territory they occupy in social space, if only because they need to sense what lies beyond the margins of the group before they can appreciate the special quality of the experience which takes place within it. Yet how do people learn about the boundaries of their community? And how do they convey this information to the generations which replace them?

---

[1]In fact, the first statement of the general notion presented here was concerned with the study of small groups. See Robert A. Dentler and Kai T. Erikson, "The Functions of Deviance in Groups," *Social Problems*, VII (Fall 1959), pp. 98-107.

To begin with, the only material found in a society for marking boundaries is the behavior of its members—or rather, the networks of interaction which link these members together in regular social relations. And the interactions which do the most effective job of locating and publicizing the group's outer edges would seem to be those which take place between deviant persons on the one side and official agents of the community on the other. The deviant is a person whose activities have moved outside the margins of the group, and when the community calls him to account for that vagrancy it is making a statement about the nature and placement of its boundaries. It is declaring how much variability and diversity can be tolerated within the group before it begins to lose its distinctive shape, its unique identity. Now there may be other moments in the life of the group which perform a similar service: wars, for instance, can publicize a group's boundaries by drawing attention to the line separating the group from an adversary, and certain kinds of religious ritual, dance ceremony, and other traditional pageantry can dramatize the difference between "we" and "they" by portraying a symbolic encounter between the two. But on the whole, members of a community inform one another about the placement of their boundaries by participating in the confrontations which occur when persons who venture out to the edges of the group are met by policing agents whose special business it is to guard the cultural integrity of the community. Whether these confrontations take the form of criminal trials, excommunication hearings, courts-martial, or even psychiatric case conferences, they act as boundary-maintaining devices in the sense that they demonstrate to whatever audience is concerned where the line is drawn between behavior that belongs in the special universe of the group and behavior that does not. In general, this kind of information is not easily relayed by the straightforward use of language. Most readers of this paragraph, for instance, have a fairly clear idea of the line separating theft from more legitimate forms of commerce, but few of them have ever seen a published statute describing these differences. More likely than not, our information on the subject has been drawn from publicized instances in which the relevant laws were applied—and for that matter, the law itself is largely a collection of past cases and decisions, a synthesis of the various confrontations which have occurred in the life of the legal order.

It may be important to note in this connection that confrontations between deviant offenders and the agents of control have always attracted a good deal of public attention. In our own past, the trial and punishment of offenders were staged in the market place and afforded the crowd a chance to participate in a direct, active way. Today, of course, we no longer parade deviants in the town square or expose them to the carnival atmosphere of a Tyburn, but it is interesting that the "reform" which brought about this change in penal practice coincided almost exactly with the development of newspapers as a medium of mass information. Perhaps this is no more than an accident of history, but it is nonetheless true that newspapers (and now radio and television) offer much the same kind of entertainment as public hangings or a Sunday visit to the local gaol. A considerable portion of what we call "news" is devoted to reports about deviant behavior and its consequences, and it is no simple matter to explain why these items should be considered newsworthy or why they should command the extraordinary atten- tion they do. Perhaps they appeal to a number of psychological perversities among the mass audience, as commentators have sug- gested, but at the same time they constitute one of our main sources of information about the normative outlines of society. In a figurative sense, at least, morality and immorality meet at the public scaffold, and it is during this meeting that the line between them is drawn.

Boundaries are never a fixed property of any community. They are always shifting as the people of the group find new ways to define the outer limits of their universe, new ways to position themselves on the larger cultural map. Sometimes changes occur within the structure of the group which require its members to make a new survey of their territory—a change of leadership, a shift of mood. Sometimes changes occur in the surrounding environment, altering the background against which the people of the group have measured their own uniqueness. And always, new generations are moving in to take their turn guarding old institutions and need to be informed about the contours of the world they are inheriting. Thus single encounters between the deviant and his community are only fragments of an ongoing social process. Like an article of common law, boundaries remain a meaningful point of reference only so long as they are repeatedly tested by persons on the fringes of the group and repeatedly defended by persons chosen to represent the group's inner morality. Each time the community moves to censure some act of deviation, then, and convenes a formal ceremony to deal with the responsible offender, it sharpens the authority of the violated norm and restates where the boundaries of the group are located.

For these reasons, deviant behavior is not a simple kind of leakage which occurs when the machinery of society is in poor working order, but may be, in controlled quantities, an important condition for preserving the stability of social life. Deviant forms of behavior, by marking the outer edges of group life, give the inner structure its special character and thus supply the framework within which the people of the group develop an orderly sense of their own cultural identity. Perhaps this is what Aldous Huxley had in mind when he wrote:

> Now tidiness is undeniably good-but a good of which it
> is easily possible to have too much and at too high a
> price . . . . The good life can only be lived in a society
> in which tidiness is preached and practised, but not too
> fanatically, and where efficiency is always haloed, as it
> were, by a tolerated margin of mess.[2]

This raises a delicate theoretical issue. If we grant that human groups often derive benefit from deviant behavior, can we then assume that they are organized in such a way as to promote this resource? Can we assume, in other words, that forces operate in the social structure to recruit offenders and to commit them to long periods of service in the deviant ranks? This is not a question which can be answered with our present store of empirical data, but one observation can be made which gives the question an interesting perspective—namely, that deviant forms of conduct often seem to derive nourishment from the very agencies devised to inhibit them. Indeed, the agencies built by society for preventing deviance are often so poorly equipped for the task that we might well ask why this is regarded as their "real" function in the first place.

It is by now a thoroughly familiar argument that many of the institutions designed to discourage deviant behavior actually operate in such a way as to perpetuate it. For one thing, prisons, hospitals, and other similar agencies provide aid and shelter to large numbers of deviant persons, sometimes giving them a certain advantage in the competition for social resources. But beyond this, such institutions gather marginal people into tightly segregated groups, give them an opportunity to teach one another the skills and attitudes of a deviant career, and even provoke them into using these skills by reinforcing their sense of alienation from the rest of society.[3] Nor is this observation a modern one:

[2]Aldous Huxley, Prisons: *The "Carceri" Etchings by Piranesi* (London: The Trianon Press, 1949), p. 13.

[3]For a good description of this process in the modern prison, see Gresham Sykes, *The Society of Captives* (Princeton, N.J.: Princeton University Press, 1958). For discussions of similar problems in two different kinds of mental hospital, see Erving Goffman, *Asylums* (New York: Bobbs-Merrill, 1962) and Kai T. Erikson, "Patient Role and Social Uncertainty: A Dilemma of the Mentally Ill," *Psychiatry*, XX (August 1957), pp. 263-274.

> The misery suffered in gaols is not half their evil; they are filled with every sort of corruption that poverty and wickedness can generate; with all the shameless and profligate enormities that can be produced by the impudence of ignominy, the rage of want, and the malignity of dispair. In a prison the check of the public eye is removed; and the power of the law is spent. There are few fears, there are no blushes. The lewd inflame the more modest; the audacious harden the timid. Everyone fortifies himself as he can against his own remaining sensibility; endeavoring to practise on others the arts that are practised on himself; and to gain the applause of his worst associates by imitating their manners.[4]

These lines, written almost two centuries ago, are a harsh indictment of prisons, but many of the conditions they describe continue to be reported in even the most modern studies of prison life. Looking at the matter from a long-range historical perspective, it is fair to conclude that prisons have done a conspicuously poor job of reforming the convicts placed in their custody; but the very consistency of this failure may have a peculiar logic of its own. Perhaps we find it difficult to change the worst of our penal practices because we *expect* the prison to harden the inmate's commitment to deviant forms of behavior and draw him more deeply into the deviant ranks. On the whole, we are a people who do not really expect deviants to change very much as they are processed through the control agencies we provide for them, and we are often reluctant to devote much of the community's resources to the job of rehabilitation. In this sense, the prison which graduates long rows of accomplished criminals (or, for that matter, the state asylum which stores its most severe cases away in some back ward) may do serious violence to the aims of its founders, but it does very little violence to the expectations of the population it serves.

These expectations, moreover, are found in every corner of society and constitute an important part of the climate in which we deal with deviant forms of behavior.

To begin with, the community's decision to bring deviant sanctions against one of its members is not a simple act of censure. It is an intricate rite of transition, at once moving the individual out of

---

[4]Written by "a celebrated" but not otherwise identified author (perhaps Henry Fielding) and quoted in John Howard, *The State of the Prisons*, London, 1777 (London: J. M. Dent and Sons, 1929), p. 10.

his ordinary place in society and transferring him into a special deviant position.[5] The ceremonies which mark this change of status, generally, have a number of related phases. They supply a formal stage on which the deviant and his community can confront one another (as in the criminal trial); they make an announcement about the nature of his deviancy (a verdict or diagnosis, for example); and they place him in a particular role which is thought to neutralize the harmful effects of his misconduct (like the role of prisoner or patient). These commitment ceremonies tend to be occasions of wide public interest and ordinarily take place in a highly dramatic setting.[6] Perhaps the most obvious example of a commitment ceremony is the criminal trial, with its elaborate formality and exaggerated ritual, but more modest equivalents can be found wherever procedures are set up to judge whether or not someone is legitimately deviant.

Now an important feature of these ceremonies in our own culture is that they are almost irreversible. Most provisional roles conferred by society—those of the student or conscripted soldier, for example—include some kind of terminal ceremony to mark the individual's movement back out of the role once its temporary advantages have been exhausted. But the roles allotted the deviant seldom make allowance for this type of passage. He is ushered into the deviant position by a decisive and often dramatic ceremony, yet is retired from it with scarcely a word of public notice. And as a result, the deviant often returns home with no proper license to resume a normal life in the community. Nothing has happened to cancel out the stigmas imposed upon him by earlier commitment ceremonies; nothing has happened to revoke the verdict or diagnosis pronounced upon him at that time. It should not be surprising, then, that the people of the community are apt to greet the returning deviant with a considerable degree of apprehension and distrust, for in a very real sense they are not at all sure who he is.

A circularity is thus set into motion which has all the earmarks of a "self-fulfilling prophesy," to use Merton's fine phrase. On the one hand, it seems quite obvious that the community's apprehensions help reduce whatever chances the deviant might otherwise have had for a successful return home. Yet at the same time, everyday experience seems to show that these suspicions are wholly

---

[5]The classic description of this process as it applies to the medical patient is found in Talcott Parsons, *The Social System* (Glencoe, Ill.: The Free Press, 1951).

[6]See Harold Garfinkel, "Successful Degradation Ceremonies," *American Journal of Sociology*, LXI (January 1956), pp. 420-424.

reasonable, for it is a well-known and highly publicized fact that many if not most ex-convicts return to crime after leaving prison and that large numbers of mental patients require further treatment after an initial hospitalization. The common feeling that deviant persons never really change, then, may derive from a faulty premise; but the feeling is expressed so frequently and with such conviction that it eventually creates the facts which later "prove" it to be correct. If the returning deviant encounters this circularity often enough, it is quite understandable that he, too, may begin to wonder whether he has fully graduated from the deviant role, and he may respond to the uncertainty by resuming some kind of deviant activity. In many respects, this may be the only way for the individual and his community to agree what kind of person he is.

Moreover this prophesy is found in the official policies of even the most responsible agencies of control. Police departments could not operate with any real effectiveness if they did not regard ex-convicts as a ready pool of suspects to be tapped in the event of trouble, and psychiatric clinics could not do a successful job in the community if they were not always alert to the possibility of former patients suffering relapses. Thus the prophesy gains currency at many levels within the social order, not only in the poorly informed attitudes of the community at large, but in the best informed theories of most control agencies as well.

In one form or another this problem has been recognized in the West for many hundreds of years, and this simple fact has a curious implication. For if our culture has supported a steady flow of deviation throughout long periods of historical change, the rules which apply to any kind of evolutionary thinking would suggest that strong forces must be at work to keep the flow intact—and this because it contributes in some important way to the survival of the culture as a whole. This does not furnish us with sufficient warrant to declare that deviance is "functional" (in any of the many senses of that term), but it should certainly make us wary of the assumption so often made in sociological circles that any well-structured society is somehow designed to prevent deviant behavior from occurring.[7]

It might be then argued that we need new metaphors to carry our thinking about deviance onto a different plane. On the whole,

[7]Albert K. Cohen, for example, speaking for a dominant strain in sociological thinking, takes the question quite for granted:
"It would seem that the control of deviant behavior is, by definition, a culture goal." See "The Study of Social Disorganization and Deviant Behavior" in Merton, et al., *Sociology Today* (New York: Basic Books, 1959), p. 465.

American sociologists have devoted most of their attention to those forces in society which seem to assert a centralizing influence on human behavior, gathering people together into tight clusters called "groups" and bringing them under the jurisdiction of governing principles called "norms" or "standards." The questions which sociologists have traditionally asked of their data, then, are addressed to the uniformities rather than the divergencies of social life: how is it that people learn to think in similar ways, to accept the same group moralities, to move by the same rhythms of behavior, to see life with the same eyes? How is it, in short, that cultures accomplish the incredible alchemy of making unity out of diversity, harmony out of conflict, order out of confusion? Somehow we often act as if the differences between people can be taken for granted, being too natural to require comment, but that the symmetry which human groups manage to achieve must be explained by referring to the molding influence of the social structure.

But variety, too, is a product of the social structure. It is certainly remarkable that members of a culture come to look so much alike; but it is also remarkable that out of all this sameness a people can develop a complex division of labor, move off into diverging career lines, scatter across the surface of the territory they share in common, and create so many differences of temper, ideology, fashion, and mood. Perhaps we can conclude, then, that two separate yet often competing currents are found in any society: those forces which promote a high degree of conformity among the people of the community so that they know what to expect from one another, and those forces which encourage a certain degree of diversity so that people can be deployed across the range of group space to survey its potential, measure its capacity, and, in the case of those we call deviants, patrol its boundaries. In such a scheme, the deviant would appear as a natural product of group differentiation. He is not a bit of debris spun out by faulty social machinery, but a relevant figure in the community's overall division of labor.

Toward a Functional Theory of Deviant Type-Scripts

Anthony R. Harris

The failure to study noncriminals proved a disaster to early work on criminal deviance. Putatively, the failure was a methodological one; in looking for a relationship between cranial shape and criminal propensity, phrenologists looked only at prisoners, thereby begging the question of how this purported relationship was distributed in the population at large (cf. Vold, 1958). The phrenologists' error, however, was almost certainly an artifact of a more fundamental conceptual blindness— the inability to imagine that rates of the "lower propensities" might be higher in the noncriminal population at large than among prisoners. Curiously, modern deviance theorists have applied the lessons learned from this sort of mistake only selectively. As a consequence, the general power of contemporary criminal deviance theory is only marginally greater than it was in the phrenologists' day. I am referring to a critical weakness resulting from the continuing failure to consider women and, consequently, the sex variable in such theory.

This failure is more than merely methodological, precisely because it means that purportedly general theories of criminal deviance are now no more than special theories of male deviance. This is no small or easily correctable problem. Its solution does not depend simply on more studies of female deviants, on adding a corollary here or a specification there in the current special theories of male criminal deviance and then applying them to

From "Sex and Theories of Deviance: Toward a Functional Theory of Deviant Type-Scripts," by Anthony R. Harris in *American Sociological Review* Vol. 42, No. 1, February, 1977, pp. 3–4, 11–16.

women, or on simply reevaluating the current evidence. The solution, or at least its beginnings, . . . most probably lie in the realization that our present conceptual blindness, like the phrenologist's, is deeply rooted in everyday assumptions about *who does what, including deviance,* in a society. Ironically, it is the distribution of these background norms about deviance which, I believe, at once accounts for our professional failure to include women in theories of criminal deviance and, more importantly, provides the single strongest causal account of the empirical differences in male and female criminality.

Such differences are striking indeed: sex appears to explain more variance in crime across cultures than any other variable. This appears so *regardless* of whether officially known or hidden ("true") rates of crime are indexed (Harris, 1976).[1] It is also worth stressing that, with the exception of age, the major social-structural predictors hitherto built into various theories of criminal deviance—class, race/ethnicity, area, and intact family background—are all strongly multicollinear. Sorting out their independent and interactive effects on crime has proved extremely difficult. This empirical morass has been paralleled by a theoretical one involving variations on the theme of structural disadvantage. However, the sex variable, to which virtually no attention has been paid, is only a trivial covariate of these major social-structural variables. The potential theoretical and empirical strategic advantages of this observation clearly have been neglected.

A . . . major goal [here] will be to . . . [develop] . . . the outlines of what I will call "a functional theory of deviant type-scripts"; toward this goal, it will be argued that the theoretical notion of greatest potential use in the necessary reconstruction of deviance theory is not one involving the idea of means or of ends or of perceived opportunity but, rather, is one involving the idea of self-attribution.

. . . Any powerful general theory of criminal deviance, if not deviance more broadly, is a theory involving the stratification of behavior and identities. From this viewpoint, the functional preservation of social dominance may be seen as resting on the assignment of readily identifiable social "types" to classes of social locales and locale-specific roles. In American society, the assignment

[1] This point is made with respect to American data. When data from less industrialized societies are considered, the point is more striking. Prior to modernization, data from third world societies yield sex ratio ranging from 900:1 to more than 20,000:1 (Nettler, 1974).

of blacks to the ghetto, women to the home and poor to the factory represent examples which have met the function of preserving white, male, middle-class dominance. Homologous legal, educational and occupational structures support such assignments and, at the level of group cognition, provide powerful expectancies by which actors come to assign themselves and others to limited classes of behavior according to social "type." Such expectancies — which specify broad behavioral sequences as well as type-to-role linkages — are referred to here as *type-scripts*. It is maintained that these scripts have important extra-logical implications, held with high social communality with respect to the perception of classes of behavior it is *likely, possible, unlikely* and *impossible* for particular types of actors to perform.

Unlike scripts for the theatre, which very precisely delimit word and action for a role but which do not specify who is to play it, type-scripts are seen not as delimiting the specific content of social roles but as specifying the types of actors who are to play them. This is not to suggest that type-scripts align a type of role with only one type of actor, or a type of actor with only one role. Rather, it is to suggest that such background expectancies align particular sets of actor types with particular sets of social roles.[2]

From the objective viewpoint, type-scripts are "normative": regardless of the social distribution of affect held for them, they would appear to have relatively high cognitive communality across both dominant and dominated groups.[3] From the subjective viewpoint, type-scripts are informative since they provide not only a limited array of role choices but also the most salient bases for a limited set of possible social identities. In these terms, besides

[2] It is proposed that this linking function is best seen as probabilistic, continuous and multi-conditional. In these terms, it would be possible to observe the conditional probability level a group held *vis à vis* the chances that a particular type of actor X — such as a woman — would hold a particular type of role Y — such as a bank presidency (i.e., the conditional "front" probability, $P(Y|X)$); or that the role Y would be held by the actor X (i.e., the conditional "back" probability, $P(X|Y)$). As suggested, such perceived probabilities are best approached as multi-conditional: while most members of this society undoubtedly hold a very low probability that a bank president would be female, there is undoubtedly a still lower perceived probability assigned the type-script of a bank president being both female and black. (In combination, however, conditional probabilities may be interactive rather than simply additive.)

[3] It is important to recognize that the aligning linkages provided by type-scripting may be at considerable variance with empirical probabilities. As anonymous reports on criminality imply, "true" rates of deviance for given types of actors are often out of line with public representations of these rates. This may be as true for public under-representations of white-collar crime as it appears to be for white, middle-class delinquency. Incongruity between alignment probabilities in type-scripts and actual empirical probabilities is not seen as a random phenomenon but,

aligning types of actors with possible classes of legitimate behaviors and identities, type-scripts also are seen as aligning types
of actors with possible classes of deviant behavior and identities.
One dominant order-maintaining function of type-scripts, then,
involves specification of what types of actors are to commit what
types of deviance in a society and — perhaps more illuminating —
what types of deviance are seen as unlikely or "impossible" for
other types of actors to commit.

Several examples illustrate the point. It is strongly type-
scripted in American society that street crimes represent the preserve of blacks and the poor. From a somewhat different slant, it is
(or was) scripted that it is nearly "impossible" for the highest officials in the land to act criminally. Similarly, and perhaps more
relevant to the present analysis, it is (still) type-scripted that it is
unlikely or "impossible" for women to attempt assassination, robbery or rape.[4]

Based on the assumption of role assignment in the interests
of the socially dominant, a functional theory of deviant type-scripts
would maintain that, over time, deviant type-scripts which preserved dominant interests in particular role arrangements also
would be preserved. From this perspective, in order to be functionally effective, deviant type-scripting must meet a special condition: *the existence or filling of legitimate roles vacated by those
actually assigned deviant status must not threaten the institutional
hegemony of the socially dominant.* Should this role-replacement condition not be met and the threat arise otherwise, the potential for
broad societal script disarray would be great and the status and
power advantages of the dominant would be severely challenged.

In these terms, ghetto males lost from legitimate roles (e.g.,
fatherhood) to prisons through crime — though a real loss to the
black family and a potential loss to the abstract interests of the

rather, as systematically related to the maintenance of dominant interests by agencies of social control.

[4] As recent attempts on the life of the American president have pointed out, it is
possible if not easier for women to engage in assassination. Similarly, it is clearly
as possible for women to commit robbery. Though most people are aware of the
"equalizing" effects of handguns, the countervailing script against female robbery
has it that females would be overpowered in robbery attempts, even if they carried
guns. The power of this deviant script or, rather, of its absence is strong — so strong
as to preclude the realization that, even if strength were the issue, women can rob
other women. Perhaps the strongest illustration of deviant scripting (or its absence), however, involves the notion of rape. Present scripting holds that rape involves vaginal penetration. On this assumption, male rape is ruled out by definition.
Clearly, alternative sexual violations consonant with the more general moral principle of rape cannot be ruled out as impossible for females to commit against males
or, for that matter, against females.

commonweal—are by no means a threat to the ongoing economic, political and symbolic interests of the socially dominant. (As literate whites can now testify, family structure in the ghetto is "matriarchal anyway"—the vacated role will presumably be filled easily by the black woman.) Similarly, given high rates of blue-collar unemployment, social members lost from blue-collar roles to prisons through crime are by no means a threat to the economic, political and symbolic interests of the socially dominant. (As many literate social scientists can testify, work in blue-collar and intensive labor occupations is to a high degree "functionally interchangeable.") In neither of these cases does the existence or filling of the vacated role pose a threat to dominant interests.

The reassignment of women from homes to prisons, however, does *not* meet the role-replacement condition. Male dominance in occupational, educational, political and legal institutions is not served by allowing the development of type-scripts which lead to putting women in jail. Rather, the prime structural mainstay of male institutional hegemony has been the continued assignment of females to the home and to the role of homemaker. Assignment of females to this locale, a modal empirical feature of every class and ethnic group within this and almost all societies, has had, among other structural implications, the major virtues of eliminating half the competition, of keeping labor supplies shorter and (male) wages higher than they would otherwise be, and of allowing males the full-time opportunity to manage extra-familial institutional control. The regular and routine assignment of females to prisons, on the other hand, would appear to challenge this advantage severely through the development of increased rates of one or more major disequilibrating outcomes: (1) the breakup of the nuclear family, (2) the maintenance of the nuclear family only with grave financial burdens entailed in hiring a full-time role replacement for the female and/or (3) the partial or full-time withdrawal from the occupational sector of males so affected.[5] It is thus argued that it is not in the interests of male dominance to allow the development of deviant type-scripts for women, both among secondary agents of social control (such as police and courts) and, at a more fundamental level, among primary agents of social control (such as parents and teachers).

[5] The threat to male hegemony posed by reassigning females from the home to prisons is not argued as varying by caste or class. It should be expected, however, that on the basis of caste and class power differentials in resisting detection, incarceration, etc.: (1) black and/or poor females will be assigned to prisons more regularly than white and/or middle-class females and (2) the hegemony of the black and/or poor male will be more threatened by such assignment than that of the white and/or middle-class male.

As outlined in these terms, the functional regulation of deviant role incumbency through the regulation of type-scripts is seen as providing a basis for distinguishing, in the most ironic sense, deviant behaviors and identities which are expected, functional and socially articulated for certain actor types from behaviors and identities which are anomalous, dysfunctional and socially inarticulate for other actor types. (Thus, where blacks and poor may be said to "become criminal," types for whom deviant scripts are unwritten may be said to "become anomalous.")

The theory outlined here . . . offers a social-structural account of who and what is to be considered deviant and why.[6] Second, it argues that the background expectancies for deviance contained in type-scripts have social communality extending across the boundary between the dominant *and* the dominated. Third, in assuming this "normative" distribution, the theory maintains an etiological scenario at the individual level. In these terms, scripts for who and what is to be considered deviant become the direct basis for deviant self-attributions. Thus, it is important to realize that the proper major target of a functional theory of deviant type-scripts is *not* secondary deviance as labeling theory would have it but, rather, is *primary deviance per se.** From this viewpoint, deviant self-attributions actualized through the perceived linkage between social "type" and deviant type-scripting become the "motivational" basis for engaging in deviant behavior *independently* of direct contact with official agents of social control.[7] Finally, in

[6] It may be objected that the development of type-scripts, though given an explanation here in terms of "why," is not explained in terms of "how." Though this apparent gap is often seen as a problem indigenous to functionalist arguments, the reader is cautioned to realize that this is properly a question of how *any* norms consonant with a given social order emerge. This general question is beyond the scope of the present paper.

* As noted by Farrell and Morrione ("Conforming to Deviance," p.416) "*secondary deviance,* as a descriptive concept for the deviant roles which result from societal reaction, was first used by Lemert (Social Pathology: A Systematic Approach to the Theory of Sociopathic Behavior. New York: McGraw-Hill Book Company, 1951; Human Deviance, Social Problems and Social Control. Englewood Cliffs, N.J.: Prentice-Hall, Inc., 1967). According to Lemert (1967:41) "the secondary deviant . . . is a person whose life and identity are organized around the facts of deviance." "Deviations remain *primary* deviations or symptomatic and situational as long as they are rationalized or otherwise dealt with as functions of a socially acceptable role . . . [However] when a person begins to employ his deviant behavior or a role based upon it as a means of defense, attack, or adjustment to the overt and covert problems created by the consequent societal reaction to him, his deviation is secondary" (Lemert, 1951: 75–76).

[7] It is not argued here that all members of a social type assigned deviant type-scripts (e.g., males, blacks, adolescents) engage in primary deviance at the same rate. On the one hand, it is not maintained that a given type is scripted for only one role. On the other hand, the issue is more properly one of explaining deviant *rate* variance

hypothesizing the direct impact of deviant self-attributions on (primary) deviant behavior, a functional theory of deviant type-scripts need not forego attention to the role of official social control. Rather, contact with official agents may be seen as homologous to previous type-scripting and, consequently, as providing: epistemological reinforcement for deviant self-typing at the individual level, stronger attendant deviant self-attributions and further organization of personality through pressure to accept the master trait of "deviance" (secondary deviance).

The theory outlined here would seem capable of starting with the sex variable and accounting for the very high amount of empirical variance it "explains" in official *and* hidden criminality. Since the theory need not be restricted by the specification of concrete socially-dominant groups, it is historically and cross-culturally flexible.[8] In these terms, despite the ubiquity of male dominance historically and cross-culturally, the degree of such dominance may easily be measured independently of sex ratios in criminal deviance and, at a minimum, the two expected to covary. Thus, even though the marked sex ratio in criminality may disappear in time, and more quickly so in post-industrial societies such as ours, the power of a general functional theory of deviant type-scripts would not be contingent upon such an occurrence.

References

Harris, A. R.
1976 "Sex, crime, and the west-acre cornfield." Unpublished manuscript, Department of Sociology, University of Massachusetts, Amherst.

---

across social types. Attempts to explain rate variance within types—analogous to the attempts by Reckless et al. (1956:16) to explain the existence of the nondelinquent slum boy—may, in part, be dealt with in the present context in terms of self-attributions which cross-cut and mitigate deviant type-scripts. The bulk of this mitigating effect is seen as a function of cross-cutting role alignments—and consequent self-attributions—based on such social-structural typologies as caste and class. From this viewpoint, and as opposed to the position of Reckless et al. (1956), the overt message, "you are a good boy, and good boys don't get into trouble with the law," is not nearly so subjectively important and sociologically significant as the covert message, "you are a white boy, and white boys don't get into trouble with the law."

[8] Though our critique has been of theories of criminal deviance, the functional theory of deviant type-scripts outlined here need not be restricted to criminal deviance.

Nettler, G.
1974 Explaining Crime. New York: McGraw-Hill.
Reckless, W. C., S. Dinitz and E. Murray
1956 "Self concept as an insulator against delinquency." American Sociological Review 21:744–6.
Vold, G. B.
1958 Theoretical Criminology. New York: Oxford University Press.

part Two

Theories Focusing on Societal Definitions

Functionalists argue that deviance is a necessary component of social systems. The articles that follow supplement this notion by focusing on the social process in which deviance has its origins. It is suggested that the creation of deviance categories is a *definitional process.*

W. I. Thomas explains that the child is born into a situation composed of social definitions. Reflecting Durkheim's formulation of the *collective conscience*, he suggests that these definitions are the cumulated norms and values of society. More specifically, they are the practical translations of these norms and values and are conveyed to the individual through the family and community. Since the modern world has brought about increased individualization, however, their transmission is never perfect. That is to say, the individual is never socialized into the total definitional network because modern society precludes such full participation. Thus, the way is open for the individual to act upon spontaneous definitions. If this action conflicts with established codes, it may be designated as deviant. Thomas felt that once persons have assigned such meaning to a situation, their behavior and some of the consequences of that behavior are determined by the ascribed meaning. Public definitions of a situation (prophecies or predictions) thus become an integral part of the situation and affect subsequent developments.

The selection by Frank Tannenbaum focuses on

the social psychological implications of these processes in the case of delinquency. He explains that the relationship between the community and the young non-conformer begins as a divergence in behavioral definitions. What to the deviant is "fun," "adventure," or "mischief" is from the community's point of view "nuisance," "evil," or "delinquent." These divergent definitions of the situation often bring the individual into conflict with the community. As this conflict increases, there occurs a gradual shift from the designation of the specific acts as evil, to a designation of the individual as evil, so that all his acts come to be looked upon with suspicion. This redefinition is accomplished through the medium of the institutions made available for the processing of delinquents, such as police and courts. The non-conformer who is exposed to these dramatizing processes may come to define himself as criminal. When this occurs, when "the person becomes the thing he is described as being," the continuation of the deviant behavior is virtually assured.

Robert Merton's discussion of the *self-fulfilling prophecy* also illustrates the power of the social definition as it shapes reality. Building on Thomas' idea, he asserts that if a situation is defined as real, it is real in its consequences, regardless of the factual base upon which it is built. As testimony to the devastating potential of the false definition of the situation, Merton uses the examples of the rumor of financial insolvency leading to the failure of hundreds of banks during the Depression and the stereotype of inferiority as limiting the attainment of equal education of blacks.

In the final selection, we argue that expectations regarding the behavior of certain portions of the population have become institutionalized in the judicial system. These expectations serve as the guiding imagery for action in the legal processing of criminal defendants. In the case of homicide, for example, individuals who conform to the stereotype of violent criminality are denied the presumption of innocence routinely accorded others. This presumption serves to justify the withholding of legal resources essential for successful defense. Denial of bail, assignment of public attorney, and a bargained settlement between prosecutor and defense ultimately produce the outcome predicted by the original imagery, award of criminal conviction. The differential treatment of persons whose class and race characteristics conform to the criminal stereotype has implications for the development and maintenance of violent behavior. Official designation as criminal leads to further isolation of those whose status in society is already marginal and to, therefore, a reaffirmed commitment to subcultural ties. Since persons thus affected may come to incorporate the stereotype of their behavior as part of their own role expectations, cultural differences between these individuals and the larger society will persist. Through the ensuing conflict of cultures, both the criminal imagery is affirmed and exclusionary legal practices legitimized.

An important assumption of this approach is the existence in society of a plurality of social definitions, definitions which lead to different behavior forms among various groups. Of equal importance is the suggestion that some groups possess the power to designate certain situations or behavior categories as deviant. These designations, in turn, have the self-fulfilling effect of creating conditions consistent with the ascriptions. From this perspective, then, deviance is seen as a socially constructed reality arising out of normal processes of differentiation and definition.

The Definition of the Situation

William I. Thomas

Preliminary to any self-determined act of behavior there is always a stage of examination and deliberation which we may call *the definition of the situation*. And actually not only concrete acts are dependent on the definition of the situation, but gradually a whole life-policy and the personality of the individual himself follow from a series of such definitions.

But the child is always born into a group of people among whom all the general types of situation which may arise have already been defined and corresponding rules of conduct developed, and where he has not the slightest chance of making his definitions and following his wishes without interference. Men have always lived together in groups. Whether mankind has a true herd instinct or whether groups are held together because this has worked out to advantage is of no importance. Certainly the wishes in general are such that they can be satisfied only in a society. But we have only to refer to the criminal code to appreciate the variety of ways in which the wishes of the individual may conflict with the wishes of society. And the criminal code takes no account of the many unsanctioned expressions of the wishes which society attempts to regulate by persuasion and gossip.

There is therefore always a rivalry between the spontaneous definitions of the situation made by the member of an organized society and the definitions

From William I. Thomas, *The Unadjusted Girl*, pp. 42–44, 49–50. Copyright © 1923 by Little, Brown and Company (Inc.).

which his society has provided for him. The individual tends to a hedonistic selection of activity, pleasure first; and society to a utilitarian selection, safety first. Society wishes its member to be laborious, dependable, regular, sober, orderly, self-sacrificing; while the individual wishes less of this and more of new experience. And organized society seeks also to regulate the conflict and competition inevitable between its members in the pursuit of their wishes. The desire to have wealth, for example, or any other socially sanctioned wish, may not be accomplished at the expense of another member of the society,—by murder, theft, lying, swindling, blackmail, etc.

It is in this connection that a moral code arises, which is a set of rules or behavior norms, regulating the expression of the wishes, and which is built up by successive definitions of the situation. In practice the abuse arises first and the rule is made to prevent its recurrence. Morality is thus the generally accepted definition of the situation, whether expressed in public opinion and the unwritten law, in a formal legal code, or in religious commandments and prohibitions.

The family is the smallest social unit and the primary defining agency. As soon as the child has free motion and begins to pull, tear, pry, meddle, and prowl, the parents begin to define the situation through speech and other signs and pressures: "Be quiet", "Sit up straight", "Blow your nose", "Wash your face", "Mind your mother", "Be kind to sister", etc. This is the real significance of Wordsworth's phrase, "Shades of the prison house begin to close upon the growing child." His wishes and activities begin to be inhibited, and gradually, by definitions within the family, by playmates, in the school, in the Sunday school, in the community, through reading, by formal instruction, by informal signs of approval and disapproval, the growing member learns the code of his society.

In addition to the family we have the community as a defining agency. At present the community is so weak and vague that it gives us no idea of the former power of the local group in regulating behavior. Originally the community was practically the whole world of its members. It was composed of families related by blood and marriage and was not so large that all the members could not come together; it was a face-to-face group. I asked a Polish peasant what was the extent of an "*okolica*" or neighborhood—how far it reached. "It reaches," he said, "as far as the report of a man reaches—as far as a man is talked about." And it was in communities of this kind that the moral code which we now recognize as valid originated. The customs of the community are "folkways", and both state and church have in their more formal codes mainly recognized and incorporated these folkways. . . .

A less formal but not less powerful means of defining the situation employed by the community is gossip. The Polish peasant's statement that a community reaches as far as a man is talked about was significant, for the community regulates the behavior of its members largely by talking about them. Gossip has a bad name because it is sometimes malicious and false and designed to improve the status of the gossiper and degrade its object, but gossip is in the main true and is an organizing force. It is a mode of defining the situation in a given case and of attaching praise or blame. It is one of the means by which the status of the individual and of his family is fixed.

The community also, particularly in connection with gossip, knows how to attach opprobrium to persons and actions by using epithets which are at the same time brief and emotional definitions of the situation. "Bastard", "whore", "traitor", "coward", "skunk", "scab", "snob", "kike", etc., are such epithets. In "Faust" the community said of Margaret, "She stinks." The people are here employing a device known in psychology as the "conditioned reflex." If, for example, you place before a child (say six months old) an agreeable object, a kitten, and at the same time pinch the child, and if this is repeated several times, the child will immediately cry at the sight of the kitten without being pinched; or if a dead rat were always served beside a man's plate of soup he would eventually have a disgust for soup when served separately. If the word "stinks" is associated on people's tongues with Margaret, Margaret will never again smell sweet. Many evil consequences, as the psychoanalysts claim, have resulted from making the whole of sex life a "dirty" subject, but the device has worked in a powerful, sometimes a paralyzing way on the sexual behavior of women.

Winks, shrugs, nudges, laughter, sneers, haughtiness, coldness, "giving the once over" are also language defining the situation and painfully felt as unfavorable recognition. The sneer, for example, is incipient vomiting, meaning, "you make me sick."

And eventually the violation of the code even in an act of no intrinsic importance, as in carrying food to the mouth with the knife, provokes condemnation and disgust. The fork is not a better instrument for conveying food than the knife, at least it has no moral superiority, but the situation has been defined in favor of the fork. To smack with the lips in eating is bad manners with us, but the Indian has more logically defined the situation in the opposite way; with him smacking is a compliment to the host.

In this whole connection fear is used by the group to produce the desired attitudes in its member. Praise is used also but more sparingly. And the whole body of habits and emotions is so much a community and family product that disapproval or separation is almost unbearable.

Definition and the Dramatization of Evil

Frank Tannenbaum

In the conflict between the young delinquent and the community there develop two opposing definitions of the situation. In the beginning the definition of the situation by the young delinquent may be in the form of play, adventure, excitement, interest, mischief, fun. Breaking windows, annoying people, running around porches, climbing over roofs, stealing from pushcarts, playing truant—all are items of play, adventure, excitement. To the community, however, these activities may and often do take on the form of a nuisance, evil, delinquency, with the demand for control, admonition, chastisement, punishment, police court, truant school. This conflict over the situation is one that arises out of a divergence of values. As the problem develops, the situation gradually becomes redefined. The attitude of the community hardens definitely into a demand for suppression. There is a gradual shift from the definition of the specific acts as evil to a definition of the individual as evil, so that all his acts come to be looked upon with suspicion. In the process of identification his companions, hang-outs, play, speech, income, all his conduct, the personality itself, become subject to scrutiny and question. From the community's point of view, the individual who used to do bad and mischievous things has now become a bad and unredeemable human being. From the individual's point of view there has taken place a similar change. He has gone slowly from a sense of

From Frank Tannenbaum, *Crime and the Community,* New York: Columbia University Press, 1938, pp. 17–22, by permission of the publisher.

grievance and injustice, of being unduly mistreated and punished, to a recognition that the definition of him as a human being is different from that of other boys in his neighborhood, his school, street, community. This recognition on his part becomes a process of self-identification and integration with the group which shares his activities. It becomes, in part, a process of rationalization; in part, a simple response to a specialized type of stimulus. The young delinquent becomes bad because he is defined as bad and because he is not believed if he is good. There is a persistent demand for consistency in character. The community cannot deal with people whom it cannot define. Reputation is this sort of public definition. Once it is established, then unconsciously all agencies combine to maintain this definition even when they apparently and consciously attempt to deny their own implicit judgment.

Early in his career, then, the incipient professional criminal develops an attitude of antagonism to the regulated orderly life that he is required to lead. This attitude is hardened and crystallized by opposition. The conflict becomes a clash of wills. And experience too often has proved that threats, punishments, beatings, commitments to institutions, abuse and defamation of one sort or another, are of no avail. Punishment breaks down against the child's stubbornness. What has happened is that the child has been defined as an "incorrigible" both by his contacts and by himself, and an attempt at a direct breaking down of will generally fails.

The child meets the situation in the only way he can, by defiance and escape—physical escape if possible, or emotional escape by derision, anger, contempt, hatred, disgust, tantrums, destructiveness, and physical violence. The response of the child is just as intelligent and intelligible as that of the schools, of the authorities. They have taken a simple problem, the lack of fitness of an institution to a particular child's needs, and have made a moral issue out of it with values outside the child's ken. It takes on the form of war between two wills, and the longer the war lasts, the more certainly does the child become incorrigible. The child will not yield because he cannot yield—his nature requires other channels for pleasant growth; the school system or society will not yield because it does not see the issues involved as between the incompatibility of an institution and a child's needs, sometimes physical needs, and will instead attempt to twist the child's nature to the institution with that consequent distortion of the child which makes an unsocial career inevitable. The verbalization of the conflict in terms of evil, delinquency, incorrigibility, badness, arrest, force, punishment,

stupidity, lack of intelligence, truancy, criminality, gives the innocent divergence of the child from the straight road a meaning that
it did not have in the beginning and makes its continuance in these
same terms by so much the more inevitable.

The only important fact, when the issue arises of the boy's
inability to acquire the specific habits which organized institutions
attempt to impose upon him, is that this conflict becomes the
occasion for him to acquire another series of habits, interests, and
attitudes as a substitute. These habits become as effective in motivating and guiding conduct as would have been those which the orderly
routine social institutions attempted to impose had they been
acquired.

This conflict gives the gang its hold, because the gang provides
escape, security, pleasure, and peace. The gang also gives room for
the motor activity which plays a large role in a child's life. The
attempt to break up the gang by force merely strengthens it. The
arrest of the children has consequences undreamed-of, for several
reasons.

First, only some of the children are caught though all may be
equally guilty. There is a great deal more delinquency practiced and
committed by the young groups than comes to the attention of the
police. The boy arrested, therefore, is singled out in specialized
treatment. This boy, no more guilty than the other members of his
group, discovers a world of which he knew little. His arrest suddenly
precipitates a series of institutions, attitudes, and experiences which
the other children do not share. For this boy there suddenly appear
the police, the patrol wagon, the police station, the other delinquents
and criminals found in the police lock-ups, the court with all its
agencies such as bailiffs, clerks, bondsmen, lawyers, probation
officers. There are bars, cells, handcuffs, criminals. He is questioned,
examined, tested, investigated. His history is gone into, his family is
brought into court. Witnesses make their appearance. The boy, no
different from the rest of his gang, suddenly becomes the center of a
major drama in which all sorts of unexpected characters play
important roles. And what is it all about? about the accustomed
things his gang has done and has been doing for a long time. In this
entirely new world he is made conscious of himself as a different
human being than he was before his arrest. He becomes classified as
a thief, perhaps, and the entire world about him has suddenly
become a different place for him and will remain different for the rest
of his life. . . .

The first dramatization of the "evil" which separates the child out of his group for specialized treatment plays a greater role in making the criminal than perhaps any other experience. It cannot be too often emphasized that for the child the whole situation has become different. He now lives in a different world. He has been tagged. A new and hitherto non-existent environment has been precipitated out for him.

The process of making the criminal, therefore, is a process of tagging, defining, identifying, segregating, describing, emphasizing, making conscious and self-conscious; it becomes a way of stimulating, suggesting, emphasizing, and evoking the very traits that are complained of. If the theory of relation of response to stimulus has any meaning, the entire process of dealing with the young delinquent is mischievous in so far as it identifies him to himself or to the environment as a delinquent person.

The person becomes the thing he is described as being. Nor does it seem to matter whether the valuation is made by those who would punish or by those who would reform. In either case the emphasis is upon the conduct that is disapproved of. The parents or the policeman, the older brother or the court, the probation officer or the juvenile institution, in so far as they rest upon the thing complained of, rest upon a false ground. Their very enthusiasm defeats their aim. The harder they work to reform the evil, the greater the evil grows under their hands. The persistent suggestion, with whatever good intentions, works mischief, because it leads to bringing out the bad behavior that it would suppress. The way out is through a refusal to dramatize the evil. The less said about it the better. The more said about something else, still better.

The hard-drinker who keeps thinking of not drinking is doing what he can to initiate the acts which lead to drinking. He is starting with the stimulus to his habit. To succeed he must find some positive interest or line of action which will inhibit the drinking series and which by instituting another course of action will bring him to his desired end.[1]

The dramatization of the evil therefore tends to precipitate the conflict situation which was first created through some innocent maladjustment. The child's isolation forces him into companionship with other children similarly defined, and the gang becomes his means of escape, his security. The life of the gang gives it special mores, and the attack by the community upon these mores merely

[1]John Dewey, *Human Nature and Conduct*, p. 35. New York, 1922.

overemphasizes the conflict already in existence, and makes it the source of a new series of experiences that lead directly to a criminal career.

In dealing with the delinquent, the criminal, therefore, the important thing to remember is that we are dealing with a human being who is responding normally to the demands, stimuli, approval, expectancy, of the group with whom he is associated. We are dealing not with an individual but with a group.

> In a study of 6,000 instances of stealing, with reference to the number of boys involved, it was found that in 90.4 per cent of the cases two or more boys were known to have been involved in the act and were consequently brought to court. Only 9.6 per cent of all the cases were acts of single individuals. Since this study was based upon the number of boys brought to court, and since in many cases not all of the boys involved were caught and brought to court, it is certain that the percentage of group stealing is therefore even greater than 90.4 per cent. It cannot be doubted that delinquency, particularly stealing, almost invariably involves two or more persons.[2]

That group may be a small gang, a gang of children just growing up, a gang of young "toughs" of nineteen or twenty, or a gang of older criminals of thirty. If we are not dealing with a gang we may be dealing with a family. And if we are not dealing with either of these especially we may be dealing with a community. In practice all these factors—the family, the gang, and the community—may be important in the development and the maintenance of that attitude towards the world which makes a criminal career a normal, an accepted and approved way of life.

Direct attack upon the individual in these circumstances is a dubious undertaking. By the time the individual has become a criminal his habits have been so shaped that we have a fairly integrated character whose whole career is in tune with the peculiar bit of the environment for which he has developed the behavior and habits that cause him to be apprehended. In theory isolation from that group ought to provide occasion for change in the individual's habit structure. It might, if the individual were transplanted to a group whose values and activities had the approval of the wider community, and in which the newcomer might hope to gain full acceptance eventually. But until now isolation has meant the group-

[2]Clifford R. Shaw and Earl D. Myers, "The Juvenile Delinquent," *The Illinois Crime Survey*, pp. 662–663. Chicago, 1929.

ing in close confinement of persons whose strongest common bond has been their socially disapproved delinquent conduct. Thus the attack cannot be made without reference to group life.

The attack must be on the whole group; for only by changing its attitudes and ideals, interests and habits, can the stimuli which it exerts upon the individual be changed. Punishment as retribution has failed to reform, that is, to change character. If the individual can be made aware of a different set of values for which he may receive approval, then we may be on the road to a change in his character. But such a change of values involves a change in stimuli, which means that the criminal's social world must be changed before he can be changed.

The point of view here developed rejects all assumptions that would impute crime to the individual in the sense that a personal shortcoming of the offender is the cause of the unsocial behavior. The assumption that crime is caused by any sort of inferiority, physiological or psychological, is here completely and unequivocally repudiated.

This of course does not mean that morphological or psychological techniques do not have value in dealing with the individual. It merely means that they have no greater value in the study of criminology than they would have in the study of any profession. If a poor IQ is a bad beginning for a career in medicine, it is also a poor beginning for a career in crime. If the psychiatrist can testify that a psychopath will make an irritable doctor he can prove the same for the criminal. But he can prove no more. The criminal differs from the rest of his fellows only in the sense that he has learned to respond to the stimuli of a very small and specialized group; but that group must exist or the criminal could not exist. In that he is like the mass of men, living a certain kind of life with the kind of companions that make that life possible.

This explanation of criminal behavior is meant to apply to those who more or less consistently pursue the criminal career. It does not necessarily presume to describe the accidental criminal or the man who commits a crime of passion. Here perhaps the theories that would seek the cause of crime in the individual may have greater application than in attempting to deal with those who follow a life of crime. But even in the accidental criminal there is a strong presumption that the accident is the outcome of a habit situation. Any habit tends to have a background of social conditioning.

A man with the habit of giving way to anger may show his habit by a murderous attack upon some one who has offended. His act is nonetheless due to habit because it occurs only once in his life. The essence of habit is an acquired predisposition to *ways* or modes of response, not to particular acts except as, under special conditions, these express a way of behaving. Habit means special sensitiveness or accessibility to certain classes of stimuli, standing predilections and aversions, rather than bare recurrence of specific acts. It means will.[3]

In other words, perhaps the accidental criminal also is to be explained in terms such as we used in discussing the professional criminal.

[3]Dewey, op. cit., p. 42

The
Self-Fulfilling Prophecy
Robert K. Merton

In a series of works seldom consulted outside the academic fraternity, W. I. Thomas, the dean of American sociologists, set forth a theorem basic to the social sciences: "If men define situations as real, they are real in their consequences." Were the Thomas theorem and its implications more widely known more men would understand more of the workings of our society. Though it lacks the sweep and precision of a Newtonian theorem, it possesses the same gift of relevance, being instructively applicable to many, if indeed not most, social processes.

The Thomas Theorem

"If men define situations as real, they are real in their consequences," wrote Professor Thomas. The suspicion that he was driving at a crucial point becomes all the more insistent when we note that essentially the same theorem had been repeatedly set forth by disciplined and observant minds long before Thomas.

When we find such otherwise discrepant minds as the redoubtable Bishop Bossuet in his passionate seventeenth-century defense of Catholic orthodoxy, the ironic Mandeville in his eighteenth-century allegory honeycombed with observations on the paradoxes of human society, the irascible genius Marx in his revision of Hegel's theory of historical change, the seminal Freud in works which have perhaps gone further than any others of his day toward modifying man's outlook on man, and the erudite, dogmatic, and occasionally sound Yale professor, William Graham Sumner, who lives on as the Karl Marx of the middle classes—when we find this mixed company (and I select from a longer if less distinguished list) agreeing on the truth and the pertinence of what is substantially the Thomas theorem, we may conclude that perhaps it is worth our attention as well.

To what, then, are Thomas and Bossuet, Mandeville, Marx, Freud and Sumner directing our attention?

The first part of the theorem provides an unceasing reminder that men respond not only to the objective features of a situation, but also, and at times primarily, to the meaning this situation has for them. And once they have assigned some meaning to the situation, their consequent behavior and some of the consequences of that behavior are determined by the ascribed meaning. But this is still rather abstract, and abstractions have a way of becoming unintelligible if they are not occasionally tied to concrete data. What is a case in point?

A Sociological Parable

It is the year 1932. The Last National Bank is a flourishing institution. A large part of its resources is liquid without being watered. Cartwright Millingville has ample reason to be proud of the banking institution over which he presides. Until Black Wednesday. As he enters his bank, he notices that business is unusually brisk. A little odd, that, since the men at the A.M.O.K. steel plant and the K.O.M.A. mattress factory are not usually paid until Saturday. Yet here are two dozen men, obviously from the factories, queued up in front of the tellers' cages. As he turns into his private office, the president muses rather compassionately: "Hope they haven't been laid off in midweek. They should be in the shop at this hour."

But speculations of this sort have never made for a thriving bank, and Millingville turns to the pile of documents upon his desk. His precise signature is affixed to fewer than a score of papers when he is disturbed by the absence of something familiar and the intrusion of something alien. The low discreet hum of bank business has given way to a strange and annoying stridency of many voices. A situation has been defined as real. And that is the beginning of what ends as Black Wednesday—the last Wednesday, it might be noted, of the Last National Bank.

Cartwright Millingville had never heard of the Thomas theorem. But he had no difficulty in recognizing its workings. He knew that, despite the comparative liquidity of the bank's assets, a rumor of insolvency, once believed by enough depositors, would result in the insolvency of the bank. And by the close of Black Wednesday—and Blacker Thursday—when the long lines of anxious depositors, each frantically seeking to salvage his own, grew to longer lines of even more anxious depositors, it turned out that he was right.

The stable financial structure of the bank had depended upon one set of definitions of the situation: belief in the validity of the interlocking system of economic promises men live by. Once depositors had defined the situation otherwise, once they questioned the possibility of having these promises fulfilled, the consequences of this unreal definition were real enough.

A familiar type-case this, and one doesn't need the Thomas theorem to understand how it happened—not, at least, if one is old enough to have voted for Franklin Roosevelt in 1932. But with the aid of the theorem the tragic history of Millingville's bank can perhaps be converted into a sociological parable which may help us understand not only what happened to hundreds of banks in the '30's but also what happens to the relations between Negro and white, between Protestant and Catholic and Jew in these days.

The parable tells us that public definitions of a situation (prophecies or predictions) become an integral part of the situation and thus affect subsequent developments. This is peculiar to human affairs. It is not found in the world of nature, untouched by human hands. Predictions of the return of Halley's comet do not influence its orbit. But the rumored insolvency of Millingville's bank did affect the actual outcome. The prophecy of collapse led to its own fulfillment.

So common is the pattern of the self-fulfilling prophecy that each of us has his favored specimen. Consider the case of the examination neurosis. Convinced that he is destined to fail, the anxious student devotes more time to worry than to study and then turns in a poor examination. The initially fallacious anxiety is transformed into an entirely justified fear. Or it is believed that war between two nations is inevitable. Actuated by this conviction, representatives of the two nations become progressively alienated, apprehensively countering each "offensive" move of the other with a "defensive" move of their own. Stockpiles of armaments, raw materials, and armed men grow larger and eventually the anticipation of war helps create the actuality.

The self-fulfilling prophecy is, in the beginning a *false* definition of the situation evoking a new behavior which makes the originally false conception come *true*. The specious validity of the self-fulfilling prophecy perpetuates a reign of error. For the prophet will cite the actual course of events as proof that he was right from the very beginning. (Yet we know that Millingville's bank was solvent, that it would have survived for many years had not the misleading rumor *created* the very conditions of its own fulfillment.) Such are the perversities of social logic.

It is the self-fulfilling prophecy which goes far toward explaining the dynamics of ethnic and racial conflict in the America of today. That this is the case, at least for relations between Negroes and whites, may be gathered from the fifteen hundred pages which make up Gunnar Myrdal's *An American Dilemma.* That the self-fulfilling prophecy may have even more general bearing upon the relations between ethnic groups than Myrdal has indicated is the thesis of the considerably briefer discussion that follows.[1]

Social Beliefs and Social Reality

As a result of their failure to comprehend the operation of the self-fulfilling prophecy, many Americans of good will (sometimes reluctantly) retain enduring ethnic and racial prejudices. They experience these beliefs, not as prejudices, not as prejudgments, but as irresistible products of their own observation. "The facts of the case" permit them no other conclusion.

Thus our fair-minded white citizen strongly supports a policy of excluding Negroes from his labor union. His views are, of course, based not upon prejudice, but upon the cold hard facts. And the facts seem clear enough. Negroes, "lately from the nonindustrial South, are undisciplined in traditions of trade unionism and the art of collective bargaining." The Negro is a strikebreaker. The Negro, with his "low standard of living," rushes in to take jobs at less than prevailing wages. The Negro is, in short, "a traitor to the working class," and should manifestly be excluded from union organizations. So run the facts of the case as seen by our tolerant but hard-headed union member, innocent of any understanding of the self-fulfilling prophecy as a basic process of society.

Our unionist fails to see, of course, that he and his kind have produced the very "facts" which he observes. For by defining the situation as one in which Negroes are held to be incorrigibly at odds

[1]Counterpart of the self-fulfilling prophecy is the "suicidal prophecy" which so alters human behavior from what would have been its course had the prophecy not been made, that it *fails* to be borne out. The prophecy destroys itself. This important type is not considered here. For examples of both types of social prophecy, see R. M. MacIver, *The More Perfect Union* (New York: Macmillan, 1948); for a general statement, see Merton, "The unanticipated consequences of purposive social action," American Sociological Review 1936, 1, 894–904.

with principles of unionism and by excluding Negroes from unions, he invited a series of consequences which indeed made it difficult if not impossible for many Negroes to avoid the role of scab. Out of work after World War I, and kept out of unions, thousands of Negroes could not resist strikebound employers who held a door invitingly open upon a world of jobs from which they were otherwise excluded.

History creates its own test of the theory of self-fulfilling prophecies. That Negroes were strikebreakers because they were excluded from unions (and from a wide range of jobs) rather than excluded because they were strikebreakers can be seen from the virtual disappearance of Negroes as scabs in industries where they have gained admission to unions in the last decades.

The application of the Thomas theorem also suggests how the tragic, often vicious, circle of self-fulfilling prophecies can be broken. The initial definition of the situation which has set the circle in motion must be abandoned. Only when the original assumption is questioned and a new definition of the situation introduced, does the consequent flow of events give the lie to the assumption. Only then does the belief no longer father the reality.

Criminal Conceptions, Legal Process, and Crime Causation

Victoria Lynn Swigert and Ronald A. Farrell

The sociology of law, by directing attention to the judicial system as a social institution, acknowledges the sensitivity of judicial decision making to the social milieu of which it is a part. The focus of study, however, has been on the development and administration of law over time, with little reference to the implications of such processes for the creation and maintenance of criminality. The system of theories and research efforts that has developed, therefore, has largely been in isolation from other areas of criminological research.* . . .

One . . . area for the exploration of . . . [the] . . . interaction . . . [between law and behavior concerns] . . . the legal treatment of criminal defendants. For it is within this . . . [arena] . . . that the confrontation of legal authorities and the various

From *Murder, Inequality, and the Law* by Victoria Lynn Swigert and Ronald A. Farrell. Lexington, Massachusetts: Lexington Books, D. C. Heath Company, 1976, pp. 89–90, 1–4, 93–101, 9–10, 102–103.

* To be sure, research does exist that recognizes structural influences in the development of behavior patterns. Little by way of formal integration of these social processes, however, may be found. Thus, for example, the societal reactions approach to deviance has introduced the possibility of legal sanction as an important factor in career deviation. At the same time, this emphasis has yet to be systematically incorporated into the perspective. Rather, arrest or conviction are seen as examples of a more inclusive range of possible societal reactions that may or may not trigger movement toward secondary deviance; see, for example, Martin S. Weinberg and Collin J. Williams, *Homosexuals and the Military* (New York: Harper and Row, 1971); and Ronald A. Farrell and Clay W. Hardin, "Legal Stigma and Homosexual Career Deviance," in Marc Riedel and Terence P. Thornberry, eds., *Crime and Delinquency: Dimensions of Deviance* (New York: Praeger, 1974).

political and social groups becomes most evident. In the pages that follow, an attempt is made to formulate a theory of legal treatment and criminal behavior by drawing from both structural and interactional processes. . . . It is argued that the differential legal treatment of offenders constitutes a causative factor in the creation and maintenance of criminal behavior . . .

The Judicial Process and Criminal Imagery

. . . It may be noted that law enforcement and adjudication are interpretive processes. At each stage, legal authorities must assess the defendant and the offense for evidence that official sanction is warranted. Such evaluation and interpretation may be guided, in part, by popular stereotypes of criminality.

Evidence that stereotypes exist in the general population is abundant. Persons asked to describe deviants do, in fact, tend to utilize highly stereotypical characterizations. Furthermore, individual descriptions of specific deviations are remarkably similar in content.[1] Thus, "the marijuana smoker stereotype emerges as an insecure escapist, lacking self-control and looking for kicks; the adulterer is immoral, promiscuous, and insecure; the homosexual is perverted and mentally ill; the political radical is ambitious, aggressive, stubborn, and dangerous."[2]

Deviance-specific stereotypes have also emerged from studies of mental illness[3] and blindness.[4] Such conceptions are perpetuated in everyday interaction and in the mass media characterizations of comic strips, television, newspapers, books, songs, and advertising. In this manner, even the very young become familiar with the stereotypes—images that continue to be reaffirmed throughout adulthood.[5] Thus, to be "crazy" is to be wild, erratic, and dangerous, while "helplessness, dependency, melancholy, docility, gravity of inner thought, aestheticism [are the] things that commonsense views tell us to expect of the blind."[6]

Stereotypes not only shape public attitudes and behavior toward deviants, but they also guide the very choice of individuals who are to be so defined and processed. Pointing out that only a fraction of those who engage in nonconforming behavior are ever labeled deviant, J. L. Simmons argues that this selection is not random, but rather is influenced by the popular images of deviance. Persons possessing characteristics associated with the stereotype of a particular deviation are more likely to be identified and reacted to as such.[7]

Furthermore, since minority groups, lower-class persons, and males more closely approximate stereotypic images, these groups are especially susceptible to their application.[8] The following account of the marijuana smoker is illustrative: ". . . a greasy Puerto Rican boy or a shaky little Skid Row bum . . . As for life led, it is shiftless, unhappy, dog eat dog for survival. I guess marijuana is used as a means of avoiding reality. The pleasure that comes from the drug outweighs the pleasure of life as it really is."[9] Crime cartoons reveal a similar bias. Typical depictions of the criminal with his "peaked 'cabbie' cap, prognathous lower face, cauliflower ears, stubbled chin, and low forehead" clearly suggest that "criminals belong to the lowest socio-economic class, a view widespread since the middle of the nineteenth century with its concept of the 'dangerous classes.' "[10]

Popular beliefs about deviants, moreover, are also found at the organizational level and may influence the application of formal labels. "Organizational practices, particularly the selection and processing of individuals by formal agencies of control, often reflect common public stereotypes or more specific organizational ideologies grounded in stereotyped thinking."[11] Thus, for example, facial stereotypes of the murderer, robber, and traitor have been found to affect evaluations of guilt for each of these criminal categories.[12] Similarly, in the case of homosexuality:

> the crucial factor influencing legal processing is not whether individuals are known to be engaging in homosexual activity, but rather if they appear to be homosexual in a stereotypic sense. . . . Such highly visible behavior may invite the intervention of police who tend to operate on 'normal' (stereotypic) cases and convince them of guilt once they have apprehended the individual. The fact that one does not display [for example] overt and effeminate behavior may [even] raise the more basic question in the minds of some as to whether he is in fact homosexual.[13]

The importance of appearance in the decision to apprehend also emerges in the case of shoplifting. Here, variation in the dress of shoplifters as either "straight" or "hippie" has been shown to exert a major influence on reporting levels.[14]

Evidence does exist, therefore, to suggest that stereotypes operate as guiding imageries for action in the treatment of deviance. Applying Goffman's theoretical discussion of the stigma to the adjudication process, it may be observed that the stereotype becomes the "means for categorizing persons and the complement of attributes felt to be ordinary and natural for members of each of these categories," the product of which is to "allow us to deal with anticipated others without special attention or thought."[15] A *legally* problematic situation would seem to be particularly prone to the use of such categorizations. Where constraints of time, personnel, and the sheer number of individuals who must be processed preclude full enforcement or extensive investigation, officials are likely to depend on shorthand methods in administrative decisions. Such methods include inspection of the offender and the offense for conformity to the popular conception of criminality.

The idea of what constitutes criminality is a product of an accumulated wisdom among legal representatives developed in their daily interaction with law violators. At every stage of the judicial process, from arrest through final conviction and sentencing, the imagery utilized in official decision making consists of configuration of characteristics relevant to the behavior in question. While class or racial status may contribute to these conceptions, they may not, in themselves, provide sufficient information for those charged with legal processing decisions. . . . Rather, these important status variables must be assessed in terms of their mediation through the criminal stereotype.*

Substitution of an interpretive imagery for class and race measures does not detract from the significance of the question of differential justice. For, the operation of a legally relevant stereotype of offenders in decisions concerning their adjudication is by far the more insidious process. Overt discrimination against persons for reasons of class or race is illegal. Official representatives charged with such misuse of office are themselves criminally accountable. Decision making in terms of a popularly accepted conception of criminality, however, is not only beyond the sanction of legal control but, in some instances, enjoys an institutionalized status. The criteria that guide bail decisions, the award of parole, and the focus of pre-sentence investigations are exemplary of the institutionalization of such conceptions as meaningful information in the legal process. The possibility that this imagery includes stereotypic assessments of certain classes and races has important implications for the distribution of justice in the United States. For the adjudication of persons on the basis of their conformity to

* Richard Quinney is to be credited with the development of the notion of *criminal conceptions*. In his own work, the criminal conception is the medium through which powerful segments of society ensure consistent definitions of criminality. Through the diffusion of popular conceptions, individuals become aware of the social characteristics of offenders, the appropriate reaction to crime, and the relevance of crime to the social system; see Richard Quinney, *The Social Reality of Crime* (Boston: Little, Brown, 1970).

criminal conceptions constitutes a patterned exclusion of portions of the population from full equality before the law. . . .

. . . Within the legal system, the expectation that individuals who conform to the criminal conception are most likely to exhibit criminal behavior constitutes a presumption of guilt. The processing of such persons, consequently, takes on a routine nature. For, when guilt is presumed, little justification can be found for providing defendants with the combatative tools essential for successful defense of their cases. The lack of legal resources that mediate between initial charge and final outcome is, in turn, instrumental in maintaining an imagery of guilt. Assignment of public counsel [for example] identifies the individual with that class of persons, the indigent, out of which the criminal stereotype is formulated; denial of bail defines the defendant as a potential danger to society; and waiver of trial by jury is self-admission of criminal involvement. Those defendants, therefore, whose access to private attorney, bail, or jury trial is blocked, are further confirmed in the stereotype of the crime within which they were originally defined. The sequence of events from designation as apparently criminal through lack of provision of legal resources for their defense produces the outcome predicted by legal wisdom — official award of criminal conviction.[16]

The Criminal Conception and the Subculture of Violence

[The use of criminal conceptions in legal processing constitutes an important link in the development of a theory of legal treatment and crime causation. The application of the stereotype of violent criminality to an analysis of homicide is illustrative.]

. . . Descriptive analyses of murder indicate that the patterns involved in such behavior are highly stable. That is, variations in the regions, time frames, and data sources studied produce minimal differences in the patterns reported in the literature. The study of the social characteristics of offenders in particular[17] has led a number of theorists to speculate on the origins of the frequency of violent behavior among certain portions of the population. Whether such theories have focused on the "inherent impulsiveness"[18] of blacks or have contributed to the more recent and popular perspective on the "subculture of violence," emphasis has been on a set of presumed characteristics said to predispose certain types of individuals to violent behavior. The substance of many of these theories suggests parallels with the criminal stereotype. . . .

By far, the most influential theory of violent behavior is that of the subculture of violence. The tendency toward excessive use of force is a reflection of participation in a subculture where there exists a normative system that "designates that in some types of social interaction a violent and physically aggressive response is either expected or required of all members sharing in that system of values."[19]

The expression of violence as a reflection of a subcultural normative system has the support of several findings in homicide research. The extent to which defendants in homicide have engaged in prior aggressive behavior[20] . . . is an indication of the diffusiveness of a violent response among these individuals. The ready access to weapons, many of which are carried as part of daily apparel, suggests an expectation for violent encounters. The types of situations and interactions for which a violent response is elicited indicates a definition of the situation that appears unshared by the dominant culture.

. . . [Commenting] . . . on the subculture of violence, Pittman and Handy, comparing aggravated assault and homicide, and noting the extent and similarities in the patterns of each, conclude that such acts are "reflective of population subgroupings which tend to externalize their aggression when confronted with conflict situations."[21] Further support for such a cultural tradition is offered by Pettigrew and Spier[22] in their research on black and white homicide rates. They report that neither immigration of blacks into an area, nor the socioeconomic deprivation and family disorganization of a population have any effect on homicide rates when homicidal culture is held constant. Blacks and lower class persons who are involved in criminal slayings are from regions where white homicide rates are also high, from regions where there exists a culture of violence.

Research on homicide, then, suggests the existence of subcultural traditions conducive to aggressive and violent behavior. The theories used to explain such patterns share in an imagery of the violent offender that bears remarkable resemblance to . . . [a more popular] . . . criminal conception. . . . Banay, for example maintains that the majority of homicides occur at:

that level of feeling, thought, and action in which the individual is accustomed to, and perhaps is incapable of adjusting to the criteria of our culture. He has the mental equipment to gauge his situation accurately, but the ethical

> perception is dulled or remains undeveloped because of
> his family or community setting, which entered into the
> formulation of his personality. A person in this subcul-
> tural group is perhaps more likely to get into situations
> where violence may occur, and has less innate equipment
> for keeping his violent tendencies in check than most of
> us.[23]

Harlan's description of the social disorganization of family
and social life and the "unsystematic and unregulated chaos in
which individual desire, choice and whim govern behavior"[24] also
reflects a view of the lower-class offender sympathetic with the
. . . [stereotype] . . .

But perhaps the closest approximation to the . . . [criminal
imagery] . . . comes from the work of Marvin Wolfgang when he
writes:

> . . . there appears to be a sub-culture where the collective
> id dominates social consciousness—i.e., where basic urges,
> drives, and impulses of the group members are less har-
> monized with each other or external reality; where basic
> drives are less inhibited, restricted, or restrained; where
> reduction of tension and satisfaction of needs are char-
> acterized by immediacy and directness; and where the
> social regulators of conduct are weak and less omnipresent
> than in the larger culture of which this collectivity is a
> part.[25]

. . . While the theoretical developments associated with the
subculture of violence reflect a social scientific approach to the
problem of causality, it [is] . . . argued in this work that a similar
imagery exists more generally in society, and, more important,
within those institutions officially charged with the control of
criminal behavior. Thus, to theorize that blacks and members of
the lower classes are prone to violent behavior is to state a specific
aspect of a more popular belief that these individuals are prone to
higher levels of criminality. To speculate on the nature of such behavior as a product of discrimination or class bias does not mitigate
the saliency of observations made throughout society that these
patterns of criminal involvement do, in fact, exist. While the symbols may vary over time from the "dangerous classes" to the
"criminal element," the imagery remains the same. A conception
exists in our society such that members of lower-status groups,
through mass media accounts and conventional wisdom, come to

be defined as criminally motivated. The scientific "discovery" of a violent subculture is testimony to the success with which this stereotype has been applied.

The self-fulfilling effect of the definition that certain groups are prone to criminality is the focus of . . . this work. In this regard, an attempt is made to explicate the processes by which the institutionalization of criminal conceptions in judicial procedures comes to influence criminal behavior patterns. Discretionary legal reaction to individuals on the basis of the criminal imagery operates as a causal influence in the development and perpetuation of a "subculture of violence." The persistence of the conception of the violent offender in both criminal behavior patterns and official decision making, finally, is instrumental in the maintenance of a legal system of differential justice. The following series of interrelated propositions constitutes a formal elaboration of this process. This theory of legal treatment and crime causation is diagrammatically illustrated in Figure 1.

A Theory of Legal Process and Crime Causation

Proposition 1:

Within the normative system of social structure there exist definitions of criminality that, by incorporating traits most characteristic of minority classes and races, reflect the differential ability of certain groups to define as deviant persons whose behavior is at variance with dominant cultural patterns.

In a pluralistic society, the social distance that separates groups produces a tendency toward the construction of stereotypes for defining the situation of others. These typifications allow the individual to anticipate and predict behavior in a situation of limited interaction. Central to the first proposition is the suggestion that the definitions of some collectivities are more pervasive and influential in establishing the normative criteria of criminality. While the behavioral patterns of all groups are a product of the same processes of socialization, then, the behavior of some, by virtue of their social location, is more likely to be defined as criminal than that of others. From this perspective, criminality may be viewed as a socially constructed phenomenon arising out of the normal processes of differentiation and definition.

Proposition 2:

The popular conceptions of criminality become institutionalized in the judicial system and serve as the guiding imagery for action regarding those to whom such definitions are applied.

Through their predominance in legislative and judicial processes, dominant group definitions come to be incorporated into legal procedure. These definitions are reflected at various levels of the judicial process and influence action relative to minority populations.

In the decision to invoke legal sanctions, official representatives assess conformity to the criminal conception as defined by dominant culture. To the extent that these conceptions are comprised of behavior forms ·characteristic of the lower classes and minority groups, the legal system may be viewed as an institutional representation of the larger societal processes of differentiation and definition. This occurs through the selective processing of individuals whose behavior or situation concurs with the criminal stereotype.

Proposition 3:

In the judicial process, those persons who are said to conform to the conception of criminality are presumed guilty to the extent that they are not provided the legal protection accorded more advantaged defendants.

Application of the stereotype in the assessment of typical offenders and normal crimes implies that a determination of guilt has been made before formal adjudication. When guilt has become the predicted outcome and the apparent circumstances do not substantiate the possibility of innocence, it becomes both unnecessary and unjustified to expend scarce resources on defense. Rather, the assessment of the social characteristics of the offender and the offense becomes the information upon which final adjudication decisions are based.

Proposition 4:

Persons who lack the legal resources for adequate defense receive the more severe dispositions by the court, dispositions that then act to confirm the original criminal conceptions.

Application of the criminal stereotype and the subsequent

withholding of legal resources has a self-fulfilling effect. Having been assigned public counsel, denied bail, and encouraged to waive trial by jury, those who are thought to conform to the stereotype are awarded the more severe convictions. Such dispositions are a product of the lack of legal protection provided in public defense and of the further confirmation of the imagery of guilt implied by pretrial detention and the utilization of a nonjury format. The award of conviction, in this situation, serves ultimately to confirm the applicability of the original belief in the criminality of those to whom the stereotype has been applied.

Proposition 5:

Official designation as criminal results in further isolation of persons from full participation in legitimate society and intensifies subcultural commitments.

The differential legal treatment of criminal defendants constitutes an act of exclusion from a major institution of society — the legal system. Similar to the effect of all discriminatory social policies, isolation from the legal standards made available to dominant social groups produces a reaffirmed commitment to original subcultural norms.

An important element of these commitments is the stereotypic attributes associated with criminality. For the diffusiveness of such images provides those so labeled with a summation of the relevant characteristics and behaviors prescribing their status. Since subcultural groups are comprised of individuals who have been exposed to and have internalized the stereotype, the characteristics associated with the imagery are continually reaffirmed. The stereotype, therefore, not only acts to exclude individuals from access to the resources essential for successful participation in the legal arena, but also acts to provide the expectations of the criminal role as defined by dominant society.

Proposition 6:

The conflict of cultures, along with the formal application of the criminal label, confirms legal representatives in their original conceptions and lends to a reaffirmation of dominant definitions of criminality.

The behavior of subcultural members and their formal designation as criminal reaffirm the belief in the necessity of isolating such persons from legitimate roles. It is the persistence of this belief that, in turn, serves to confirm legal representatives in their discretionary and punitive treatment of the culturally different. The subsequent exclusion produced by such institutionalized discrimination precludes full opportunity for enculturation to dominant norms and behaviors. The net effect of this process is a continuously renewed cycle of conflict with the larger society. Thus, the interaction between the criminally defined and the legal system results in a renewal of deviance-defining processes that ultimately contribute to the persistence of the original subcultures.

In sum, the theory suggests the existence of cultural definitions of criminality based on class- and race-related characteristics. These definitions are institutionalized in the judicial system and have important implications for the legal treatment of criminal defendants. In the assessment of cases, those persons whose behavior and situation conform to the conception of criminality are denied the presumption of innocence routinely accorded more advantaged defendants. The imagery of guilt within which they are processed leads to a denial of the legal resources essential for successful defense, the outcome of which is the award of more severe dispositions by the court.

This process of differential adjudication is an important aspect in the creation and maintenance of criminal behavior patterns among the lower classes and minority groups. For, discretionary treatment in such an important institutional arena constitutes a form of social isolation conducive to subcultural development. These subcultures serve to reinforce the behaviors of those who conform to the criminal conception, and, thus, to intensify the original cultural differences. The ensuing conflict, along with the process of adjudication itself, acts to validate the criminal imagery.

Implications of the Theory for Violent Behavior

In the case of homicide, . . . [there exists a conception of the violent offender which] . . . represents the institutionalization of a criminal stereotype in judicial procedures. This conception is a product of an accumulation of observations and impressions concerning the characteristics typically associated with homicide. . . . [Such an offender] is seen as one whose social and cultural background predispose him to violent behavior. Living under disorganized . . . conditions, his response to any situation of personal challenge is aggression.

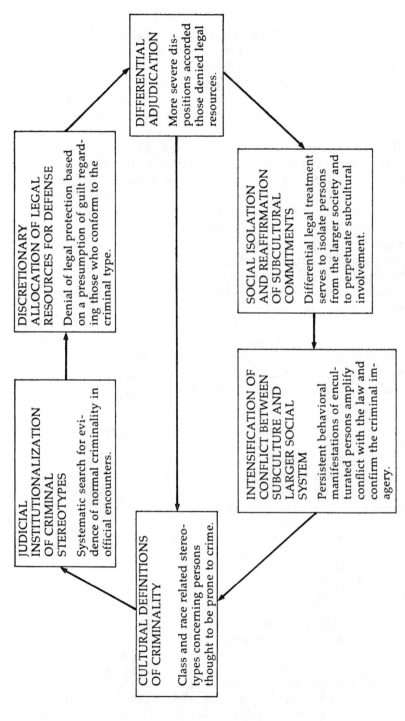

Figure 1. Legal Process and Crime Causation.

The boxes in the figure contain the following text:

JUDICIAL INSTITUTIONALIZATION OF CRIMINAL STEREOTYPES
Systematic search for evidence of normal criminality in official encounters.

DISCRETIONARY ALLOCATION OF LEGAL RESOURCES FOR DEFENSE
Denial of legal protection based on a presumption of guilt regarding those who conform to the criminal type.

DIFFERENTIAL ADJUDICATION
More severe dispositions accorded those denied legal resources.

SOCIAL ISOLATION AND REAFFIRMATION OF SUBCULTURAL COMMITMENTS
Differential legal treatment serves to isolate persons from the larger society and to perpetuate subcultural involvement.

INTENSIFICATION OF CONFLICT BETWEEN SUBCULTURE AND LARGER SOCIAL SYSTEM
Persistent behavioral manifestations of enculturated persons amplify conflict with the law and confirm the criminal imagery.

CULTURAL DEFINITIONS OF CRIMINALITY
Class and race related stereotypes concerning persons thought to be prone to crime.

It has been posited that decisions to invoke legal sanctions involve assessments of conformity to such criminal conceptions. Once the applicability of the stereotype is determined, the assurance of legal safeguards becomes superfluous. The absence of these resources further confirms the imagery of criminal responsibility and disadvantages the defense to the extent that more severe dispositions are meted out by the court. . . .

It has also been suggested that differential legal treatment has important consequences for the development of violent behavior. Such discrimination acts to perpetuate the subcultural patterns conducive to violence. This is a result of exclusion from legitimate definitions and opportunities, on the one hand, and adherence to subculturally derived norms and values, on the other. Central to the argument is the contention that the popular conception of criminality acts to shape behavior within these isolated segments of the population. Expectations that membership in the black and lower classes will produce a propensity to violence, then, takes on meaning not only for the larger society but for those involved in such subcultures as well. Without the social opportunities and information necessary for enculturation to dominant norms and behaviors, subcultural manifestations of stereotypical behavior patterns are likely to produce a continuously renewed cycle of conflict with, and exclusion from, the dominant culture . . . .

Notes

1. J. L. Simmons, "Public Stereotypes of Deviants," *Social Problems* 13, 2 (Fall 1965), p. 226.
2. Ibid., p. 228. © 1965 by The Society for the Study of Social Problems.
3. J. C. Nunnally, Jr., *Popular Conceptions of Mental Health* (New York: Holt, 1961); Thomas J. Scheff, *Being Mentally Ill* (Chicago: Aldine, 1966).
4. Robert A. Scott, *The Making of Blind Men: A Study of Adult Socialization* (New York: Russell Sage, 1969).
5. Albert C. Cain, "On the Meaning of 'Playing Crazy' in Borderline Children," *Psychiatry* 27 (1964), pp. 278–289; Scheff, op. cit., p. 64.
6. Scott, op. cit., p. 4.
7. Simmons, op. cit., p. 226.
8. Ibid., p. 226.
9. Ibid., p. 226.
10. Albert G. Hess and Dorothy A. Mariner, "On the Sociology of Crime Cartoons," *International Journal of Criminology and Penology* 3 (1975), p. 255.
11. Edwin M. Schur, *Labeling Deviant Behavior: Its Sociological Implications* (New York: Harper and Row, 1971), p. 51.
12. Donald J. Shoemaker, Donald R. South, and Jay Lowe, "Facial Stereotypes of Deviants and Judgments of Guilt or Innocence," *Social Forces*

51 (June 1973), pp. 427–433.

13. Ronald A. Farrell and Clay W. Hardin, "Legal Stigma and Homosexual Career Deviance," in Marc Riedel and Terence P. Thornberry, eds., *Crime and Delinquency: Dimensions of Deviance* (New York: Praeger, 1974), pp. 134–135. © 1974 Praeger Publishers.

14. Darrell J. Steffensmeier and Robert M. Terry, "Deviance and Respectability: An Observational Study of Reactions to Shoplifting," *Social Forces* 51 (June 1973), pp. 417–426.

15. Erving Goffman, *Stigma: Notes on the Management of Spoiled Identity* (Englewood Cliffs, N. J.: Prentice-Hall, 1963), p. 2.

16. [For an empirical examination of the role of criminal conceptions in legal processing, see Victoria Lynn Swigert and Ronald A. Farrell, *Murder, Inequality, and the Law* (Lexington, Mass.: Heath, 1976), and "Normal Homicides and the Law," *American Sociological Review* 42, 1 (February 1977), pp. 16–32.]

17. Robert C. Bensing and Oliver Schroeder, Jr., *Homicide in an Urban Community* (Springfield, Ill.,: Charles C Thomas, 1960); J. V. De Porte and Elizabeth Parkhurst, "Homicide in New York State: A Statistical Study of the Victims and Criminals in Thirty-Seven Counties in 1921–1930," *Human Biology* 7 (1935), pp. 47–73; Howard Harlan, "Five Hundred Homicides," *Journal of Criminal Law, Criminology and Police Science* 40 (March-April 1950), pp. 736–752; Alex D. Porkorny, "A Comparison of Homicides in Two Cities," *Journal of Criminal Law, Criminology and Police Science* 56, 4 (December 1965), pp. 479–487; Calvin F. Schmid, "A Study of Homicides in Seattle, 1914–1924," *Social Forces* 4 (June 1926), pp. 745–756; Harwin L. Voss and John R. Hepburn, "Patterns in Criminal Homicide in Chicago," *Journal of Criminal Law, Criminology and Police Science* 59, 4 (December 1968), pp. 499–508; Marvin Wolfgang, *Patterns in Criminal Homicide* (Philadelphia: University of Pennsylvania Press, 1958).

18. Charles S. Johnson et. al., *The Negro in American Civilization* (New York: Holt, 1930).

19. Marvin E. Wolfgang and Franco Ferracuti, *The Subculture of Violence* (London: Methaen, 1967), pp. 150–163.

20. Wolfgang, op. cit., pp. 177–178; Swigert and Farrell, 1976, op. cit., pp. 44–46.

21. David J. Pittman and William Handy, "Patterns of Criminal Aggravated Assault," *Journal of Criminal Law, Criminology and Police Science* 55, 4 (December 1964), p. 470.

22. Thomas F. Pettigrew and Rosalind Barclay Spier, "The Ecological Structure of Negro Homicide," *American Journal of Sociology* 67, 6 (May 1962), p. 624.

23. Ralph S. Banay, "Study in Murder," *Annals of the American Academy of Political and Social Science* 364 (1966), p. 26.

24. Harlan, op. cit., pp. 738–739.

25. Wolfgang, op. cit., p. 329.

part Three

The Interactionist Perspective

In the preceding sections we examined the functional relationship between deviance and the social system and the definitional processes that create deviance categories. The following section, based on *the interactionist perspective,* focuses on the impact that these structural and definitional processes have on the individual deviant.

The first selection by Charles Horton Cooley deals with the role of the social structure and definitional processes in the development of the self. Cooley defines the *social self* as a "system of ideas, drawn from the communicative life, that the mind cherishes as its own." This definition contains three principal elements: "the imagination of our appearance to the other person; the imagination of his judgment of that appearance; and some sort of self feeling, such as pride or mortification." In short, the person tends to become, for the time, his interpretation of what the other thinks he is. Thus, if he perceives rejection from others, he is likely to view himself negatively. Cooley points out that persons with deviant traits are especially subject to such responses and self feelings.

Developing these ideas into a systematic explanation of deviance, Edwin Lemert maintains that if deviant acts are severely sanctioned, they may be incorporated as part of the *ME* of the individual and the integration of existing roles may be disrupted, and reorganization based on a deviant role may occur. He refers to these latter roles as *secondary deviation* and suggests that they develop as means of adjustment to the problems created by the societal reaction to the original or specific *(primary)* deviation. A crucial element in becoming a secondary deviant, then, is the reorganization of identity around the deviation and its associated roles. The contribution of the theorists that follow Lemert expand upon the concept of secondary deviation.

Howard Becker suggests that the person who is labeled as a deviant is ascribed a new status with an institutionalized set of role expectations. Regardless of the other positions he may occupy, the status of deviant often remains the *master status,* since one who occupies it will be identified deviant before other identifications are made. He points out, furthermore, that the possession of a single deviant trait also may have a generalized symbolic value, so that people assume that its bearer possesses other undesirable traits thought to be associated with it. On the basis of the original and specific deviation, then, they impute to the individual a wide range of imperfections. Becker argues that treating a person as though he were generally rather than specifically deviant produces a self-fulfilling prophecy. Isolation from participation in conventional groups exerts pressure on the deviant to identify with the status that the reacting society provides for him.

The generalizability of deviant characteristics is also the subject of the selection by Erving Goffman. He contends that through the construction of a *stigma theory,* or stereotype, particularized deviant behavior is seen as contaminating other aspects of the individual's identity. The effect of the stigma theory, says Goffman, is that the very humanity of the deviant is brought into question.

The concept of the stereotype has been applied by Thomas Scheff to an explanation of mental illness. Because of the existence of the stereotypic definition of mental illness, persons who perceive being defined and reacted to as such are likely to be very much aware of the institutionalized set of role expectations that go along with their new status. In essence, the stereotype acts as a summation of the characteristics assumed relevant to the deviation. Holding that the stereotype is learned in childhood and continually reaffirmed in everyday interaction, Scheff asserts that such popular conceptions of mental disorder serve as the social definition for action not only for persons reacting to the deviant, but also for the deviant himself. Thus stereotypic definitions and reactions cause those who are labeled eventually to organize their identity and behavior around the stereotype of their deviation.

Self-conscious identification with the deviant status results in behavioral patterns that are best described in terms of Marvin Scott and Stanford Lyman's *game-theoretic model.* Using the homosexual as an example, they point out that the status of deviant and the attempt of the socially stigmatized individual to "pass" in society creates increased sensitivity to the language, cues, and gestures of others. Situations that are routinely encountered by normals become problematic for the deviant. In such a heightened awareness context, suspicion of the motives and actions of others is likely to result in paranoid-like responses. This suspicion, contend Scott and Lyman, is not unfounded but rather is in accordance with "their perception of the nature, rules, and problems of the 'game' in which they find themselves."

Edwin Schur discusses the process of *retrospective interpretation* as it pertains to deviance. This involves the reinterpretation of the individual's past in light of his deviance, thus invalidating his prior identity and giving increased meaning to the deviation. Speaking to the dynamics of this process, he points out that such reinterpretation allows others to reestablish an historical continuity between the individual's past and his present behavior.

Harold Garfinkel's description of the *status degradation ceremony* provides a powerful illustration of retrospective interpretation and the *formal* transformation of identity. He explains that the community's action toward the deviant is like a sharp rite of transition, at once removing him from his normal position and into the deviant role. Garfinkel emphasizes that more formalized reactions in particular are likely to have this effect. Discussing these ceremonies, he states that "the work of the denunciation effects the recasting of the objective character of the perceived other: The other person becomes in the eyes of his condemners literally a different and *new* person."

The second selection by Schur deals with *role engulfment* as it relates to deviance. Schur says that role engulfment lies at the heart of Becker's formulation of the concept of *master status* and represents one step in Lemert's conceptualization of movement from primary to *secondary deviation;* very generally, it applies to the organization of one's identity around the social definition of his deviance. Role engulfment also implies *stereotyping* and *retrospective interpretation.* The immersion of a non-conformist into the role of his deviance, as that role has become defined by stereotyping processes, is an effort at validating his identity. That is to say that the deviant, cut off from legitimate roles and faced with the stereotypic expectations of others, may become engulfed in the deviant role as a means of stabilizing his self-concept. The result is for the individual to become preoccupied with the fact of his deviance to the exclusion of identification with other social roles.

Role engulfment, retrospective interpretation, stereotyping, and the designation of deviance as a master status are interrelated processes in the creation of secondary deviance. Each involves the symbolic interaction of the deviant and reacting conformist toward the creation of a mutually understood and shared definition of what constitutes deviant characteristics. In addition, each contributes to the stability and persistence of a deviant identity by systematically isolating the non-conformer from legitimate roles and non-stereotypic interaction.

The
Social Self
Charles Horton Cooley

The social self is simply any idea, or system of ideas, drawn from the communicative life, that the mind cherishes as its own. Self-feeling has its chief scope *within* the general life, not outside of it; the special endeavor or tendency of which it is the emotional aspect finds its principal field of exercise in a world of personal forces, reflected in the mind by a world of personal impressions. . . .

That the "I" of common speech has a meaning which includes some sort of reference to other persons is involved in the very fact that the word and the ideas it stands for are phenomena of language and the communicative life. It is doubtful whether it is possible to use language at all without thinking more or less distinctly of some one else, and certainly the things to which we give names and which have a large place in reflective thought are almost always those which are impressed upon us by our contact with other people. Where there is no communication there can be no nomenclature and no developed thought. What we call "me," "mine," or "myself" is, then, not something separate from the general life, but the most interesting part of it, a part whose interest arises from the very fact that it is both general and individual. That is, we care for it just because it is that phase of the mind that is living and striving in the common life, trying to impress itself upon the minds of others. "I" is a militant social tendency, working to hold and enlarge its place in the general current of tendencies. So far as it can it waxes, as all life does. To think of it as apart from society is a palpable absurdity of which no one could be guilty who really *saw* it as a fact of life. . . .

From *Human Nature and the Social Order* by Charles Horton Cooley. Charles Scribner's Sons, 1902, pp. 179–185, 259–260.

The reference to other persons involved in the sense of self may be distinct and particular, as when a boy is ashamed to have his mother catch him at something she has forbidden, or it may be vague and general, as when one is ashamed to do something which only his conscience, expressing his sense of social responsibility, detects and disapproves; but it is always there. There is no sense of "I," as in pride or shame, without its correlative sense of you, or he, or they. Even the miser gloating over his hidden gold can feel the "mine" only as he is aware of the world of men over whom he has secret power; and the case is very similar with all kinds of hid treasure. Many painters, sculptors, and writers have loved to withhold their work from the world, fondling it in seclusion until they were quite done with it; but the delight in this, as in all secrets, depends upon a sense of the value of what is concealed.

. . . We think of the body as "I" when it comes to have social function or significance, as when we say "I am looking well to-day," or "I am taller than you are." We bring it into the social world, for the time being, and for that reason put our selfconsciousness into it. Now it is curious, though natural, that in precisely the same way we may call any inanimate object "I" with which we are identifying our will and purpose. This is notable in games, like golf or croquet, where the ball is the embodiment of the player's fortunes. You will hear a man say, "I am in the long grass down by the third tee," or "I am in position for the middle arch." So a boy flying a kite will say "I am higher than you," or one shooting at a mark will declare that he is just below the bullseye.

In a very large and interesting class of cases the social reference takes the form of a somewhat definite imagination of how one's self—that is any idea he appropriates—appears in a particular mind, and the kind of self-feeling one has is determined by the attitude toward this attributed to that other mind. A social self of this sort might be called the reflected or looking-glass self:

> "Each to each a looking-glass
> Reflects the other that doth pass."

As we see our face, figure, and dress in the glass, and are interested in them because they are ours, and pleased or otherwise with them according as they do or do not answer to what we should like them to be; so in imagination we perceive in another's mind some thought of our appearance, manners, aims, deeds, character, friends, and so on, and are variously affected by it.

A self-idea of this sort seems to have three principal elements:

the imagination of our appearance to the other person; the imagination of his judgment of that appearance, and some sort of self-feeling, such as pride or mortification. The comparision with a looking-glass hardly suggests the second element, the imagined judgment, which is quite essential. The thing that moves us to pride or shame is not the mere mechanical reflection of ourselves, but an imputed sentiment, the imagined effect of this reflection upon another's mind. This is evident from the fact that the character and weight of that other, in whose mind we see ourselves, makes all the difference with our feeling. We are ashamed to seem evasive in the presence of a straightforward man, cowardly in the presence of a brave one, gross in the eyes of a refined one, and so on. We always imagine, and in imagining share, the judgments of the other mind. A man will boast to one person of an action—say some sharp transaction in trade—which he would be ashamed to own to another.

It should be evident that the ideas that are associated with self-feeling and form the intellectual content of the self cannot be covered by any simple description, as by saying that the body has such a part in it, friends such a part, plans so much, etc., but will vary indefinitely with particular temperaments and environments. The tendency of the self, like every aspect of personality, is expressive of far-reaching hereditary and social factors, and is not to be understood or predicted except in connection with the general life. Although special, it is in no way separate—speciality and separateness are not only different but contradictory, since the former implies connection with a whole. The object of self-feeling is affected by the general course of history, by the particular development of nations, classes, and professions, and other conditions of this sort.

The truth of this is perhaps most decisively shown in the fact that even those ideas that are most generally associated or colored with the "my" feeling, such as one's idea of his visible person, of his name, his family, his intimate friends, his property, and so on, are not universally so associated, but may be separated from the self by peculiar social conditions. . . .

[Cooley felt that if one perceives in the actions of others coldness or contempt instead of kindness and deference, he is likely to experience fear and see himself as a helpless outcast. He pointed out, furthermore, that persons possessing deviant aims or attributes are particularly subject to negative self feelings. Commenting on such persons, he wrote:]

The peculiar relations to other persons attending any marked personal deficiency or peculiarity are likely to aggravate, if not to produce, abnormal manifestations of self-feeling. Any such trait sufficiently noticeable to interrupt easy and familiar intercourse with others, and make people talk and think *about* a person or *to* him rather than *with* him, can hardly fail to have this effect. If he is naturally inclined to pride or irritability, these tendencies, which depend for correction upon the flow of sympathy, are likely to be increased. One who shows signs of mental aberration is, inevitably perhaps, but cruelly, shut off from familiar, thoughtless intercourse, partly excommunicated; his isolation is unwittingly proclaimed to him on every countenance by curiosity, indifference, aversion, or pity, and in so far as he is human enough to need free and equal communication and feel the lack of it, he suffers pain and loss of a kind and degree which others can only faintly imagine, and for the most part ignore. He finds himself apart, "not in it," and feels chilled, fearful, and suspicious. Thus "queerness" is no sooner perceived than it is multiplied by reflection from other minds. The same is true in some degree of dwarfs, deformed or disfigured persons, even the deaf and those suffering from the infirmities of old age.

Secondary Deviance and Role Conceptions
Edwin M. Lemert

Primary and Secondary Deviation

There has been an embarrassingly large number of theories, often without any relationship to a general theory, advanced to account for various specific pathologies in human behavior. For certain types of pathology, such as alcoholism, crime, or stuttering, there are almost as many theories as there are writers on these subjects. This has been occasioned in no small way by the preoccupation with the origins of pathological behavior and by the fallacy of confusing *original* causes with *effective* causes. All such theories have elements of truth, and the divergent viewpoints they contain can be reconciled with the general theory here if it is granted that original causes or antecedents of deviant behaviors are many and diversified. This holds especially for the psychological processes leading to similar pathological behavior, but it also holds for the situational concomitants of the initial aberrant conduct. A person may come to use excessive alcohol not only for a wide variety of subjective reasons but also because of diversified situational influences, such as the death of a loved one, business failure, or participating in some sort of organized group activity calling for heavy drinking of liquor. Whatever the original reasons for violating the norms of the community, they are important only for certain research purposes, such as assessing the extent of the "social problem" at a given time or determining the requirements for a rational program of social control. From a narrower sociological viewpoint the deviations are not significant until they are organized subjectively and transformed into active roles and become the social criteria for assigning status. The deviant individuals must react symbolically to their own behavior aberrations and fix them in their sociophyschological patterns. The deviations remain primary deviations or symptomatic and situational as long as they are rationalized or otherwise dealt with as functions of a socially acceptable role. Under such conditions normal and pathological behaviors remain strange and somewhat tensional bedfellows in the same person. Undeniably a vast amount of such segmental and partially integrated pathological behavior exists in our society and has impressed many writers in the field of social pathology.

Just how far and for how long a person may go on dissociating his sociopathic tendencies so that they are merely troublesome adjuncts of normally conceived roles is not known. Perhaps it depends upon the number of alternative definitions of the same overt behavior that he can develop; perhaps certain physiological factors (limits) are also involved. However, if the deviant acts are repetitive and have a high visibility, and if there is a severe societal reaction, which, through a process of identification is incorporated as part of the "me" of the individual, the probability is greatly increased that the integration of existing roles will be disrupted and that reorganization based upon a new role or roles will occur. (The "me" in this context is simply the subjective aspect of the societal reaction.) Reorganization may be the adoption of another normal role in which the tendencies previously defined as "pathological" are given a more acceptable social expression. The other general possibility is the assumption of a deviant role, if such exists; or, more rarely, the person may organize an aberrant sect or group in which he creates a special role of his own. *When a person begins to employ his deviant behavior or a role based upon it as a means of defense, attack, or adjustment to the overt and covert problems created by the consequent societal reaction to him, his deviation is secondary.* Objective evidences of this change will be found in the symbolic appurtenances of the new role, in clothes, speech, posture, and mannerisms, which in some cases heighten social visibility, and which in some cases serve as symbolic cues to professionalization.

Role Conceptions of the
Individual Must Be Reinforced
by Reactions of Others

It is seldom that one deviant act will provoke a sufficiently strong societal reaction to bring about secondary deviation, unless in the process of introjection the individual imputes or projects meanings into the social situation which are not present. In this case anticipatory fears are involved. For example, in a culture where a child is taught sharp distinctions between "good" women and "bad" women, a single act of questionable morality might conceivably have a profound meaning for the girl so indulging. However, in the absence of reactions by the person's family, neighbors, or the larger community, reinforcing the tentative "bad-girl" self-definition, it is questionable whether a transition to secondary deviation would take place. It is also doubtful whether a temporary exposure to a severe punitive reaction by the community will lead a person to identify himself with a pathological role, unless, as we have said, the experience is highly traumatic. Most frequently there is a progressive reciprocal relationship between the deviation of the individual and the societal reaction, with a compounding of the societal reaction out of the minute accretions in the deviant behavior, until a point is reached where ingrouping and outgrouping between society and the deviant is manifest.[1] At this point a stigmatizing of the deviant occurs in the form of name calling, labeling, or stereotyping.

The sequence of interaction leading to secondary deviation is roughly as follows: (1) primary deviation; (2) social penalties; (3) further primary deviation; (4) stronger penalties and rejections; (5) further deviation, perhaps with hostilities and resentment beginning to focus upon those doing the penalizing; (6) crisis reached in the tolerance quotient, expressed in formal action by the community stigmatizing of the deviant; (7) strengthening of the deviant conduct as a reaction to the stigmatizing and penalties; (8) ultimate acceptance of deviant social status and efforts at adjustment on the basis of the associated role.

As an illustration of this sequence the behavior of an errant schoolboy can be cited. For one reason or another, let us say excessive energy, the schoolboy engages in a classroom prank. He is

[1]Mead, G., "The Psychology of Punitive Justice," *American Journal of Sociology*, 23, March, 1918, pp. 577–602.

penalized for it by the teacher. Later, due to clumsiness, he creates another disturbance and again he is reprimanded. Then, as sometimes happens, the boy is blamed for something he did not do. When the teacher uses the tag "bad boy" or "mischief maker" or other invidious terms, hostility and resentment are excited in the boy, and he may feel that he is blocked in playing the role expected of him. Thereafter, there may be a strong temptation to assume his role in the class as defined by the teacher, particularly when he discovers that there are rewards as well as penalties deriving from such a role. There is, of course, no implication here that such boys go on to become delinquents or criminals, for the mischief-maker role may later become integrated with or retrospectively rationalized as part of a role more acceptable to school authorities.[2] If such a boy continues this unacceptable role and becomes delinquent, the process must be accounted for in the light of the general theory of this volume. There must be a spreading corroboration of a sociopathic self-conception and societal reinforcement at each step in the process.

The most significant personality changes are manifest when societal definitions and their subjective counterpart become generalized. When this happens, the range of major role choices becomes narrowed to one general class.[3] This was very obvious in the case of a young girl who was the daughter of a paroled convict and who was attending a small Middle Western college. She continually argued with herself and with the author, in whom she had confided, that in reality she belonged on the "other side of the railroad tracks" and that her life could be enormously simplified by acquiescing in this verdict and living accordingly. While in her case there was a tendency to dramatize her conflicts, nevertheless there was enough societal reinforcement of her self-conception by the treatment she received in her relationship with her father and on dates with college boys to lend it a painful reality. Once these boys took her home to the shoddy dwelling in a slum area where she lived with her father, who was often in a drunken condition, they abruptly stopped seeing her again or else became sexually presumptive.

[2]Evidence for fixed or inevitable sequences from predelinquency to crime is absent. Sutherland, E. H., *Principles of Criminology*, 1939, 4th ed., p. 202.

[3]Sutherland seems to say something of this sort in connection with the development of criminal behavior. *Ibid.*, p. 86.

Deviance
as a
Master Status
Howard S. Becker

One of the most crucial steps in the process of building a stable pattern of deviant behavior is likely to be the experience of being caught and publicly labeled as a deviant. Whether a person takes this step or not depends not so much on what he does as on what other people do, on whether or not they enforce the rule he has violated. . . . First of all, even though no one else discovers the nonconformity or enforces the rules against it, the individual who has committed the impropriety may himself act as an enforcer. He may brand himself as deviant because of what he has done and punish himself in one way or another for his behavior. This is not always or necessarily the case, but may occur. Second, there may be cases like those described by psychoanalysts in which the individual really wants to get caught and perpetrates his deviant act in such a way that it is almost sure he will be.

In any case, being caught and branded as deviant has important consequences for one's further social participation and self-image. The most important consequence is a drastic change in the individual's public identity. Committing the improper act and being publicly caught at it place him in a new status. He has been revealed as a different kind of person from the kind he was supposed to be. He is labeled a "fairy," "dope fiend," "nut" or "lunatic," and treated accordingly.

In analyzing the consequences of assuming a deviant identity let us make use of Hughes' distinction between master and auxiliary status traits.[1] Hughes notes that most statuses have one key trait which serves to distinguish those who belong from those who do not. Thus the doctor, whatever else he may be, is a person who has a certificate stating that he has fulfilled certain requirements and is licensed to practice medicine; this is the master trait. As Hughes points out, in our society a doctor is also informally expected to have a number of auxiliary traits: most people expect him to be upper middle class, white, male, and Protestant. When he is not there is a sense that he has in some way failed to fill the bill. Similarly, though skin color is the master status trait determining who is Negro and who is white, Negroes are informally expected to have certain status traits and not to have others; people are surprised and find it anomalous if a Negro turns out to be a doctor or a college professor. People often have the master status trait but lack some of the auxiliary, informally expected characteristics; for example, one may be a doctor but be female or Negro.

Hughes deals with this phenomenon in regard to statuses that are well thought of, desired and desirable (noting that one may have the formal qualifications for entry into a status but be denied full entry because of lack of the proper auxiliary traits), but the same process occurs in the case of deviant statuses. Possession of one deviant trait may have a generalized symbolic value, so that people automatically assume that its bearer possesses other undesirable traits allegedly associated with it.

To be labeled a criminal one need only commit a single criminal offense, and this is all the term formally refers to. Yet the word carries a number of connotations specifying auxiliary traits characteristic of anyone bearing the label. A man who has been convicted of housebreaking and thereby labeled criminal is presumed to be a person likely to break into other houses; the police, in rounding up known offenders for investigation after a crime has been committed, operate on this premise. Further, he is considered likely to commit other kinds of crimes as well, because he has shown himself to be a person without "respect for the law." Thus, apprehension for one deviant act exposes a person to the likelihood that he will be regarded as deviant or undesirable in other respects.

There is one other element in Hughes' analysis we can borrow with profit: the distinction between master and subordinate

[1]Everett C. Hughes, "Dilemmas and Contradictions of Status," *American Journal of Sociology*, L (March, 1945), 353–359.

statuses.[2] Some statuses, in our society as in others, override all other statuses and have a certain priority. Race is one of these. Membership in the Negro race, as socially defined, will override most other status considerations in most other situations; the fact that one is a physician or middle-class or female will not protect one from being treated as a Negro first and any of these other things second. The status of deviant (depending on the kind of deviance) is this kind of master status. One receives the status as a result of breaking a rule, and the identification proves to be more important than most others. One will be identified as a deviant first, before other identifications are made. The question is raised: "What kind of person would break such an important rule?" And the answer is given: "One who is different from the rest of us, who cannot or will not act as a moral human being and therefore might break other important rules." The deviant identification becomes the controlling one.

Treating a person as though he were generally rather than specifically deviant produces a self-fulfilling prophecy. It sets in motion several mechanisms which conspire to shape the person in the image people have of him.[3] In the first place, one tends to be cut off, after being identified as deviant, from participation in more conventional groups, even though the specific consequences of the particular deviant activity might never of themselves have caused the isolation had there not also been the public knowledge and reaction to it. For example, being a homosexual may not affect one's ability to do office work, but to be known as a homosexual in an office may make it impossible to continue working there. Similarly, though the effects of opiate drugs may not impair one's working ability, to be known as an addict will probably lead to losing one's job. In such cases, the individual finds it difficult to conform to other rules which he had no intention or desire to break, and perforce finds himself deviant in these areas as well. The homosexual who is deprived of a "respectable" job by the discovery of his deviance may drift into unconventional, marginal occupations where it does not make so much difference. The drug addict finds himself forced into other illegitimate kinds of activity, such as robbery and theft, by the refusal of respectable employers to have him around.

When the deviant is caught, he is treated in accordance with

[2] *Ibid.*
[3] See Marsh Ray, "The Cycle of Abstinence and Relapse Among Heroin Addicts," *Social Problems,* 9 (Fall, 1961), 132–140.

the popular diagnosis of why he is that way, and the treatment itself may likewise produce increasing deviance. The drug addict, popularly considered to be a weak-willed individual who cannot forego the indecent pleasures afforded him by opiates, is treated repressively. He is forbidden to use drugs. Since he cannot get drugs legally, he must get them illegally. This forces the market underground and pushes the price of drugs up far beyond the current legitimate market price into a bracket that few can afford on an ordinary salary. Hence the treatment of the addict's deviance places him in a position where it will probably be necessary to resort to deceit and crime in order to support his habit.[4] The behavior is a consequence of the public reaction to the deviance rather than a consequence of the inherent qualities of the deviant act.

[4]See *Drug Addiction: Crime or Disease?* Interim and Final Reports of the Joint Committee of the American Bar Association and the American Medical Association on Narcotic Drugs (Bloomington, Indiana: Indiana University Press, 1961).

Stigma and
Social Identity
Erving Goffman

Preliminary Conceptions

Society establishes the means of categorizing persons and the complement of attributes felt to be ordinary and natural for members of each of these categories. Social settings establish the categories of persons likely to be encountered there. The routines of social intercourse in established settings allow us to deal with anticipated others without special attention or thought. When a stranger comes into our presence, then, first appearances are likely to enable us to anticipate his category and attributes, his "social identity"—to use a term that is better than "social status" because personal attributes such as "honesty" are involved, as well as structural ones, like "occupation."

We lean on these anticipations that we have, transforming them into normative expectations, into righteously presented demands.

Typically, we do not become aware that we have made these demands or aware of what they are until an active question arises as to whether or not they will be fulfilled. It is then that we are likely to realize that all along we had been making certain assumptions as to what the individual before us ought to be. Thus, the demands we make might better be called demands made "in effect," and the character we impute to the individual might better be seen as an imputation made in potential retrospect—a characterization "in effect," a *virtual social identity*. The category and attributes he could in fact be proved to possess will be called his *actual social identity*.

From Erving Goffman, *STIGMA: Notes on the Management of Spoiled Identity*, © 1963. Reprinted by permission of Prentice-Hall, Inc., Englewood Cliffs, New Jersey, pp. 2-9.

While the stranger is present before us, evidence can arise of his possessing an attribute that makes him different from others in the category of persons available for him to be, and of a less desirable kind—in the extreme, a person who is quite thoroughly bad, or dangerous, or weak. He is thus reduced in our minds from a whole and usual person to a tainted, discounted one. Such an attribute is a stigma, especially when its discrediting effect is very extensive; sometimes it is also called a failing, a shortcoming, a handicap. It constitutes a special discrepancy between virtual and actual social identity. Note that there are other types of discrepancy between virtual and actual social identity, for example the kind that causes us to reclassify an individual from one socially anticipated category to a different but equally well-anticipated one, and the kind that causes us to alter our estimation of the individual upward. Note, too, that not all undesirable attributes are at issue, but only those which are incongruous with our stereotype of what a given type of individual should be.

The term stigma, then, will be used to refer to an attribute that is deeply discrediting, but it should be seen that a language of relationships, not attributes, is really needed. An attribute that stigmatizes one type of possessor can confirm the usualness of another, and therefore is neither creditable nor discreditable as a thing in itself. For example, some jobs in America cause holders without the expected college education to conceal this fact; other jobs, however, can lead the few of their holders who have a higher education to keep this a secret, lest they be marked as failures and outsiders. Similarly, a middle class boy may feel no compunction in being seen going to the library; a professional criminal, however, writes:

I can remember before now on more than one occasion, for instance, going into a public library near where I was living, and looking over my shoulder a couple of times before I actually went in just to make sure no one who knew me was standing about and seeing me do it.[1]

So, too, an individual who desires to fight for his country may conceal a physical defect, lest his claimed physical status be discredited; later, the same individual, embittered and trying to get out of the army, may succeed in gaining admission to the army hospital, where he would be discredited if discovered in not really having an

[1]T. Parker and R. Allerton, *The Courage of His Convictions* (London: Hutchinson & Co., 1962), p. 109.

acute sickness.[2] A stigma, then, is really a special kind of relationship between attribute and stereotype, although I don't propose to continue to say so, in part because there are important attributes that almost everywhere in our society are discrediting.

The term stigma and its synonyms conceal a double perspective: does the stigmatized individual assume his differentness is known about already or is evident on the spot, or does he assume it is neither known about by those present nor immediately perceivable by them? In the first case one deals with the plight of the *discredited*, in the second with that of the *discreditable*. This is an important difference, even though a particular stigmatized individual is likely to have experience with both situations. I will begin with the situation of the discredited and move on to the discreditable but not always separate the two.

Three grossly different types of stigma may be mentioned. First there are abominations of the body—the various physical deformities. Next there are blemishes of individual character perceived as weak will, domineering or unnatural passions, treacherous and rigid beliefs, and dishonesty, these being inferred from a known record of, for example, mental disorder, imprisonment, addiction, alcoholism, homosexuality, unemployment, suicidal attempts, and radical political behavior. Finally there are the tribal stigma of race, nation, and religion, these being stigma that can be transmitted through lineages and equally contaminate all members of a family.[3] In all of these various instances of stigma, however . . . the same sociological features are found: an individual who might have been received easily in ordinary social intercourse possesses a trait that can obtrude itself upon attention and turn those of us whom he meets away from him, breaking the claim that his other attributes have on us. He possesses a stigma, an undesired differentness from what we had anticipated. We and those who do not depart negatively from the particular expectations at issue I shall call the *normals*.

The attitudes we normals have toward a person with a stigma, and the actions we take in regard to him, are well known, since these responses are what benevolent social action is designed to soften and

[2]In this connection see the review by M. Meltzer, "Countermanipulation through Malingering," in A. Biderman and H. Zimmer, eds., *The Manipulation of Human Behavior* (New York: John Wiley & Sons, 1961), pp. 277–304.

[3]In recent history, especially in Britain, low class status functioned as an important tribal stigma, the sins of the parents, or at least their milieu, being visited on the child, should the child rise improperly far above his initial station. The management of class stigma is of course a central theme in the English novel.

ameliorate. By definition, of course, we believe the person with a stigma is not quite human. On this assumption we exercise varieties of discrimination, through which we effectively, if often unthinkingly, reduce his life chances. We construct a stigma-theory, an ideology to explain his inferiority and account for the danger he represents, sometimes rationalizing an animosity based on other differences, such as those of social class.[4] We use specific stigma terms such as cripple, bastard, moron in our daily discourse as a source of metaphor and imagery, typically without giving thought to the original meaning.[5] We tend to impute a wide range of imperfections on the basis of the original one,[6] and at the same time to impute some desirable but undesired attributes, often of a supernatural cast, such as "sixth sense," or "understanding":[7]

> For some, there may be a hesitancy about touching or steering the blind, while for others, the perceived failure to see may be generalized into a gestalt of disability, so that the individual shouts at the blind as if they were deaf or attempts to lift them as if they were crippled. Those confronting the blind may have a whole range of belief that is anchored in the stereotype. For instance, they may think they are subject to unique judgment, assuming the blinded individual draws on special channels of information unavailable to others.[8]

Further, we may perceive his defensive response to his situation as a direct expression of his defect, and then see both defect and response as just retribution for something he or his parents or his tribe did, and hence a justification of the way we treat him.[9]

---

[4]D. Riesman, "Some Observations Concerning Marginality," *Phylon*, Second Quarter, 1951, 122.

[5]The case regarding mental patients is presented by T. J. Scheff in a forthcoming paper.

[6]In regard to the blind, see E. Henrich and L. Kriegel, eds., *Experiments in Survival* (New York: Association for the Aid of Crippled Children, 1961), pp. 152 and 186; and H. Chevigny, *My Eyes Have a Cold Nose* (New Haven, Conn.: Yale University Press, paperbound, 1962), p. 201.

[7]In the words of one blind woman, "I was asked to endorse a perfume, presumably because being sightless my sense of smell was super-discriminating." See T. Keitlen (with N. Lobsenz), *Farewell to Fear* (New York: Avon, 1962), p. 10.

[8]A. G. Gowman, *The War Blind in American Social Structure* (New York: American Foundation for the Blind, 1957), p. 198.

[9]For examples, see F. Macgregor *et al.*, *Facial Deformities and Plastic Surgery* (Springfield, Ill.: Charles C Thomas, 1953).

Now turn from the normal to the person he is normal against. It seems generally true that members of a social category may strongly support a standard of judgment that they and others agree does not directly apply to them. Thus it is that a businessman may demand womanly behavior from females or ascetic behavior from monks, and not construe himself as someone who ought to realize either of these styles of conduct. The distinction is between realizing a norm and merely supporting it. The issue of stigma does not arise here, but only where there is some expectation on all sides that those in a given category should not only support a particular norm but also realize it.

Also, it seems possible for an individual to fail to live up to what we effectively demand of him, and yet be relatively untouched by this failure; insulated by his alienation, protected by identity beliefs of his own, he feels that he is a full-fledged normal human being, and that we are the ones who are not quite human. He bears a stigma but does not seem to be impressed or repentant about doing so. This possibility is celebrated in exemplary tales about Mennonites, Gypsies, shameless scoundrels, and very orthodox Jews.

In America at present, however, separate systems of honor seem to be on the decline. The stigmatized individual tends to hold the same beliefs about identity that we do; this is a pivotal fact. His deepest feelings about what he is may be his sense of being a "normal person," a human being like anyone else, a person, therefore, who deserves a fair chance and a fair break.[10] (Actually, however phrased, he bases his claims not on what he thinks is due *everyone*, but only everyone of a selected social category into which he unquestionably fits, for example, anyone of his age, sex, profession, and so forth.) Yet he may perceive, usually quite correctly, that whatever others profess, they do not really "accept" him and are not ready to make contact with him on "equal grounds."[11] Further, the standards he has incorporated from the wider society equip him to be intimately alive to what others see as his failing, inevitably causing

---

[10]The notion of "normal human being" may have its source in the medical approach to humanity or in the tendency of large-scale bureaucratic organizations, such as the nation state, to treat all members in some respects as equal. Whatever its origins, it seems to provide the basic imagery through which laymen currently conceive of themselves. Interestingly, a convention seems to have emerged in popular life-story writing where a questionable person proves his claim to normalcy by citing his acquisition of a spouse and children, and, oddly, by attesting to his spending Christmas and Thanksgiving with them.

[11]A criminal's view of this nonacceptance is presented in Parker and Allerton, *op. cit.*, pp. 110–111.

him, if only for moments, to agree that he does indeed fall short of what he really ought to be. Shame becomes a central possibility, arising from the individual's perception of one of his own attributes as being a defiling thing to possess, and one he can readily see himself as not possessing.

The immediate presence of normals is likely to reinforce this split between self-demands and self, but in fact self-hate and self-derogation can also occur when only he and a mirror are about:

> When I got up at last . . . and had learned to walk again, one day I took a hand glass and went to a long mirror to look at myself, and I went alone. I didn't want anyone . . . to know how I felt when I saw myself for the first time. But there was no noise, no out cry; I didn't scream with rage when I saw myself. I just felt numb. That person in the mirror *couldn't* be me. I felt inside like a healthy, ordinary, lucky person—oh, not like the one in the mirror! Yet when I turned my face to the mirror there were my own eyes looking back, hot with shame . . . when I did not cry or make any sound, it became impossible that I should speak of it to anyone, and the confusion and the panic of my discovery were locked inside me then and there, to be faced alone, for a very long time to come.[12]

> Over and over I forgot what I had seen in the mirror. It could not penetrate into the interior of my mind and become an integral part of me. I felt as if it had nothing to do with me; it was only a disguise. But it was not the kind of disguise which is put on voluntarily by the person who wears it, and which is intended to confuse other people as to one's identity. My disguise had been put on me without my consent or knowledge like the ones in fairy tales, and it was I myself who was confused by it, as to my own identity. I looked in the mirror, and was horror-struck because I did not recognize myself. In the place where I was standing, with that persistent romantic elation in me, as if I were a favored fortunate person to whom everything was possible, I saw a stranger, a little, pitiable, hideous figure, and a face that became, as I stared at it, painful and blushing with shame. It was only a disguise, but it

[12]K. B. Hathaway, *The Little Locksmith* (New York: Coward-McCann, 1943), p. 41, in B. Wright, *Physical Disability-A Psychological Approach* (New York: Harper & Row, 1960), p. 157.

was on me, for life. It was there, it was there, it was real. Every one of those encounters was like a blow on the head. They left me dazed and dumb and senseless everytime, until slowly and stubbornly my robust persistent illusion of well-being and of personal beauty spread all through me again, and I forgot the irrelevant reality and was all unprepared and vulnerable again.[13]

The central feature of the stigmatized individual's situation in life can now be stated. It is a question of what is often, if vaguely, called "acceptance." Those who have dealings with him fail to accord him the respect and regard which the uncontaminated aspects of his social identity have led them to anticipate extending, and have led him to anticipate receiving; he echoes this denial by finding that some of his own attributes warrant it.

[13]*Ibid.*, pp. 46–47. For general treatments of the self-disliking sentiments, see K. Lewin, *Resolving Social Conflicts*, Part III (New York: Harper & Row, 1948); A. Kardiner and L. Ovesey, *The Mark of Oppression: A Psychosocial Study of the American Negro* (New York: W. W. Norton & Company, 1951); and E. H. Erikson, *Childhood and Society* (New York: W. W. Norton & Company, 1950).

The Social Institution of Insanity
Thomas J. Scheff

Learning and Maintaining Role-Imagery

What are the beliefs and practices that constitute the social institution of insanity? And how do
they figure in the development of mental disorder?
Two propositions concerning beliefs about mental
disorder in the general public will now be considered.

1. STEREOTYPED IMAGERY OF MENTAL DISORDER IS LEARNED IN EARLY CHILDHOOD

Although there are no substantiating studies in
this area, scattered observations lead the author to
conclude that children learn a considerable amount
of imagery concerning deviance very early, and that
much of the imagery comes from their peers rather
than from adults. The literal meaning of "crazy," a
term now used in a wide variety of contexts, is
probably grasped by children during the first years
of elementary school. Since adults are often vague
and evasive in their responses to questions in this
area, an aura of mystery surrounds it. In this socialization the grossest stereotypes that are heir to childhood fears, e.g., of the "boogie man," survive. . . .

Assuming that hypothesis #1 is sound, what
effect does early learning have on the shared conceptions of insanity held in the community? In early
childhood much fallacious material is learned that is
later discarded when more adequate information
replaces it. This question leads to Hypothesis 2.

Reprinted from Thomas J. Scheff, *Being Mentally Ill* (Chicago:
Aldine Publishing Company, 1966); Copyright © 1966 by Thomas
J. Scheff. Reprinted by permission of the author and Aldine
Publishing Company, 64, 67-68, 74, 82-88, 92-93.

2. THE STEREOTYPES OF INSANITY ARE CONTINUALLY REAFFIRMED, INADVERTENTLY, IN ORDINARY SOCIAL INTERACTION

Although many adults become acquainted with medical concepts of mental illness, the traditional stereotypes are not discarded, but continue to exist alongside the medical conceptions, because the stereotypes receive almost continual support from the mass media and in ordinary social discourse. In mental health education campaigns, televised lectures by psychiatrists and others, magazine articles and newspaper feature stories, medical discussions of mental illness occur from time to time. These types of discussions, however, seem to be far outnumbered by stereotypic references. . . .

Reaffirmation of the stereotype of insanity occurs not only in the mass media but indirectly in ordinary conversation: in jokes, anecdotes, and even in conventional phrases. Such phrases as "are you crazy?" or "it would be a madhouse," or "it's driving me out of my mind," or "we were chatting like crazy," or "he was running like mad," and literally hundreds of others occur frequently in informal conversations. In this usage, insanity itself is seldom the topic of conversation, and the discussants do not mean to refer to the topic of insanity, and are usually unaware that they are doing so. . . .

In a crisis, when the deviance of an individual becomes a public issue, the traditional stereotype of insanity becomes the guiding imagery for action, both for those reacting to the deviant and, at times, for the deviant himself. When societal agents and persons around the deviant react to him uniformly in terms of the traditional stereotypes of insanity, his amorphous and unstructured rule-breaking tends to crystallize in conformity to these expectations, thus becoming similar to the behavior of other deviants classified as mentally ill, and stable over time. The process of becoming uniform and stable is completed when the traditional imagery becomes a part of the deviant's orientation for guiding his own behavior.

The idea that cultural stereotypes may stabilize residual rule-breaking and tend to produce uniformity in symptoms, is supported by cross-cultural studies of mental disorder. Although some observers insist there are underlying similarities, many agree that there are enormous differences in the manifest symptoms of stable mental disorder *between* societies, and great similarity *within* societies.[1]

These considerations suggest that the labeling process is a

---

[1]P. M. Yap, "Mental Diseases Peculiar to Certain Cultures: A Survey of Comparative Psychiatry," *Journal of Mental Science*, 97 (April, 1951), pp. 313-327.

crucial contingency in most careers of residual deviance. Thus Glass, who observed that neuropsychiatric casualties may not become mentally ill if they are kept with their unit, goes on to say that military experience with psychotherapy has been disappointing. Soldiers who are removed from their unit to a hospital, he states, often go on to become chronically impaired.[2] That is, their deviance is stabilized by the labeling process, which is implicit in their removal and hospitalization. A similar interpretation can be made by comparing the observations of childhood disorders among Mexican-Americans with those of "Anglo" children. Childhood disorders such as *susto* (an illness believed to result from fright) sometimes have damaging outcomes in Mexican-American children.[3] Yet the deviant behavior involved is very similar to that which seems to have high incidence among Anglo children, with permanent impairment virtually never occurring. Apparently through cues from his elders the Mexican-American child, behaving initially much like his Anglo counterpart, learns to enter the sick role, at times with serious consequences.[4]

Acceptance of the Deviant Role

From this point of view, most mental disorder can be considered to be a social role. This social role complements and reflects the status of the insane in the social structure. It is through the social processes which maintain the status of the insane that the varied rule-breaking from which mental disorder arises is made uniform and stable. The stabilization and uniformization of residual deviance are completed when the deviant accepts the role of the insane as the framework within which he organizes his own behavior. Three hypotheses are stated below which suggest some of the processes which cause the deviant to accept such a stigmatized role.

[2]A. J. Glass, "Psychotherapy in the Combat Zone," in Symposium on Stress (Washington, DC: Army Medical Service Graduate School, 1953). For a contrary view, See E. Ginzberg, *The Ineffective Soldier* (New York: Columbia University Press, 1959).

[3]L. Saunders, *Cultural Difference and Medical Care* (New York: Russell Sage Foundation, 1954), p. 142.

[4]For discussion, with many illustrative cases, of the process in which persons play the "dead role" and subsequently die, see C. C. Herbert, "Life-Influencing Interactions," in A. Simon *et al.* (eds.), *The Physiology of the Emotions* (Springfield, Ill.: Charles C Thomas, 1961).

3. LABELED DEVIANTS MAY BE REWARDED FOR PLAYING THE STEREOTYPED DEVIANT ROLE

Ordinarily patients who display "insight" are rewarded by psychiatrists and other personnel. That is, patients who manage to find evidence of "their illness" in their past and present behavior, confirming the medical and societal diagnosis, receive benefits. This pattern of behavior is a special case of a more general pattern that has been called the "apostolic function" by Balint, in which the physician and others inadvertently cause the patient to display symptoms of the illness the physician thinks the patient has. The apostolic function occurs in the context of bargaining between the patient and the doctor over what shall be decided to be the nature of the patient's illness:

> Some of the people who, for some reason or other, find it difficult to cope with problems of their lives resort to becoming ill. If the doctor has the opportunity of seeing them in the first phases of their being ill, i.e. before they settle down to a definite "organized" illness, he may observe that these patients, so to speak, offer or propose various illnesses, and that they have to go on offering new illnesses until between doctor and patient an agreement can be reached resulting in the acceptance by both of them of one of the illnesses as justified.[5]

It is in this fluid situation that Balint believes the doctor influences the manifestations of illness:

> Apostolic mission or function means in the first place that every doctor has a vague, but almost unshakably firm, idea of how a patient ought to behave when ill. Although this idea is anything but explicit and concrete, it is immensely powerful, and influences, as we have found, practically every detail of the doctor's work with his patients. *It was almost as if every doctor had revealed knowledge of what was right and what was wrong for patients to expect and to endure, and further, as if he had a sacred duty to convert to his faith all the ignorant and unbelieving among his patients.*[6]

Not only physicians but other hospital personnel and even

[5]M. Balint, The Doctor, His Patient, and the Illness (New York: International Universities Press, 1957), p. 18.

[6]*Ibid.*, p. 216.

other patients, reward the deviant for conforming to the stereotypes. Caudill, who made observations of ward life in the guise of being a patient, reports various pressures from fellow patients. In the following excerpt, for example, there is the suggestion in the advice of the other patients that he should realize that he is a sick man:

On the second day, following a conference with his therapist, the observer expressed resentment over not having going-out privileges to visit the library and work on his book—his compulsive concern over his inability to finish this task being (according to his simulated case history) one of the factors leading to his hospitalization. Immediately two patients, Mr. Hill and Mrs. Lewis, who were later to become his closest friends, told him he was being "defensive"; since his doctor did not wish him to do such work, it was probably better "to lay off it." Mr. Hill went on to say that one of his troubles when he first came to the hospital was thinking of things that he had to do or thought he had to do. He said that now he did not bother about anything. Mrs. Lewis said that at first she had treated the hospital as a sort of hotel and had spent her therapeutic hours "charming" her doctor, but it had been pointed out to her by others that this was a mental hospital and that she should actively work with her doctor if she expected to get well.[7]

In the California mental hospital in which the author conducted a study in 1959, a common theme in the discussions between patients on the admissions wards was the "recognition" of one's illness. This interchange, which took place during a ward meeting on a female admission ward, provides an extreme example:

New Patient: "I don't belong here. I don't like all these crazy people. When can I talk to the doctor? I've been here four days and I haven't seen the doctor. I'm not crazy."

Another Patient: "She says she's not crazy." (Laughter from patients.)

Another Patient: "Honey, what I'd like to know is, if you're not crazy, how did you get your ass in this hospital?"

New Patient: "It's complicated, but I can explain. My husband and I. . . . "

First Patient: "That's what they all say." (General laughter.)

[7]W. Caudill, F. C. Redlich, H. R. Gilmore, and E. B. Brody, "Social Structure and Interaction Processes on a Psychiatric Ward," *American Journal of Orthopsychiatry,* 22 (April, 1952), pp. 314-334.

Thus there is considerable pressure on the patient to accept the role of the mentally ill as part of his self-conception.

4. LABELED DEVIANTS ARE PUNISHED WHEN THEY ATTEMPT THE RETURN TO CONVENTIONAL ROLES

The second process operative is the systematic blockage of entry to nondeviant roles once the label has been publicly applied.[8] Thus the former mental patient, although he is urged to rehabilitate himself in the community, usually finds himself discriminated against in seeking to return to his old status and on trying to find a new one in the occupational, marital, social, and other spheres.

Recent studies have shown that former mental patients, like ex-convicts, may find it difficult to find employment, even when their behavior and qualifications are unexceptionable. In an experimental study, Phillips has shown that the rejection of the mentally ill is largely a matter of stigmatization, rather than an evaluation of their behavior:

> Despite the fact that the "normal" person is more an "ideal type" than a normal person, when he is described as having been in a mental hospital he is rejected more than psychotic individuals described as not seeking help or as seeing a clergyman, and more than a depressed-neurotic seeing a clergyman. Even when the normal person is described as (only) seeing a psychiatrist, he is rejected more than a simple schizophrenic who seeks no help, (and) more than a phobic-compulsive individual seeking no help or seeing a clergyman or physician.[9]

Propositions 3 and 4, taken together, suggest that to a degree the labeled deviant is rewarded for deviating, and punished for attempting to conform.

5. IN THE CRISIS OCCURRING WHEN A RESIDUAL RULE-BREAKER IS PUBLICLY LABELED, THE DEVIANT IS HIGHLY SUGGESTIBLE, AND MAY ACCEPT THE PROFFERED ROLE OF THE INSANE AS THE ONLY ALTERNATIVE

When gross rule-breaking is publicly recognized and made an issue, the rule-breaker may be profoundly confused, anxious, and

[8]E. M. Lemert, Social Pathology (New York: McGraw-Hill, 1951), provides an extensive discussion of this process under the heading of "Limitation of Participation," pp. 434-440.

[9]D. L. Phillips, "Rejection: A Possible Consequence of Seeking Help for Mental Disorder," American Sociological Review, 28 (December, 1963), pp. 963-973.

ashamed. In this crisis it seems reasonable to assume that the rule-breaker will be suggestible to the cues that he gets from the reactions of others toward him.[10] But those around him are also in a crisis; the incomprehensible nature of the rule-breaking, and the seeming need for immediate action lead them to take collective action against the rule-breaker on the basis of the attitude which all share—the traditional stereotypes of insanity. The rule-breaker is sensitive to the cues provided by these others and begins to think of himself in terms of the stereotyped role of insanity, which is part of his own role vocabulary also, since he, like those reacting to him, learned it early in childhood. In this situation his behavior may begin to follow the pattern suggested by his own stereotypes and the reactions of others. That is, when a residual rule-breaker organizes his behavior within the framework of mental disorder, and when his organization is validated by others, particularly prestigeful others such as physicians, he is "hooked" and will proceed on a career of chronic deviance. . . .

The preceding . . . hypotheses form a basis for the final causal hypothesis.

6. AMONG RESIDUAL RULE-BREAKERS, LABELING IS THE SINGLE MOST IMPORTANT CAUSE OF CAREERS OF RESIDUAL DEVIANCE

This hypothesis assumes that most residual rule-breaking, if it does not become the basis for entry into the sick role, will not lead to a deviant career.[11] The most usual case, according to the argument that has been advanced here, is that there will be few if any social consequences of residual rule-breaking.

[10]This proposition receives support from K. T. Erikson, "Patient Role and Social Uncertainty—A Dilemma of the Mentally Ill," Psychiatry, 20 (August, 1957), pp. 263-274.

[11]Sociologically, an occupational career can be defined as "the sequence of movements from one position to another in an occupational system made by any individual who works in that system" (H. S. Becker, Outsider [New York: Free Press, 1963] p. 24). Similarly, a deviant career is the sequence of movements from one stigmatized position to another in the sector of the larger social system that functions to maintain social control. For example, the frequently cited progression of young men from probation through detention centers and reform schools to prison, with intervening times spent out of prison, might be considered as [a] recurring deviant career. For Becker's discussion of deviant careers, see op. cit., pp. 25-39.

Paranoia, Homosexuality and Game Theory

Marvin B. Scott / Stanford M. Lyman

Sociologists studying deviant behavior are increasingly thinking about labeled deviants (Becker, 1963; Kitsuse, 1964; Freidson, n.d.; Scheff, 1966), but few are studying what labeled deviants are thinking.

It has proved fruitful to ask, who gets labeled and what are the fateful consequences for those so labeled. But, in pursuing this question, recent investigators have neglected the qualities of consciousness of the deviants themselves. There are at least two reasons for this neglect. First, the very concern with states of consciousness is considered to be within the psychological rather than sociological realm of inquiry, and only of peripheral or *a priori* interest to the sociologist; second, sociological theory apparently lacks a framework within which to investigate the problem. However, we shall argue that sociological theory is both appropriate and equipped to investigate what may appear as a psychological or psychiatric concern.

We hold that the model most fruitful for exploring the qualities of consciousness of deviants in general and paranoids and homosexuals in particular is that derived from recent thought in game theory (Schelling, 1963).* First we shall present the components of a game model, then illustrate its usefulness in comprehending the behavior of normals in abnormal situations. Finally, we shall describe two

From "Paranoia, Homosexuality and Game Theory" by Marvin B. Scott and Stanford M. Lyman in *The Journal of Health and Social Behavior*, Vol. 9, Sept. 1968, pp. 179-180, 182-187. By permission of the authors and The American Sociological Association.

deviant types—paranoids and homosexuals—and suggest that their presumed quality of consciousness might best be analyzed in terms of the game model.

The Game Model

Any encounter between two or more individuals may be analyzed as a game if the following condition holds true: at least one of the interactants is aware or capable of being made aware that, in realizing his aims in an encounter, he must take into account the others' expectations of him, the others' expectations of what he expects of them, and vice versa.

Two problems have beset the game framework analysis of social relationships: the problem of consciousness, and the problem of goals and goal orientation, sometimes called the problem of rationality. One can easily exaggerate these problems, however. To begin with, consciousness is not in fact a problem of the model, but a potential condition of the empirical situation. True, encounters ordinarily proceed without the consciousness of the rules of the game so long as behavior follows along the lines of "the recipes for living" that "everyone knows" (Schutz, 1964:64-88, esp. pp. 72-76). But once an interruption or breakdown of these "recipes," or "background expectancies," occurs there arises in the minds of the interactants a heightened awareness context in which the expectations of self, others, and the scanning of reciprocal meanings becomes manifest (Goffman, 1956:473-474). To put it another way, the awareness of self—and the need to properly interpret the language, signs, and gestures of others—becomes conscious when the situation is made problematic. We will shortly return to this point.

Similarly, the so-called problem of rationality need not be perceived as an obstacle to the adoption of a game framework for analysis. As Boulding (1963) has noted, all behavior—including that of the "irrational" man—is characterized by the actor's having an image of the state of things and a preferential ordering of behavior patterns in accordance with that image. (The principal differentiation between rational and irrational behavior is that the latter is charac-

---

*Credit for the idea of applying a game-like model to the analysis of certain kinds of deviance goes to Erving Goffman. His unpublished manuscript, "Communication and Strategic Interaction," consists—among other things—of an explication of Schelling's work and a brilliant application of game-theoretic notions for the analysis of a variety of diverse social structures. We are deeply indebted to Goffman's paper for many of the ideas presented here.

terized by a rigid orientation, unmodified by further information, and an inconsistent and shifting order of preferences governing behavior choices [Boulding, 1963:150-151].) Furthermore, the game model can be employed to recognize that the goals of men are variable and not necessarily reducible to the material benefits so dear to users of the *homo economicus model.* Men may choose goals involving sacrifice, long term gains for short term losses, deferred gratifications, and so on. These are all empirical properties of encounters and as such merely represent the raw data to which the game framework model is applied.

As these remarks suggest, one unit in which a game model may be fruitfully employed for analysis is a focused gathering or an encounter. Goffman (1961b:17) has defined this unit as existing when for the participants there is "a single visual and cognitive focus of attention; a mutual and preferential openness to verbal communication; a heightened mutual relevance of acts; an eye-to-eye ecological huddle that maximizes each participant's opportunity to perceive the other participants' monitoring of him." Such a unit may proceed on the course of interaction without any of the members becoming especially conscious of any game being involved in their own or others' behavior. But should obtrusive information, unexpected events, or untoward behavior intrude on the proceedings, a situation having all the properties of a game might then become a conscious as well as an active part of the encounter. Moreover, within any focused gathering one or more of the participants might be more or less conscious than others of their presentation of social selves. Thus, the game properties of a situation may be a greater or lesser part of the awareness contexts (Glaser and Strauss, 1964) of the actors in such a gathering.

Focused gatherings in which games may be observed are circumscribed by time, space, and boundary rules. Such gatherings have an episodic character so that the actions carried on may be observed by both actors and analysts as having a beginning and an ending. Despite their temporal boundaries, episodic events provide the occasion for the actors to reconstruct their own and others' biographies. And it is the mutually established biographies of the actors that constitute the social selves involved in a game. These include the actor's perception of the self he is presenting, alter's perception of that self, and both actor's and alter's estimation of that biographical self.

Once a game has consciously begun (that is, once at least one of the actors in the encounter realizes he has a stake in the outcome of the situation) he becomes consciously aware of rules of conduct appropriate to the situation—rules which define what and how other actors and objects are relevant to the stakes at issue (Goffman, 1961b:19-34), and which indicate appropriate norms of conduct. These rules of relevance and rectitude constitute what for both the actor and analyst are the game parameters.

Furthermore, the goal-directed actions undertaken by an actor constitute the "moves" of the game. When an actor conceives and executes or attempts to execute a set of moves—which in context take into account the moves, including countermoves, of those with whom he is interacting—he is carrying out a strategy.

A game may be said to be underway, then, when at least one actor in an encounter perceives a situation as problematic, estimates his own and others' construction of self and situation, and undertakes a line of action designed to achieve a goal or goals with respect to the situation. . . .

Homosexuals and the Game Framework

. . . There are some persons who continually regard their social world as problematic and who thus exhibit a heightened awareness. Among these are the *stigmatized.* As a result of possessing a stigma, an individual (Goffman, 1963:111)

may be led into placing brackets around a spate of casual social interaction so as to examine what is contained therein for general themes. He can become "situation conscious" while normals present are spontaneously involved *within* the situation, the situation itself constituting for these normals a background of unattended matters.
This extension of consciousness on the part of the stigmatized persons is reinforced . . . by his special aliveness to the contingencies of acceptance and disclosure, contingencies to which normals will be less alive.

Among the stigmatized a particularly significant issue is "passing," that is, concealing from others that portion of one's identity that is discreditable. Negroes who "pass" for whites, spies who pose as ordinary citizens, and homosexuals who move in heterosexual circles must take special precautions to preserve their secret identity against disclosure. Because of this danger of discovery "passers" must develop a more heightened awareness and a sharper perspective on ordinary affairs and everyday encounters than those for whom concealment is not an issue.

It is a[s] "passer" that the homosexual exhibits the behavior sometimes called "paranoid" by clinical investigators. The situations that are quite routine for normals become problematic for him. Thus one homosexual reports, "You know what was really hard? Watching television with my folks. I'd catch myself saying, 'There's a good-looking boy'" (McCall and Simmons, 1966:190). Another homosexual reported his fear that a request to the landlord for more heat in the apartment he shared with his friend might lead to discovery and even arrest (Westwood, 1960:147).

As these cases illustrate, the "passing" homosexual must be more cognizant of all those "little things" that might give him away. Thus, his manner of dress and speech, his mobilization of gestures, especially those of the eyes, and his indications of interests and avocations are all potential clues to his "real" identity. The same is true for the heterosexual who thinks that others think he is a homosexual. The case of R. R., a young Negro man, illustrates the point nicely (Kardiner and Ovesey, 1962:179-190). Outwardly, according to the psychiatrists that treat him, R. R. displays a masculine appearance. Yet he is troubled by doubts about his own sexuality, and by his belief that others think him to be homosexual. Therefore he calculates the impressions others get of him and behaves so as to belie the imagined identity of homosexual.

> I try to make myself appear to others what I really am not. If they could see into my mind, they would get a different impression than they have. . . . I just wonder what in my appearance now suggests a feminine person? (Kardiner and Ovesey, 1962:185-186)

Further, R. R. is alive to those events in his everyday life that suggest a homosexual identity to ordinary persons, even if his psychiatrists are not. Thus he reports about radio listening:

> Yesterday I was sitting and listening to music on one radio at work. Everybody else was at another radio listening to the ball game. A person came in and said, "Get up. Let's listen to the game." I said, "I would rather listen to music." The boss came in and said, "I always thought something was wrong with you. Now, I know it." He wouldn't have said it if he didn't have something in the back of his mind."

And R. R. adopts a game strategic—or to the psychiatrists, a "paranoid"—interpretation of these events:

To him [i.e., the boss] my behavior is not usual. Maybe
to him it isn't normal for a young man to prefer music
to a baseball game. Evidently, people have formulated
ideas and opinions that I have an unusual personality.
Rather than being a strong young man interested in
athletics and sports, I am more interested in light
things. I must appear effeminate to them. (Kardiner and
Ovesey, 1962:186)

The strategies open to R. R., once he begins to gauge the
meanings his peers attach to events like listening to the radio, are
many and varied. He might try to convince his fellow workers that
love of music is not unmasculine. He might try to "compensate" for
his one "feminine" trait by excelling in another activity that demon-
strates masculinity—use of obscene language, for example. He
might confine his music listening to the privacy of his home, join his
co-workers in listening to ball games, feigning interest in the
subject, even reading up on it in private to be able to validate his
meretricious interest. He might purchase a tiny portable radio
outfitted with an earphone so that his taste in radio programs will be
unknown to his peers, but actually tune it to the ball game so that
when asked he can prove he is a "man" by handing the earphone to
the interrogator. And he might—and in fact, R. R. does—avoid as
much as possible any social contact with his peers. In other words,
once a problem is recognized in the interaction, R. R. might carefully
evaluate the seemingly innocuous items in the encounter environment for their meanings and utility. He may seek to reorganize his
own image or environment to convey a new or different image from
that which he presently suspects he is giving. He may correctly or
incorrectly implement his strategy, make wise or inept tactical
moves, succeed or fail to achieve his objective. He might, indeed,
play a game.

"Passing" poses another kind of problem for the homosexual,
namely, communicating the secret identity he is trying to conceal in
order to make contact with a fellow homosexual "passer." The
successful homosexual "passer" must be able to mobilize his sign
equipment so that a double identity is available—a normal one for
"straight" people, and a homosexual one for those seeking his sexual
services. However, the indicators of homosexuality must be capable
of withdrawal or redefinition should he have to revert to the "pure"
version of the passing identity. The elements of this situation
amount to a special kind of information game in which A, a
homosexual, seeks to outwardly manifest a heterosexual identity to
B, a suspected homosexual, but provide the latter with the necessary

information to suggest A's identity as a homosexual and thus invite B to disclose his own homosexual identity. Of course should B turn out to be "straight," A is left with the problem of managing the clues already given off to his own true identity so as not to give himself away. Ideally the situation amounts to a reciprocally escalating presentation of relevant information by which each actor enhances the risk of revealing himself in order to ascertain the definite and unambiguous identity of the other. The game is concluded either when both actors recognize one another as homosexuals and drop all pretense as heterosexuals, or when one actor concludes that the other is "straight" and determines upon a strategy to salvage his own "passing" identity.

To repeat the important point: the exigencies of "passing" necessitate that the real or suspected homosexual take as problematic what others take for granted. He must take into account the nuances of verbal meaning, the symbolic definitions of objects, and the fact that others are (or may be) taking into account his taking them into account. He operates in a context of "suspicion awareness" (Glaser and Strass, 1964:669-679), asking: Do they know? How are they reacting to me? When can I stop observing them observing me observing them? This is the orientation of professional spies, an orientation not employed in everyday life.

The awareness contexts of the interactants may vary; consequently, the strategies may vary in accordance with them. Thus homosexuals may encounter one another or "straights" when each is openly aware of the other's identity and aware that the other knows his identity; when one is unaware of the other's identity and also unaware of the other's knowledge of his own identity; when one or both suspects the true identity of the other and that the other suspects his own; and when each is aware of the other's identity but pretending ignorance of it (Glaser and Strauss, 1964). Homosexuals must ascertain which awareness context they are in (or if they are in multiple contexts simultaneously), and then mobilize the sign equipment appropriate to the context. Thus, unlike many straights in the same situation, passing homosexuals or ambivalent males must be more game aware.

The game-theoretic perspective is a model of strategic man playing with hyperconsciousness of the opponent's moves. It is a normative model in the sense of what a thinking actor must do to defeat an opponent and not an empirical model of how people in fact typically experience their social world. However, in the case of the passing homosexual or the ambivalent heterosexual, it approaches an empirical model.

Paranoids and the Game Framework

What we have said about homosexuals in particular applies to paranoids and paranoid-like states in general. Certain individuals—especially but not exclusively persons with something to hide, or bearers of discrediting stigmas—may come to see all or part of their world in terms of a conspiracy in which they must constantly be on guard against physical or financial harm, exploitation, or loss of status. Unlike normals, "paranoids" are more aware of social realities, more alive to contingencies and nuances, more strategic in their responses.

Until recently a paranoid was regarded as a person who had fashioned and come to inhabit a "pseudo-community" directed against himself; a person who aroused the concern of the actual community only after having struck out at it in his vengeful reaction to the unreal world in which he lived (Cameron, 1959:52-58). The researches of Lemert (1967:197-211) suggest that this definition and sequence is questionable, if not wholly wrong. Lemert's study of paranoids points out that the allegedly paranoid state of mind grows out of the context of a *real* community of suspicion, hostility and exclusion in which the "paranoid" finds himself actually alone, under suspicion, and the object of secret conversations, closed-door sessions, and extra-curricular plans. The incidents reported by Lemert indicate the kind of events that make up this dynamic exclusionary process. An office research team used huddles around the water cooler to discuss an unwanted associate; a researcher's interview schedule was changed at a conference arranged without him; office rules against extraneous conversation were introduced with the connivance of superiors in order to isolate an unwanted worker. Plans may be made that affect the after-hours situation of the excluded person. In one instance, reported by Lemert, fellow workers considered the possibility of placing an all night watch in front of their perceived malefactor's home. The conspiracy said to be imagined by the paranoid may not then be due originally to a malfunction in his interior mental processes, but rather it may arise out of an actual conspiratorial setting.

Kitsuse's (1964:92-93) study of the grounds for which a person is designated "homosexual" provides further evidence of the dynamics of the conspiratorial and exclusionist process. Among the incidents respondents recalled as indicating to them that a person was a sex deviant were that an officer "spent more time with the enlisted men than is expected of an officer"; that a tennis coach offered to give a back rub to the guest invited for dinner; that a stranger in a bar expressed interest in the fact that the person sitting next to him was studying psychology. Following their interpretation of these events as signs of homosexuality, the "normals" either watched the person closely, or withdrew hastily from the encounter. Thus the labeled deviant was given an indication of a problem in his interaction with others, an indication that might make him react with game-awareness responses.

Once a person establishes for himself that he is in a con-spiratorial setting, it is likely that he will begin to be suspiciously aware of just those items and events that "everyone else" takes for granted. Thus, R. R., suspecting that his fellow workers harbor doubts about his masculinity, watches closely the events that follow a conversation:

> I feel that people when they are in groups are talking about me. Especially if a person I have just been talking to goes over to another and they laugh. I feel they are talking about me. (Kardiner and Ovesey, 1962:186)

The paranoid is suspicious of objects in his social environment. For him, the taken-for-granted world is placed under suspicion. The strategic concerns and hyper-awareness of alternative meanings routinely manifested by the theorist in a game of conflict are found among the paranoid, except now the entire social environment is the opponent. Like an intelligence officer continually engaged in doping out the opponent's real intentions, the paranoid is hyper-conscious of others' motives. Note that in the literature of paranoid schizo-phrenia, we find a recurrent theme depicting the paranoid as possessing a "mysterious intuition" (Stanton and Schwartz, 1964:200), as engaging in a kind of "emotional eavesdropping" (Fromm-Reichmann, 1950), as being "diffusely vigilant" (Cameron, 1959:54). The paranoid, as Cameron describes him, "watches every-thing uneasily; he listens alertly for clues; he looks everywhere for hidden meanings." Jackson (1953:5) nicely illustrates the point:

> A therapist and his patient had inadvertently occupied another doctor's office. When the owner of the office appeared at the door, the therapist apologized. The second physician remarked it was "perfectly all right" and retired. The patient immediately told his therapist, "Gosh, Dr. X was angry." The therapist had not de-tected such a reaction in his colleague, but on checking later he discovered that the patient was correct. In-deed, therapists are sometimes a little frightened and

disconcerted to learn that their schizophrenic patients have an uncanny way of nosing out things about their personalities which they have unconsciously tried to cover up.

The paranoid explores, in game-theoretic fashion, the possibilities of all encounters. To illustrate, in one case reported by Laing and Esterson (1964) a girl feared her father was going to kill her; and so when she was given a sedative, she believed it was poison, for if her father was indeed out to kill her, he could—from her viewpoint—do no better than attempt to poison her while presumably offering her a sedative. Like a good game theorist, the paranoid ascribes to the opponent just the kind of rationality necessary to make the best strategic move (Laing and Esterson, 1964:16f).

The paranoid—again, like a good intelligence officer—becomes attuned to concealment and detection. The pathological component develops from the shift in interest in "what really is going on" to the conviction that "something is going on behind my back." Thus: (Stanton and Schwartz, 1964:203)

Patients maintained delusional misinterpretations by continually overemphasizing an inferred, implied, concealed meaning (the "real" meaning) and discarding the obvious or superficial content of a statement or action of a staff member.

Otherwise put, the paranoid schizophrenic is routinely engaged in interpreting the world in terms of a game-theoretic model.

Now if we ask, how is it that some people routinely put together their world in these terms, we are approaching the etiology of paranoia. And in this regard, the work of Bateson and his associates (1956:251-264) is highly suggestive. Consider this illustration:

For example, if mother begins to feel hostile (or affectionate) toward her child and also feels compelled to withdraw from him, she might say, "Go to bed, you're very tired and I want you to get your sleep." This overtly loving statement is intended to deny a feeling which could be verbalized as "Get out of my sight because I'm sick of you." If the child correctly discriminates her meta-communicative signals, he would have to face the fact that she both doesn't want him and is deceiving him by her loving behavior. He would be "punished" for learning to discriminate orders of messages accurately. He therefore would tend to accept the idea that he is tired rather than recognize his mother's deception. This means that he must deceive himself about his own internal state in order to support mother in her deception. To survive with her he must falsely discriminate his own internal message as well as falsely discriminate the messages of others.

Laing's work on family and schizophrenia is a rich source of examples illustrating the "double bind" hypothesis of Bateson and associates. His main point of emphasis is the family's negation of the child's perceived reality. Only one example, the case of Maya, need be mentioned here (1964:26).

She was frightened that her parents knew that she had sexual thoughts about them. She tried to tell them about this, but they told her *she did not have any thoughts of that kind.* She told them she masturbated *and they told her that she did not.* What happened then is of course inferred, but *when she told her parents in the presence of the interviewer that she still masturbated, her parents simply told her she did not!*

Of course the family is not the only group of significant others having a consequential impact in the etiology of the paranoid interpretive framework. Lemert's (1967) study of the onset of paranoia focuses on the conspiratorial denial of reality that emerges in the small, informal groups embedded in the bureaucratic milieu.

The empirical investigations of Bateson (1956), Laing (1964) and Lemert (1967) converge on this point: The constellation of significant others that systematically negates reality for an individual is engaged in producing persons who routinely place their world under suspicion. Whether the product of such a constellation will be identified as "ill" will depend on "career contingencies" (Goffman, 1961a:134ff), a discussion of which would take us beyond our immediate interests.

Conclusion

The game-theoretic model provides a framework whereby the quality of consciousness of many who would clinically occupy the categories of homosexual and paranoid is made sociologically intelligible. The game framework is a model of behavior of man under consciously problematic situations trying to make sense of and plans for that and future situations of a similar nature. The model suggests the contextual establishment of identities, the situation-oriented aliveness to objects and events, and the calculation of strategies.

The game model may not be suited to the analyses of all behavior, but rather to those situations having the properties of games—namely, imagination of the interactant's identities, motives, and strategies, and the development of counter-strategies, contingency tactics, and rescue operations.

While all persons are cast into game-potential situations whenever an interruption in ordinary activities occurs, certain persons are in them as routine matters of their everyday lives. Homosexuals, who have sometimes been treated as clinically paranoid, can be seen as persons embedded in a permanently problematic environment so long as they inhabit heterosexually oriented societies. Their allegedly paranoid behavior—indicated by a heightened suspiciousness, conspiratorial interpretation of events, and strategies of deviance disavowal or concealment—can be seen as behavior oriented to their peculiar problematic status. The game framework, a model of a thinking man in a win-lose-draw situation, not only provides the model for distinguishing the elements of the homosexual's behavior, but also by inference suggests the "normal" nature of this behavior.

Paranoids, typically treated as inhabitants of an unreal world, may manifest their unusual behavior pattern because of the dynamics of exclusion and conspiracy which constitute their actual environment. Like homosexuals, their behavior, especially in its early stages, may be analyzed in terms of that of a game player. The persistence of a game environment in their actual lives may be the factor that brings about the clinically diagnosed symptoms of paranoia.

Homosexuals and paranoids have a heightened awareness. Beyond this, their awareness is patterned in accordance with their perception of the nature, rules, and problems of the "game" in which they find themselves. . . .

Finally, our paper suggests that problematic environments are stable features of life for certain groups in society. In addition to homosexuals and paranoids, minority groups, physically disabled persons, the blind and the deaf are some that might be suggested. It may be that these groups are more sensitized to game situations than others and more subject to being labelled as mentally ill when they exhibit their awareness of the game aspects of life.

References

Bateson, G., et al.
1956 "Toward a theory of schizophrenia." Behavioral Science 1 (October): 251-264.

Becker, H. S.
1963 Outsiders. New York: The Free Press of Glencoe.

Boulding, K.
1963 Conflict and Defense: A General Theory. New York: Harper and Row Torchbook.

Cameron, N.
1959 "The paranoid pseudo-community revisited." American Journal of Sociology 65:52-58.

Freidson, E.
n.d. "Disability as Social Deviance." in Marvin B. Sussman (ed.), Sociology and Rehabilitation. Washington: American Sociological Association.

Fromm-Reichmann, F.
1950 Principles of Intensive Psychotherapy. Chicago: University of Chicago Press.

Glaser, Barney G., and Anselm L. Strauss
1964 "Awareness contexts and social interaction." American Sociological Review 29:669-679.

Goffman, E.
1956 "The nature of deference and demeanor." American Anthropologist (June):473-474.
1961a Asylums. Garden City, New York: Anchor paperback.
1961b Encounters: Two Studies in the Sociology of Interaction. Indianapolis: Bobbs-Merrill.
1963 Stigma. Englewood Cliffs, N.J.: Prentice-Hall Spectrum paperback.
1965 "Communication and Strategic Interaction." Unpublished manuscript. Jackson, D.D.
1953 "Psychotherapy for schizophrenia." Scientific American (January):5.

Kardiner, Abram, and Lionel Ovesey
1962 The Mark of Oppression. Cleveland: Meridian Books.

Kitsuse, J. I.
1964 "Societal Reaction to Deviant Behavior." in Howard S. Becker (ed.), The Other Side. New York: The Free Press of Glencoe.

Laing, R. D., and A. Esterson
1964 Sanity, Madness, and the Family, Vol. I. London: Tavistock Publications.

Lemert, E.
1967 "Paranoia and the Dynamics of Exclusion." in Human Deviance, Social Problems and Social Control. Englewood Cliffs, N.J.: Prentice-Hall.

McCall, George J., and J. L. Simmons
1966 Identities and Interactions: An Examination of Human Associations in Everyday Life. New York: Free Press of Glencoe.

Scheff, T.
  1966 Being Mentally Ill. Chicago: Aldine Press.
Schelling, T. C.
  1963 Strategy of Conflict. New York: Galaxy Books.
Schutz, A.
  1964 "The problem of rationality in the social world." in Collected Papers,
  Vol. II. The Hague, Martinus Nijhoff.
Stanton, Alfred H., and Morris S. Schwartz.
  1964 The Mental Hospital. New York: Basic Books.
Westwood, G.
  1960 A Minority. London: Longmans, Green and Co.

Retrospective Interpretation
Edwin M. Schur

. . . Retrospective interpretation, involves the mechanisms by which reactors come to view deviators or suspected deviators "in a totally new light." Undoubtedly the most glaring examples are found in such public "status-degradation ceremonies"[1] as the criminal trial. Sociologists have long been aware of the social-psychological processes by which an individual perceived one day as simply John Doe can (as a result of conviction at trial or even of having been held as a suspect) become "a murderer" or "a rapist" the next. Yet again it has remained for scholars using the labeling approach to focus research and analysis directly on this reconstitution of individual character or identity.

Such reassessment of the deviator and the attendant re-"placing" of him socially are not at all limited to public ceremonies. In his interesting research on reactions to deviance, John Kitsuse asked his respondents (mostly students) whether or not they had ever known individuals who had been involved in various specified kinds of deviation and, if so, to trace the circumstances under which they had recognized the deviance, what they had thought of it, and how they reacted to it. In analyzing the responses related to imputed homosexuality, Kitsuse noted a process by which the subject re-interprets the

[1]See Harold Garfinkel, "Conditions of Successful Degradation Ceremonies," *American Journal of Sociology,* 61 (March 1956), 420–424.

individual's past behavior in the light of the new information concerning his sexual deviance . . . The subjects indicate that they reviewed their past interactions with the individuals in question, searching for subtle cues and nuances of behavior which might give further evidence of the alleged deviance. This retrospective reading generally provided the subjects with just such evidence to support the conclusion that "this is what was going on all the time."[2]

Kitsuse's research produced similar findings about such other forms of deviation as drug addiction. In those instances too he found that perception of individuals as deviators had usually come first (in the drug cases often through public disclosure) and that *then* the respondents questioned in the study had "recognized" apparent "indicators" of such deviation in earlier behavior.

The ramifications of such rereading of an individual are basic to the way in which the labeling process "creates" deviants. Harold Garfinkel's early statement remains the most succinct and forcible description of what is involved:

The work of the denunciation effects the recasting of the objective character of the perceived other: The other person becomes in the eyes of his condemners literally a different and *new* person. It is not that the new attributes are added to the old "nucleus." He is not changed, he is reconstituted. The former identity, at best, receives the accent of mere appearance . . . the former identity stands as accidental; the new identity is the "basic reality." What he is now is what, "after all," he was all along.[3]

One of the most intriguing and systematic forms of retrospective interpretation of deviance occurs in the organizational processing of deviators and involves the use of the "case record," or "case history." This version is especially apparent of course in psychiatric treatment; theories of mental illness usually come close to *requiring* thoroughgoing scrutiny of each patient's past life. As Erving Goffman has pointed out, the actual function of case records seems to be almost entirely to support current diagnoses, to reinforce the formal definition of patients as mentally ill, and to deny their rationaliza-

---

[2]John I. Kitsuse, "Societal Reactions to Deviant Behavior: Problems of Theory and Method," *Social Problems*, 9 (Winter 1962), 253.

[3]Garfinkel, *op. cit.*, pp. 421-422.

tions and counterassertions. He has commented that the patient's dossier is not regularly used

> to record occasions when the patient showed capacity to cope honorably and effectively with difficult life situations. Nor is the case record typically used to provide a rough average or sampling of his past conduct. One of its purposes is to show the ways in which the patient is sick and the reasons why it was right to commit him and is right currently to keep him committed, and this is done by extracting from his whole life course a list of those incidents that have or might have had "symptomatic" significance.[4]

In discussing the various kinds of items that are brought together in the dossier to produce a picture rather heavily weighted toward discrediting the individual, Goffman has not meant to suggest that the items are collected for ulterior reasons. In fact, most of the information in the case record is probably true, but—a most important point—it is probably also true "that almost anyone's life course could yield up enough denigrating facts to provide grounds for the record's justification of commitment."[5] Basically the case record provides a retrospective rationalization, or substantiation, of the present diagnosis and, according to Goffman, "a new view of the patient's 'essential' character."

In such "biographical reconstructions," John Lofland has argued,

> we see most clearly the social need of Others to render Actors as consistent objects . . . there must be a *special* history that *specially* explains current imputed identity. Relative to deviance, the *present evil* of current character must be related to *past evil* that can be discovered in biography.

From this point of view such professionals as psychologists and psychiatrists often serve as "specialists in biographical reconstruction" (or, as Lofland has phrased it elsewhere, "consistency" or "imputational" specialists).[6] This aspect of their role as agents of

---

[4]Goffman, "The Moral Career of the Mental Patient," in Goffman, *Asylums* (Garden City, N.Y.: Doubleday Anchor, 1961), pp. 155-156; also "The Medical Model and Mental Hospitalization," in *Asylums,* pp. 323-386.

[5]Goffman, "The Moral Career of the Mental Patient," p. 159.

[6]John Lofland, *Deviance and Identity* (Englewood Cliffs, N.J.: Prentice-Hall, 1966), pp. 150, 155-158.

social control represents, according to Lofland, merely a formaliza-
tion and elaboration of similar efforts at maintaining consistency
through biographical reconstruction that all of us engage in continually in our everyday interactions.

Lofland has explored some of the public ramifications of
retrospective interpretation, by analyzing newspaper coverage of two
recent and widely publicized crimes.[7] He has noted that early
research on Richard Speck, charged with the murder of eight student
nurses in Chicago in 1966, had uncovered mostly favorable information about the suspect and had consequently warranted only back-
page treatment. It was not until four days after Speck's apprehension
that "enough appropriate material was available to credibly present
the 'right' biography on the front page." (Lofland has reprinted the
front page story from the Detroit *Free Press,* headlined "Richard
Speck's Twisted Path" and noting all his past derelictions and
character failings.) In the instance of Charles Whitman, who in 1966
shot fourteen people from a tower at the University of Texas,
newsmen were hard put to render a consistent biography of a
"deviant." Whitman's history—as a boy he had been an Eagle Scout,
and later he had served honorably in the American armed forces and
had done well in college—was difficult to square with the image of
"mad murderer." Some people who knew Whitman had questioned
his all-American image, but these doubts were not really convincing
enough to warrant frontpage banner headlines. Lofland has concluded:

The problem posed in the effort to reconstruct consistently Whitman's biography possibly explains the later
popularity of attributing his acts to an alleged brain
tumor. When social and psychological explanations
fail, one can always try biological or physiological ones.
Regardless of the character of the account, Actor must
be accounted for.[8]

    . . . It should be apparent from the discussion so far that the
potential force of retrospective interpretation lies in the attendant
social refusal to validate the prior identity that the labeled individual
seeks to maintain. Peter Berger has nicely expressed this general
point:

One cannot be human all by oneself and, apparently,
one cannot hold on to any particular identity all by

[7]*Ibid.,* pp. 150-151.
[8]*Ibid.,* p. 151.

oneself. The self-image of the officer as an officer [referring to an earlier example] can be maintained only in a social context in which others are willing to recognize him in this identity. If this recognition is suddenly withdrawn, it usually does not take very long before the self-image collapses.[9]

At the same time individual vulnerability to imputational processes may be highly variable, depending upon situational factors, social position, power resources, and the like.

[9]Peter L. Berger, *Invitation to Sociology* (Garden City, N.Y.: Doubleday Anchor, 1963), p. 100.

Conditions
of Successful
Degradation Ceremonies
Harold Garfinkel

Any communicative work between persons, whereby the public identity of an actor is transformed into something looked on as lower in the local scheme of social types, will be called a "status degradation ceremony." Some restrictions on this definition may increase its usefulness. The identities referred to must be "total" identities. That is, these identities must refer to persons as "motivational" types rather than as "behavioral" types,[1] not to what a person may be expected to have done or to do (in Parsons' term,[2] to his "performances") but to what the group holds to be the ultimate "grounds" or "reasons" for his performance.[3]

The grounds on which a participant achieves what for him is adequate understanding of why he or another acted as he did are not treated by him in a utilitarian manner. Rather, the correctness of an imputation is decided by the participant in accordance with socially valid and institutionally re-

[1]These terms are borrowed from Alfred Schutz , "Common Sense and Scientific Interpretation of Human Action," *Philosophy and Phenomenological Research*, Vol. XIV, No. 1 (September, 1953).

[2]Talcott Parsons and Edward Shils, "Values, Motives, and Systems of Action," in Parsons and Shils (eds.), *Toward a General Theory of Action* (Cambridge: Harvard University Press, 1951).

[3]Cf. the writings of Kenneth Burke, particularly *Permanence and Change* (Los Altos, Calif.: Hermes Publications, 1954), and *A Grammer of Motives* (New York: Prentice-Hall, Inc., 1945).

commended standards of "preference." With reference to these standards, he makes the crucial distinctions between appearances and reality, truth and falsity, triviality and importance, accident and essence, coincidence and cause. Taken together, the grounds, as well as the behavior that the grounds make explicable as the other person's conduct, constitute a person's identity. Together, they constitute the other as a social object. Persons identified by means of the ultimate "reasons" for their socially categorized and socially understood behavior will be said to be "totally" identified. The degradation ceremonies here discussed are those that are concerned with the alteration of total identities.

It is proposed that only in societies that are completely demoralized, will an observer be unable to find such ceremonies, since only in total anomie are the conditions of degradation ceremonies lacking. Max Scheler[4] argued that there is no society that does not provide in the very features of its organization the conditions sufficient for inducing shame. It will be treated here as axiomatic that there is no society whose social structure does not provide, in its routine features, the conditions of identity degradation. Just as the structural conditions of shame are universal to all societies by the very fact of their being organized, so the structural conditions of status degradation are universal to all societies. In this framework the critical question is not whether status degradation occurs or can occur within any given society. Instead, the question is: Starting from any state of a society's organization, what program of communicative tactics will get the work of status degradation done?

First of all, two questions will have to be decided, at least tentatively: *What are we referring to behaviorally when we propose the product of successful degradation work to be a changed total identity?* And *what are we to conceive the work of status degradation to have itself accomplished or to have assumed as the conditions of its success?*

I

Degradation ceremonies fall within the scope of the sociology of moral indignation. Moral indignation is a social affect. Roughly speaking, it is an instance of a class of feelings particular to the more

---

[4]Richard Hays Williams, "Scheler's Contributions to the Sociology of Affective Action, with Special Attention to the Problem of Shame," *Philosophy and Phenomenological Research*, Vol. II, No. 3 (March, 1942).

or less organized ways that human beings develop as they live out their lives in one another's company. Shame, guilt, and boredom are further important instances of such affects.

Any affect has its behavioral paradigm. That of shame is found in the withdrawal and covering of the portion of the body that socially defines one's public appearance—prominently, in our society, the eyes and face. The paradigm of shame is found in the phrases that denote removal of the self from public view, i.e., removal from the regard of the publicly identified other: "I could have sunk through the floor; I wanted to run away and hide; I wanted the earth to open up and swallow me." The feeling of guilt finds its paradigm in the behavior of self-abnegation—disgust, the rejection of further contact with or withdrawal from, and the bodily and symbolic expulsion of the foreign body, as when we cough, blow, gag, vomit, spit, etc.

The paradigm of moral indignation is *public* denunciation. We publicly deliver the curse: "I call upon all men to bear witness that he is not as he appears but is otherwise and *in essence*[5] of a lower species."

The social affects serve various functions both for the person as well as for the collectivity. A prominent function of shame for the person is that of preserving the ego from further onslaughts by withdrawing entirely its contact with the outside. For the collectivity shame is an "individuator." One experiences shame in his own time.

Moral indignation serves to effect the ritual destruction of the person denounced. Unlike shame, which does not bind persons together, moral indignation may reinforce group solidarity. In the market and in politics, a degradation ceremony must be counted as a secular form of communion. Structurally, a degradation ceremony bears close resemblance to ceremonies of investiture and elevation. How such a ceremony may bind persons to the collectivity we shall see when we take up the conditions of a successful denunciation. Our immediate question concerns the meaning of ritual destruction.

In the statement that moral indignation brings about the ritual destruction of the person being denounced, destruction is intended literally. The transformation of identities is the destruction of one social object and the constitution of another. The transformation does not involve the substitution of one identity for another, with the terms of the old one loitering about like the overlooked parts of a

---

[5]The man at whose hands a neighbor suffered death becomes a "murderer." The person who passes on information to enemies is really, i.e., "in essence," "in the first place," "all along," "in the final analysis," "originally," an informer.

fresh assembly, any more than the woman we see in the depart-
ment-store window that turns out to be a dummy carries with it the
possibilities of a woman. It is not that the old object has been
overhauled; rather it is replaced by another. One declares, "*Now*, it
was otherwise in the first place."

The work of the denunciation effects the recasting of the
objective character of the perceived other: The other person becomes
in the eyes of his condemners literally a different and *new* person. It
is not that the new attributes are added to the old "nucleus." He is
not changed, he is reconstituted. The former identity, at best,
receives the accent of mere appearance. In the social calculus of
reality representations and test, the former identity stands as accidental; the new identity is the "basic reality," What he is now is
what, "after all," he was all along.[6]

The public denunciation effects such a transformation of essence by substituting another socially validated motivational scheme
for that previously used to name and order the performances of the
denounced. It is with reference to this substituted, socially validated
motivational scheme as the essential grounds, i.e., the *first principles*, that his performances, past, present, and prospective, according to the witnesses, are to be properly and necessarily understood.[7]
Through the interpretive work that respects this rule, the denounced
person becomes in the eyes of the witnesses a different person.

II

How can one make a good denunciation?[8] To be successful, the
denunciation must redefine the situations of those that are witnesses
to the denunciation work. The denouncer, the party to be denounced

[6]Two themes commonly stand out in the rhetoric of denunciation: (1) the irony
between what the denounced appeared to be and what he is seen now really to be
where the new motivational scheme is taken as the standard and (2) a re-examination
and redefinition of origins of the denounced. For the sociological relevance of the
relationship between concerns for essence and concerns for origins see particularly
Kenneth Burke, *A Grammar of Motives.*

[7]While constructions like "substantially a something" or "essentially a something"
have been banished from the domain of scientific discourse, such constructions have
prominent and honored places in the theories of motives, persons, and conduct that
are employed in handling the affairs of daily life. Reasons can be given to justify the
hypothesis that such constructions may be lost to a group's "terminology of motives"
only if the relevance of socially sanctioned theories to practical problems is suspended.
This can occur where interpersonal relations are trivial (such as during play) or, more
interestingly, under severe demoralization of a system of activities. In such organizational states the frequency of status degradation is low.

[8]Because the paper is short, the risk must be run that, as a result of excluding certain
considerations, the treated topics may appear exaggerated. It would be desirable, for

(let us call him the "perpetrator"), and the thing that is being blamed on the perpetrator (let us call it the "event") must be transformed as follows:[9]

1. Both event and perpetrator must be removed from the realm of their everyday character and be made to stand as "out of the ordinary."

2. Both event and perpetrator must be placed within a scheme of preferences that shows the following properties:

A. The preferences must not be for event A over event B, but for event of *type* A over event of *type* B. The same typing must be accomplished for the perpetrator. Event and perpetrator must be defined as instances of a uniformity and must be treated as a uniformity throughout the work of the denunciation. The unique, never recurring character of the event or perpetrator should be lost. Similarly, any sense of accident, coincidence, indeterminism, chance, or monetary occurrence must not merely be minimized. Ideally, such measures should be inconceivable; at least they should be made false.

B. The witnesses must appreciate the characteristics of the typed person and event by referring the type to a dialectical counterpart. Ideally, the witnesses should not be able to contemplate the features of the denounced person without reference to the counterconception, as the profanity of an occurrence or a desire or a character trait, for example, is clarified by the references it bears to its opposite, the sacred. The features of the mad-dog murderer reverse the features of the peaceful citizen. The confessions of the Red can be read to [t]each the meanings of patriotism. There are many contrasts available, and any aggregate of witnesses this side of a complete war of each against all

example, to take account of the multitude of hedges that will be found against false denunciation; of the rights to denounce; of the differential apportionment of these rights, as well as the ways in which a claim, once staked out, may become a vested interest and may tie into the contests for economic and political advantage. Further, there are questions centering around the appropriate arenas of denunciation. For example, in our society the tribal council has fallen into secondary importance; among lay persons the denunciation has given way to the complaint to the authorities.

[9]These are the effects that the communicative tactics of the denouncer must be designed to accomplish. Put otherwise, in so far as the denouncer's tactics accomplish the reordering of the definitions of the situation of the witnesses to the denunciatory performances, the denouncer will have succeeded in effecting the transformation of the public identity of his victim. The list of conditions of this degrading effect are the determinants of the effect. Viewed in the scheme of a project to be rationally pursued, they are the adequate means. One would have to choose one's tactics for their efficiency in accomplishing these effects.

will have a plethora of such schemata for effecting a "familiar," "natural," "proper," ordering of motives, qualities, and other events.

From such contrasts, the following is to be learned. If the denunciation is to take effect, the scheme must not be one in which the witness is allowed to elect the preferred. Rather, the alternatives must be such that the preferred is morally required. Matters must be so arranged that the validity of his choice, its justification, is maintained by the fact that he makes it.[10] The scheme of alternatives must be such as to place constraints upon his making a selection "for a purpose." Nor will the denunciation succeed if the witness is free to look beyond the fact that he makes the selection for evidence that the correct alternative has been chosen, as, for example, by the test of empirical consequences of the choice. The alternatives must be such that, in "choosing," he takes it for granted and beyond any motive for doubt that not choosing can mean only preference for its opposite.

3. The denouncer must so identify himself to the witnesses that during the denunciation they regard him not as a private but as a publicly known person. He must not portray himself as acting according to his personal, unique experiences. He must rather be regarded as acting in his capacity as a public figure, drawing upon communally entertained and verified experience. He must act as a bona fide participant in the tribal relationships to which the witnesses subscribe. What he says must not be regarded as true for him alone, not even in the sense that it can be regarded by denouncer and witnesses as matters upon which they can become agreed. In no case, except in a most ironical sense, can the convention of true-for-reasonable-men be invoked. What the denouncer says must be regarded by the witnesses as true on the grounds of a socially employed metaphysics whereby witnesses assume that witnesses and denouncer are alike in essence.[11]

4. The denouncer must make the dignity of the supra-personal values of the tribe salient and accessible to view, and his denunciation must be delivered in their name.

5. The denouncer must arrange to be invested with the right to speak in the name of these ultimate values. The success of the denunciation will be undermined if, for his authority to de-

---

[10]Cf. Gregory Bateson and Jurgen Ruesch, *Communication: The Social Matrix of Psychiatry* (New York: W. W. Norton & Co., 1951), pp. 212-27.

[11]For bona fide members it is not that these are the grounds upon which we are agreed but upon which we are *alike,* consubstantial, in origin the same.

nounce, the denouncer invokes the personal interests that he may have acquired by virtue of the wrong done to him or someone else. He must rather use the wrong he has suffered as a tribal member to invoke the authority to speak in the name of these ultimate values.

6.   The denouncer must get himself so defined by the witnesses that they locate him as a supporter of these values.

7.   Not only must the denouncer fix his distance from the person being denounced, but the witnesses must be made to experience their distance from him also.

8.   Finally, the denounced person must be ritually separated from a place in the legitimate order, i.e., he must be defined as standing at a place opposed to it. He must be placed "outside," he must be made "strange."

These are the conditions that must be fulfilled for a successful denunciation. If they are absent, the denunciation will fail. Regardless of the situation when the denouncer enters, if he is to succeed in degrading the other man, it is necessary to introduce these features.[12]

Not all degradation ceremonies are carried on in accordance with publicly prescribed and publicly validated measures. Quarrels which seek the humiliation of the opponent through personal

[12]Neither of the problems of possible communicative or organizational conditions of their effectiveness have been treated here in systematic fashion. However, the problem of communicative tactics in degradation ceremonies is set in the light of systematically related conceptions. These conceptions may be listed in the following statements:

1. The definition of the situation of the witnesses (for ease of discourse we shall use the letter S) always bears a time qualification.

2. The S at t_2 is a function of the S at t_1. This function is described as an operator that transforms the S at t_1.

3. The operator is conceived as communicative work.

4. For a successful denunciation, it is required that the S at t_2 show specific properties. These have been specified previously.

5. The task of the denouncer is to alter the S's of the witnesses so that these S's will show the specified properties.

6. The "rationality" of the denouncer's tactics, i.e., their adequacy as a means for effecting the set of transformations necessary for effecting the identity transformation, is decided by the rule that the organizational and operational properties of the communicative net (the social system) are determinative of the size of the discrepancy between an intended and an actual effect of the communicative work. Put otherwise, the question is not that of the temporal origin of the situation but always and only how it is altered over time. The view is recommended that the definition of the situation at time 2 is a function of the definition at time 1 where this function consists of the communicative work conceived as a set of operations whereby the altered situation at time 1 is the situation at time 2. In strategy terms the function consists of the program of procedures that a denouncer should follow to effect the change of state S_{t_1} to S_{t_2}. In this paper S_{t_1} is treated as an unspecified state.

invective may achieve degrading on a limited scale. Comparatively few persons at a time enter into this form of communion, few benefit from it, and the fact of participation does not give the witness a definition of the other that is standardized beyond the particular group or scene of its occurrence.

The devices for effecting degradation vary in the feature and effectiveness according to the organization and operation of the system of action in which they occur. In our society the arena of degradation whose product, the redefined person, enjoys the widest transferability between groups has been rationalized, at least as to the institutional measures for carrying it out. The court and its officers have something like a fair monopoly over such ceremonies, and there they have become an occupational routine. This is to be contrasted with degradation undertaken as an immediate kinship and tribal obligation and carried out by those who, unlike our professional degraders in the law courts, acquire both right and obligation to engage in it through being themselves the injured parties or kin to the injured parties.

Factors conditioning the effectiveness of degradation tactics are provided in the organization and operation of the system of action within which the degradation occurs. For example, timing rules that provide for serial or reciprocal "conversations" would have much to do with the kinds of tactics that one might be best advised to use. The tactics advisable for an accused who can answer the charge as soon as it is made are in contrast with those recommended for one who had to wait out the denunciation before replying. Face-to-face contact is a different situation from that wherein the denunciation and reply are conducted by radio and newspaper. Whether the denunciation must be accomplished on a single occasion or is to be carried out over a sequence of "tries," factors like the territorial arrangements and movements of persons at the scene of the denunciation must be accomplished on a single occasion or is to be carried out over a sequence of "tries," factors like the territorial and power allocations among participants, all should influence the outcome.

In short, the factors that condition the success of the work of degradation are those that we point to when we conceive the actions of a number of persons as group-governed. Only some of the more obvious structural variables that may be expected to serve as predicters of the characteristics of denunciatory communicative tactics have been mentioned. They tell us not only how to construct an effective denunciation but also how to render denunciation useless.

Role Engulfment
Edwin M. Schur

One major consequence of the processes through which deviant identity is imputed is the tendency of the deviator to become "caught up in" a deviant role, to find that it has become highly salient in his overall personal identity (or concept of self), that his behavior is increasingly organized "around" the role, and that cultural expectations attached to the role have come to have precedence, or increased salience relative to other expectations, in the organization of his activities and general way of life. Lemert's term "secondary deviance" is intended to label this tendency, but we shall reserve it for use in a more inclusive sense—to cover not only the impact of labeling on the individual's self-concept but also secondary expansion of deviance problems at the situational and societal levels. "Role engulfment" seems a satisfactory term for the social-psychological impact on the individual. It should be viewed not as an alternative to "secondary deviance" but rather as a subconcept denoting one, narrower facet of the secondary expansion of deviation through societal reaction processes.

Accepting Deviant Identity

In considering role engulfment, we should keep in mind two major points of reference: how others define the actor and how the actor defines himself. Very crudely we can say that, as role engulfment increases, there is a tendency for the actor to define himself as others define him. Yet, a person can be "engulfed," at least in a practical sense by a deviant role, despite his definition of himself as non-deviant. The increasing difficulty of continuing to view himself as non-deviant, as more and more people treat him more and more of the time as if he were "deviant," is a central problem. Basically the problem is one of validating identity . . . Indeed, the notion of role engulfment is implicit in, or integral to, a number of concepts and processes [relevant to deviance]. Both stereotyping and retrospective interpretation seem to imply role engulfment almost by definition. The concept of master status lies at the heart of role engulfment, for it is the increased salience or primacy of the deviant role for the individual that is the hallmark of such engulfment. And deviant roles generally seem to have a kind of built-in primacy, or master status, relative at least to certain other kinds of roles. It should be noted, though, that we may also be able to distinguish between particular deviant roles according to the overall likelihood that they will acquire primacy. Similarly, there may be systematic differences between particular categories of individuals in the likelihood that deviant roles generally or specific deviant roles will become primary. That is, individuals have socially patterned, or categoric, variations in their susceptibility and resistance to engulfment in deviant roles generally and in particular deviant roles.

What kinds of events (or what kinds of information acquired by others) are particularly likely to precipitate or to accelerate the process of role engulfment? Labeling analysts like Becker have emphasized rather strongly the event of public identification and labeling. One difficulty in this emphasis, as well as in that on formal degradation ceremonies, is the possible suggestion that role engulfment occurs "all at once." It is true that a criminal trial, hospitalization for mental illness, or entrance into various other screening and treatment procedures seems to have special impact. Life is no longer the same as it was, and the individual inevitably comes to be viewed in a new light; he can thus hardly help but see himself in new terms. Yet, although such an event can theoretically occur "out of the blue," only rarely does it do so. Ordinarily if we are to understand public definition of a "deviant," we must view it within a context of continuous interaction, involving numerous relevant patterns of action and response and constantly shifting definitions of situations.

In important research on family reactions to mental illness[1] Marian Yarrow and her associates found that the open definition of a

[1]Marian Radke Yarrow et al., 'The Psychological Meaning of Mental Illness in the Family," *Journal of Social Issues*, 11 (1955), 12–24.

family member as mentally ill and direct action based on such a definition are often preceded by a long period of accommodation, during which the individual's disturbing behavior is "normalized"— that is, its pathological nature is denied or otherwise explained away. It is only after a gradual process of redefinition, in which behavior is finally accepted as symptomatic of illness, that such a seemingly abrupt and decisive step as hospitalization occurs. Nor is it true that being "publicly caught and labeled" ends the process of societal reaction to deviation. On the contrary, as Kitsuse's study of responses to homosexuality has shown, such an event is likely to encourage others who interact with the individual to reassess their conceptions of him. Their subsequent relations with him are likely to be altered, in turn, thus adding to the cumulative processes at work. In this connection, we may also recall the "hidden deviant," who is neither publicly caught and labeled nor recognized as a deviator by those with whom he interacts but who nonetheless may well find his self-concept and behavior affected by his knowledge that he could be so labeled and by his awareness of others' views of people "like" himself.

Other interesting research findings have indicated still further the quite diverse sorts of "cues" (information about individuals) that may activate or propel the process of role engulfment. The field study of "legal stigma" by Richard Schwartz and Jerome Skolnick,[2] in which prospective employers at resort hotels were shown employment "dossiers" on job applicants (which included systematically varied information about "criminal records" of varying degrees), has shown that merely being accused of a deviating act can be seriously discrediting, even though the accusation has been "disproved" (as when "acquittal" records were included in the dossiers). Derek Phillips' research on rejection of the mentally ill has disclosed that an individual's effort to seek particular kinds of help in connection with behavior that is troubling him and that others may view as deivant may itself be a discrediting factor.[3] Respondents in Phillips' sample of several hundred adults were shown five cards, each of which contained a description of an individual exhibiting a certain pattern of behavior. The cards were constructed to represent a paranoid schizophrenic, an individual suffering from simple schizophrenia, an anxious and depressed person, a phobic individual with compulsive

[2]Richard D. Schwartz and Jerome Skolnick, "Two Studies of Legal Stigma," *Social Problems*, 10 (Fall 1962), 133–142.

[3]Derek L. Phillips, "Rejection: A Possible Consequence of Seeking Help for Mental Disorders," *American Sociological Review*, 28 (December 1963), 963–972.

features, and a "normal" person. These abstracts were presented in systematically varied combinations with information about what source of help the person was using (none, a clergyman, an ordinary physician, a psychiatrist, or a mental hospital). After reading the combined descriptions of behavior and help source, respondents were asked a series of questions comprising a social-distance scale.

Although Phillips found a significant association between the kind of behavior displayed by the individual and the extent to which he was rejected by respondents, he also found that an individual displaying a given type of behavior was rejected least when he sought no help and most when he was hospitalized in a mental institution. Interestingly, when an individual depicted as "normal" was described as having been in a mental hospital, he was rejected more frequently than was a psychotic individual described as not having sought help from a professional or as seeing a clergyman and more frequently than was a depressed neurotic seeing a clergyman. The association between the source of help and rejection was maintained within age groups, socioeconomic-status categories, and groups showing different levels of authoritarianism. The basic findings thus did not appear to reflect differences among respondents in any of these factors. Phillips did find that respondents who had had relatives who had sought help for mental disorders deviated from the general rejection pattern; they were likely to reject individuals who did not seek help more than they rejected those who consulted clergymen, ordinary physicians, or psychiatrists. He also found that respondents who did not accept a "norm of self-reliance" were less likely to reject seekers of help than were those who strongly or even mildly professed such a norm.

Deviance Disavowal

A major aspect of role engulfment . . . is the difficulty that the deviating individual experiences in trying to alter his situation, or to reduce the "engulfment" (at least when the process has reached an advanced stage). The problems involved in efforts at "deviance disavowal" were recognized early by Frank Tannenbaum. . . . As he has noted, once the individual has been stigmatized as a delinquent or criminal, "the community expects him to live up to his reputation, and will not credit him if he does not live up to it."[4] Similarly, recent

---

[4]Frank Tannenbaum, *Crime and the Community* (Boston: Ginn, 1938), p. 477.

studies using social-distance scales (for example, Simmons' research on stereotyping and the Phillips study just discussed) suggest that, once one has a "record" of recognized deviation, negative reactions set in; we must assume that these reactions are difficult to overcome. Indeed, treatment personnel and others professionally concerned with the practical problems of former deviators of various kinds have emphasized the extreme difficulties that such individuals face in seeking employment, establishing themselves in non-deviant communities, and generally in trying to lead "normal" lives.

The difficulties of the ex-convict, the former mental patient, and the drug addict released from institutional treatment have all been documented at some length. Such people encounter serious problems in convincing significant others that they are "no longer like that." Their success in managing both practical problems and relations with others bears heavily upon their ability to maintain non-deviant conceptions of themselves. As Marsh Ray has observed, the drug addict who has undergone withdrawal treatment and who seeks to remain abstinent "now enters a period which might best be characterized as a 'running struggle' with his problems of social identity." The ex-addict who is successful in this endeavor "relates to new groups of people, participates in their experience and to some extent begins to evaluate the conduct of his former associates (and perhaps his own when he was an addict) in terms of the values of the new group."[5] As this quotation suggests—and as should be emphasized—it is by no means impossible for particular individuals to "shake off" imputed deviant characters or identities Furthermore, that individuals can sometimes successfully disavow deviant identities in no way provides an argument against the labeling perspective. Recently Harrison Trice and Paul Roman have suggested that, at the very least, the labeling approach slights possibilities of "delabeling" and "relabeling"—as exemplified by the rather successful efforts of Alcoholics Anonymous.[6] Although it is certainly true that labeling analysts have paid less attention to these processes than to those of negative labeling, it is far from true that the existence of such processes is itself inconsistent or a challenge to the labeling orientation. On the contrary, that success in removing stigma requires such delabeling and relabeling tends to confirm the labeling thesis.

[5]Marsh B. Ray, "The Cycle of Abstinence and Relapse Among Heroin Addicts," *Social Problems*, 9 (Fall 1961), 136.

[6]Harrison M. Trice and Paul M. Roman, "Delabeling, Relabeling, and Alcoholics Anonymous," *Social Problems*, 17 (Spring 1970), 538–546.

Although disavowal of deviance is, then, not impossible, it is nonetheless difficult and uncertain, and the difficulties are exacerbated by the very widespread belief that changes in character are impossible (for example, "once an addict, always an addict"). The self-fulfilling nature of such beliefs and the attendant interpersonal reactions, including erection of barriers to various practical opportunities, should be obvious. It is worth emphasizing too that, even apart from conscious efforts to reverse negative imputations of deviance, role and identity changes frequently occur in deviating individuals over the course of time. We know that not all those juveniles who are or who might be adjudged "delinquent" go on to become hardened criminal offenders. And even among "hard core" drug addicts, a "maturing out" process, in which drug use appears to be a "stage" that loses its importance for the individual as new life styles and possible courses of action emerge, has been noted.

A related phenomenon involves the various efforts of individuals currently engaged in deviation to insulate themselves from the demoralization and negative self-concepts that often follow from being labeled as deviant. Many of the techniques cited by Goffman in his study of stigma,[7] like the various forms of "information control" aimed at the "management of spoiled identity," illustrate such efforts. In part they are designed to refute the negative imputations that produce deviant identities, though at some point they become primarily devices for learning to "live with" deviant identities that have been pretty much accepted. Similarly, Gresham Sykes and David Matza have perceptively analyzed the "techniques of neutralization" (denial of serious injury, assertion that there is no real "victim," and so on) by which delinquent youths frequently rationalize their offending behavior and maintain positive self-concepts.[8] Youths who engage in homosexual acts for money rely heavily upon similar insulating mechanisms. As Albert Reiss has noted, some very explicit norms govern such encounters, norms that function to define these situations as only transactions and by virtue of which "the peer hustler in the peer-queer relationship develops no conception of himself either as prostitute or as homosexual." Reiss has found that, as long as such a youth conforms to the role expectations built into his activities (for example, maintenance of affective neutrality, emphasis on money as the goal, and restriction

[7]Erving Goffman, *Stigma: Notes on the Management of Spoiled Identity* (Englewood Cliffs, N.J.: Prentice-Hall, 1963).

[8]Gresham M. Sykes and David Matza, "Techniques of Neutralization: A Theory of Delinquency," *American Sociological Review*, 22 (December 1957), 664–670.

to specific sexual acts), his peers do not view him as homosexual, which seems to be the crucial factor influencing his own self-concept.[9]

James Bryan's studies of call girls provide another example of the ways in which neutralizing and justifying mechanisms can be used to preserve deviators' self-respect and resistance to the negative evaluations of others. He found that parts of the "ideology" that trainers sought to instill in the girls during an "apprenticeship" period were discarded as they became less valuable (as, for example, the value of cooperation with fellow girls declined) but that other themes, like those relating to the "functions" of prostitution, persisted. The potential for disavowal or neutralization of deviance in such themes is apparent from these statements by girls whom Bryan interviewed.

> We girls see, like I guess you call them perverts of some sort, you know, little freaky people and if they didn't have girls to come to like us that are able to handle them and make it a nice thing, there would be so many rapes and . . . nutty people really . . .

> I could say that a prostitute has held more marriages together as part of their profession than any divorce counselor . . . .

> I don't regret doing it because I feel I help people. A lot of men that come over to see me don't come for sex. They come over for companionship, someone to talk to . . . a lot of them have problems.[10]

Deviant Subcultures

Clearly these statements suggest a close relation between a labeling analysis of deviance (in this instance focusing on efforts to insulate the self against negative imputations) and a "functional" analysis. Some of our discussion also indicates certain links between emphases of the labeling orientation and those of the traditional analysis of deviant subcultures (itself largely influenced by functionalist theory). We can sense from some of these research findings a few of the major functions of deviant subcultures. In varying degrees a given type of deviant subculture (one organized around a specific

[9]Albert J. Reiss, Jr., "The Social Integration of Queers and Peers," *Social Problems,* 9 (Fall 1961), 102–120.

[10]James H. Bryan, "Occupational Ideologies and Individual Attitudes of Call Girls," *Social Problems,* 13 (Spring 1966), 443; see also Bryan, "Apprenticeships in Prostitution," *Social Problems,* 12 (Winter 1965), 287–297.

deviation) usually serves one or both aspects of a dual function. On one hand, involvement in the subculture facilitates access to and immersion in deviant roles that "members" either feel a need for or find pleasurable or desirable. (A good indication that not all deviant roles are undesirable ones into which individuals are pressured is provided by Becker's studies of marihuana users.) On the other hand, the subculture serves, often simultaneously, a kind of "defensive," or "protective," function, shielding individuals from the negative attitudes of outsiders, from the quite practical problems posed by outsiders' reactions (including legal ones), or from both.

Another set of related functions involves enhancement of in-group solidarity and measures for at least informal social control within the group itself. In connection with group solidarity and the morale of individual deviators, Goffman has discussed the support provided by being with one's own "kind" or with others who are "wise" to the deviation, and has analyzed the functions of "back places" where the deviator can relax and let down his guard.[11] Weinberg's studies of nudist camps[12]—in which a response often regarded as almost instinctual, that is, the sexual provocation inherent in nudity, can be controlled through socialization to a generally unfamiliar set of norms—demonstrate the provision of internal social control. The need to control behavior within a group, particularly when it has important bearing on outsiders' views of the group, may be a factor in the content of some deviant subcultures. Another facet of the operations of subcultures is apparent in instances of political deviation or esoteric cults, in which complex and unusual belief systems are central to the patterns of deviation; the very survival of those patterns may depend heavily upon the kinds of support that the subcultures can provide.[13]

Most of these comments pertain primarily to what we have called the "positive" or "facilitative" aspect of subculture. But we can rather easily find various examples of defensive subcultural elaboration and involvement. Becker has shown how learning the norms of marihuana use (and the close association with other users required) helps the user to deal with the problems of supply, secrecy, and societal definition to which his behavior gives rise. Similarly, many

[11]Goffman, *Stigma.*

[12]Weinberg, "Sexual Modesty and the Nudist Camp," *Social Problems,* 12 (Winter 1965), 311–318; see also Weinberg, "Becoming a Nudist," *Psychiatry,* 29 (February 1966).

[13]Simmons, "Maintaining Deviant Belief Systems: A Case Study," *Social Problems,* 11 (Winter 1964), 250–256.

of the subcultural features surrounding heroin addiction serve an even more direct defensive function, permitting the addict to deal with the substantial and very serious enforcement efforts designed to block his access to drugs and to identify and isolate him.

Almost always we find combinations of these diverse functions. For example, the homosexual subculture clearly facilitates the deviator's relaxed association with others of his own kind; yet to some extent it also provides a kind of protective segregation from police harassment and other interference by the "straight" world. In an interesting analysis of "bottle gangs" (groups of indigent street drinkers created for the purpose of purchasing and sharing bottles of liquor), Rubington has noted internal control functions (making sure that the members making the purchases do return with the bottles), general facilitative functions (shaping a pleasant cooperative experience, and helping to order the members' daily round), and defensive functions (shielding participants from police scrutiny).[14]

Although immersion in a deviant subculture may be one prime indicator of role engulfment, it does not at all follow that such immersion is a necessary condition of the individual's developing a strong deviant self-concept. As we have noted elsewhere, whether or not a given kind of deviation gives rise to a special subculture depends in part upon "the need for continuous contact with other like individuals in order for the basic deviant acts to be carried out."[15] But, even without such a need, the deviating individual often experiences role engulfment when he confronts strong negative social reactions, whatever form they may take. The crucial point has been highlighted in Lemert's classic statement:

When a person begins to employ his deviant behavior or a role based upon it as a means of defense, attack, or adjustment to the overt and covert problems created by the consequent societal reaction to him, his deviation is secondary.[16]

It is not the particular form of deviation or the specific content of the societal reaction that determines role engulfment so much as simply that there is a sufficient "progressive reciprocal relationship" between the two. As Lemert has further remarked, the development

[14]Rubington, "Variations in Bottle-Gang Controls," in Rubington and Weinberg eds., *Deviance: The Interactionist Perspective* (New York: Macmillan, 1968), pp. 303–316.

[15]Edwin M. Schur, *Crimes Without Victims* (Englewood Cliffs, N.J.: Prentice-Hall, 1965), pp. 172–173.

[16]Lemert, *Social Pathology* (New York: McGraw-Hill, 1951), p. 76.

of secondary deviation usually involves a sequence of interaction along these approximate lines:

> . . . (I) primary deviation; (2) social penalties; (3) further primary deviation; (4) stronger penalties and rejections; (5) further deviation, perhaps with hostilities and resentment beginning to focus upon those doing the penalizing; (6) crisis reached in the tolerance quotient, expressed in formal action by the community stigmatizing the deviant; (7) strengthening of the deviant conduct as a reaction to the stigmatizing and penalties; (8) ultimate acceptance of deviant social status and efforts at adjustment on the basis of the associated role.[17]

The "content" of those actions and reactions and the point reached on the continuum, ranging from initial acts of deviation, to full elaboration of patterns of secondary deviance, will be highly variable, according to the particular deviation, the individual, and the social context.

Substantial possibility of individual role engulfment in a situation in which subcultural elaboration is not very likely is illustrated by the condition of stuttering. Lemert has referred to adult stuttering as representing in many respects the "pure case" of secondary deviance,

> because stuttering thus far has defied efforts at causative explanation. It appears to be exclusively a process-product in which . . . normal speech variations, or at most, minor abnormalities of speech (primary stuttering) can be fed into an interactional or evaluational process and come out as secondary stuttering.[18]

As Lemert has pointed out, early reactions to childhood speech difficulties—on the part of family, peers, schoolteachers, and so on—seem to determine whether or not the difficulty persists and expands. Research findings indicate that merely calling a child a "stutterer" does not necessarily ensure persistent adult stuttering; rather, a substantial elaboration of interaction between the individual's speech difficulties and certain kinds of negative response seems required. Lemert has also observed that the age levels at which various situational pressures are experienced may be an important factor; as a child grows older the primacy of the stuttering role

[17]*Ibid.*, p. 77.

[18]Lemert, *Human Deviance, Social Problems, and Social Control* (Englewood Cliffs, N.J.: Prentice-Hall, 1967), p. 56.

apparently increases. For our purposes, Lemert's comments on the role of speech therapy in fostering, rather than in impeding, the development of secondary stuttering are particularly interesting:

. . . we may safely say that going to a speech clinic in all cases confronts the individual with a clear-cut societal definition of the stuttering self. The association with other stutterers and with speech cases in the clinic situation has a clear implication for self and role, as well as the knowledge that other students or members of the community know the function of the clinic. One well-known clinic, at a Middle Western college, makes it more or less of a prerequisite for treatment of adult stutterers that they make frank avowals in speech and behavior that they are stutterers. This is done by having the stutterers practice blocks in front of mirrors, exaggerate them, copy one another's blocks, and have or fake blocks in public situations. While there are several objectives behind this procedure, one of its chief consequences is to instill an unequivocal self-definition in the stutterer as one who is different from others. . . .[19]

[19]Lemert, *Social Pathology*, p. 159.

part Four

Anomie
Theory

Interaction theorists emphasized the effects of societal reaction to deviant behavior on the formation of the self concept. Implied in the process of adopting a deviant identity is the notion of social psychological strain; the self label and perceived societal reaction may operate as a stigma which produces frustration and a tendency toward some mode of adaptation. *Anomie theory* offers further explanation of the causes of such strain and, even more importantly in terms of its contribution to the development of an integrative theory, it provides an understanding of the processes of adaptation.

The selection by Emile Durkheim defines and elaborates the concept of *anomie*. Durkheim defined anomie as a condition of the social system that is characterized by a lack of normative regulation of behavior. Utilizing a structural functional analysis, he locates its source in an imperfect integration of certain social structural variables. Durkheim maintained that human needs and desires, in their unrestrained state, are insatiable. Without the regulation of limits by normative constraint, life would be unbearable. For "to pursue a goal which is by definition unattainable is to condemn oneself to a state of perpetual unhappiness." A social system for the most part enjoys normative limiting of needs and desires. There occur, however, periods in the life of the system when rapid or sudden changes disrupt regulation. This lack of regulation, and the consequent surge of desires, Durkheim calls anomie.

While Durkheim was concerned with a general condition of anomie as effected by changes in the social system, the theorists that follow him are concerned with a more persistent form that affects only certain segments of the population. In this latter situation, groups and individuals are not only faced with the deregulative effects of anomie that make normative behavior problematic, but are also under pressure (from those who are relatively unaffected by imperfect structural integration) to conform to that normative behavior. Thus, in addition to the description of the lack of structural integration, these theorists focus on the modes of adaptation made to alleviate the resultant social psychological strain.

Robert Merton attributes the development of strain to a malintegration of the cultural goals and institutionalized means of a social structure. Persons who experience strain are those who, because of their normative reference group identifications, have internalized the societal goals but lack legitimate means for their attainment. He accounts for the specific modes of adaptation by the relative strength of internalization of goals and means, as well as by the availability of alternative means within the structure.

Expanding upon Merton's idea and incorporating it into a more general theory of social interaction, Talcott Parsons similarly views deviance as an adaptation to the strain that develops when the actions of others relative to the individual do not conform to the norms governing their relationship. This strain occurs because these persons are important to the individual to the extent that he views their actions as sanctions of his behavior, and because he has internalized the norms of their relationship to become part of his own needs. If others persist in their actions, and if he is unable to transfer cathexis to other non-deviants, or restructure his need dispositions through the mechanisms of defense or by redefining his expectations of others, he may develop ambivalence toward the normative patterns of this relationship and restructure his present orientation through some deviant mode of adaptation.

Synthesizing ideas from Merton and Parsons, Albert Cohen emphasizes the role of reference group identification in adapting to strain. Deviant behavior, he states, is a response to ambivalence relative to institutionalized expectations. Such ambivalence occurs when conformity to these expectations is strongly motivated but difficult to attain. The resolution to this problem depends upon reference group loyalties. If the individual continues to hold conforming members of society as his reference group, he is likely to conform to their expectations despite continued frustration. Or, he may break relations with these groups and continue in his behavior without the support of persons whose norms legitimize the behavior; Cohen calls this "going it alone." Finally, as a third alternative, the deviant may select a new reference group which is sympathetic to his problems and eventually become immersed in their subculture.

The second selection by Cohen further expands upon the notion of reference group identification as it applies to the development of these subcultures. The genesis of the subculture, he writes, is a process of effective communication among a number of individuals sharing similar problems of adjustment. Such problems evolve largely out of the difficulties of obtaining status in one's reference group. Persons lacking characteristics necessary for achievement, as determined by group norms, are likely to experience stress. The creation of alternative norms, then, arises out of hesitant and exploratory gestures made by these individuals as they work toward a mutually acceptable solution. The tendency is "to gravitate toward one another and jointly to establish new norms, new criteria of status which define as meritorious the characteristics they *do* possess, the kinds of conduct of which they *are* capable."

Anomie theory, then, points out the relationship that exists between social structure and individual behavior. Social systems may be organized in such a way as to preclude full or satisfying participation of certain of their members. If those affected in this way have also internalized the norms of such systems, feelings of relative deprivation may result. The tendency is for persons to attempt to restore equilibrium to their relationships through various modes of adaptation. Such adaptations often involve a shift in reference identifications to groups wherein the attainment of status and a more positive identity may be realized.

Anomie
Emile Durkheim

No living being can be happy or even exist unless his needs are sufficiently proportioned to his means. In other words, if his needs require more than can be granted, or even merely something of a different sort, they will be under continual friction and can only function painfully. Movements incapable of production without pain tend not to be reproduced. Unsatisfied tendencies atrophy, and as the impulse to live is merely the result of all the rest, it is bound to weaken as the others relax.

In the animal, at least in a normal condition, this equilibrium is established with automatic spontaneity because the animal depends on purely material conditions. All the organism needs is that the supplies of substance and energy constantly employed in the vital process should be periodically renewed by equivalent quantities; that replacement be equivalent to use. When the void created by existence in its own resources is filled, the animal, satisfied, asks nothing further. Its power of reflection is not sufficiently developed to imagine other ends than those implicit in its physical nature. On the other hand, as the work demanded of each organ itself depends on the general state of vital energy and the needs of organic equilibrium, use is regulated in turn by replacement and the balance is automatic. The limits of one are those of the other; both are fundamental to the constitution of the existence in question, which cannot exceed them.

This is not the case with man, because most of his needs are not dependent on his body or not to the same degree. Strictly speaking, we may consider

Reprinted with permission of Macmillan Publishing Co., Inc. and Routledge & Kegan Paul, Ltd. from *Suicide* by Emile Durkheim, trans. by John A. Spaulding and George Simpson. Copyright 1952 by The Free Press, pp. 246–254.

that the quantity of material supplies necessary to the physical maintenance of a human life is subject to computation, though this be less exact than in the preceding case and a wider margin left for the free combinations of the will; for beyond the indispensable minimum which satisfies nature when instinctive, a more awakened reflection suggests better conditions, seemingly desirable ends craving fulfillment. Such appetites, however, admittedly sooner or later reach a limit which they cannot pass. But how determine the quantity of well-being, comfort or luxury legitimately to be craved by a human being? Nothing appears in man's organic nor in his psychological constitution which sets a limit to such tendencies. The functioning of individual life does not require them to cease at one point rather than at another; the proof being that they have constantly increased since the beginnings of history, receiving more and more complete satisfaction, yet with no weakening of average health. Above all, how establish their proper variation with different conditions of life, occupations, relative importance of services, etc.? In no society are they equally satisfied in the different stages of the social hierarchy. Yet human nature is substantially the same among all men, in its essential qualities. It is not human nature which can assign the variable limits necessary to our needs. They are thus unlimited so far as they depend on the individual alone. Irrespective of any external regulatory force, our capacity for feeling is in itself an insatiable and bottomless abyss.

But if nothing external can restrain this capacity, it can only be a source of torment to itself. Unlimited desires are insatiable by definition and insatiability is rightly considered a sign of morbidity. Being unlimited, they constantly and infinitely surpass the means at their command; they cannot be quenched. Inextinguishable thirst is constantly renewed torture. It has been claimed, indeed, that human activity naturally aspires beyond assignable limits and sets itself unattainable goals. But how can such an undetermined state be any more reconciled with the conditions of mental life than with the demands of physical life? All man's pleasure in acting, moving and exerting himself implies the sense that his efforts are not in vain and that by walking he has advanced. However, one does not advance when one walks toward no goal, or—which is the same thing—when his goal is infinity. Since the distance between us and it is always the same, whatever road we take, we might as well have made the motions without progress from the spot. Even our glances behind and our feeling of pride at the distance covered can cause only deceptive satisfaction, since the remaining distance is not proportionately reduced. To pursue a goal which is by definition unattainable is to condemn oneself to a state of perpetual unhappiness. Of course, man may hope contrary to all reason, and hope has its pleasures even when unreasonable. It may sustain him for a time; but it cannot survive the repeated disappointments of experience indefinitely. What more can the future offer him than the past, since he can never reach a tenable condition nor even approach the glimpsed ideal? Thus, the more one has, the more one wants, since satisfactions received only stimulate instead of filling needs. Shall action as such be considered agreeable? First, only on condition of blindness to its uselessness. Secondly, for this pleasure to be felt and to temper and half veil the accompanying painful unrest, such unending motion must at least always be easy and unhampered. If it is interfered with only restlessness is left, with the lack of ease which it, itself, entails. But it would be a miracle if no insurmountable obstacle were never encountered. Our thread of life on these conditions is pretty thin, breakable at any instant.

To achieve any other result, the passions first must be limited. Only then can they be harmonized with the faculties and satisfied. But since the individual has no way of limiting them, this must be done by some force exterior to him. A regulative force must play the same role for moral needs which the organism plays for physical needs. This means that the force can only be moral. The awakening of conscience interrupted the state of equilibrium of the animal's dormant existence; only conscience, therefore, can furnish the means to re-establish it. Physical restraint would be ineffective; hearts cannot be touched by physio-chemical forces. So far as the appetites are not automatically restrained by physiological mechanisms, they can be halted only by a limit that they recognize as just. Men would never consent to restrict their desires if they felt justified in passing the assigned limit. But, for reasons given above, they cannot assign themselves this law of justice. So they must receive it from an authority which they respect, to which they yield spontaneously. Either directly and as a whole, or through the agency of one of its organs, society alone can play this moderating role; for it is the only moral power superior to the individual, the authority of which he accepts. It alone has the power necessary to stipulate law and to set the point beyond which the passions must not go. Finally, it alone can estimate the reward to be prospectively offered to every class of human functionary, in the name of the common interest.

As a matter of fact, at every moment of history there is a dim perception, in the moral consciousness of societies, of the respective value of different social services, the relative reward due to each, and the consequent degree of comfort appropriate on the average to workers in each occupation. The different functions are graded in public opinion and a certain coefficient of well-being assigned to each, according to its place in the hierarchy. According to accepted ideas, for example, a certain way of living is considered the upper limit to which a workman may aspire in his efforts to improve his existence, and there is another limit below which he is not willingly permitted to fall unless he has seriously demeaned himself. Both differ for city and country workers, for the domestic servant and the day-laborer, for the business clerk and the official, etc. Likewise the man of wealth is reproved if he lives the life of a poor man, but also if he seeks the refinements of luxury overmuch. Economists may protest in vain; public feeling will always be scandalized if an individual spends too much wealth for wholly superfluous use, and it even seems that this severity relaxes only in times of moral disturbance.[1] A genuine regimen exists, therefore, although not always legally formulated, which fixes with relative precision the maximum degree of ease of living to which each social class may legitimately aspire. However, there is nothing immutable about such a scale. It changes with the increase or decrease of collective revenue and the changes occurring in the moral ideas of society. Thus what appears luxury to one period no longer does so to another; and the well-being which for long periods was granted to a class only by exception and supererogation, finally appears strictly necessary and equitable.

Under this pressure, each in his sphere vaguely realizes the extreme limit set to his ambitions and aspires to nothing beyond. At least if he respects regulations and is docile to collective authority, that is, has a wholesome moral constitution, he feels that it is not well to ask more. Thus, an end and goal are set to the passions. Truly, there is nothing rigid nor absolute about such determination. The economic ideal assigned each class of citizens is itself confined to certain limits, within which the desires have free range. But it is not infinite. This relative limitation and the moderation it involves, make men contented with their lot while stimulating them moderately to improve it; and this average contentment causes the feeling of calm, active happiness, the pleasure in existing and living which characterizes health for societies as well as for individuals. Each person is then at least, generally speaking, in harmony with his condition, and

[1] Actually, this is a purely moral reprobation and can hardly be judicially implemented. We do not consider any reestablishment of sumptuary laws desirable or even possible.

desires only what he may legitimately hope for as the normal reward of his activity. Besides, this does not condemn man to a sort of immobility. He may seek to give beauty to his life; but his attempts in this direction may fail without causing him to despair. For, loving what he has and not fixing his desire solely on what he lacks, his wishes and hopes may fail of what he has happened to aspire to, without his being wholly destitute. He has the essentials. The equilibrium of his happiness is secure because it is defined, and a few mishaps cannot disconcert him.

But it would be of little use for everyone to recognize the justice of the hierarchy of functions established by public opinion, if he did not also consider the distribution of these functions just. The workman is not in harmony with his social position if he is not convinced that he has his desserts. If he feels justified in occupying another, what he has would not satisfy him. So it is not enough for the average level of needs for each social condition to be regulated by public opinion, but another, more precise rule, must fix the way in which these conditions are open to individuals. There is no society in which such regulation does not exist. It varies with times and places. Once it regarded birth as the almost exclusive principle of social classification; today it recognizes no other inherent inequality than hereditary fortune and merit. But in all these various forms its object is unchanged. It is also only possible, everywhere, as a restriction upon individuals imposed by superior authority, that is, by collective authority. For it can be established only by requiring of one or another group of men, usually of all, sacrifices and concessions in the name of the public interest.

Some, to be sure, have thought that this moral pressure would become unnecessary if men's economic circumstances were only no longer determined by heredity. If inheritance were abolished, the argument runs, if everyone began life with equal resources and if the competitive struggle were fought out on a basis of perfect equality, no one could think its results unjust. Each would instinctively feel that things are as they should be.

Truly, the nearer this ideal equality were approached, the less social restraint will be necessary. But it is only a matter of degree. One sort of heredity will always exist, that of natural talent. Intelligence, taste, scientific, artistic, literary or industrial ability, courage and manual dexterity are gifts received by each of us at birth, as the heir to wealth receives his capital or as the nobleman formerly received his title and function. A moral discipline will therefore still be required to make those less favored by nature accept the lesser advantages which they owe to the chance of birth. Shall it be demanded that all have an equal share and that no advantage be given those more useful and deserving? But then there would have to be a discipline far stronger to make these accept a treatment merely equal to that of the mediocre and incapable.

But like the one first mentioned, this discipline can be useful only if considered just by the peoples subject to it. When it is maintained only by custom and force, peace and harmony are illusory; the spirit of unrest and discontent is latent; appetites superficially restrained are ready to revolt. This happened in Rome and Greece when the faiths underlying the old organization of the patricians and plebeians were shaken, and in our modern societies when aristocratic prejudices began to lose their old ascendancy. But this state of upheaval is exceptional; it occurs only when society is passing through some abnormal crisis. In normal conditions the collective order is regarded as just by the great majority of persons. Therefore, when we say that an authority is necessary to impose this order on individuals, we certainly do not mean that violence is the only means of establishing it. Since this regulation is meant to restrain individual passions, it must come from a power which dominates individuals; but this power must also be obeyed through respect, not fear.

It is not true, then, that human activity can be released from all restraint. Nothing in the world can enjoy such a privilege. All existence being a part of the universe is relative to the remainder; its nature and method of manifestation accordingly depend not only on itself but on other beings, who consequently restrain and regulate it. Here there are only differences of degree and form between the mineral realm and the thinking person. Man's characteristic privilege is that the bond he accepts is not physical but moral; that is, social. He is governed not by a material environment brutally imposed on him, but by a conscience superior to his own, the superiority of which he feels. Because the greater, better part of his existence transcends the body, he escapes the body's yoke, but is subject to that of society.

But when society is disturbed by some painful crisis or by beneficent but abrupt transitions, it is momentarily incapable of exercising this influence; thence come the sudden rises in the curve of suicides . . . .

In the case of economic disasters, indeed, something like a declassification occurs which suddenly casts certain individuals into a lower state than their previous one. Then they must reduce their requirements, restrain their needs, learn greater self-control. All the advantages of social influence are lost so far as they are concerned; their moral education has to be recommenced. But society cannot adjust them instantaneously to this new life and teach them to practice the increased self-repression to which they are unaccustomed. So they are not adjusted to the condition forced on them, and its very prospect is intolerable; hence the suffering which detaches them from a reduced existence even before they have made trial of it.

It is the same if the source of the crisis is an abrupt growth of power and wealth. Then, truly, as the conditions of life are changed, the standard according to which needs were regulated can no longer remain the same; for it varies with social resources, since it largely determines the share of each class of producers. The scale is upset; but a new scale cannot be immediately improvised. Time is required for the public conscience to reclassify men and things. So long as the social forces thus freed have not regained equilibrium, their respective values are unknown and so all regulation is lacking for a time. The limits are unknown between the possible and the impossible, what is just and what is unjust, legitimate claims and hopes and those which are immoderate. Consequently, there is no restraint upon aspirations. If the disturbance is profound, it affects even the principles controlling the distribution of men among various occupations. Since the relations between various parts of society are necessarily modified, the ideas expressing these relations must change. Some particular class especially favored by the crisis is no longer resigned to its former lot, and, on the other hand, the example of its greater good fortune arouses all sorts of jealousy below and about it. Appetites, not being controlled by a public opinion become disoriented, no longer recognize the limits proper to them. Besides, they are at the same time seized by a sort of natural erethism simply by the greater intensity of public life. With increased prosperity desires increase. At the very moment when traditional rules have lost their authority, the richer prize offered these appetites stimulates them and makes them more exigent and impatient of control. The state of de-regulation or anomy is thus further heightened by passions being less disciplined, precisely when they need more disciplining.

But then their very demands make fulfillment impossible. Overweening ambition always exceeds the results obtained, great as they may be, since there is no warning to pause here. Nothing gives satisfaction and all this agitation is uninterruptedly maintained without appeasement. Above all, since this race for an unattainable goal can give no other pleasure but that of the race itself, if it is one, once it is interrupted the participants are left empty-handed. At the same time the struggle grows more violent and painful, both from being less controlled and because competition is greater. All classes contend among themselves because no established classification any longer exists. Effort grows, just when it becomes less productive. How could the desire to live not be weakened under such conditions?

This explanation is confirmed by the remarkable immunity of poor countries. Poverty protects against suicide because it is a restraint in itself. No matter how one acts, desires have to depend upon resources to some extent; actual possessions are partly the criterion of those aspired to. So the less one has the less he is tempted to extend the range of his needs indefinitely. Lack of power, compelling moderation, accustoms men to it, while nothing excites envy if no one has superfluity. Wealth, on the other hand, by the power it bestows, deceives us into believing that we depend on ourselves only. Reducing the resistance we encounter from objects, it suggests the possibility of unlimited success against them. The less limited one feels, the more intolerable all limitation appears. Not without reason, therefore, have so many religions dwelt on the advantages and moral value of poverty. It is actually the best school for teaching self-restraint. Forcing us to constant self-discipline, it prepares us to accept collective discipline with equanimity, while wealth, exalting the individual, may always arouse the spirit of rebellion which is the very source of immorality. This, of course, is no reason why humanity should not improve its material condition. But though the moral danger involved in every growth of prosperity is not irremediable, it should not be forgotten.

Social Structure and Anomie
Robert K. Merton

There persists a notable tendency in sociological theory to attribute the malfunctioning of social structure primarily to those of man's imperious biological drives which are not adequately restrained by social control. In this view, the social order is solely a device for "impulse management" and the "social processing" of tensions. These impulses which break through social control, be it noted, are held to be biologically derived. Nonconformity is assumed to be rooted in original nature.[1] Conformity is by implication the result of an utilitarian calculus or unreasoned conditioning. This point of view, whatever its other deficiences, clearly begs one question. It provides no basis for determining the nonbiological conditions which induce deviations from prescribed patterns of conduct. In this paper, it will be suggested that certain phases of social structure generate the circumstances in which infringement of social codes constitutes a "normal" response.[2]

The conceptual scheme to be outlined is de-

[1]E.g., Ernest Jones, *Social Aspects of Psychoanalysis*, 28, London, 1924. If the Freudian notion is a variety of the "original sin" dogma, then the interpretation advanced in this paper may be called the doctrine of "socially derived sin."

[2]"Normal" in the sense of a culturally oriented, if not approved, response. This statement does not deny the relevance of biological and personality differences which may be significantly involved in the *incidence* of deviate conduct. Our focus of interest is the social and cultural matrix; hence we abstract from other factors. It is in this sense, I take it, that James S. Plant speaks of the "normal reaction of normal people to abnormal conditions." See his *Personality and the Cultural Pattern*, 248, New York, 1937.

From "Social Structure and Anomie" by Robert K. Merton in *American Sociological Review*, Vol. 3, Oct. 1938, pp. 672–682. By permission of the author and The American Sociological Association.

signed to provide a coherent, systematic approach to the study of socio-cultural sources of deviate behavior. Our primary aim lies in discovering how some social structures *exert a definite pressure* upon certain persons in the society to engage in nonconformist rather than conformist conduct. The many ramifications of the scheme cannot all be discussed; the problems mentioned outnumber those explicitly treated.

Among the elements of social and cultural structure, two are important for our purposes. These are analytically separable although they merge imperceptibly in concrete situations. The first consists of culturally defined goals, purposes, and interests. It comprises a frame of aspirational reference. These goals are more or less integrated and involve varying degrees of prestige and sentiment. They constitute a basic, but not the exclusive, component of what Linton aptly has called "designs for group living." Some of these cultural aspirations are related to the original drives of man, but they are not determined by them. The second phase of the social structure defines, regulates, and controls the acceptable modes of achieving these goals. Every social group invariably couples its scale of desired ends with moral or institutional regulation of permissible and required procedures for attaining these ends. These regulatory norms and moral imperatives do not necessarily coincide with technical or efficiency norms. Many procedures which from the standpoint of *particular individuals* would be most efficient in securing desired values, e.g., illicit oil-stock schemes, theft, fraud, are ruled out of the institutional area of permitted conduct. The choice of expedients is limited by the institutional norms.

To say that these two elements, culture goals and institutional norms, operate jointly is not to say that the ranges of alternative behaviors and aims bear some constant relation to one another. The emphasis upon certain goals may vary independently of the degree of emphasis upon institutional means. There may develop a disproportionate, at times, a virtually exclusive, stress upon the value of specific goals, involving relatively slight concern with the institutionally appropriate modes of attaining these goals. The limiting case in this direction is reached when the range of alternative procedures is limited only by technical rather than institutional considerations. Any and all devices which promise attainment of the all important goal would be permitted in this hypothetical polar case.[3] This

[3]Contemporary American culture has been said to tend in this direction. See André Siegfried, *America Comes of Age*, 26–37, New York, 1927. The alleged extreme(?) emphasis on the goals of monetary success and material prosperity leads to dominant concern with technological and social instruments designed to produce the desired result, inasmuch as institutional controls become of secondary importance. In such a

constitutes one type of cultural malintegration. A second polar type is found in groups where activities originally conceived as instrumental are transmuted into ends in themselves. The original purposes are forgotten and ritualistic adherence to institutionally prescribed conduct becomes virtually obsessive.[4] Stability is largely ensured while change is flouted. The range of alternative behaviors is severely limited. There develops a tradition-bound, sacred society characterized by neophobia. The occupational psychosis of the bureaucrat may be cited as a case in point. Finally, there are the intermediate types of groups where a balance between culture goals and institutional means is maintained. These are the significantly integrated and relatively stable, though changing, groups.

An effective equilibrium between the two phases of the social structure is maintained as long as satisfactions accrue to individuals who conform to both constraints, viz., satisfactions from the achievement of the goals and satisfactions emerging directly from the institutionally canalized modes of striving to attain these ends. Success, in such equilibrated cases, is twofold. Success is reckoned in terms of the product and in terms of the process, in terms of the outcome and in terms of activities. Continuing satisfactions must derive from sheer *participation* in a competitive order as well as from eclipsing one's competitors if the order itself is to be sustained. The occasional sacrifices involved in institutionalized conduct must be compensated by socialized rewards. The distribution of statuses and roles through competition must be so organized that positive incentives for conformity to roles and adherence to status obligations are provided *for every position* within the distributive order. Aberrant conduct, therefore, may be viewed as a symptom of dissociation between culturally defined aspirations and socially structured means.

Of the types of groups which result from the independent variation of the two phases of the social structure, we shall be

---

situation, innovation flourishes as the *range of means* employed is broadened. In a sense, then, there occurs the paradoxical emergence of "materialists" from an "idealistic" orientation. Cf. Durkheim's analysis of the cultural conditions which predispose toward crime and innovation, both of which are aimed toward efficiency, not moral norms. Durkheim was one of the first to see that "contrairement aux idées courantes le criminel n'apparait plus comme un etre radicalement insociable, comme une sorte d'element parasitaire, de corps etranger et inassimilable, introduit au sein de la societe; c'est un agent regulier de la vie sociale." See *Les Regles de la Methode Sociologique*, 86–89, Paris, 1927.

[4]Such ritualism may be associated with a mythology which rationalizes these actions so that they appear to retain their status as means, but the dominant pressure is in the direction of strict ritualistic conformity, irrespective of such rationalizations. In this sense, ritual has proceeded farthest when such rationalizations are not even called forth.

primarily concerned with the first, namely, that involving a disproportionate accent on goals. This statement must be recast in a proper
perspective. In no group is there an absence of regulatory codes
governing conduct, yet groups do vary in the degree to which these
folkways, mores, and institutional controls are effectively integrated
with the more diffuse goals which are part of the culture matrix.
Emotional convictions may cluster about the complex of socially
acclaimed ends, meanwhile shifting their support from the culturally
defined implementation of these ends. As we shall see, certain
aspects of the social structure may generate countermores and
antisocial behavior precisely because of differential emphases on
goals and regulations. In the extreme case, the latter may be so
vitiated by the goal-emphasis that the range of behavior is limited
only by considerations of technical expediency. The sole significant
question then becomes, which available means is most efficient in
netting the socially approved value?[5] The technically most feasible
procedure, whether legitimate or not, is preferred to the institutionally prescribed conduct. As this process continues, the integration of
the society becomes tenuous and anomie ensues.

Thus, in competitive athletics, when the aim of victory is shorn
of its institutional trappings and success in contests becomes construed as "winning the game" rather than "winning through circumscribed modes of activity," a premium is implicitly set upon the use
of illegitimate but technically efficient means. The star of the
opposing football team is surreptitiously slugged; the wrestler fur-
tively incapacitates his opponent through ingenious but illicit techniques; university alumni covertly subsidize "students" whose tal-
ents are largely confined to the athletic field. The emphasis on the
goal has so attenuated the satisfactions deriving from sheer participation in the competitive activity that these satisfactions are
virtually confined to a successful outcome. Through the same
process, tension generated by the desire to win in a poker game is
relieved by successfully dealing oneself four aces, or, when the cult
of success has become completely dominant, by sagaciously shuf-
fling the cards in a game of solitaire. The faint twinge of uneasiness
in the last instance and the surreptitious nature of public delicts

[5]In this connection, one may see the relevance of Elton Mayo's paraphrase of the title
of Tawney's well known book. "Actually the problem *is not that of the sickness of an
acquisitive society; it is that of the acquisitiveness of a sick society.*" *Human Problems of
an Industrial Civilization,* 153, New York, 1933. Mayo deals with the process through
which wealth comes to be a symbol of social achievement. He sees this as arising from
a state of anomie. We are considering the unintegrated monetary-success goal as an
element in producing anomie. A complete analysis would involve both phases of this
system of interdependent variables.

indicate clearly that the institutional rules of the game *are known* to those who evade them, but that the emotional supports of these rules are largely vitiated by cultural exaggeration of the success-goal.[6] They are microcosmic images of the social macrocosm.

Of course, this process is not restricted to the realm of sport. The process whereby exaltation of the end generates a *literal demoralization*, i.e., a deinstitutionalization, of the means is one which characterizes many[7] groups in which the two phases of the social structure are not highly integrated. The extreme emphasis upon the accumulation of wealth as a symbol of success[8] in our own society militates against the completely effective control of institutionally regulated modes of acquiring a fortune.[9] Fraud, corruption, vice, crime, in short, the entire catalogue of proscribed behavior, becomes increasingly common when the emphasis on the *culturally induced* success-goal becomes divorced from a coordinated institutional emphasis. This observation is of crucial theoretical importance in examining the doctrine that antisocial behavior most frequently derives from biological drives breaking through the restraints imposed by society. The difference is one between a strictly utilitarian interpretation which conceives man's ends as random and an analysis which finds these ends deriving from the basic values of the culture.[10]

Our analysis can scarcely stop at this juncture. We must turn to

[6]It is unlikely that interiorized norms are completely eliminated. Whatever residuum persists will induce personality tensions and conflict. The process involves a certain degree of ambivalence. A manifest rejection of the institutional norms is coupled with some latent retention of their emotional correlates. "Guilt feelings," "sense of sin," "pangs of conscience" are obvious manifestations of this unrelieved tension; symbolic adherence to the nominally repudiated values or rationalizations constitute a more subtle variety of tensional release.

[7]"Many," and not all, unintegrated groups, for the reason already mentioned. In groups where the primary emphasis shifts to institutional means, i.e., when the range of alternatives is very limited, the outcome is a type of ritualism rather than anomie.

[8]Money has several peculiarities which render it particularly apt to become a symbol of prestige divorced from institutional controls. As Simmel emphasized, money is highly abstract and impersonal. However acquired, through fraud or institutionally, it can be used to purchase the same goods and services. The anonymity of metropolitan culture, in conjunction with this peculiarity of money, permits wealth, the sources of which may be unknown to the community in which the plutocrat lives, to serve as a symbol of status.

[9]The emphasis upon wealth as a success-symbol is possibly reflected in the use of the term "fortune" to refer to a stock of accumulated wealth. This meaning becomes common in the late sixteenth century (Spenser and Shakespeare). A similar usage of the Latin *fortuna* comes into prominence during the first century B.C. Both these periods were marked by the rise to prestige and power of the "bourgeoisie."

[10]See Kingsley Davis, "Mental Hygiene and the Class Structure," *Psychiatry*, 1928, I, esp. 62–63; Talcott Parsons, *The Structure of Social Action*, 59–60, New York, 1937.

other aspects of the social structure if we are to deal with the social genesis of the varying rates and types of deviate behavior characteristic of different societies. Thus far, we have sketched three ideal types of social orders constituted by distinctive patterns of relations between culture ends and means. Turning from these types of *culture patterning*, we find five logically possible, alternative modes of adjustment or adaptation *by individuals* within the culture-bearing society or group.[11] These are schematically presented in the following table, where (+) signifies "acceptance," (−) signifies "elimination" and (±) signifies "rejection and substitution of new goals and standards."

	Culture Goals	Institutionalized Means
I. Conformity	+	+
II. Innovation	+	−
III. Ritualism	−	+
IV. Retreatism	−	−
V. Rebellion[12]	±	±

Our discussion of the relation between these alternative responses and other phases of the social structure must be prefaced by the observation that persons may shift from one alternative to another as they engage in different social activities. These categories refer to role adjustments in specific situations, not to personality *in toto*. To treat the development of this process in various spheres of conduct would introduce a complexity unmanageable within the confines of this paper. For this reason, we shall be concerned primarily with economic activity in the broad sense, "the production, exchange, distribution and consumption of goods and services" in our competitive society, wherein wealth has taken on a highly symbolic cast. Our task is to search out some of the factors which exert pressure upon individuals to engage in certain of these logically possible alternative responses. This choice, as we shall see, is far from random.

[11]This is a level intermediate between the two planes distinguished by Edward Sapir; namely, culture patterns and personal habit systems. See his "Contribution of Psychiatry to an Understanding of Behavior in Society," *Amer. J. Sociol.*, 1937, 42:862–70.

[12]This fifth alternative is on a plane clearly different from that of the others. It represents a *transitional* response which seeks to *institutionalize* new procedures oriented toward revamped cultural goals shared by the members of the society. It thus involves efforts to *change* the existing structure rather than to perform accommodative actions *within* this structure, and introduces additional problems with which we are not at the moment concerned.

In every society, Adaptation I (conformity to both culture goals and means) is the most common and widely diffused. Were this not so, the stability and continuity of the society could not be maintained. The mesh of expectancies which constitutes every social order is sustained by the modal behavior of its members falling within the first category. Conventional role behavior oriented toward the basic values of the group is the rule rather than the exception. It is this fact alone which permits us to speak of a human aggregate as comprising a group or society.

Conversely, Adaptation IV (rejection of goals and means) is the least common. Persons who "adjust" (or maladjust) in this fashion are, strictly speaking, *in* the society but not *of* it. Sociologically, these constitute the true "aliens." Not sharing the common frame of orientation, they can be included within the societal population merely in a fictional sense. In this category are *some* of the activities of psychotics, psychoneurotics, chronic autists, pariahs, outcasts, vagrants, vagabonds, tramps, chronic drunkards and drug addicts.[13] These have relinquished, in certain spheres of activity, the culturally defined goals, involving complete aim-inhibition in the polar case, and their adjustments are not in accord with institutional norms. This is not to say that in some cases the source of their behavioral adjustments is not in part the very social structure which they have in effect repudiated nor that their very existence within a social area does not constitute a problem for the socialized population.

This mode of "adjustment" occurs, as far as structural sources are concerned, when both the culture goals and institutionalized procedures have been assimilated thoroughly by the individual and imbued with affect and high positive value, but where those institutionalized procedures which promise a measure of successful attainment of the goals are not available to the individual. In such instances, there results a twofold mental conflict insofar as the moral obligation for adopting institutional means conflicts with the pressure to resort to illegitimate means (which may attain the goal) and inasmuch as the individual is shut off from means which are both legitimate *and* effective. The competitive order is maintained, but the frustrated and handicapped individual who cannot cope with this

[13]Obviously, this is an elliptical statement. These individuals may maintain some orientation to the values of their particular differentiated groupings within the larger society or, in part, of the conventional society itself. Insofar as they do so, their conduct cannot be classified in the "passive rejection" category (IV). Nels Anderson's description of the behavior and attitudes of the bum, for example, can readily be recast in terms of our analytical scheme. See *The Hobo*, 93–98, *et passim*, Chicago, 1923.

order drops out. Defeatism, quietism and resignation are manifested in escape mechanisms which ultimately lead the individual to "escape" from the requirements of the society. It is an expedient which arises from continued failure to attain the goal by legitimate measures and from an inability to adopt the illegitimate route because of internalized prohibitions and institutionalized compulsives, *during which process the supreme value of the success-goal has as yet not been renounced.* The conflict is resolved by eliminating *both* precipitating elements, the goals and means. The escape is complete, the conflict is eliminated and the individual is a socialized.

Be it noted that where frustration derives from the inaccessibility of effective institutional means for attaining economic or any other type of highly valued "success," that Adaptations II, III and V (innovation, ritualism and rebellion) are also possible. The result will be determined by the particular personality, and thus, the *particular* cultural background, involved. Inadequate socialization will result in the innovation response whereby the conflict and frustration are eliminated by relinquishing the institutional means and retaining the success-aspiration; an extreme assimilation of institutional demands will lead to ritualism wherein the goal is dropped as beyond one's reach but conformity to the mores persists; and rebellion occurs when emancipation from the reigning standards, due to frustration or to marginalist perspectives, leads to the attempt to introduce a "new social order."

Our major concern is with the illegitimacy adjustment. This involves the use of conventionally proscribed but frequently effective means of attaining at least the simulacrum of culturally defined success,—wealth, power, and the like. As we have seen, this adjustment occurs when the individual has assimilated the cultural emphasis on success without equally internalizing the morally prescribed norms governing means for its attainment. The question arises, Which phases of our social structure predispose toward this mode of adjustment? We may examine a concrete instance, effectively analyzed by Lohman,[14] which provides a clue to the answer. Lohman has shown that specialized areas of vice in the near north side of Chicago constitute a "normal" response to a situation where the cultural emphasis upon pecuniary success has been absorbed, but where there is little access to conventional and legitimate means for attaining such success. The conventional occupational opportunities of persons in this area are almost completely limited to manual labor.

[14]Joseph D. Lohman, "The Participant Observer in Community Studies," *Amer. Sociol. Rev.*, 1937, 2:890–98.

Given our cultural stigmatization of manual labor, and its correlate, the prestige of white collar work, it is clear that the result is a strain toward innovational practices. The limitation of opportunity to unskilled labor and the resultant low income can not compete *in terms of conventional standards of achievement* with the high income from organized vice.

For our purposes, this situation involves two important features. First, such antisocial behavior is in a sense "called forth" by certain conventional values of the culture *and* by the class structure involving differential access to the approved opportunities for legitimate, prestige-bearing pursuit of the culture goals. The lack of high integration between the means-and-end elements of the cultural pattern and the particular class structure combine to favor a heightened frequency of antisocial conduct in such groups. The second consideration is of equal significance. Recourse to the first of the alternative responses, legitimate effort, is limited by the fact that actual advance toward desired success-symbols through conventional channels is, despite our persisting open-class ideology,[15] relatively rare and difficult for those handicapped by little formal education and few economic resources. The dominant pressure of group standards of success is, therefore, on the gradual attenuation of legitimate, but by and large ineffective, strivings and the increasing use of illegitimate, but more or less effective, expedients of vice and crime. The cultural demands made on persons in this situation are incompatible. On the one hand, they are asked to orient their conduct toward the prospect of accumulating wealth and on the other, they are largely denied effective opportunities to do so institutionally. The consequences of such structural inconsistency are psychopathological personality, and/or antisocial conduct, and/or revolutionary activities. The equilibrium between culturally designated means and ends becomes highly unstable with the progressive emphasis on attaining the prestige-laden ends by any means whatsoever. Within this context, Capone represents the triumph of amoral intelligence over morally prescribed "failure," when the

[15]The shifting historical role of this ideology is a profitable subject for exploration. The "office-boy-to-president" stereotype was once in approximate accord with the facts. Such vertical mobility was probably more common then than now, when the class structure is more rigid. (See the following note.) The ideology largely persists, however, possibly because it still performs a useful function for maintaining the *status quo*. For insofar as it is accepted by the "masses," it constitutes a useful sop for those who might rebel against the entire structure, were this consoling hope removed. This ideology now serves to lessen the probability of Adaptation V. In short, the role of this notion has changed from that of an approximately valid empirical theorem to that of an ideology, in Mannheim's sense.

channels of vertical mobility are closed or narrowed[16] *in a society which places a high premium on economic affluence and social ascent for all its members.*[17]

This last qualification is of primary importance. It suggests that other phases of the social structure besides the extreme emphasis on pecuniary success, must be considered if we are to understand the social sources of antisocial behavior. A high frequency of deviate behavior is not generated simply by "lack of opportunity" or by this exaggerated pecuniary emphasis. A comparatively rigidified class structure, a feudalistic or caste order, may limit such opportunities far beyond the point which obtains in our society today. It is only when a system of cultural values extols, virtually above all else, certain *common* symbols of success *for the population at large* while its social structure rigorously restricts or completely eliminates access to approved modes of acquiring these symbols *for a considerable part of the same population*, that antisocial behavior ensues on a considerable scale. In other words, our egalitarian ideology denies by implication the existence of noncompeting groups and individuals in the pursuit of pecuniary success. The same body of success-symbols is held to be desirable for all. These goals are held to *transcend class lines*, not to be bounded by them, yet the actual social organization is such that there exist class differentials in the accessibility of these *common* success-symbols. Frustration and thwarted aspiration lead to the search for avenues of escape from a culturally

[16]There is a growing body of evidence, though none of it is clearly conclusive, to the effect that our class structure is becoming rigidified and that vertical mobility is declining. Taussig and Joslyn found that American business leaders are being *increasingly* recruited from the upper ranks of our society. The Lynds have also found a "diminished chance to get ahead" for the working classes in Middletown. Manifestly, these objective changes are not alone significant; the individual's subjective evaluation of the situation is a major determinant of the response. The extent to which this change in opportunity for social mobility has been recognized by the least advantaged classes is still conjectural, although the Lynds present some suggestive materials. The writer suggests that a case in point is the increasing frequency of cartoons which observe in a tragi-comic vein that "my old man says everybody can't be President. He says if ya can get three days a week steady on W.P.A. work ya ain't doin' so bad either." See F. W. Taussig and C. S. Joslyn, *American Business Leaders*, New York, 1932; R. S. and H. M. Lynd, *Middletown in Transition*, 67 ff., chap. 12, New York, 1937.

[17]The role of the Negro in this respect is of considerable theoretical interest. Certain elements of the Negro population have assimilated the dominant caste's values of pecuniary success and social advancement, but they also recognize that social ascent is at present restricted to their own caste almost exclusively. The pressures upon the Negro which would otherwise derive from the structural inconsistencies we have noticed are hence not identical with those upon lower class whites. See Kingsley Davis, *op. cit.*, 63; John Dollard, *Caste and Class in a Southern Town*, 66 ff., New Haven, 1936; Donald Young, *American Minority Peoples*, 581, New York, 1932.

induced intolerable situation; or unrelieved ambition may eventuate in illicit attempts to acquire the dominant values.[18] The American stress on pecuniary success and ambitiousness for all thus invites exaggerated anxieties, hostilities, neuroses and antisocial behavior.

This theoretical analysis may go far toward explaining the varying correlations between crime and poverty.[19] Poverty is not an isolated variable. It is one in a complex of interdependent social and cultural variables. When viewed in such a context, it represents quite different states of affairs. Poverty as such, and consequent limitation of opportunity, are not sufficient to induce a conspicuously high rate of criminal behavior. Even the often mentioned "poverty in the midst of plenty" will not necessarily lead to this result. Only insofar as poverty and associated disadvantages in competition for the culture values approved for *all* members of the society is linked with the assimilation of a cultural emphasis on monetary accumulation as a symbol of success is antisocial conduct a "normal" outcome. Thus, poverty is less highly correlated with crime in southeastern Europe than in the United States. The possibilities of vertical mobility in these European areas would seem to be fewer than in this country, so that neither poverty *per se* nor its association with limited opportunity is sufficient to account for the varying correlations. It is only when the full configuration is considered, poverty, limited opportunity and a commonly shared system of success symbols, that we can explain the higher association between poverty and crime in our society than in others where rigidified class structure is coupled with *differential class symbols of achievement.*

In societies such as our own, then, the pressure of prestige-bearing success tends to eliminate the effective social constraint over means employed to this end. "The-end-justifies-the-means" doc-

[18]The psychical coordinates of these processes have been partly established by the experimental evidence concerning *Anspruchsniveaus* and levels of performance. See Kurt Lewin, *Vorsatz, Willie und Bedurfnis*, Berlin, 1926; N. F. Hoppe, "Erfolg und Misserfolg," *Psychol. Forschung*, 1930, 14:1–63; Jerome D. Frank, "Individual Differences in Certain Aspects of the Level of Aspiration," *Amer. J. Psychol.*, 1935, 47:119–28.

[19]Standard criminology texts summarize the data in this field. Our scheme of analysis may serve to resolve some of the theoretical contradictions which P. A. Sorokin indicates. For example, "not everywhere nor always do the poor show a greater proportion of crime . . . many poorer countries have had less crime than the richer countries . . . The [economic] improvement in the second half of the nineteenth century, and the beginning of the twentieth, has not been followed by a decrease of crime." See his *Contemporary Sociological Theories*, 560–61, New York, 1928. The crucial point is, however, that poverty has varying social significance in different social structures, as we shall see. Hence, one would not expect a linear correlation between crime and poverty.

trine becomes a guiding tenet for action when the cultural structure unduly exalts the end and the social organization unduly limits possible recourse to approved means. Otherwise put, this notion and associated behavior reflect a lack of cultural coordination. In international relations, the effects of this lack of integration are notoriously apparent. An emphasis upon national power is not readily coordinated with an inept organization of legitimate, i.e., internationally defined and accepted, means for attaining this goal. The result is a tendency toward the abrogation of international law, treaties become scraps of paper, "undeclared warfare" serves as a technical evasion, the bombing of civilian populations is rationalized,[20] just as the same societal situation induces the same sway of illegitimacy among individuals.

The social order we have described necessarily produces this "strain toward dissolution." The pressure of such an order is upon outdoing one's competitors. The choice of means within the ambit of institutional control will persist as long as the sentiments supporting a competitive system, i.e., deriving from the possibility of outranking competitors and hence enjoying the favorable response of others, are distributed throughout the entire system of activities and are not confined merely to the final result. A stable social structure demands a balanced distribution of affect among its various segments. When there occurs a shift of emphasis from the satisfactions deriving from competition itself to almost exclusive concern with successful competition, the resultant stress leads to the breakdown of the regulatory structure.[21] With the resulting attenuation of the institutional imperatives, there occurs an approximation of the situation erroneously held by utilitarians to be typical of society generally wherein calculations of advantage and fear of punishment are the sole regulating agencies. In such situations, as Hobbes observed, force and fraud come to constitute the sole virtues in view of their relative efficiency in attaining goals,—which were for him, of course, not culturally derived.

It should be apparent that the foregoing discussion is not pitched on a moralistic plane. Whatever the sentiments of the writer or reader concerning the ethical desirability of coordinating the means-

[20]See M. W. Royse, *Aerial Bombardment and the International Regulation of War*, New York, 1928.

[21]Since our primary concern is with the socio-cultural aspects of this problem, the psychological correlates have been only implicitly considered. See Karen Horney, *The Neurotic Personality of Our Time*, New York, 1937, for a psychological discussion of this process.

and-goals phases of the social structure, one must agree that lack of such coordination leads to anomie. Insofar as one of the most general functions of social organization is to provide a basis for calculability and regularity of behavior, it is increasingly limited in effectiveness as these elements of the structure become dissociated. At the extreme, predictability virtually disappears and what may be properly termed cultural chaos or anomie intervenes.

This statement, being brief, is also incomplete. It has not included an exhaustive treatment of the various structural elements which predispose toward one rather than another of the alternative responses open to individuals; it has neglected, but not denied the relevance of, the factors determining the specific incidence of these responses; it has not enumerated the various concrete responses which are constituted by combinations of specific values of the analytical variables; it has omitted, or included only by implication, any consideration of the social functions performed by illicit responses; it has not tested the full explanatory power of the analytical scheme by examining a large number of group variations in the frequency of deviate and conformist behavior; it has not adequately dealt with rebellious conduct which seeks to refashion the social framework radically; it has not examined the relevance of cultural conflict for an analysis of culture-goal and institutional-means malintegration. It is suggested that these and related problems may be profitably analyzed by this scheme.

Deviant Behavior
Talcott Parsons

It is a cardinal principle of the present analysis that all motivational processes are processes in the personalities of individual actors. The processes by which the motivational structure of an individual personality gets to be what it is are, however, mainly social processes, involving the interaction of ego with a plurality of alters. Thus the sectors of the motivation of the individual which are concerned with his motivation to deviant behavior, are the outcome of his processes of social interaction in the past and the whole problem must therefore be approached in social interaction terms. In the analysis of deviance as well as of socialization we must focus on the interactive processes as it influences the orientation of the individual actor in his situation and in orientation to the situation itself, including above all the significant social objects, and to the normative patterns which define the expectations of his roles.

Deviance and the mechanisms of social control may be defined in two ways, according to whether the individual actor or the interactive system is taken as the point of reference. In the first context deviance is a motivated tendency for an actor to behave in contravention of one or more institutionalized normative patterns, while the mechanisms of social control are the motivated processes in the behavior of this actor, and of the others with whom he is in interaction, by which these tendencies to deviance tend in turn to be counteracted. In the second context, that of the interactive system, deviance is the tendency on the part of one or more of the component actors to behave in such a way as to disturb the equilibrium of the interactive process (whether a static or a moving equilibrium). Deviance therefore is defined by its tendency to result either in change in the state of the interactive system, or in re-equilibration by counteracting forces, the latter being the mechanisms of social control. It is presumed here that such an equilibrium always implies integration of action with a system of normative patterns which are more or less institutionalized.

It is clearly the conception of deviance as a disturbance of the equilibrium of the interactive system, which is the more important perspective for the analysis of social systems. But we must still be quite clear that it is essential to be able to follow this analysis from the level of ascertaining uniformities in the processes of change in the structure of the social system, to that of analyzing the relevant motivational processes in the personalities of the individual actors. Hence there is always *also* a reference to the first context implied.

It should also be made clear that there is a certain relativity in the conceptions of conformity and deviance. These are concepts which refer to problems of the integration and malintegration of social systems and sub-systems. It is therefore not possible to make a judgment of deviance or lack of it without specific reference to the system or sub-system to which it applies. The structure of normative patterns in any but the simplest sub-system is always intricate and usually far from fully integrated; hence singling out one such pattern without reference to its interconnections in a system of patterns can be very misleading, e.g., the judgment that a person who tells a "white lie" as a way out of a conflict situation is a "dishonest person." Similarly the concrete individual actor never acts in one role only, but in a plurality of roles and situations, with complex possibilities of variation in the expectations and tensions to which they subject the actor. Furthermore, there is the problem of the time sector which is taken as relevant to the analysis of a system. Actions are mortised together in time sequence as well as in other respects, and conflicts can focus on time-allocation as well as on the conflicting claims of different interaction-partners.

These are all problems of the first importance and must be made as clear and explicit as possible. Nevertheless the fact remains that all social action is normatively oriented, and that the value-orientations embodied in these norms must to a degree be common to the actors in an institutionally integrated interactive system. It is this circumstance which makes the problem of conformity and deviance a major axis of the analysis of social systems. The fact that in its working out it is highly complex, does not imply that it can be safely ignored or cannot be satisfactorily analyzed. The crucial significance of this problem focus derives as we have seen from two fundamental considerations; first that the frame of reference of action makes the concept of orientation a primary focus of analysis and second, the fact that we are dealing with the "boundary-maintaining" type of system, which defines what we must mean by the concept of integration of the system.

Interaction and the Genesis of Deviant Motivation

Let us go back then to the fundamental paradigm of social interaction including the assumption . . . that a stably established interactive process, that is, one in equilibrium, tends to continue unchanged. We will further assume that ego and alter have, in their interaction, developed mutual cathectic attachments to each other, so that they are sensitive to each other's attitudes, i.e., attitudes are fundamental as sanctions, and that the interaction is integrated with a normative pattern of value-orientation, both ego and alter, that is, have internalized the value-pattern. We have stated many times that such an interaction system is characterized by the complementarity of expectations, the behavior and above all the attitudes of alter conform with the expectations of ego and vice versa.

This paradigm provides the setting for the analysis of the genesis of motivation to deviance. Let us assume that, from whatever source, a disturbance is introduced into the system, of such a character that what alter does leads to a frustration, in some important respects, of ego's expectation-system vis-à-vis alter. This failure of the fulfillment of ego's expectations places a "strain" upon him, that is, presents him with a problem of "adjustment" in the terms which we have used. There are always, we may presume, three terms to this problem. First ego's expectations in the interaction system are part of his own system of need-dispositions which in some sense press for gratification. Second, these expectations are organized to include an attachment to alter as a cathected object, and third the value-pattern governing the relationship has been internalized and violation of its prescriptions is directly a frustration of some of ego's need-dispositions. In so far as the adjustment problem is "serious," in that alter's disturbing behavior is more than momentary and in that it touches some strategic area of ego's orientation system, ego will be forced to restructure his orientation in one or more of these three respects. He can first restructure his own need-dispositions, by inhibition and by one or more of the mechan-isms of defense, such as simply repressing the needs which are no longer gratified. He can, secondly, seek to transfer his cathexis to a new object and relieve the strain that way and, finally, he can renounce or seek to redefine the value-orientation pattern with which alter is no longer conforming.

In any one or more of these three directions there may be resolution of the strain by a successful learning process; ego may learn to inhibit his need-disposition, he may cathect a new object which will fulfill his expectations, or he may extinguish or alter the value-pattern. This would be the obverse of alter abandoning his changed behavior. In either case equilibrium would be re-established, in one case with a changed state of the system, in the other with a restoration of the old state.

But another outcome is possible, and in many cases very likely. That is that, in one or more of the above three respects, a "com-promise" solution should be reached. Our primary interest is not in the internal integration of the personality but in ego's adjustment to social objects and to normative patterns. Hence first, ego may not abandon his cathexis of alter by substituting an alternative object, but may retain his cathexis, but this cathexis can no longer be "undisturbed." Ego must have some reaction to the frustration which alter has imposed upon him, some resentment or hostility.[1] In other words the cathectic orientation acquires an ambivalent charac-ter, there is still the need to love or admire alter, but there is also the product of his frustration in the form of negative and in some sense hostile attitudes toward alter. In so far as this happens of course ego is put in an emotional conflict in his relation to alter. Similarly, the integration of ego's expectations with the value-pattern has been disturbed by alter's failure to conform with it, the pattern may be too strongly internalized for ego to be able to abandon it and accept one in conformity with alter's behavior. Here again ego may devel p an ambivalent attitude structure, at the same time adhering to the normative pattern and resenting the "cost" of this adherence in that it involves him in conflict with alter and with aspects of his own personality.

There are many complications involved in the possibilities of handling the strains inherent in such an ambivalent motivational structure. For our purpose, however, they may be related to two fundamental alternatives. The first is repression of one side of the

---

[1]Another very important phenomenon of reaction to strain is the production of phantasies.

ambivalent structure so that only the other side receives overt expression. If it is the negative side which is repressed, ego will continue to be attached to alter and/or to be motivated to conform with the normative pattern in question. If the positive side is repressed, conversely ego will tend to abandon his attachment to alter, in the sense of giving it overt expression, and to refuse to conform with the normative pattern. The second fundamental possibility is for ego to try to find a way to gratify both sides of his ambivalent motivation. Presumably in the same concrete relationship this is impossible[2] since the two are in conflict. But in a more extensive and complex interaction system there may be such possibilities either because contexts and occasions can be segregated, or because it is possible to find alternative objects for one or both sides of the need-disposition structure. This latter possibility will become very important to the discussion of the social structuring of deviance later in this chapter. But for the present let us adhere to the simpler case.

The negative component of such an ambivalent motivational structure relative to a system of complementary expectations will be called an *alienative* need-disposition, the positive component, a *conformative* need-disposition. It should be noted that in these theoretical terms alienation is conceived *always* to be part of an ambivalent motivational structure, while conformity need not be. Where there is no longer *any* attachment to the object and/or internalization of the normative pattern, the attitude is not alienation but *indifference.* Both social object and pattern have become only neutral objects of the situation which are no longer a focus of ego's cathectic need-system. The conflict in such a case would have been solved by full resolution, through substitution of a new object, through inhibition or extinction of the need-disposition, and/or through internalization of a new normative pattern.

Where alienative motivation is present, but the conformative component is dominant over the alienative, we may speak of *compulsive conformity*, where on the other hand the alienative component is dominant over the conformative, we may speak of *compulsive alienation*. The psychological reasons for using these terms are not far to seek. The essential point is that ego is subject not only to a strain in his relations with alter, but to an internal conflict

[2]It is of course possible within limits through time allocation. At certain times ego's resentment may break through into hostile acts (including verbal) and the positive attitude then regain ascendancy.

in his own need-disposition system. Precisely because he has a negative feeling toward alter, but at the same time a powerful need to retain his relation to alter and to the normative pattern, he must "defend himself" against his need to express his negative feelings, with the attendant risk of disturbing his relation to alter still further or provoking him to retaliatory action, in the more extreme case, of losing alter. This is, indeed, in relation to social interaction relationships, the basis of the defense mechanism of reaction formation. The pattern is to "accentuate the positive," to be compulsively careful to conform with what ego interprets as alter's expectations (which by institutionalization are also his own) so as to minimize the risk of disturbing the relationship still further.

Conversely, if the alienative component is dominant, the fact that the attachment to alter as a person and to the normative pattern is still a fundamental need, means that ego must defend himself against the tendency to express this need-disposition. He must therefore not only express his negative reaction, but be doubly sure that the conformative element does not gain the upper hand and risk his having to inhibit the negative again. Therefore his refusal to conform with alter's expectations becomes compulsive. This defense against the repressed component is in both cases the primary basis of resistance against the abandonment of "symptoms," even though they involve ego in serious negative sanctions in his social relationships.

It is here that we have the focus of the well-known vicious circle in the genesis of deviant behavior patterns, whether they be neurotic or psycho-somatic illness, criminality or others. It may be presumed that the reaction of ego to the change in alter's behavior, which resulted in resort to adjustive and defensive mechanisms involving ambivalence, will be in some way complementary to the change alter introduced. For example, alter, instead of recognizing the merit of a piece of work ego has done, may have shown marked disapproval, which ego felt to be in contravention of the value-pattern with respect to competent achievement shared by both. Ego reacted to this with resentment which, however, he repressed and became compulsively anxious to secure alter's approval. This compulsive element in ego's motivation makes him excessively "demanding" in his relation to alter. He both wants to be approved, to conform, and his need for approval is more difficult to satisfy because of his anxiety that alter may not give it. This in turn has its effect on alter. Whatever his original motivation to withhold the approval ego expected, ego has now put him in a position where it is more difficult than it was before for him to fulfill ego's expectations; the same level of approval which would have sufficed before is no longer sufficient. Unless a mechanism of social control is operating, then, the tendency will be to drive alter to approve even less, rather than more as ego hopes. This will still further increase the strain on ego and intensify his resentment, hence, if the alienative component does not break through, it will add to the compulsiveness of his motivation to seek approval through conformity with alter's expectations. The pressure of ego's conflict may also of course lead to cognitive distortion so that he thinks that alter's expectations are more extreme than they really are, and that therefore he is being held to intolerable standards.

This is the essential structure of the generation of cumulative motivation to deviance through the interaction of complementary ambivalences in the motivational systems of ego and alter. Of course this is a highly simplified and abstract paradigm. The "direct line" of development of the vicious circle could not empirically proceed far without some modification for two sets of reasons. First the need-dispositions of ego and alter which are the focus of the developing conflict are only parts of a complicated system of need-dispositions in the personalities of each. The alterations in these parts growing out of the interaction process would lead to repercussions in the rest of the personality systems which would modify the development of the interaction itself. Secondly, the interaction of ego and alter on which we have focused is only a sector of a larger system of social interaction which involves other actors than ego and alter, and perhaps their interaction in other roles. These complications must duly be taken into account, and are of course extremely important for the mechanisms of social control. But the vicious circle in the interaction of two actors is the fundamental paradigm of the genesis of the motivation for deviant behavior.

The Directions of Deviant Orientation

We may now return to the question of what are the most important further differentiations in the direction of deviant motivation itself, whether it be in the compulsively conformative or alienative direction. Two such further differentiations appear to be particularly important. In the first place, the differentiation between activity and passivity, is of generally recognized psychological significance.[3] If the conformative and the alienative types each be subdivided according to whether the orientation is primarily active or passive, we derive the following four-fold classification:

	Activity	*Passivity*
Conformative Dominance	Compulsive Performance Orientation.	Compulsive Acquiescence in Status-Expectations.
Alienative Dominance	Rebelliousness.	Withdrawal.

This classification is of interest, not only because of its direct derivation from the analysis of the interaction, paradigm, but because it restates, from the motivational point of view, in essentials the classification put forward some years ago by Merton in his well-known paper on Social Structure and Anomie.[4] What Merton calls "conformity" is clearly what we here mean by the equilibrated condition of the interactive system without conflict on either side or alienative motivation. Merton's "innovation" and "ritualism" are our two compulsively conformative types, while "rebellion" and "retreatism" are clearly the two alienative types. Since Merton's

[3]There may be a variety of aspects and sources of this distinction. For present purposes it may, however, be regarded as a direct derivative of the fundamental paradigm of interaction itself. The conformity-alienation dimension of possible deviance concerns, as we have just seen, the orientation of any actor to the pattern aspect of the established system of expectations—or any part of it—which is institutionalized and internalized in the interaction system. Activity-passivity, on the other hand, is the dimension concerned with one primary aspect of the mutual orientation of ego and alter to each other *as objects*. The point of reference is, as always, a stabilized system of interaction. The concept of "activity" defines deviation from the role of an actor in this stabilized process in the direction of taking more "initiative," of taking a larger degree of control over the interaction process, than the role-expectations call for. "Passivity," on the other hand, is the obverse, it is the direction of taking less initiative, of letting alter control the situation and himself, to a larger degree than the role-expectations call for.

There is a third dimension of the possibilities of deviance, which will be discussed presently. This concerns relative primacies, in the orientation of the actors, as between the pattern element and the social object element of the interaction system. A stabilized interaction system always involves a balance between these. This balance can be upset, on the one hand by giving a greater primacy to the pattern—either by insisting on conformity or by alienative resistance to it—on the other hand to orientation to alter as a social object positively or negatively. All three of these dimensions are thus grounded in the essential structure of the interactive relationship system.

[4]Revised and extended version in his *Social Theory and Social Structure*, Chapter III.

paradigm was formulated in terms of relations to institutionalized goals and means, it is interesting to find that the active emphasis puts the primary stress on goals—as its relation to the achievement pole of the pattern variable of ascription-achievement would lead one to expect—while the passive emphasis puts the stress on means. In each case, however, we may infer, the compulsive element puts a strain on genuine conformity with institutionalized expectations, but in the two cases the primary incidence varies. We may surmise that Merton's paradigm is most readily applicable to a social system where achievement values are prominent, then because achievement goals are highly institutionalized, the actively ambivalent person can find the easiest "way out" in accentuated goal striving. Where ascriptive values were institutionalized, especially in combination with particularism, this outlet would largely be closed. Because of this element of culture-boundness of the Merton paradigm, and because of the inclusion of the motivational element, we may presume that the version presented here is the more general one, of which Merton's is a very important special case.

The second further differentiation of the directions of deviant motivation which needs to be introduced concerns the possibility of differentiation between focusing on one or the other of the two fundamental components of the interactive system beside ego's own need-disposition system, namely alter as a person, i.e., a social object, and the normative pattern which integrates their interaction. Both are, as in the case of ambivalence, inevitably involved. But there may be dominance of compulsive concern in one direction or the other. The introduction of this further differentiation yields the eightfold classification presented in Table 1.

Where the conformative element is dominant and ego's primary concern is with his relations to alter as person, anxiety focuses on disturbance of the relation, on the possibility that alter may turn his favorable attitude into an unfavorable one and may aggressively punish ego or withdraw from the relationship. There are, fundamentally, two ways in which ego can seek to cope with the situation, in relation both to his own anxiety and to alter. He may, if he is actively oriented, seek to put alter in a position where it is impossible for him to do anything but fulfill ego's expectations, that is, to *dominate him.* If, on the other hand, he is passively inclined, he may seek to protect his interest in the relationship by acquiescing in alter's every wish, lest failure to do so jeopardize the relationship, that is, he may be *submissive* to alter.

If the alienative component of ego's motivation is dominant he

Table 1

	Activity		Passivity	
	COMPULSIVE PERFORMANCE ORIENTATION		COMPULSIVE ACQUIESCENCE	
	Focus on Social Objects	Focus on Norms	Focus on Social Objects	Focus on Norms
Conformative Dominance	Dominance	Compulsive Enforce-ment	Submission	Perfectionistic Observance (Merton's Ritualism)
	REBELLIOUSNESS		WITHDRAWAL	
Alienative Dominance	Aggressive-ness toward Social Ob-jects	Incorrigi-bility	Compulsive Independ-ence	Evasion

is by definition less concerned with preserving alter's favorable attitudes than he is with expressing his alienative need-dispositions. Hence in the active case he will tend to act *aggressively* toward alter, to "pick a fight" with him relatively regardless of the risk of alienating alter, to seek a "showdown." If, on the other hand, he is passively inclined, his tendency will be, not aggressively to force a "showdown" but to avoid exposure to uncongenial expectations on alter's part, to be *compulsively independent,* in the extreme case to break the relationship altogether by withdrawing from it. The four cases may be grouped together by saying that both dominance and submission are expressions of a compulsive dependency need, to avoid losing alter as an object at almost any cost, while aggressive-ness and passive compulsive independence have in common that they are motivated by a compulsive need for independence, a need to avoid giving way to the dependency need at almost any cost.

Turning to the cases where the normative pattern is the primary focus of the conflict, on the conformative side we may differentiate according to activity and passivity, a compulsive need to enforce the norm on alter, and a compulsive need for perfectionistic observance on the part of ego himself. An alternative to compulsive enforcement on alter is, for the actively oriented, to develop a compulsive achievement drive for himself. He may of course mani-fest both tendencies as in the familiar case of the compulsive achiever who is merciless in his demands on his subordinates. The passively inclined will tend to evade demands for active achievement or control and focus his compulsiveness on the details of conformity-expectations.

Finally, where the alienative component is dominant, the active type is the "incorrigible," the one who flouts rules and laws apparently "for its own sake," whose attitude is "try and do anything about it." The passive type on the other hand tends to evasion of conformity with the normative pattern, to do his best to avoid situations in which the expectations can be implemented, or sanctions applied.

These are, of course, definitions of the direction of deviant tendencies. First it must not be forgotten that they are *always* relative to a particular set of complementary role-expectations, to a particular alter or class of alters, and to a particular normative pattern or sub-system of them. In some cases the ambivalence may, in the personality of the actor, be highly "localized" in its application. But it may also under certain circumstances become more or less highly generalized, transferred by substitution from the original objects and normative patterns. In the extreme cases we may have personalities with a highly generalized need-disposition for rebellion or for withdrawal. It is not possible to go into all the complications here.

Secondly, of course, the actual behavior patterns which will result are not a function only of the ways in which deviant motivation comes to be built into the motivational structure of the personality, but of the nature of the situations in which the actors are placed. As noted, this always involves third persons, and also a variety of features of the normative pattern system and the sanction system. What we have presented is only the barest beginning of a dynamic analysis of these complex processes.

Reference Group Identification and Deviant Behavior
Albert K. Cohen

We define deviant behavior as behavior which violates institutionalized expectations—that is, expectations which are shared and recognized as legitimate within a social system. The implications of this commonplace definition are not always clearly appreciated.

First, we here define deviant behavior in terms of the relationship of action to institutionalized expectations, not in terms of its relationship to personality structure. Behavior which is psychotic, neurotic, maladjusted, or otherwise pathological from a psychiatric or mental-hygiene point of view is defined in terms of its dependence upon or consequences for personality structure. Therefore, the pathology of personality is not, as such, subject matter for the sociology of deviant behavior.

This is not to say that personality structure is irrelevant to sociology. What goes on in a social system obviously depends upon the personalities it has to work with, so to speak, even if those personalities do not, as such, constitute the system. It does not follow, however, either by definition or as a matter of empirical fact, that the pathology of personalities is any more relevant to deviant behavior than is normality. Much—probably most—deviant behavior is produced by clinically normal people. This would be true, for example, of most illicit sexual behavior. On the other hand, many clinically abnormal people, confronted by sexual temptation and

From Chapter 21 of *Sociology Today*, by Robert K. Merton, Leonard Broom, Leonard S. Cottrell, Jr., © 1959 Basic Books, Inc., Publishers, New York, pp. 462-474.

opportunity to which many normal people would succumb, are incapable, in consequence of their pathological anxieties concerning sex, of anything but virtue. In order to build a sociology of deviant behavior, we must always keep as our point of reference deviant behavior, not kinds of people. A major task before us is to get rid of the notion, so pervasive in sociological thinking, that the deviant, the abnormal, the pathological, and, in general, the deplorable always come wrapped in a single package.

A second implication: Since the sociology of deviant behavior is concerned with explaining the departure of behavior from institutionalized expectations, it follows that the sociology of deviant behavior is not the sociology of prostitution plus the sociology of drug addiction plus the sociology of suicide, etc., *in general.* This is so, first, because no behavior is *per se* and universally deviant, and, secondly, because any behavior can be subject matter for many different sociological fields, of which the sociology of deviant behavior is but one. One reason for the undeveloped state of the sociology of deviant behavior is the tendency to focus on a few kinds of behavior that are usually deviant in our society and to study these in a diffuse and encyclopedic way, rather than to concentrate on the theoretical problems inherent in the fact of deviance itself.

A theory of deviant behavior not only must account for the occurrence of deviant behavior; it must also account for its failure to occur, or conformity. In fact, the explanation of one necessarily implies the explanation of the other. Therefore "the sociology of deviant behavior" is elliptical for "the sociology of deviant behavior and conformity"; it includes the explanation of the prevention, reduction, and elimination of deviant behavior.

Merton's well-known paper on "Social Structure and Anomie"[1] and the relevant chapters in Parsons' *The Social System*[2] are deserving of special comment because they are among the few attempts to formulate a general theory of deviant behavior which addresses itself to the generic property of deviance, its variant forms, and their determinants.

AN ILLUSTRATION: MERTON

Merton's typology of modes of individual adaptation is couched in terms of "culture goals" and "institutionalized means," either of which can be accepted or rejected. Any act, whatever its concrete content, can be described in terms of this scheme; what the scheme

[1] In Robert K. Merton, *Social Theory and Social Structure,* Free Press, 1957.
[2] Talcott Parsons, *The Social System,* Free Press, 1951, esp. Chap. 7.

abstracts from the concrete content is the relationship of the act to the institutionalized value system. Furthermore, "acceptance or rejection of goals" and "acceptance or rejection of means" constitute, in effect, two dichotomous variables; in terms of the values of these variables, we can specify at least five logically possible modes of adaptation to institutionalized expectations, one of which is conformity, the others, distinctive modes of deviance.

What concerns us here is the way in which this scheme illustrates our criterion of a sociological field of deviant behavior. The starting point, let it be noted, is not a definition of deviant behavior, but the specification of two dimensions along which behavior may vary. The class of all points that can be located in these two dimensions defines the full scope of a sociological field which comprehends both conformity and deviant behavior. Furthermore, the varieties of deviant behavior are not described in terms of their unique and incommensurable concrete characteristics but are derived from the logic of the classification itself and stated in terms of the same conceptual scheme. Also, the scheme is a way of classifying actions, not personalities. The widespread use of this scheme testifies to the felt need for such a scheme; the near monopoly it has enjoyed testifies to the paucity of original thinking in this field.

Merton's conceptual scheme, however, although obviously valuable for taxonomic purposes, does not in itself constitute a *theory* of deviant behavior-conformity. Such a theory would be a system of propositions which would make it possible to account for the actual choices among the possibilities given by the scheme. The same paper by Merton also contains the beginnings of a theory. Paraphrasing liberally—and Merton is not to be held accountable for this formulation—we suggest that the central idea is socially structured strain, defined as ambivalence relative to institutionalized expectations. This strain or ambivalence arises out of tension or malintegration between culture goals and institutionalized means. This is the general situation which generates deviant motivation. The specific direction of deviant behavior is accounted for, in part, by the relative strength of internalization of goals and means, respectively, and the socially structured availability of alternative means. Of particular note is the fact that strain and the circumstances that determine responses to strain are treated as elements which are variously distributed in the social system and the distribution of which is a function of societal mechanisms.

Note also how Merton's scheme lends itself to the conceptualizing of social control. It would seem that the control of deviant behavior is, by definition, a culture goal. For any given form of deviant behavior, there are institutionally appropriate means of control. In short, the responses to deviant behavior may be conceptualized in terms of the same scheme applied to deviant behavior itself.[3] Whether this extension of Merton's scheme is more than idle play with a sociological toy remains to be seen. It is certain, however, that a sociology of deviant behavior–conformity will have to devise ways of conceptualizing responses to deviant behavior from the standpoint of their relevance to the production or extinction of deviant behavior.

AN ILLUSTRATION: PARSONS

For our present purposes, we shall only point out briefly the ways in which Parsons' work goes beyond Merton's. First, Parsons distinguishes several aspects of the concept "strain" and several ways in which strain may arise.[4] The tension between culture goals and institutionalized means which, for Merton, appears to define strain becomes, for Parsons, a special case of strain. Strain, for Parsons, may take various other forms, including, for example, failure of the actor's expectations concerning himself to correspond to the expectations which others have concerning him, or inability of the actor to make certain institutionally expected object-attachments (e.g., with persons of the opposite sex).

Secondly, although Parsons also formulates a classification of the directions of deviant behavior, based on the same logic as Merton's, he postulates a set of three variables as opposed to Merton's two, and the combinations of these variables yield eight varieties of deviant behavior. The classification is based on the predominance of alienative or conformative need-dispositions within the ambivalent motivational structure, of active or passive orienta-

[3]Merton's Conformity would be represented by the use of institutionally expected means in the interest of social control. His Innovation would be represented by disregard of institutionalized limitations on the choice of means—for example, McCarthyism, third-degree methods, wiretapping. Ritualism is a preoccupation with the minutiae of procedure without regard to its effectiveness as a means to an end—legalism, if you will. It would also consist in affirmations and gestures of indignation, by means of which one aligns oneself symbolically with the angels without having to take up cudgels against the devil. Retreatism would take the form of refusal to concern oneself with the fact of deviant behavior or to do anything about it. Lastly, Rebellion would be represented by seduction, so to speak, by the deviant—that is, acceptance of the deviant's goals and substitution of means which support and facilitate his deviant behavior. It might be illustrated by corrupt alliances among police, politicians, and racketeers.

[4]Parsons, op. cit., p. 252; Talcott Parsons and Edward A. Shils (eds.), Toward a General Theory of Action, Harvard University Press, 1952, pp. 151-52.

tions, and of concern with social objects—that is, with one's relationships to persons and collectivities—or with normative patterns. It is not possible to present and interpret this classification intelligibly in a brief space. However, it appears to subsume Merton's types under a wider range of alternatives. Merton's "Ritualism," for example, becomes Parsons' "Perfectionistic Observance," the product of conformative dominance, passivity, and focus on normative patterns. On the other hand, Parsons' scheme includes distinctions, such as that between "Perfectionistic Observance" and "Submission" (in which the focus is on social objects), that do not appear in Merton's scheme.

Thirdly, Parsons has given us much more than a taxonomy of deviant behavior–conformity. More than any other person, he has contributed to the clarification of the substantive theoretical problems. I shall make no effort to summarize; suffice it to say that the discussion which follows is so heavily indebted to him as to preclude detailed acknowledgment, point for point, of my indebtedness.

Deviant Behavior-Conformity as Interaction Process

Deviant behavior and conformity are kinds of behavior that evolve in the course of an interaction process. When we say that deviant behavior is an attempt to reduce strain or to solve a problem of adjustment, we do not mean that an actor finds himself in an awkward spot, considers a number of alternatives, and then makes a choice. The break with the routine and the institutionalized is more typically half-conscious, tentative, and groping. Ambivalence motivates exploratory but noncommittal gestures. The gestures elicit from others responses which tend to reduce the original strain, responses which only make matters worse, responses which signify that further movement in the same direction will receive a cold welcome, or responses which guardedly suggest that alter has problems akin to ego's and would like to explore with ego the possibility of new solutions. Whether incipient deviant behavior is checked before it becomes fully conscious, or becomes explicit and the actors more fully committed in a vicious circle of progressively deviant behavior, accompanied by realignments and coalitions with the system, alter contributes as much to the outcome as ego. In short, the outcome is a cumulative and collective product, and the history of the deviant act is the history of an interactional system, not of the actor who happened to author the act. It follows that research and theory must address themselves to the following questions: What is the detailed structure of this process of progressive commitment? What are the characteristics of the points of no return? What sets in motion the reverse cycles of restoration of conformity? And, implicit in all these questions: In what ways do alter's values affect the course of these processes? In particular, to what kinds of strain is alter subject, and what are the consequences to alter of ego's deviant behavior? When does incipient deviant behavior seduce the ambivalent and lead to deviant coalitions? When does it excite indignation, sanctimony, and hostility? When does it elicit sympathy, emotional support, and nonpunitive efforts to restore ego to conformity?

How, furthermore, does the significance of an event for deviant behavior depend upon the stage of the interaction process? Since the stimulus value of any event depends upon the perspectives on which it impinges, and since the perspectives of participants in a system change with their experience in the system, we cannot say that certain kinds of events or circumstances are pressures for or against behavior without reference to the stage of the interaction process. The rebuke which brings the incipient deviant back into line may further alienate the deviant who is somewhat further advanced. Can we, however, move beyond the platitudinous statement that "the stage of the interaction process makes a difference" and state just what kind of difference it makes under various conditions?

Alternative Responses to Strain

Deviant behavior is a response to strain, which we have defined as ambivalence relative to institutionalized expectations. Such ambivalence occurs whenever conformity to institutionalized expectations is positively motivated and, at the same time, somehow frustrating or unacceptable. It is probably inherent in the nature of social systems that most of the members are subject to such strain in various degrees. However, most of us conform most of the time. Therefore, deviant behavior is not the only response to strain, and there must be ties to the institutional order that are powerful enough to override deviant motivation most of the time. In other words, social systems must be so organized that deviant behavior tends to produce, more often than not, tensions greater than those produced by conformity. The following discussion of these ties to the institutional order, the restraining forces they exert on deviant behavior, and the possible modes of adaptation in the face of such restraining forces will yield, we think, a systematic formulation of the major theoretical problems of a sociology of deviant behavior.

Let us begin with an example of an individual who is seeking, consciously or unconsciously, to resolve his ambivalence relative to some institutionalized expectation: a doctor considering whether to perform illegal abortions, a police officer debating whether to accept a "cut" from a brothel keeper, or a person with homosexual inclinations hesitating about yielding to those inclinations. In each case the temptation is attractive but institutionally forbidden.

A satisfactory resolution will have certain characteristics. It will be one which the individual can square with his own moral standards and which is symbolically consistent with the roles in terms of which he defines himself. Thus, overt homosexuality may not only be unacceptable because it is seen as "wrong" and "sinful"; it may also be symbolically inappropriate in the sense that it signifies a denial of manhood. (By the same token, to throw stones at street lights may be "wrong" for boy and man alike. For the latter, however, it is "kid stuff" and threatening to his self-conception as an "adult"; for the former, it serves to validate his claim to being "all boy.")

The adequacy of a response in both these respects depends very much on what have been called the actor's "normative reference groups." It is difficult to be persuaded of the moral rightness of a choice when our judgment does not agree with that of groups which we have come to regard as authoritative with respect to the issue involved. Such reference groups will always be, to some extent, participants in the institutional order. To the degree that this is so, we cannot indulge in behavior that violates their expectations without moral uncertainty, guilt, or ambivalence. Similarly, the symbolism of an act, as of language, depends upon the usages of a community which the actor regards as authoritative in such matters. Thus, whether I consider myself a "square" or a "cat"—assuming that it is important to me whether I am the one or the other—depends upon the role symbolism of what I say and do, and this symbolism is defined by my normative reference groups. The role symbolism that these reference groups confer on institutionally expected behavior will usually, although not necessarily, be congruent with the self-conceptions that the actor is trying to fulfill. Conversely, behavior that violates the institutionally expected is likely to signify roles with which the actor seeks to avoid identification.

One problem for an individual who is confronted with a situation of strain and is consequently tempted to behave in deviant ways is to come to terms with the moral conceptions and role definitions of his normative reference groups, which, as we have said, are generally ranged on the side of the institutional order.

There are three possible resolutions of this problem, one of them conformist, two deviant.

One alternative is for our hypothetical subject to continue to conform, despite continued frustration, because conformity is the only alternative that is morally and symbolically validated by his reference groups. It is probable, as a matter of fact, that most people carry a chronic load of frustration but nevertheless continue to conform because the frustration is easier to bear than moral uncertainty or unfavorable role significance.

A second alternative is for him to break with his reference groups and acknowledge other reference groups, whose norms legitimize deviant solutions and attribute favorable role symbolism to them. This solution may involve "shopping around" to find such reference groups or joining forces with others in the same position to create new reference groups. These processes can be observed in the fields of unethical medical practice, police corruption, and homosexuality. Clearly, we are here talking about processes by means of which subcultures are created and perpetuated. Of these processes we have only the most elementary understanding. The development of a theory of subcultures is a general theoretical problem of the greatest possible import for a sociology of deviant behavior.

A third alternative is for the individual to "go it alone," violating the institutionalized expectations without the legitimation and validation that come from consensus. This would appear to be the most costly and, on current theoretical grounds, the most improbable alternative, but it occurs. In view of the enormous importance attributed to reference-group support by current sociological theory, the conditions under which this response occurs pose a crucial theoretical problem.

The question of whether to conform or not resolves itself, in part, into a choice among these three alternative responses to the problem of what to do about reference-group support in the areas of moral validity and role symbolism. To the extent that this is so, the task of theory is to clarify what is entailed in each of these responses and to account for choices among them.

However, the actor must deal with yet another type of problem, the responses to which take the form of a very similar set of alternatives. This type of problem concerns, not the assessment of morality and meaning, but the objective consequences of the act in terms of the satisfaction or deprivation of the individual's needs or wants. These needs or wants do not exist in pure or disembodied form but are attached or directed to particular objects or classes of objects. Satisfaction consists in acquiring, using, or establishing some sort of relationship to these objects. Some of these needs may be called social-emotional; gratification of needs in this category consists in the establishment of certain kinds of relationships with social objects (persons or collectivities). Those with whom we value such relationships have been called our "status reference groups"— "status," in this context, signifying the whole class of gratifying emotional responses from others.

By definition, satisfaction of social-emotional needs depends upon the responses of others. More specifically, it depends upon the standards and criteria current in the individual's reference groups in terms of which these groups evaluate his personal qualities and conduct. To the degree to which his status reference groups are themselves integrated into the institutional order, the individual's social-emotional security depends upon his conformity to institutionalized expectations, for such conformity is always among the conditions upon which the favorable response is contingent.

In addition to its consequences for gratification-deprivation in the social-emotional area, any act has consequences for the gratification or deprivation of needs and wants attached to nonsocial objects—a residual category commonly called goods and services. These are multitudinous, including food, clothing, shelter, money, drugs and medical care, transportation, and entertainment. Some of these are directly gratifying, some are instrumental to other satisfactions. The important point is that the consequences of an act in terms of want satisfaction depend upon the way in which it articulates with the established systems of interaction through which goods and services are produced and distributed. Families, businesses, fraternal organizations, churches, governmental agencies, and universities are such systems. To obtain the goods and services they offer, the individual must participate in them on their own terms. He must assume responsible roles in these systems and perform them appropriately—that is, in accordance with the institutionalized expectations of the other participants. The systems themselves may generate needs that cannot be legitimately or even illegitimately satisfied within the systems, but this fact does not mean that the individual can lightly turn his back on the systems and refuse to conform to their expectations. For it is characteristic of social systems that through each of them we satisfy not one but many wants. Therefore, the loss of good standing in our family, our neighborhood, or our business community may result in the denial of satisfaction of not one but a whole set of wants. In still another way, therefore, dependence upon the institutional order encourages us to conform, even under conditions of strain.

Again, the question of whether to conform or not resolves itself into a choice among three alternative responses to the problem of what to do about our dependence upon the institutional order for satisfaction of social-emotional and other needs.

First, an individual confronted with this choice may continue to conform rather than risk shame, contumely, loss of love, or the denial or deprivation of goods and services.

Secondly, he can, so to speak, take his business elsewhere. He can seek out or participate in the creation—together with similarly disaffected individuals—of status reference groups which are disposed to reward behavior that would otherwise result in social rejection. To obtain goods and services which he has forfeited by refusal to meet the demands of the institutionalized order, he may participate in or help to create, together with other individuals who stand to profit from such cooperative endeavors, systems which are geared to the satisfaction of illicit wants or which provide mechanisms through which culturally approved wants can be satisfied through illegitimate means.

This second type of response parallels the creation of or participation in subcultures. The subcultural response, however, deals with the problems of meaning and moral validity. The present response deals with the problem of finding or effecting practical arrangements that are capable of gratifying our needs and wants.

A third type of response is to violate the institutionalized expectations and put up with the consequent denial and frustration of needs which can be gratified only through playing a responsible role in a cooperative social concern.

The process of becoming a deviant, therefore, involves coming to terms with a number of problems. A deviant solution which is acceptable on one criterion may not be acceptable on others. Stable deviant solutions usually consist of complex social arrangements that are capable of resolving strain in several areas. Becoming a marihuana user, for example, is a gradual process of induction, step by step, into an elaborate deviant substructure which makes it possible to be a marihuana user and at the same time to cope with all the problems arising out of alienation from the conventional or institutional order.[5] What is it about the structure of the larger society that generates such deviant substructures—and there is a large family of

[5]Howard S. Becker, "Marihuana Use and Social Control," *Soc. Prob.*, 3 (1955), 35-44.

them—and makes it possible for them to survive? What kinds of interactive process produce awareness of, access to, and progressive involvement in such substructures? These are problems generic to the sociology of deviant behavior, not to marihuana use alone.

On the other hand, consider a (somewhat idealized) Skid Row bum who, to all appearances, is isolated and despised, who has lost his self-respect, whose behavior is neither rewarded by response from people whose response he values nor sanctioned by reference groups whose authority he respects, and whose behavior, further, is instrumentally ineffective to the point that even his liquor supply is precarious. In this case, the choice—if the word "choice" is appropriate—seems to be the third alternative. The theory we evolve must be able to make sense of this sort of behavior. To state that deviant behavior and conformity represent resolutions of a threefold dilemma in each of several areas may be a fruitful way of approaching what we are here attempting to explain.

Linkages Among Forms of Deviant Behavior

There is a strong tendency for sociologists to treat the various forms of deviant behavior as somehow interrelated—either as protean symptoms or manifestations of a single underlying pathology, or as cause and consequence of one another.

It is true that varieties of deviant behavior may be linked in a number of ways. Various kinds of deviant behavior—for example, aggressive "acting out" and passive withdrawal—may tend to cluster because they represent different ways of coping with the same situation. One kind of deviant behavior may be instrumental to another—as, for example, in the case of the drug addict who is forced to steal in order to maintain his habit. One kind may be a device for evading the consequences of another; for example, the rapist may be a killer because his victim is his witness. Or again, various kinds of deviant specialties may aid and abet one another. Those who are already involved in deviant behavior exert pressure upon all those who are in a position to affect their operations adversely or to render them services to become their accessories. Thus slot-machine rackets, labor racketeering, political corruption, police graft, and organized gambling tend to encourage one another, to become symbiotically linked, and to come under common control because each serves the interests of the others.

One of the tasks of a sociology of deviant behavior is to classify and elucidate the mechanisms by means of which one kind of deviant behavior generates others. But this is not to say that the sources of deviant behavior are always to be found in the abnormal, the pathological, and the deplorable. They may also be found in the institutionally expected and the sacred. Implicit in the very idea of a system is the fact that whatever is found in it is a function of its total structure. The consequences of any particular feature of a system for deviant behavior or conformity depend not on its moral or hygienic status but on its context. The same strains which help to produce deviant behavior also help to produce the behavior we most admire and applaud. For example, the characteristic American belief that a man should "make something of himself" encourages the hard work, self-discipline, and productivity that we so much admire; at the same time, it makes failure all the more ego-involved and humiliating and, if the writer's analysis[6] is correct, helps to motivate delinquent subcultures in American society. If Kingsley Davis[7] is correct, the sanctity of the marriage institution and the high value placed upon female chastity help to explain prostitution as well as sexual continence. If Chein and Rosenfeld[8] are correct, teen-age drug use may result from the impact upon a certain kind of personality of age-graded expectations which motivate other young people to assume the responsibilities of adulthood. Furthermore; much that is deviant can be largely attributed to efforts, some of them nobly motivated, to control deviant behavior. For example, efforts to prevent the consumption of liquor and narcotics and to prevent gambling have fostered the growth of large-scale criminal organizations for the provision of these goods and services, and these organizations in turn have contributed to the corruption of politics and law enforcement. In short, that which we deplore and that which we cherish are not only part of the same seamless web; they are actually woven of the same fibers.

[6]Albert K. Cohen, *Delinquent Boys, the Culture of the Gang,* Free Press, 1955.

[7]Kingsley Davis, "The Sociology of Prostitution," *Amer. Sociol. Rev.,* 2 (1937), 744-55.

[8]Isidor Chein and Eva Rosenfeld, "Juvenile Narcotics Use," *Law Contemp. Prob.,* 22 (1957), 59-63.

A Theory of Subcultures
Albert K. Cohen

. . . The crucial condition for the emergence
of new cultural forms is the existence, *in effective
interaction with one another, of a number of actors
with similar problems of adjustment.* These may be
the entire membership of a group or only certain
members, similarly circumstanced, within the
group. Among the conceivable solutions to their
problems may be one which is not yet embodied in
action and which does not therefore exist as a
cultural model. This solution, except for the fact that
it does not already carry the social criteria of validity
and promise the social rewards of consensus, might
well answer more neatly to the problems of this
group and appeal to its members more effectively
than any of the solutions already institutionalized.
For each participant, this solution would be adjustive
and adequately motivated provided that he could
anticipate a simultaneous and corresponding transformation in the frames of reference of his fellows.
Each would welcome a sign from the others that a
new departure in this direction would receive approval and support. But how does one *know* whether
a gesture toward innovation will strike a responsive
and sympathetic chord in others or whether it will
elicit hostility, ridicule and punishment? *Potential*
concurrence is always problematical and innovation
or the impulse to innovate a stimulus for anxiety.

The paradox is resolved when the innovation is
broached in such a manner as to elicit from others
reactions suggesting their receptivity; and when, at
the same time, the innovation occurs by increments
so small, tentative and ambiguous as to permit the

actor to retreat, if the signs be unfavorable, without having become identified with an unpopular position. Perhaps all social actions have, in addition to their instrumental, communicative and expressive functions, this quality of being *exploratory gestures*. For the actor with problems of adjustment which cannot be resolved within the frame of reference of the established culture, each response of the other to what the actor says and does is a clue to the directions in which change may proceed further in a way congenial to the other and to the direction in which change will lack social support. And if the probing gesture is motivated by tensions common to other participants it is likely to initiate a process of *mutual* exploration and *joint* elaboration of a new solution. My exploratory gesture functions as a cue to you; your exploratory gesture as a cue to me. By a casual, semi-serious, noncommittal or tangential remark I may stick my neck out just a little way, but I will quickly withdraw it unless you, by some sign of affirmation, stick *yours* out. I will permit myself to become progressively committed but only as others, by some visible sign, become likewise committed. The final product, to which we are jointly committed, is likely to be a compromise formation of all the participants to what we may call a cultural process, a formation perhaps unanticipated by any of them. Each actor may contribute something directly to the growing product, but he may also contribute indirectly by encouraging others to advance, inducing them to retreat, and suggesting new avenues to be explored. The product cannot be ascribed to any one of the participants; it is a real "emergent" on a group level.

We may think of this process as one of mutual conversion. The important thing to remember is that we do not first convert ourselves and then others. The acceptability of an idea to oneself depends upon its acceptability to others. Converting the other is part of the process of converting oneself. . . .

The emergence of these "group standards" of this shared frame of reference, is the emergence of a new subculture. It is cultural because each actor's participation in this system of norms is influenced by his perception of the same norms in other actors. It is *sub*cultural because the norms are shared only among those actors who stand somehow to profit from them and who find in one another a sympathetic moral climate within which these norms may come to fruition and persist. In this fashion culture is continually being created, re-created and modified wherever individuals sense in one another like needs, generated by like circumstances, not shared generally in the larger social system. Once established, such a subcultural system may persist, but not by sheer inertia. It may achieve a life which outlasts that of the individuals who participated in its creation, but only so long as it continues to serve the needs of those who succeed its creators.

Subcultural Solutions to Status Problems

One variant of this cultural process interests us especially because it provides the model for our explanation of the subculture. [This process deals with subcultural solutions to status problems.] Status problems are problems of achieving respect in the eyes of one's fellows. Our ability to achieve status depends upon the criteria of status applied by our fellows, that is, the standards or norms they go by in evaluating people. These criteria are an aspect of their cultural frames of reference. If we lack the characteristics or capacities which give status in terms of these criteria, we are beset by one of the most typical and yet distressing of human problems of adjustment. One solution is for individuals who share such problems to gravitate toward one another and jointly to establish new norms, new criteria of status which define as meritorious the characteristics they *do* possess, the kinds of conduct of which they *are* capable. It is clearly necessary for each participant, if the innovation is to solve his status problem, that these new criteria be shared with others, that the solution be a group and not a private solution. If he "goes it alone" he succeeds only in further estranging himself from his fellows. Such new status criteria would represent new subcultural values different from or even antithetical to those of the larger social system. . . .

part Five

Social and Cultural Support Theory

In the preceding section we examined the ideas of theorists who dealt with individual and group adaptations to strain. Central to the discussion was the concept of reference group orientation. Merton emphasized the role of the reference group in his discussion of the relative degree of the person's internalization of cultural goals and institutionalized means for their attainment. Parsons focused on the norms and expectations of the interpersonal relationship as they became part of the need-dispositions of the individual. And Cohen explained the development of the deviant subcultures as a reaction to failure in meeting the demands of the larger society. Further, says Cohen, the success of subcultural adaptations to the ambivalence between expectation and opportunity depends on the deviant's ability to choose a new reference group which is supportive of his behavior.

Dealing principally with crime, social and cultural support theorists also have recognized the centrality of the reference group in the development of deviant behavior. They contend that all behavior, conforming or non-conforming, is socially located. That is, behavior is a product of a defining social environment. Offering one of the earliest statements on this assumption, Gabriel Tarde describes the development of behavioral patterns in terms of *imitation*. Through the example of others, individuals acquire the skills necessary for participation in social life. The domination of example in the construction of social acts applies to such diverse phenomena as procreation, assassination, and the violence of mobs.

The first systematic explanation of this process in the case of criminal behavior is offered by Edwin Sutherland in his *theory of differential association*. Referring to ideas like those contained in anomie theory (especially in the work of Merton), he states that although crime may be an expression of general needs and values, such as striving for success and experiencing frustration, it is not entirely explained in this manner. Persons must be exposed to a supportive social and cultural environment in order to adopt such behavior. He thus constructs his theory around the fundamental proposition that criminal behavior, like conforming behavior, is learned. Further, he contends that the techniques of committing crimes, as well as criminal motives, drives, attitudes, and rationalizations are learned in primary group interaction wherein there is an excess of definitions favorable to violation of the

law. Whether the individual internalizes these definitions, says Sutherland, depends upon the frequency,
duration, priority, and intensity of the associations.

Clifford Shaw and Henry McKay apply this general
principle in their analysis of delinquency in urban
areas. They point out that the opportunities for participation in delinquent groups are differentially distributed on the basis of geographical area, the high
opportunity areas being the slums near the center of
the city. These areas are characterized by the simultaneous existence of conflicting moral values. Such a
situation is brought about by the migration of religious,
educational, and recreational institutions out of the
urban slum and into the middle class suburb. Since
such organizations are designed to protect and perpetuate a stable value system, attitudes and behavior are
likely to be homogeneous in areas in which they are
more prevalent. Delinquent areas, on the other hand,
with their relative absence of such organizations, establish deviant traditions which are often transmitted
intergenerationally. Behavior in both slum and suburb,
then, is a product of the pursuit of human needs and
satisfactions as they are defined by local norms and
traditions. Because the behaviors promoted in the slum
are more likely to conflict with conventional norms,
they are more often designated delinquent.

Daniel Glaser adds still another dimension to
Sutherland's theory in his statement on *differential
identification.* He explains that while group association
may be sufficient for identification with criminal patterns, such association may not always be necessary.
Applying the concept of *role-taking*, he states that the
individual may learn criminality through an identification with persons whom he perceives as accepting such
behavior.

The articles by C. R. Jeffery and by Robert Burgess
and Ronald Akers reformulate the principles of differential association theory in terms of recent developments in learning theory. Jeffery maintains that the
acquisition of non-conforming behavior patterns does
not depend entirely on criminal association or identification. Rather he suggests that the sources of rein-

forcement for the deviant are both social and material. That is, not only does the support of reference associations contribute to the formation and stability of nonconforming behavior, but so also do the material gains acquired during the criminal act. Burgess and Akers systematically reformulated the propositions of Sutherland's theory by utilizing the principles of operant conditioning. They argue that the translation and reformulation of differential association theory in terms of the concepts of learning theory provide a more accurate and useful tool for the analysis of criminal behavior.

Stressing a variable that is only implied in differential association theory, Richard Cloward and Lloyd Ohlin state that motivation and pressure are not sufficient causes of conforming or non-conforming behavior. Rather, there is also operative a differential access to the learning environments and means required for the performance of such roles. Reflecting Robert Merton's discussion of the availability of institutionalized means for conforming behavior, Cloward and Ohlin maintain that there is also a parallel opportunity structure for non-conforming behavior, one composed of learning and performance structures. Access to these structures depends upon a variety of factors, such as age, sex, and social class.

Gresham Sykes and David Matza elaborate on Sutherland's suggestion that an important part of the learning process in the case of crime is the acquisition of rationalizations for one's behavior. They suggest that the necessity for such learning rests on the fact that the individual who is socialized into a deviant group is never completely immune from confrontations with conforming members of society. In such circumstances, in order to maintain a positive self concept, the deviant engages in various techniques of neutralization. These are rationalizations to justify the deviant acts. Sykes and Matza list "denial of responsibility," "denial of injury," "denial of the victim," "condemnation of the condemners," and "appeal to higher loyalties" as the major techniques used to neutralize non-conforming behavior.

Complementing ideas concerning the differential learning of deviant behavior, Travis Hirschi has proposed that non-conformity is a product of the failure of the social bond. Through the *attachment* of individuals to others, conformity is assured. When such attachments fail to develop or when they are disrupted, the internalization of legitimate norms becomes problematic. *Commitment* to conventional lines of action and *involvement* in conventional activities have similar effects. As persons increasingly organize their lives around conforming roles and behaviors, the possibility of deviant alternatives is proportionately diminished. The concept of the social bond constitutes an important addition to social and cultural support theory. The failure of social control, that is the release of individuals from legitimate attachments, commitments, and involvements, may constitute a necessary condition in the development of ties with groups wherein there are found definitions more favorable to deviant behavior.

In sum, social and cultural support theorists emphasize reference group association and identification as instrumental to the development of deviant behavior. The acquisition and enactment of these behavior forms depends on performance as well as learning structures which provide rewards compatible with deviant group definitions. Very generally these theorists view deviance as resulting from socialization to a definitional framework conducive to such behavior. The processes occurring here are essentially the same as those involved in learning conforming behavior.

Tendency
Toward Imitation
Gabriel Tarde

All the important acts of social life are carried out under the domination of example. One procreates or one does not procreate, because of imitation; the statistics of the birth rate have shown us this. One kills or one does not kill, because of imitation; would we today conceive of the idea of fighting a duel or of declaring war, if we did not know that these things had always been done in the country which we inhabit? One kills oneself or one does not kill oneself, because of imitation; it is a recognized fact that suicide is an imitative phenomenon to the very highest degree; at any rate it is impossible to refuse to give this character to those "suicides in large numbers of conquered peoples escaping by means of death the shame of defeat and the yoke of the stranger, like that of the Sidonians who were defeated by Artaxerxes Orchus, of the Tyrians defeated by Alexander, of the Sagontines defeated by Scipio, of the Achaeans defeated by Metellus, etc."[1]

After this how can we doubt but that one steals or does not steal, one assassinates or does not assassinate, because of imitation? But it is especially in the great tumultuous assemblages of our cities that this characteristic force of the social world ought to be studied. The great scenes of our revolutions cause it to break out, just as great storms are a manifestation of the presence of the electricity in the atmosphere, while it remains unperceived though none the less a reality in the intervals between them.

[1]"Le suicide dans l'armée," by *Mesnier*.

From Gabriel Tarde, *Penal Philosophy* (1928; reprinted as Publication No. 16, Patterson Smith Series in Criminology, Law Enforcement and Social Problems, Montclair, N.J., 1970).

A *mob* is a strange phenomenon. It is a gathering of heterogeneous elements, unknown to one another;[2] but as soon as a spark of passion, having flashed out from one of these elements, electrifies this confused mass, there takes place a sort of sudden organization, a spontaneous generation. This incoherence becomes cohesion, this noise becomes a voice, and these thousands of men crowded together soon form but a single animal, a wild beast without a name, which marches to its goal with an irresistible finality. The majority of these men had assembled out of pure curiosity, but the fever of some of them soon reached the minds of all, and in all of them there arose a delirium. The very man who had come running to oppose the murder of an innocent person is one of the first to be seized with the homicidal contagion, and moreover, it does not occur to him to be astonished at this.

There is no need for me to recall certain never to be forgotten pages of Taine's dealing with the fourteenth of July and its consequences in the provinces.[3] How can these things be so? In the most simple manner imaginable. The manner in which the mob acts shows us the force under the domination of which it became organized. Let us imagine ourselves carried back to the time of the Commune; a man wearing a white blouse, crossing a square, passes close to an over-excited crowd; he looks like a suspicious person to someone. In a moment, with the rapidity of a conflagration, this suspicion spreads, and instantly, what happens? "*A suspicion is enough*, all protest is useless, every proof is a delusion; *the conviction is profound.*"[4] Supposing that each one of these people had been alone in his own house, never could a mere suspicion in the mind of each one of them, without proofs to support it, have been changed into a conviction. But they are together, and the suspicion of each of them, by virtue of imitative force, keener, and acting more promptly in times of emotion, is reinforced by the suspicions of all the others; the result of which ought to be that, from being very weak, a belief in the guilt of the unfortunate fellow suddenly becomes very strong,

[2]Of course, it necessarily follows that these men assembled together should resemble one another on some essential points such as nationality, religion, social class.

[3]Read again what is said about the massacres of September ("Revolution," vol. IV, pp. 295 *et seq.*). Among the Septemberists "some having come with good intentions are seized with vertigo at the contact of the bloody whirlwind, and, by a sudden stroke of revolutionary feeling, are converted to the religion of murder. A certain Grapin, delegated by his section to save two prisoners, sits down beside Maillard, and passes sentences with him during sixty hours."—There must without doubt also have been many such men as Grapin during the night of St. Bartholomew.

[4]Maxime du Camp.

without the shadow of an argument being necessary. Reciprocal imitation, when it is exercised over *similar* beliefs, and, generally speaking, over *similar* psychological states, is a true multiplication of the intensity proper to these beliefs, to these various states, in each one of those who feel them simultaneously.

When, on the contrary, in imitating one another, several persons exchange *different* states, which is what ordinarily takes place in social life, when, for example, one communicates to the other a taste for Wagnerian music and in return the other communicates to him a love for realistic fiction; these persons no doubt establish between themselves a bond of mutual assimilation, just as when they express to each other two similar ideas or needs which take root in this manner. But in the first case, the assimilation is, for each of them, a *complication* of their internal state—this is essentially an effect of civilization—and in the second case the assimilation is, for each of them, a mere *reinforcement* of their inner life. Between these two cases there is the musical interval between unison and a chord. A mob has the simple and deep power of a large unison. This explains why it is so dangerous to associate too much with minds which reflect one's own thoughts and one's own feelings; in doing this one soon arrives at the *sect spirit,* which is entirely analogous to the *mob spirit.*

Differential Association
Edwin H. Sutherland

The scientific explanation of a phenomenon may be stated either in terms of the factors which are operating at the moment of the occurrence of a phenomenon or in terms of the processes operating in the earlier history of that phenomenon. In the first case the explanation is mechanistic, in the second historical or genetic; both are desirable. The physical and biological scientists favor the first of these methods and it would probably be superior as an explanation of criminal behavior. Efforts at explanations of the mechanistic type have been notably unsuccessful, perhaps largely because they have been concentrated on the attempt to isolate personal and social pathologies. Work from this point of view has, at least, resulted in the conclusion that the immediate factors in criminal behavior lie in the person-situation complex. Person and situation are not factors exclusive of each other, for the situation which is important is the situation as defined by the person who is involved. The tendencies and inhibitions at the moment of the criminal behavior are, to be sure, largely a product of the earlier history of the person, but the expression of these tendencies and inhibitions is a reaction to the immediate situation as defined by the person. The situation operates in many ways, of which perhaps the least important is the provision of an opportunity for a criminal act. A thief may steal from a fruit stand when the owner is not in sight but refrain when the owner is in sight; a bank burglar may attack a bank which is poorly protected but refrain from attacking a bank protected by watchmen and burglar alarms. A corporation which manufactures automobiles seldom or never

From *Principles of Criminology* by Edwin H. Sutherland. Reprinted by permission of the publisher, J. B. Lippincott Company. Copyright © 1947, pp. 5–9.

violates the Pure Food and Drug Law but a meat-packing corporation violates this law with great frequency.

The second type of explanation of criminal behavior is made in terms of the life experience of a person. This is an historical or genetic explanation of criminal behavior. This, to be sure, assumes a situation to be defined by the person in terms of the inclinations and abilities which the person has acquired up to that date. The following paragraphs state such a genetic theory of criminal behavior on the assumption that a criminal act occurs when a situation appropriate for it, as defined by a person, is present.

Genetic Explanation of Criminal Behavior

The following statement refers to the process by which a particular person comes to engage in criminal behavior.

1. *Criminal behavior is learned.* Negatively, this means that criminal behavior is not inherited, as such; also, the person who is not already trained in crime does not invent criminal behavior, just as a person does not make mechanical inventions unless he has had training in mechanics.
2. *Criminal behavior is learned in interaction with other persons in a process of communication.* This communication is verbal in many respects but includes also "the communication of gestures."
3. *The principal part of the learning of criminal behavior occurs within intimate personal groups.* Negatively, this means that the impersonal agencies of communication, such as picture shows and newspapers, play a relatively unimportant part in the genesis of criminal behavior.
4. *When criminal behavior is learned, the learning includes (a) techniques of committing the crime, which are sometimes very complicated, sometimes very simple; (b) the specific direction of motives, drives, rationalizations, and attitudes.*
5. *The specific direction of motives and drives is learned from definitions of the legal codes as favorable or unfavorable.* In some societies an individual is surrounded by persons who invariably define the legal codes as rules to be observed, while in others he is surrounded by persons whose definitions are favorable to the violation of the legal codes. In our American society these definitions are almost always mixed and consequently we have culture conflict in relation to the legal codes.

6. *A person becomes delinquent because of an excess of definitions favorable to violation of law over definitions unfavorable to violation of law.* This is the principle of differential association. It refers to both criminal and anti-criminal associations and has to do with counteracting forces. When persons become criminal, they do so because of contacts with criminal patterns and also because of isolation from anti-criminal patterns. Any person inevitably assimilates the surrounding culture unless other patterns are in conflict; a Southerner does not pronounce "r" because other Southerners do not pronounce "r." Negatively, this proposition of differential association means that associations which are neutral so far as crime is concerned have little or no effect on the genesis of criminal behavior. Much of the experience of a person is neutral in this sense, e.g., learning to brush one's teeth. This behavior has no negative or positive effect on criminal behavior except as it may be related to associations which are concerned with the legal codes. This neutral behavior is important especially as an occupier of the time of a child so that he is not in contact with criminal behavior during the time he is so engaged in the neutral behavior.

7. *Differential associations may vary in frequency, duration, priority, and intensity.* This means that associations with criminal behavior and also associations with anti-criminal behavior vary in those respects. "Frequency" and "duration" as modalities of associations are obvious and need no explanation. "Priority" is assumed to be important in the sense that lawful behavior developed in early childhood may persist throughout life, and also that delinquent behavior developed in early childhood may persist throughout life. This tendency, however, has not been adequately demonstrated, and priority seems to be important principally through its selective influence. "Intensity" is not precisely defined but it has to do with such things as the prestige of the source of a criminal or anti-criminal pattern and with emotional reactions related to the associations. In a precise description of the criminal behavior of a person these modalities would be stated in quantitative form and a mathematical ratio be reached. A formula in this sense has not been developed and the development of such a formula would be extremely difficult.

8. *The process of learning criminal behavior by association with criminal and anti-criminal patterns involves all of the mechanisms that are involved in any other learning.* Negatively, this means that the learning of criminal behavior is not restricted to the

process of imitation. A person who is seduced, for instance, learns criminal behavior by association but this process would not ordinarily be described as imitation.

9. *While criminal behavior is an expression of general needs and values, it is not explained by those general needs and values since non-criminal behavior is an expression of the same needs and values.* Thieves generally steal in order to secure money, but likewise honest laborers work in order to secure money. The attempts by many scholars to explain criminal behavior by general drives and values, such as the happiness principle, striving for social status, the money motive, or frustration, have been and must continue to be futile since they explain lawful behavior as completely as they explain criminal behavior. They are similar to respiration, which is necessary for any behavior but which does not differentiate criminal from non-criminal behavior.

It is not necessary, at this level of explanation, to explain why a person has the associations which he has; this certainly involves a complex of many things. In an area where the delinquency rate is high a boy who is sociable, gregarious, active, and athletic is very likely to come in contact with the other boys in the neighborhood, learn delinquent behavior from them, and become a gangster; in the same neighborhood the psychopathic boy who is isolated, introvert, and inert may remain at home, not become acquainted with the other boys in the neighborhood, and not become delinquent. In another situation, the sociable, athletic, aggressive boy may become a member of a scout troop and not become involved in delinquent behavior. The person's associations are determined in a general context of social organization. A child is ordinarily reared in a family; the place of residence of the family is determined largely by family income; and the delinquency rate is in many respects related to the rental value of the houses. Many other factors enter into this social organization, including many of the small personal group relationships.

The preceding explanation of criminal behavior was stated from the point of view of the person who engages in criminal behavior. It is possible, also, to state theories of criminal behavior from the point of view of the community, nation, or other group. The problem, when thus stated, is generally concerned with crime rates and involves a comparison of the crime rates of various groups or the crime rates of a particular group at different times. One of the best explanations of crime rates from this point of view is that a high crime rate is due to social disorganization. The term "social disorganization" is not entirely satisfactory and it seems preferable to substitute for it the term "differential social organization." The postulate on which this theory is based, regardless of the name, is that crime is rooted in the social organization and is an expression of that social organization. A group may be organized for criminal behavior or organized against criminal behavior. Most communities are organized both for criminal and anti-criminal behavior and in that sense the crime rate is an expression of the differential group organization. Differential group organization as an explanation of a crime rate must be consistent with the explanation of the criminal behavior of the person, since the crime rate is a summary statement of the number of persons in the group who commit crimes and the frequency with which they commit crimes.

Differential
Systems
of Values

Clifford R. Shaw / Henry D. McKay

In general, the more subtle differences between types of communities in Chicago may be
encompassed within the general proposition that in
the areas of low rates of delinquents there is more or
less uniformity, consistency, and universality of
conventional values and attitudes with respect to
child care, conformity to law, and related matters;
whereas in the high-rate areas systems of competing
and conflicting moral values have developed. Even
though in the latter situation conventional traditions
and institutions are dominant, delinquency has developed as a powerful competing way of life. It
derives its impelling force in the boy's life from the
fact that it provides a means of securing economic
gain, prestige, and other human satisfactions and is
embodied in delinquent groups and criminal organizations, many of which have great influence,
power, and prestige.

In the areas of high economic status where the
rates of delinquents are low there is, in general, a
similarity in the attitudes of the residents with
reference to conventional values, as has been said,
especially those related to the welfare of children.
This is illustrated by the practical unanimity of
opinion as to the desirability of education and con-
structive leisure-time activities and of the need for a
general health program. It is shown, too, in the
subtle, yet easily recognizable, pressure exerted
upon children to keep them engaged in conventional

activities, and in the resistance offered by the community to behavior which threatens the conventional values. It does not follow that all the activities participated in by members of the community are lawful; but, since any unlawful pursuits are likely to be carried out in other parts of the city, children living in the low-rate communities are, on the whole, insulated from direct contact with these deviant forms of adult behavior.

In the middle-class areas and the areas of high economic status, moreover, the similarity of attitudes and values as to social control is expressed in institutions and voluntary associations designed to perpetuate and protect these values. Among these may be included such organizations as the parent-teachers associations, women's clubs, service clubs, churches, neighborhood centers, and the like. Where these institutions represent dominant values, the child is exposed to, and participates in a significant way in one mode of life only. While he may have knowledge of alternatives, they are not integral parts of the system in which he participates.

In contrast, the areas of low economic status, where the rates of delinquents are high, are characterized by wide diversity in norms and standards of behavior. The moral values range from those that are strictly conventional to those in direct opposition to conventionality as symbolized by the family, the church, and other institutions common to our general society. The deviant values are symbolized by groups and institutions ranging from adult criminal gangs engaged in theft and the marketing of stolen goods, on the one hand, to quasi-legitimate businesses and the rackets through which partial or complete control of legitimate business is sometimes exercised, on the other. Thus, within the same community, theft may be defined as right and proper in some groups and as immoral, improper, and undesirable in others. In some groups wealth and prestige are secured through acts of skill and courage in the delinquent or criminal world, while in neighboring groups any attempt to achieve distinction in this manner would result in extreme disapprobation. Two conflicting systems of economic activity here present roughly equivalent opportunities for employment and for promotion. Evidence of success in the criminal world is indicated by the presence of adult criminals whose clothes and automobiles indicate unmistakably that they have prospered in their chosen fields. The values missed and the greater risks incurred are not so clearly apparent to the young.

Children living in such communities are exposed to a variety of contradictory standards and forms of behavior rather than to a relatively consistent and conventional pattern.[1] More than one type of moral institution and education are available to them. A boy may be familiar with, or exposed to, either the system of conventional activities or the system of criminal activities, or both. Similarly, he may participate in the activities of groups which engage mainly in delinquent activities, those concerned with conventional pursuits, or those which alternate between the two worlds. His attitudes and habits will be formed largely in accordance with the extent to which he participates in and becomes identified with one or the other of these several types of groups.

Conflicts of values necessarily arise when boys are brought in contact with so many forms of conduct not reconcilable with conventional morality as expressed in church and school. A boy may be found guilty of delinquency in the court, which represents the values of the larger society, for an act which has had at least tacit approval in the community in which he lives. It is perhaps common knowledge in the neighborhood that public funds are embezzled and that favors and special consideration can be received from some public officials through the payment of stipulated sums; the boys assume that all officials can be influenced in this way. They are familiar with the location of illegal institutions in the community and with the procedures through which such institutions are opened and kept in operation; they know where stolen goods can be sold and the kinds of merchandise for which there is a ready market; they know what the rackets are; and they see in fine clothes, expensive cars, and other lavish expenditures the evidences of wealth among those who openly engage in illegal activities. All boys in the city have some knowledge of these activities; but in the inner-city areas they are known intimately, in terms of personal relationships, while in other sections they enter the child's experience through more impersonal forms of communication, such as motion pictures, the newspaper, and the radio.

Other types of evidence tending to support the existence of diverse systems of values in various areas are to be found in the data on delinquency and crime. . . . When translated into its significance for children, the presence of a large number of adult criminals in certain areas means that children there are in contact with crime as a career and with the criminal way of life, symbolized by organized crime. In this type of organization can be seen the delegation of

[1]Edwin H. Sutherland has called this process "differential association." See E. H. Sutherland, *Principles of Criminology* (Chicago: J. B. Lippincott Co., 1939), chap. i.

authority, the division of labor, the specialization of function, and all the other characteristics common to well-organized business institutions wherever found.

Similarly, the delinquency data . . . give plausibility to the existence of a coherent system of values supporting delinquent acts. In making these interpretations it should be remembered that delinquency is essentially group behavior. A study of boys brought into the Juvenile Court of Cook County during the year 1928[2] revealed that 81.8 per cent of these boys committed the offenses for which they were brought to court as members of groups. And when the offenses were limited to stealing, it found that 89 per cent of all offenders were taken to court as group or gang members. In many additional cases where the boy actually committed his offense alone, the influence of companions was, nevertheless, apparent. This point is illustrated in certain cases of boys charged with stealing from members of their own families, where the theft clearly reflects the influence and instigation of companions, and in instances where the problems of the boy charged with incorrigibility reveal conflicting values, those of the family competing with those of the delinquent group for his allegiance.

The heavy concentration of delinquency in certain areas means, therefore, that boys living in these areas are in contact not only with individuals who engage in proscribed activity but also with groups which sanction such behavior and exert pressure upon their members to conform to group standards. . . . In contrast with the areas of concentration of delinquents, there are many other communities where the cases are so widely dispersed that the chances of a boy's having intimate contact with other delinquents or with delinquent groups are comparatively slight.

The importance of the concentration of delinquents is seen most clearly when the effect is viewed in a temporal perspective. . . . Year after year, decade after decade, the same areas have been characterized by these concentrations. This means that delinquent boys in these areas have contact not only with other delinquents who are their contemporaries but also with older offenders, who in turn had contact with delinquents preceding them, and so on back to the earliest history of the neighborhood. This contact means that the

[2]Clifford R. Shaw and Henry D. McKay, *Social Factors in Juvenile Delinquency,* Vol. II of *Report on the Causes of Crime,* National Commission on Law Observance and Enforcement, Report No. 13 (Washington, D.C.: U.S. Government Printing Office, 1931), pp. 191–99.

traditions of delinquency can be and are transmitted down through successive generations of boys, in much the same way that language and other social forms are transmitted.

The cumulative effect of this transmission of tradition is seen in two kinds of data, which will be presented here only very briefly. The first is a study of offenses, which reveals that certain types of delinquency have tended to characterize certain city areas. The execution of each type involves techniques which must be learned from others who have participated in the same activity. Each involves specialization of function, and each has its own terminology and standards of behavior. Jack-rolling, shoplifting, stealing from junk-men, and stealing automobiles are examples of offenses with well-developed techniques, passed on by one generation to the next.

The second body of evidence on the effects of the continuity of tradition within delinquent groups comprises the results of a study of the contacts between delinquents, made through the use of official records.[3] The names of boys who appeared together in court were taken, and the range of their association with other boys whose names appeared in the same records was then analyzed and charted. It was found that some members of each delinquent group had participated in offenses in the company of other older boys, and so on, backward in time in an unbroken continuity as far as the records were available. The continuity thus traced is roughly comparable to that which might be established among baseball players through their appearance in official lineups or regularly scheduled games. In baseball it is known that the techniques are transmitted through practice in back yards, playgrounds, sand lots, and in other places where boys congregate. Similarly in the case of delinquency traditions, if an unbroken continuity can be traced through formal institutions such as the Juvenile Court, the actual contacts among delinquents in the community must be numerous, continuous, and vital.

The way in which boys are inducted into unconventional behavior has been revealed by large numbers of case studies of youths living in areas where the rates of delinquents are high. Through the boy's own life-story the wide range of contacts with other boys has been revealed. These stories indicate how at early ages the boys took part with older boys in delinquent activities, and how, as they themselves acquired experience, they initiated others

[3]"Contacts between Successive Generations of Delinquent Boys in a Low-Income Area in Chicago" (unpublished study by the Department of Sociology, Illinois Institute for Juvenile Research, 1940).

into the same pursuits. These cases reveal also the steps through which members are incorporated into the delinquent group organization. Often at early ages boys engage in malicious mischief and simple acts of stealing. As their careers develop, they become involved in more serious offenses, and finally become skilled workmen or specialists in some particular field of criminal activity. In each of these phases the boy is supported by the sanction and the approbation of the delinquent group to which he belongs.

Differential Identification
Daniel Glaser

We describe identification somewhat unconventionally as "the choice of another, from whose perspective we view our own behavior." What we have called "differential identification" reconceptualizes Sutherland's theory in role-taking imagery, drawing heavily on Mead as well as on later refinements of role theory."[1] Most persons in our society are believed to identify themselves with both criminal and non-criminal persons in the course of their lives. Criminal identification may occur, for example, during direct experience in delinquent membership groups, through positive reference to criminal roles portrayed in mass media, or as a negative reaction to forces opposed to crime. The family probably is the principal non-criminal reference group, even for criminals. It is supplemented by many other groups of anti-criminal "generalized others."

The theory of differential identification, in essence, is that *a person pursues criminal behavior to the extent that he identifies himself with real or imaginary persons from whose perspective his criminal behavior seems acceptable.* Such a theory focuses attention on the interaction in which choice of models occurs, including the individual's interaction

[1]Cf. D. Glaser, "A Reconsideration of Some Parole Prediction Factors," *American Sociological Review,* XIX (June, 1954), 335–41; G. H. Mead, *Mind, Self, and Society* (Chicago: University of Chicago Press, 1934); N. N. Foote, "Identification as the Basis for a Theory of Motivation," *American Sociological Review,* XVI (February, 1951), 14–22; C. W. Mills, "Situated Actions and Vocabularies of Motive," *American Sociological Review,* V (December, 1940), 904–913; T. Shibutani, "Reference Groups as Perspectives," *American Journal of Sociology,* LX (May, 1955), 562–69.

with himself in rationalizing his conduct. This focus makes differential identification theory integrative, in that it provides a criterion of the relevance, for each individual case of criminality, of economic conditions, prior frustrations, learned moral creeds, group participation, or other features of an individual's life. These features are relevant to the extent that they can be shown to affect the choice of the other from whose perspective the individual views his own behavior. The explanation of criminal behavior on the basis of its imperfect correlation with any single variable of life-situations, if presented without specifying the intervening identification, evokes only a disconnected image of the relationship between the life-situation and the criminal behavior.

Sutherland supported the differential association theory by evidence that a major portion of criminality is learned through participation in criminal groups. Differential identification is a less disconnected explanation for such learning, and it also does not seem vulnerable to most of the objections to differential association. Because opposing and divisive roles frequently develop within groups, because our identification may be with remote reference groups or with imaginary or highly generalized others, and because identifications may shift rapidly with dialectical processes of role change and rationalization during social interaction, differential association, as ordinarily conceived, is insufficient to account for all differential identification.

In practice, the use of differential identification to explain lone crimes the source of learning which is not readily apparent (such as extremes of brutality or other abnormality in sex crimes) gives rise to speculation as to the "others" involved in the identification. The use of this theory to explain a gang member's participation in a professional crime against property presents fewer difficulties. In so far as the former types of offense are explained by psychiatrists without invoking instincts or other mystical forces, they usually are interpreted, on a necessarily speculative basis, in terms of the self conception which the offender develops in supporting his behavior and the sources of that self-conception. Such differential identification, in the case of most unusual and compulsive crimes, offers a less disconnected explanation than explanations derived from the alternative theories.[2]

[2]For an outstanding illustration of what becomes differential identification rather than the usual conception of differential association, applied to compulsive crimes, see Donald R. Cressey, "Differential Association and Compulsive Crimes," *Journal of Criminal Law, Criminology, and Police Science,* XLV (May–June, 1954), 29–40.

The one objection to the theory of differential association which cannot be met by differential identification is that it does not account for "accidental" crimes. Differential identification treats crime as a form of voluntary (i.e., anticipatory) behavior, rather than as an accident. Indeed, both legal and popular conceptions of "crime" exclude acts which are purely accidental, except for some legislation on felonious negligence, to which our discussion of criminality must be considered inapplicable. Even for the latter offenses, however, it is noteworthy that the consequences of accidentally committing a crime may be such as to foster identification with criminal-role models (whether one is apprehended for the accidental crime or not).

During any period, *prior identifications* and *present circumstances* dictate the selection of the persons with whom we identify ourselves. Prior identifications which have been pleasing tend to persist, but at any time the immediate circumstances affect the relative ease (or salience) of alternative identifications. That is why membership groups so frequently are the reference groups, although they need not be. That, too, is why those inclined to crime usually refrain from it in situations where they play satisfying conventional roles in which crime would threaten their acceptance. From the latter situations their identification with non-criminal others may eventually make them anticriminal. This is the essence of rehabilitation.[3]

There is evidence that, with the spread of urban secularism, social situations are becoming more and more deliberately rather than traditionally organized. Concurrently, roles are increasingly adjusted on the basis of the apparent authority or social pressure in each situation.[4] Our culture is said to give a common level of aspiration but different capacities of attainment according to socioeconomic class. At the same time, it is suggested, economic sources of status are becoming stronger while non-economic sources are becoming weaker. Therefore, when conventional occupational avenues of upward mobility are denied, people are more and more willing to seek the economic gains anticipated in crime, even at the risk of

[3]Cf. Donald R. Cressey, "Contradictory Theories in Correctional Group Therapy Programs," *Federal Probation*, XVIII (June, 1954), 20–26.

[4]This evidence has come most dramatically from recent studies of race relations. Cf. Joseph D. Lohman and Dietrich C. Reitzes, "Note on Race Relations in Mass Society," *American Journal of Sociology*, LVIII (November, 1952), 240–46; Dietrich C. Reitzes, "The Role of Organizational Structures," *Journal of Social Issues*, IX, No. 1 (1953), 37–44; William C. Bradbury, "Evaluation of Research in Race Relations," *Inventory of Research in Racial and Cultural Relations*, V (winter-spring, 1953), 99–133.

losing such non-economic sources of status as acceptance by non-criminal groups.[5] All these alleged features of urbanism suggest a considerable applicability of differential identification to "situational" and "incidental" crimes; focus on differential identification with alternative reference groups may reveal "situational imperatives" in individual life-histories.

Differential identification may be considered tautological, in that it may seem merely to make "crime" synonymous with "criminal identification." It is more than a tautology, however, if it directs one to observations beyond those necessary merely for the classification of behavior as criminal or noncriminal. It is a fruitful empirical theory leading one to proceed from the legalistic classification to the analysis of behavior as identification and role-playing.[6]

[5]Cf. Merton, *Social Theory and Social Structure* (Glencoe, Ill.: Free Press, 1949), chap. iv. It may be noteworthy here that classification of Illinois parolees by status ratings of the jobs to which they were going was more predictive than classification by the status of their father's occupation or by whether their job was of higher, lower, or equal status than their father's occupation. Regardless of their class background, the parolee's infractions seemed primarily to be a function of their failure to approach middle-class status (cf. Daniel Glaser, "A Reformulation and Testing of Parole Prediction Factors" [unpublished Ph.D. dissertation, University of Chicago, 1954], pp. 253–59).

[6]A number of examples of useful tautologies in social science are presented in Arnold Rose, *Theory and Method in the Social Sciences* (Minneapolis: University of Minnesota Press, 1954), pp. 328–38. In so far as a proposition is of heuristic use, however, one may question whether it is appropriately designated a "tautology."

Criminal Behavior and Learning Theory

C. R. Jeffery

Differential Association

One of the most popular theories of criminal behavior, especially among sociologists and social psychologists, is the notion that criminal behavior is learned behavior. The theory of differential association, put forth by Edwin H. Sutherland (1), is a learning theory which formulates the process as one whereby criminal behavior is learned in association with those who have criminal attitudes and values, as compared to associations with those who have noncriminal attitudes and values.

Sutherland's theory is now over thirty years old, and there has been no major theoretical revision nor any empirical verification of the theory during its lifespan (2). The purpose of this paper is to apply modern learning theory to differential association in order to place it in modern dress and to place it in a form which is empirically testable. The theory of differential association is not valid in its present form because, though it is basically sound in asserting that criminal behavior is learned, it does not make use of the learning principles which are now available as a result of experimental laboratory research.

Reprinted by special permission of the *Journal of Criminal Law, Criminology and Police Science,* copyright © by Northwestern University School of Law, Vol. 56, No. 3. pp. 294–300.

The principles were not available when Sutherland wrote, and it is therefore necessary to reappraise and reformulate his theory in terms of laboratory research carried on from 1940 to 1964.

Operant Behavior

Learning theory has revolved around the concept of conditioning, wherein behavior (responses) is related to the environment in which it occurs (stimuli). The Pavlovian type of classical conditioning is based upon a stimulus eliciting a response, the stimulus occurring before the response. Such conditioning procedures are of minor importance to sociologists since the behaviors involved are usually eye blinks, salivation, and galvanic skin responses. Much more important are operant behaviors, those behaviors emitted in the presence of given stimulus conditions and maintained by their consequences, that is, the changes they produce in the environment (3). The stimulus follows the response. Examples of operant behavior include verbal behavior, sexual behavior, driving a car, writing an article, wearing clothing, or living in a house. The concept of operant behavior is important to sociologists because most social behavior is of an operant nature. Social interaction is maintained by the effect it has on other people. Homans has used the concept of operant behavior to discuss what he calls elementary forms of social behavior (4).

Theory of Differential Reinforcement

Criminal behavior is operant behavior; that is, it is maintained by the changes it produces on the environment. A criminal response can produce money, a car, a radio, sex gratification, or the removal of an enemy. Most crimes are property offenses, and there the reinforcing stimulus is the stolen item. Crimes against the person may involve negative reinforcement, that is the removal of an aversive stimulus. Murder and assault are behaviors of this type. Voyeurism, fetishism, exhibitionism, and homosexuality are behaviors that are maintained by their consequences on the environment, though the nature of the reinforcement and the conditioning which led to this association of sex gratification with such consequences is not well understood at this time. What is involved, however, is the association of sex behavior with a forbidden sex object, such as occurs in the case of fetishism or homosexuality. The homosexual selects a male

rather than a female as the sex object because of his past conditioning history in the sexual area. Narcotics and alcohol are reinforcing
stimuli because of the biochemical changes they produce in the body.
In the case of narcotics addiction negative reinforcement is involved,
that is, the removal of an aversive stimulus (withdrawal distress).

Coupled with reinforcement for criminal behavior, however, is
punishment. Society through its legal system attaches aversive
consequences to criminal behavior. A criminal act may lead to
reinforcement, but it also may lead to punishment. The theory of
differential reinforcement states that a criminal act occurs in an
environment in which in the past the actor has been reinforced for
behaving in this manner, and the aversive consequences attached to
the behavior have been of such a nature that they do not control or
prevent the response. Criminal behavior is under the control of
reinforcing stimuli. An act of robbery produces money; it also may
produce being shot at by the victim or the police, being arrested,
being imprisoned, etc. However, if the aversive consequences of the
act control the behavior, then the behavior does not occur, e.g., if a
thief regards the consequences of his act as being shot or arrested, he
will not steal in that particular situation.

The theory assumes that (1) The reinforcing quality of different
stimuli differ for different actors depending on the past conditioning
history of each; (2) some individuals have been reinforced for
criminal behavior whereas other individuals have not been; (3) some
individuals have been punished for criminal behavior whereas other
individuals have not been; and (4) an individual will be intermittently
reinforced and/or punished for criminal behavior, that is, he will not
be reinforced or punished every time he commits a criminal act.
However, intermittent reinforcement will maintain a response pattern, and a large part of our social behavior is maintained on an
intermittent schedule of reinforcement. For example, if one man
steals and another does not under similar circumstances, at least
three variables can be noted immediately: (1) the reinforcing quality
of the stolen item; (2) past stealing responses which have been
reinforced; and (3) past stealing responses which have been punished. One of the criticisms often leveled at the theory of differential
association is that it does not adequately account for the differences
in behavior of those living in the same social environment: same
family, same slum area, same ethnic group, and so forth. There are
people living in high delinquency areas who are not delinquent;
there are Negroes who are not delinquent; and there are young adult
males who are not delinquent, though from a statistical point of view

these social factors are important. This is a very selective process, the reason being that each individual has a different conditioning history even though he is in an environment similar to others.

Criminal Associations

Sutherland's theory states that other human beings act as reinforcers for criminal activities. Human beings often act as social agents for reinforcers such as food, sex gratification, employment, medical aid, housing, trips, entertainment, and the like. We associate with those from whom we receive reinforcement.

In the case of criminal activity, other people can reinforce the behavior in several ways. They can use verbal praise to strengthen criminal behavior, which is what is meant by a reputation in a criminal or delinquent gang. Delinquents talk a great deal about their exploits and conquests in order to be praised. Another person can also act as a confederate in the commission of a criminal act, or can be an accessory after the fact: hiding the criminal, "fencing" stolen goods, and so forth. People also apply aversive consequences to criminal behavior by verbally reprimanding, arresting, or shooting the criminal. These behaviors constitute what Sutherland calls "attitudes" favorable or unfavorable to the commission of a criminal act.

A research problem presented by the theory of differential association is the problem of what environmental consequences maintain criminal behavior. Is it the material gain, or is it the social approval and group membership? Sutherland's theory assumes that the important variable is social reinforcement, and his theory ignores the obvious fact that money, cars, and sex are in themselves powerful reinforcers in our society. For this reason whenever one attempts to test the theory of differential association one discovers cases of criminals without criminal associations, or noncriminals with criminal associations. Criminal behavior can be maintained by money or cars without social approval. A man without prior association with criminals may murder his wife after a quarrel or when he discovers she has a lover. This act cannot be explained by the theory of differential association; it can be explained by the theory of differential reinforcement, since the removal of an aversive stimulus is negative reinforcement. The husband's interaction with his wife is crucial in this act of murder, but this interaction is not of a criminal nature until after the husband has killed his wife.

Stealing is reinforcing in and by itself whether other people know about it and reinforce it socially or not. Sutherland limited the learning of criminal behavior to situations involving criminal attitudes and associations. A stimulus for a criminal response need not involve a criminal component. A person learns to respond to food in legitimate ways. As a baby he was fed, and gradually he learns a series of behaviors associated with the acquisition of food—buying food, cooking food, verbally requesting food, and so forth. Among the responses which may in time be associated with or conditioned to food might be a response called "stealing food". If a boy asks his mother for a cookie and she refuses his request, he learns he can raid the cookie jar when mother is not looking. Stealing a cookie is reinforced by the cookie, not by the mother or a delinquent gang. This child has had no contact with a delinquent pattern, and yet learning has taken place which later on can generalize to other situations.

A person rides in an automobile as a child. He learns to drive a car as an adolescent. If an automobile is available to him either because he can afford one or because his father owns one, then there is no need to steal automobiles. However, if access to automobiles is only by stealing, then he steals. A girl can get a fur coat by working for it, by having a rich parent, by marrying a rich man, or by exchanging sex favors for a fur coat. Criminal behavior is learned, though this does not imply as Sutherland did that the learning process itself involves criminal associations.

The theory of differential association limits the learning process to criminal attitudes; the theory discussed in this paper states that criminal behavior can be learned in situations not containing criminals or criminal attitudes. For this reason a person living in a criminal environment will often not be a criminal, while criminals are found in noncriminal environments.

Other individuals are probably as important, if not more important, in the behavioral process as discriminative stimuli rather than reinforcing stimuli; that is, the presence of a given person will signal that a given act will or will not be reinforced. It is a well established sociological fact that individuals behave differently in the presence of certain people than in the absence of these same people. A man behaves differently when his wife is in the room than when she is absent; a worker behaves differently in the presence of the boss, and so forth. The reason is obvious; certain behaviors are reinforced or punished in the presence of a given person, and not in his absence. An obvious example from the area of criminology is the fact that people often behave differently in the presence of a policeman than in his absence. Motorists try to figure out when the patrolman is around and when he is not. A father may send his son out to commit criminal acts, or a delinquent companion may serve as a stimulus for a delinquent act. Certain criminal acts are reinforced or punished in the presence or absence of a given person. Associates therefore help to maintain criminal behavior either as reinforcing stimuli or as discriminative stimuli.

Social Variables and Conditioning

Most official criminal and delinquent acts are committed by young adult males who are members of a minority group and who live in slum areas. One of the characteristics of a slum area is deprivation; the inhabitants are without the important social reinforcers in our economy. They are not reinforced for lawful behavior. A middle class person can secure food, clothing, and automobiles by noncriminal means.

Behavior theory takes into account the level of deprivation and satiation of the actor. A person deprived of food will respond to food in a manner in which a satiated person will not. A sexually deprived person will respond to stimuli which will not arouse a sex response in a sexually satiated person. In prison camps inmates eat rats and engage in homosexual acts which they do not do when they have access to beefsteak and females.

Young adults are more criminalistic than older adults for the reason that they lack the responses necessary to produce reinforcement. If they develop acceptable responses for the reinforcers they want, the criminal responses are extinguished. Also, if they persist in a pattern of criminal behavior they are likely to come to the attention of the police and a new series of contingencies come to control the behavior, such as imprisonment.

The influence of television and comic books upon behavior is also better understood in terms of conditioning principles. Let us take, for example, one hundred wives watching a television show wherein a wife murders her husband. After viewing the program ninety-nine wives go back to their chores, the hundredth wife kills her husband. Ignoring for a moment the fact that we cannot really relate the behavior to a specific situation such as a television show (she might have killed her husband even if she did not see the show), we must further ask the question: "Why was it reinforcing for this woman to kill her husband, but not for the other ninety-nine?" We can assume that because of the nature of her relationship with her husband she wished to have him out of the way. She was responding as people do respond to aversive situations—she was removing the aversive stimulus.

It is sometimes assumed that if a child watches violence on television he will then behave in a violent manner. This argument assumes that the stimuli controlling the behavior are those presented on a television screen, whereas in fact the controlling stimuli are those in the child's own environment. Generalization of responses from a television program to those who observe the television program depends upon the extent to which the two environments are the same or similar, and upon the past conditioning of the observer. If we watch a television program in which Jewish children are placed in a gas chamber, this does not mean we are going out and place Jewish children in a gas chamber. We might, rather than imitating the Nazi, behave in such a manner as to prevent such acts from taking place in the future. The belief that a television stimulus will produce a given response in a viewer is based on the classical Pavlovian Stimulus-Response paradigm; however, the behaviors involved are usually operant rather than classical responses, and as such they depend upon environmental contingencies for their existence, not upon the television set.

Punishment

As was stated earlier, punishment is defined as the withdrawal of a reinforcing stimulus or the presentation of an aversive stimulus. There are several contradictory notions concerning the effect of punishment on behavior.

Punishment will reduce a response rate but, unless it is severe, punishment will not eliminate a response rate. Once the punishment is discontinued, the rate of response will return to its normal pattern. Some authors have stated that punishment is not the opposite of reinforcement, since the withdrawal of punishment results in an increase in the response that was formerly punished. However, it should be remembered that the withdrawal of a positive reinforcer results in a decrease in a response that was formerly reinforced.

The problem lies in the fact that punishment is usually paired with a response that is strongly maintained by other reinforcing stimuli, whereas a reinforced response is not paired with other contingencies. There are two stimuli—not one—controlling a punished response: the reinforcing stimulus (food), and the aversive stimulus (shock). If we punish a food response, we can expect that the response will continue because of the strength of food as a reinforcer. The removal of food as a reinforcer will eliminate the response. Punishment will completely elimate the response if food is not contingent on the response. Is the elimination of the food response due, however, to the removal of food (extinction), or is it due to punishment? Since we can accomplish the same results without punishment, we must conclude that the effective control is one based on extinction. We must, however, provide an alternative response pattern for obtaining food. Under these conditions punishment is an adequate control of behavior. Given two responses, one of which leads to food, the other to food and punishment, the organism will soon cease responding in the latter and respond only in the former situation (5).

Continuous punishment will not control behavior either, for satiation takes place the same as with a reinforcing stimulus. Food and money are not effective reinforcers except as they are placed on an intermittent schedule. Likewise, to control a delinquent by punishing him 24 hours a day is like trying to control him by feeding him ice-cream 24 hours a day.

Holz and Azrin have shown that punishment can become a discriminative stimulus if it is followed by reinforcement (6). If a rat is shocked before the food mechanism operates, it will administer a shock to itself in order to get food. This experiment led to the so-called masochistic rat. The statement is often made in psychiatric circles that masochistic people "like pain" or "must punish themselves" in order to get rid of guilt feelings. The literature is filled with case histories of men who committed crimes so that they would be punished. Such notions must be questioned in the face of experimental evidence. A person will not punish himself unless this punishment is paired with reinforcement. A child who is punished and then comforted or given candy will in future misbehave in order to get attention or sweets. Abrahamsen cites the example of a masochistic delinquent, a boy whose mother would punish him and then reward him with candy or ice-cream (7).

Mild punishment will be followed by a reduction in a response rate *if* it is a discriminative stimulus for non-reinforcement. Heavy punishment will be followed by an increase in a response rate *if* it is a discriminative stimulus for reinforcement.

These observations help to explain many of the contradictory statements about punishment and human behavior. *Under no condition, however, will punishment increase a response rate.* The Holz-Azrin experiment is often cited as evidence of the increase in response rate through punishment. Likewise, experimental work in the area of brain stimulation has led to observations of pleasure centers in the brain. A rat will shock itself at a high rate if an electrode is implanted in the proper area of the brain. This is used as another example of increasing the response rate by administering punishment. The problem here lies in the fact that the experimenter has classified shock as a painful stimulus. Rather the psychologist should talk about electrical stimulation to a given area of the brain as reinforcing, since it increases the rate of response. It is a well established fact that the stimulation of a nerve center can be pleasurable or reinforcing under some conditions but painful under others. A warm bath, for example, is reinforcing; but to be boiled alive is painful.

The Holz-Azrin experiment could be repeated wherein food was an S^D for shock—food would be presented and followed five seconds later by a shock. Under such conditions food would become a conditioned aversive stimulus, and the presentation of food would result in anxiety and conditioned suppression. Punishment is defined procedurally as a decrease in the response rate due to the presentation of an aversive stimulus contingent on the response. Yet punishment is followed by an increase in the response when punishment is a discriminative stimulus for reinforcement. The increase in the response rate is due to reinforcement (food) and not to punishment; and, since reinforcement is defined in terms of an increase in the response rate, there is no contradiction in such statements.

The experimental evidence supports the classical school (Bentham-Beccaria) of criminology in its statement that it is the certainty of punishment—not the severity—that deters people from criminal acts. One of the basic principles learned by every student of criminology is that "punishment does not deter". It is pointed out that for hundreds of years criminals have been punished by execution; yet we have an increasing rate of crime. Such statements are in gross error concerning the influence of punishment on behavior.

The statistical evidence on capital punishment reveals the source of one difficulty. About one percent of those eligible to be executed are thus punished. The *uncertainty* of capital punishment is one major factor in the system. Another factor is the *time* element. A consequence must be applied immediately if it is to be effective; yet in Chessman's case the consequence was applied eleven years after the behavior. Such punishment does not recondition or rehabilitate. There is also present the fact that execution makes further rehabilitation impossible. The lesson to be learned from capital punishment is not that punishment does not deter, but that the improper and sloppy use of punishment does not deter or rehabilitate.

The immediate consequence of a crime—rape, murder, robbery, burglary—is the presentation of a reinforcing stimulus: money, sex gratification, or the removal of an enemy or hated individual. When one commits a criminal act, the behavior, like all behavior, is under the control of reinforcing stimuli. There are no aversive stimuli in the environment at that moment. If a robber is caught in the act and is immediately punished, then the effect of punishment on behavior is radically different.

These statements on punishment are not to be interpreted as supporting any wholesale drive to pass laws that inflict heavier penalities on criminals. Increasing the penalties for crimes has the negative effect of making the punishment less certain. Throughout the history of penology an increase in punitive measures has been accompanied by an increase in measures, legal and otherwise, by which punishment is avoided. Severity of punishment can be gained only by sacrificing certainty. The Holz-Azrin experiment definitely established the fact that mild punishment can control a response, whereas heavy punishment under different conditions will not control the response. Legislators think in terms of severity of punishment, which is an inappropriate and harmful way to use punishment.

The use of punishment as it is currently administered by the legal system does not eliminate criminal behavior, although undoubtedly it does reduce the crime rate; but it does shape other behaviors, known as *avoidance responses*. An organism will respond in such a way as to avoid an aversive consequence. This, of course, is negative reinforcement. Escape responses, which are like avoidance responses except that they terminate an aversive stimulus rather than avoid it, likewise increase in rate in the face of aversive stimuli.

The avoidance and escape responses available to the criminal are many: avoid detection, don't leave fingerprints, hire a good lawyer, bribe the police, plead guilty to a reduced charge, plead insanity, tell the probation officer the right kind of story, etc. Law enforcement procedures shape a great deal of avoidance and escape behavior, but this can be quite unrelated to the behavior the law is trying to prevent and control.

It must also be kept in mind that the effects of punishment upon different people differ according to what they have to lose as a result. As an example, a university professor who was accused of a misdemeanor (contributing to the delinquency of a minor) was dismissed from his position, lost status in his professional community, and was divorced by his wife. He was never convicted, and he never served a day for this minor offense, and yet the aversive consequences to this man were much greater than a five to ten year sentence would be to a felon who had already served three terms in a prison.

Delinquent Subcultures

The theoretical work of Cohen, Cloward and Ohlin, Miller, Bloch and Niederhoffer, and Yablonsky could be reformulated in terms of reinforcement principles (8). The work of Cloward and Ohlin comes closest to the theoretical scheme presented in this paper; in fact, some readers might feel that it is a new way of talking about means, ends, and opportunities. A goal or end is obviously a general term referring to the environmental contingencies which have been labeled herein reinforcers. When Cloward and Ohlin note that different behaviors emerge in different subcultural groups, they are saying that in certain environments a response is reinforced, whereas in other environments it is not. There is nothing in the Cloward and Ohlin treatment of delinquency that contradicts what has been said in this paper concerning criminal behavior as learned behavior. The difference is that this paper attempts to look with a microscope at individual responses in a given envrionment, whereas Cloward and Ohlin were looking at social organization rather than individual behavior.

However, if we wish to deal with delinquent behavior, we must deal with individual behavior. We now know a great deal about the environment from which delinquents come; we know very little about the variables in this environment controlling individual responses. A systematic application of learning principles to criminal behavior might be appropriate at this stage in the development of criminology since criminality involves both an environment and a response to an environment. Research in learning processes has provided us with some principles with which we can investigate in greater detail the interaction of the criminal with his environment.

Summary

Criminal behavior is learned behavior. Sutherland's theory of differential association is basically correct; however, it needs to be revised in terms of recent advances in the psychology of learning. Operant behavior is behavior that is maintained by its consequences.

Criminal behavior is maintained by its consequences, both material and social. Such social variables as age, sex, social class, ethnic membership, and residential area influence the manner in which criminal behavior is conditioned.

Punishment decreases a response rate only if it is used in a consistent manner, and is applied near the time of the occurrence of the forbidden act. As it is used to control criminal behavior, punishment is likely to create avoidance and escape behaviors rather than law abiding behaviors.

References

1. SUTHERLAND & CRESSEY, PRINCIPLES OF CRIMINOLOGY 74 (5th ed. 1955).
2. Cressey, *Epidemiology and Individual Conduct,* PACIFIC SOC. REV. (Fall, 1960) 47; *The Theory of Differential Association,* SOCIAL PROBLEMS (Summer, 1960) 2; Glaser, *Criminality Theories and Behavioral Images,* AM. J. SOC. (March, 1956) 433.
3. SIDMAN, TACTICS OF SCIENTIFIC RESEARCH (1961); NURNBERGER, FERSTER, & BRADY, AN INTRODUCTION TO A SCIENCE OF HUMAN BEHAVIOR (1963); BACHRACH, EXPERIMENTAL FOUNDATIONS OF CLINICAL PSYCHOLOGY (1962); HILL, LEARNING (1963); LAWSON, LEARNING AND BEHAVIOR (1960); STAATS (Arthur & Carolyn), COMPLEX HUMAN BEHAVIOR (1963); WOLPE, THE CONDITIONING THERAPIES (1964).
4. HOMANS, SOCIAL BEHAVIOR: ITS ELEMENTARY FORMS (1961).
5. AZRIN, Punishment and Recovery during Fixed-Ratio Performance, 2 JOURNAL OF THE EXPERIMENTAL ANALYSIS OF BEHAVIOR 301–305 (1959); Azrin & Holz, *Punishment During Fixed-Interval Reinforcement,* 4 *Ibid.* 343–347 (1961).
6. HOLZ & AZRIN, *Discriminative Properties of Punishment,* 4 JOURNAL OF THE EXPERIMENTAL ANALYSIS OF BEHAVIOR 225–232 (1961); Holz & Azrin, *Inner Actions Between the Discriminative and Aversive Properties of Punishment,* 5 *Ibid.* 229–234 (1962).
7. ABRAHAMSEN, THE PSYCHOLOGY OF CRIME 65 (1960).
8. COHEN, DELINQUENT BOYS (1955); BLOCH & NIEDERHOFFER, THE GANG (1958); KVARACEUS & MILLER, DELINQUENT BEHAVIOR (1959); CLOWARD & OHLIN, DELINQUENCY AND OPPORTUNITY (1960); YABLONSKY, THE VIOLENT GANG (1962).

A Differential Association— Reinforcement Theory of Criminal Behavior
Robert L. Burgess / Ronald L. Akers

The nine formal propositions in which Sutherland expressed his theory of differential association may be analyzed in terms of behavior theory and research any may be reformulated as seven new propositions. (See Table 1).

I. "Criminal behavior is learned." VIII. "The process of learning criminal behavior by association with criminal and anti-criminal patterns involves all of the mechanisms that are involved in any other learning."

Since both the first and eighth sentences in the theory obviously form a unitary idea, it seems best to state them together. Sutherland was aware that these statements did not sufficiently describe the learning process,[1] but these two items leave no doubt that differential association theory was meant to fit into a general explanation of human behavior and, as much is unambiguously stated in the prefatory remarks of the theory: an "explanation of criminal behavior should be a specific part of a general theory of behavior."[2] Modern behavior theory as a general theory provides us with a

[1] Donald R. Cressey, "Epidemiology and Individual Conduct: A Case from Criminology," *Pacific Sociological Review*, 3 (Fall, 1960), p. 54.

[2] Edwin H. Sutherland and Donald R. Cressey, *Principles of Criminology*, 6th ed., Chicago: J. B. Lippincott Co., 1960, p. 75.

From "A Differential Association-Reinforcement Theory of Criminal Behavior," by Robert L. Burgess and Ronald L. Akers in *Social Problems*, Vol. 14, No. 2 (Fall, 1968), pp. 132–147. By permission of the authors and The Society for the Study of Social Problems.

good idea of what the mechanisms are that are involved in the process of acquiring behavior.[3]

According to this theory, there are two major categories of behavior. On the one hand, there is reflexive or *respondent* behavior which is behavior that is governed by the stimuli that elicit it. Such behaviors are largely associated with the autonomic system. The work of Pavlov is of special significance here. On the other hand, there is *operant* behavior: behavior which involves the central nervous system. Examples of operant behavior include verbal behavior, playing ball, driving a car, and buying a new suit. It has been found that this class of behavior is a function of its past and present environmental consequences. Thus, when a particular operant is followed by certain kinds of stimuli, that behavior's frequency of occurrence will increase in the future. These stimuli are called reinforcing stimuli or reinforcers[4] and include food, money, clothes, objects of various sorts, social attention, approval, affection and social status. This entire process is called positive reinforcement. One distinguishing characteristic of operant behavior as opposed to respondent behavior, then, is that the latter is a function of its

---

[3] It should be mentioned at the outset that there is more than one learning theory. The one we will employ is called Behavior Theory. More specifically, it is that variety of behavior theory largely associated with the name of B. F. Skinner. (*Science and Human Behavior*, New York: Macmillan, 1953.) It differs from other learning theories in that it restricts itself to the relations between observable, measurable behavior and observable, measurable conditions. There is nothing in this theory that denies the existence, or importance, or even the inherent interest of the nervous system or brain. However, most behavioral scientists in this area are extremely careful in hypothesizing intervening variables or constructs, whether they are egos, personalities, response sets, or some sort of internal computers. Generally they adopt the position that the only real value of a construct is its ability to improve one's predictions. If it does not, then it must be excluded in accordance with the rule of parsimony.

[4] It has been said by some that a tautology is involved here. But there is nothing tautological about classfying events in terms of their effects. As Skinner, *op. cit.*, pp. 72-73, has noted, this criterion is both empirical and objective. There is only one sure way of telling whether or not a given stimulus event is reinforcing to a given individual under given conditions and that is to make a direct test: observe the frequency of a selected behavior, then make a stimulus event contingent upon it and observe any change in frequency. If there is a change in frequency then we may classify the stimulus as reinforcing to the individual under the stated conditions. Our reasoning would become circular, however, if we went on to assert that a given stimulus strengthens the behavior *because* it is reinforcing. Furthermore, not all stimuli, when presented, will increase the frequency of the behavior which *produced* them. Some stimuli will increase the frequency of the behavior which *removes* them, still others will neither strengthen nor weaken the behavior which produced them. See Robert L. Burgess, Ronald L. Akers. "Are Operant Principles Tautological?" *The Psychological Record*, 16 (July, 1966), pp. 305-312.

antecedent stimuli, whereas the former is a function of its antecedent environmental consequences.

Typically, operant and respondent behaviors occur together in an individual's everyday behavior, and they interact in extremely intricate ways. Consequently, to fully understand any set of patterned responses, the investigator should observe the effects of the operants on the respondents as well as the effects of the respondents on the operants. The connections between operant and respondent behaviors are especially crucial to an analysis of attitudes, emotional and conflict behaviors.

In everyday life, different consequences are usually contingent upon different classes of behavior. This relationship between behavior and its consequences functions to alter the rate and form of behavior as well as its relationship to many features of the environment. The process of operant reinforcement is the most important process by which behavior is generated and maintained. There are, in fact, six possible environmental consequences relative to the Law of Operant Behavior. (1) A behavior may produce certain stimulus events and thereby increase in frequency. As we have indicated above, such stimuli are called positive reinforcers and the process is called positive reinforcement. (2) A behavior may remove, avoid, or terminate certain stimulus events and thereby increase in frequency. Such stimuli are termed negative reinforcers and the process, negative reinforcement. (3) A behavior may produce certain stimulus events and thereby decrease in frequency. Such stimuli are called aversive stimuli or, more recently, punishers.[5] The entire behavioral process is called positive punishment. (4) A behavior may remove or terminate certain stimulus events and thereby decrease in frequency. Such stimuli are positive reinforcers and the process is termed negative punishment. (5) A behavior may produce or remove certain stimulus events which do not change the behavior's frequency at all. Such stimuli are called neutral stimuli. (6) A behavior may no longer produce customary stimulus events and thereby decrease in frequency. The stimuli which are produced are neutral stimuli, and the process, extinction. When a reinforcing stimulus no longer functions to increase the future probability of the behavior which produced it, we say the individual is satiated. To restore the reinforcing property of the stimulus we need only deprive the individual of it for a time.[6]

[5] N. H. Azrin and D. F. Hake, "Conditioned Punishment," *Journal of the Experimental Analysis of Behavior*, 8 (September, 1965), pp. 279-293.
[6] See Jacob L. Gewirtz and Donald M. Baer, "Deprivation and Satiation of Social

The increase in the frequency of occurrence of a behavior that is reinforced is the very property of reinforcement that permits the fascinating variety and subtlety that occur in operant as opposed to respondent behavior. Another process producing the variety we see in behavior is that of *conditioning*. When a primary or unconditioned reinforcing stimulus such as food is repeatedly paired with a neutral stimulus, the latter will eventually function as a reinforcing stimulus as well. An illustration of this would be as follows. The milk a mother feeds to her infant is an unconditioned reinforcer. If the food is repeatedly paired with social attention, affection, and approval, these latter will eventually become reinforcing as will the mother herself as a stimulus object. Later these *conditioned reinforcers* can be used to strengthen other behaviors by making these reinforcers contingent upon those new behaviors.

Differential reinforcement may also alter the form of a response. This process is called *shaping* or *response* differentiation. It can be exemplified by a child learning to speak. At first, the parent will reinforce any vocalization, but as time wears on, and as the child grows older, the parent will differentially reinforce only those responses which successfully approximate certain criteria. The child will be seen to proceed from mere grunts to "baby-talk" to articulate speech.[7]

Of course, organisms, whether pigeons, monkeys or people, do not usually go around behaving in all possible ways at all possible times. In short, behavior does not occur in a vacuum; a given behavior is appropriate to a given situation. By appropriate we mean that reinforcement has been forthcoming only under these conditions and it is under these conditions that the behavior will occur. In other words, differential reinforcement not only increases the probability of a response, it also makes that response more probable upon the recurrence of conditions the same as or similar to those that were present during previous reinforcement. Such a process is called *stimulus control* or *stimulus discrimination*. For example, a child when he is first taught to say "daddy" may repeat it when any male is present, or even, in the very beginning, when any adult is present. But through differential reinforcement, the child will eventually only speak the word "daddy" when his father is present or in other

Reinforcers as Drive Conditions," *Journal of Abnormal and Social Psychology*, 57, 1958, pp. 165–172.

[7] This seems to be the process involved in learning to become a marihuana user. By successive approximations, the user learns (from others) to close on the appropriate techniques and effects of using marihuana. See Howard S. Becker, *Outsiders*, Glencoe, Ill.: The Free Press, 1963, pp. 41-58.

"appropriate" conditions. We may say that the father as a stimulus object, functions as a discriminative stimulus (S^D) setting the occasion for the operant verbal response "daddy" because in the past such behavior has been reinforced under such conditions.

It has also been discovered that the pattern or schedule of reinforcement is as important as the amount of reinforcement. For example, a *fixed-interval* schedule of reinforcement, where a response is reinforced only after a certain amount of time has passed, produces a lower rate of response than that obtained with reinforcement based on a *fixed-ratio* schedule where a response is reinforced only after a certain number of responses have already been emitted. Similarly a response rate obtained with a fixed-ratio schedule is lower than that obtained with a *variable-ratio* schedule, where reinforcement occurs for a certain proportion of responses randomly varied about some central value. A schedule of reinforcement, then, refers to the response *contingencies* upon which reinforcement depends. All of the various schedules of reinforcement, besides producing lawful response characteristics, produce lawful extinction rates, once reinforcement is discontinued. Briefly, behavior reinforced on an intermittent schedule takes longer to extinguish than behavior reinforced on a continuous schedule.

This concept, schedules of reinforcement, is one the implications of which are little understood by many behavioral scientists, so a few additional words are in order. First of all, social reinforcements are for the most part intermittent. One obvious result of this fact is the resistance to extinction and satiation of much social behavior, desirable as well as undesirable. This is not peculiar to human social behavior, for even lower organisms seldom are faced with a continuous reinforcement schedule. Nevertheless, reinforcements mediated by another organism are probably much less reliable than those produced by the physical environment. This is the case because social reinforcement depends upon behavioral processes in the reinforcer which are not under good control by the reinforcee. A more subtle, though essentially methodological, implication of this is that because most social behaviors are maintained by complex intermittent schedules which have been shaped over a long period of time, a social observer, newly entering a situation may have extreme difficulty in immediately determining exactly what is maintaining a particular behavior or set of behaviors. Nor can the individual himself be expected to be able to identify his own contingencies of reinforcement.[8]

[8] Cressey encountered this problem in trying to get trust violators to reconstruct past associations. Cressey, *Other People's Money*, Glencoe, Ill.: The Free Press, 1953, p. 149.

An important aspect of this theory is the presentation of the general ways that stimuli and responses can be formed into complex constellations of stimulus-response events. Although the basic principles are simple and must be separated to distinguish and study them, in actual life the principles function in concert, and consist of complex arrays and constellations.[9] Such complexity can be seen in the fact that single S-R events may be combined into sequences on the basis of conditioning principles. That is, responses can be thought to have stimulus properties. In addition, more than one response may come under the control of a particular stimulus. Thus, when the stimulus occurs, it will tend to set the occasion for the various responses that have been conditioned to it. These responses may be competitive, that is, only one or the other can occur. When this is so, the particular response which does occur may also depend upon other discriminative stimuli present in the situation that control only one or the other response. Finally, while some of the stimuli to which an individual responds emanate from the external environment, social and otherwise, some come from his own behavior. An individual is, then, not only a source of responses, he is also a source of some stimuli—stimuli that can effect his own behavior.

The most general behavioral principle is the Law of Operant Behavior which says that behavior is a function of its past and current environmental consequences. There have been numerous studies with children[10] as well as adults[11] which indicate that individual behavior conforms to this law. Of much more interest to sociologists is an experiment designed by Azrin and Lindsley in 1956[12] to investigate cooperative social behavior. Their study demonstrated that cooperative behavior could be developed, maintained, eliminated and reinstated solely through the manipulation of the contingency between reinforcing stimuli and the cooperative response. This basic finding has received much subsequent support. It has also been demonstrated that not only cooperative behavior, but also competitive behavior and leading and following behavior are a function of their past and present consequences.

[9] Arthur Staats, "An Integrated-Functional Learning Approach to Complex Human Behavior," *Technical Report 28*, Contract ONR and Arizona State University, 1965.

[10] See, for example, S. W. Bijou and P. T. Sturges, "Positive Reinforcers for Experimental Studies with Children—Consumables and Manipulatables," *Child Development*, 30, 1959, pp. 151-170.

[11] J. G. Holland, "Human Vigilance," *Science*, 128, 1959, pp. 61-67; Harold Weiner, "Conditioning History and Human Fixed-Interval Performance," *Journal of the Experimental Analysis of Behavior*, 7 (September, 1964), pp. 383-385.

[12] N. H. Azrin and O. R. Lindsley, "The Reinforcement of Cooperation Between Children," *The Journal of Abnormal and Social Psychology*, 52 (January, 1956).

Another of the behavioral principles we mentioned was that of stimulus discrimination. A discriminative stimulus is a stimulus in the presence of which a particular operant response is reinforced. Much of our behavior has come under the control of certain environmental, including social stimuli because in the past it has been reinforced in the presence of those stimuli. In an experiment by Donald Cohen,[13] a normal 13-year-old boy named Justin, when placed under identical experimental conditions emitted different behaviors depending upon whether his partner was his mother, brother, sister, friend, or a stranger. The results of this investigation demonstrated that Justin's social behavior was differentially controlled by reinforcement; but it also demonstrated that his behavior was different depending upon the social stimuli present, thus reaffirming the principle of stimulus discrimination. In other words, the dynamic properties of his social behavior, whether cooperative, competitive, leading or following, were controlled by his previous extra-experimental history with his teammates, although the experimenter could change those behaviors by experimentally altering the contingencies of reinforcement. It is, of course, almost a truism to say that an individual behaves differently in the presence of different people. The significance of this experiment, however, is that the investigator was able to isolate the determining variables and the principles by which they operated to produce this common phenomenon.

While this is by no means a complete survey of the relevant experimental tests of the behavioral principles outlined above, it may serve to point out that many forms of "normal" social behavior function according to the Law of Operant Behavior. But what about "deviant" behavior? Can we be sure these same principles are operating here? Unfortunately there have been no studies which attempt to test directly the relevance of these behavioral principles to criminal behavior. But there have been several experimental investigations of deviant behaviors emitted by mental patients. For example, in a study by Ayllon and Michael,[14] it was shown that the bizarre behaviors of psychotics functioned according to these learning principles. In this particular study various behavioral problems of psychotic patients were "cured" through the manipulation of rein-

[13] Donald J. Cohen, "Justin and His Peers: an Experimental Analysis of a Child's Social World," *Child Development*, 33, 1962.

[14] T. Ayllon and J. Michael, "The Psychiatric Nurse as a Behavioral Engineer," *Journal of the Experimental Analysis of Behavior*, 2, 1959, pp. 323–334.

forcement contingencies. Such principles as extinction, negative and positive reinforcement, and satiation were effectively utilized to eliminate the unwanted behaviors.[15] This study was one of the first experimental tests of the contention that not only conforming but also many unusual, inappropriate, or undesirable behaviors are shaped and maintained through social reinforcement. In another experiment Isaacs, Thomas, and Goldiamond[16] demonstrate that complex adjustive behaviors can be operantly conditioned in long-term psychotics by manipulating available reinforcers.

In yet another investigation,[17] the personnel of a mental hospital ward for schizophrenics recorded the behavior of the patients and provided consequences to it according to certain preestablished procedures. Without going into the many important details of this long investigation, we may note that in each of the six experiments that were carried out, the results demonstrate that reinforcement was effective in maintaining desired performances, even though these were "back-ward" psychotics who had resisted all previous therapy, including psychoanalysis, electroshock therapy, lobotomies and so forth.

> In each experiment, the performance fell to a near zero level when the established response-reinforcement relation was discontinued. . . . The standard procedure for reinforcement had been to provide tokens . . . [exchanged] for a variety of reinforcers. Performance decreased when this response-reinforcement relation was disrupted (1) by delivering tokens independently of the response while still allowing exchange of tokens for the reinforcers (Exp II and III), (2) by discontinuing the token system entirely but providing continuing access to the reinforcers (Exp IV), or (3) by discontinuing the delivery of tokens for a previously reinforced response while simultaneously providing tokens for a different, alternative response

[15] There is, of course, no intention on our part to equate "mental" illness or similarly severe behavior problems with criminal behavior. The only connection that we are making is that both may be seen to function according to the same basic behavioral principles and both may be in opposition to established norms.

[16] W. Isaacs, J. Thomas, and I. Goldiamond, "Application of Operant Conditioning to Reinstate Verbal Behavior in Psychotics," *Journal of Speech and Disorders*, 25, 1960, pp. 8–12.

[17] T. Ayllon and N. Azrin, "The Measurement and Reinforcement of Behavior of Psychotics," *Journal of the Experimental Analysis of Behavior*, 8 (November, 1965), pp. 357–383.

(Exp. I and VI). Further, the effectiveness of the re-inforcement procedure did not appear to be limited to an all-or-none basis. Patients selected and performed the assignment that provided the larger number of tokens when reinforcement was available for more than one assignment (Exp V).[18]

Again, we cannot review all of the relevant literature, yet perhaps the three investigations cited will serve to emphasize that many forms of deviant behavior are shaped and maintained by various contingencies of reinforcement.[19] Given this experimental evidence we would amend Sutherland's first and eighth propositions to read:

I. Criminal behavior is learned according to the principles of operant conditioning.

II. "Criminal behavior is learned in interaction with other persons in the process of communication."

As DeFleur and Quinney have noted, the major implication of this proposition is that symbolic interaction is a necessary condition for the learning of criminal behavior.[20] Of direct relevance to this is an experiment designed to test the relative significance of verbal instructions and reinforcement contingencies in generating and maintaining a certain class of behaviors.[21] In brief, the results indicated that behavior could not be maintained solely through verbal instructions. However, it was also discovered that it was an extremely arduous task to shape a set of complex behaviors without using verbal instructions as discriminative stimuli. Behavior was quickly and effectively developed and maintained by a combination of verbal instructions *and* reinforcement consequences. Symbolic interaction is, then, not enough, contingencies of reinforcement must also be present.

From the perspective of modern behavior theory, two aspects

[18] *Ibid.*, p. 381.

[19] See also J. J. Eysenck (ed.), *Experiments in Behaviour Therapy,* New York: Pergamon Press, The Macmillan Company, 1964. L. Krasner and L. Ullman, *Research in Behavior Modification,* New York: Holt, Rinehart and Winston, 1965. L. Ullman and L. Krasner, *Case Studies in Behavior Modification,* New York: Holt, Rinehart and Winston, 1964.

[20] Melvin DeFleur and Richard Quinney, "A Reformulation of Sutherland's Differential Association Theory and a Strategy for Empirical Verification," *Journal of Research in Crime and Delinquency,* 3 (January, 1966), p. 3.

[21] T. Ayllon and N. Azrin, "Reinforcement and Instructions with Mental Patients," *Journal of the Experimental Analysis of Behavior,* 7, 1964, pp. 327–331.

of socialization are usually considered to distinguish it from other processes of behavioral change: (1) Only those behavioral changes occurring through learning are considered relevant; (2) only the changes in behavior having their origins in interaction with other persons are considered products of socialization.[22] Sutherland's theory may, then, be seen to be a theory of differential socialization since he, too, restricted himself to learning having its origin in interaction with other persons. While social learning is, indeed, important and even predominant, it certainly does not exhaust the learning process. In short, we may learn (and, thus, our behavior would be modified) without any direct contact with another person. As such, Sutherland's theory may be seen to suffer from a significant lacuna in that it neglected the possibility of deviant behavior being learned in nonsocial situations. Consequently, to be an adequate theory of deviant behavior, the theory must be amended further to include those forms of deviant behavior that are learned in the absence of social reinforcement. Other people are not the only source of reinforcement although they are the most important. As Jeffery[23] has aptly noted, stealing is reinforcing in and by itself whether other people know about it and reinforce it socially or not. The same may be said to apply to many forms of aggressive behaviors.[24]

There are many studies which are relevant to social interaction and socialization on the one hand, and Sutherland's second proposition on the other. For example, in a study by Lott and Lott[41] it was found that when child A was reinforced in the presence of child B, child A would later select child B as a companion. The behavior of selecting child B was not the behavior that was reinforced. The experimental conditions simply paired child B with positive reinforcement. In accordance with the principle of conditioning, child B had become a conditioned positive reinforcer. As such any behavior which produced the presence of child B would be strengthened, such behaviors, for example, as verbal responses requesting child B's

[22] Paul E. Secord and Carl W. Backman, *Social Psychology*, New York: McGraw-Hill, 1964.

[23] C. R. Jeffery, "Criminal Behavior and Learning Theory," *The Journal of Criminal Law, Criminology and Police Science*, 56 (September, 1965), pp. 294–300.

[24] For some evidence that aggressive behavior may be of a respondent as well as an operant nature, see N. Azrin, R. Hutchinson, and R. McLaughlin, "The Opportunity for Aggression as an Operant Reinforcer during Aversive Stimulation," *Journal of the Experimental Analysis of Behavior*, 8 (May, 1965), pp. 171–180.

[25] B. E. Lott and A. J. Lott, "The Formation of Positive Attitudes Toward Group Members," *The Journal of Abnormal and Social Psychology*, 61, 1960, pp. 297–300.

company. Thus, as Staats[26] has noted, the results of this study indicate that the concepts of reinforcing stimuli and group cohesion are related when analyzed in terms of an integrated set of learning principles.

Glaser[27] has attempted to reformulate Sutherland's differential association theory in terms of social identification. It should be recognized, however, that identification as well as modeling and imitative behavior (which are usually associated with identification) comprise just one feature of the socialization process. Furthermore, such behavior may be analyzed quite parsimoniously with the principles of modern behavior theory. For example, in a study by Bandura and Ross,[28] a child experienced the pairing of one adult with positive reinforcers. Presumably this adult would become a conditioned reinforcer. And indeed, later it was found that the child imitated this adult more than he did an adult who was not paired with positive reinforcers. That is, the one adult, as he became a stronger reinforcer, had also become a stronger S^D for imitating or following behavior. Thus, Bandura's and Ross's results demonstrate that imitating or following behavior is at least in part a function of the reinforcing value of people as social stimuli.

> On the basis of these results it is suggested that a change in the reinforcing value of an individual will change his power as a stimulus controlling other people's behavior in various ways. An increase in the reinforcing value of an individual will increase verbal and motor approach, or companionable responses, respectful responses, affectionate behavior, following behavior, smiling, pleasant conversation, sympathetic responses and the like.[29]

The relevance of these studies is that they have isolated some of the determining variables whereby the behavior of one person is influenced or changed by the behavior of another as well as the principles by which these variables operate. We have, of course, only scratched the surface. Many other variables are involved. For in-

[26] Arthur Staats, *Human Learning*, New York: Holt, Rinehart and Winston, 1964, p. 333.

[27] Daniel Glaser, "Criminality Theories and Behavioral Images," *American Journal of Sociology*, 61 (March, 1965), pp. 433–444.

[28] A. Bandura, D. Ross, and S. Ross, "A Comparative Test of the Status Envy, Social Power and the Secondary Reinforcement Theories of Identification Learning," *Journal of Abnormal and Social Psychology*, 67, 1963, pp. 527–534.

[29] Staats, 1964, *op. cit.*, p. 333.

stance, not all people are equally effective in controlling or influencing the behavior of others. The person who can mediate the most reinforcers will exercise the most power. Thus, the parent, who controls more of his child's reinforcers, will exercise more power than an older sibling or the temporary "baby sitter." As the child becomes older and less dependent upon the parent for many of his reinforcers, other individuals or groups such as his peers may exercise more power. Carrying the analysis one step further, the person who has access to a large range of aversive stimuli will exert more power than one who has not. Thus a peer group may come to exercise more power over a child's behavior than the parent even though the parent may still control a large share of the child's positive reinforcers.

In addition to the reinforcing function of an individual or group, there is, as seen in the Cohen and the Bandura and Ross studies, the discriminative stimulus function of a group. For example, specific individuals as physical stimuli may acquire discriminative control over an individual's behavior. The child in our example above is reinforced for certain kinds of behaviors in the presence of his parent, thus the parent's presence may come to control this type of behavior. He is reinforced for different behaviors in the presence of his peers, who then come to set the occasion for this type of behavior. Consequently this proposition must be amended to read:

II. Criminal behavior is learned both in nonsocial situations that are reinforcing or discriminative, and through that social interaction in which the behavior of other persons is reinforcing or discriminative for criminal behavior.

III. "The principal part of the learning of criminal behavior occurs within intimate personal groups."

In terms of our analysis, the primary group would be seen to be the major source of an individual's social reinforcements. The bulk of behavioral training which the child receives occurs at a time when the trainers, usually the parents, possess a very powerful system of reinforcers. In fact, we might characterize a primary group as a generalized reinforcer (one associated with many reinforcers, conditioned as well as unconditioned). And, as we suggested above, as the child grows older, groups other than the family may come to control a majority of an individual's reinforcers, e.g., the adolescent peer group.

To say that the primary group is the principal molder of an individual's behavioral repertoire is not to ignore social learning which may occur in other contexts. As we noted above, learning from social models can be adequately explained in terms of these behavioral principles. The analysis we employed there can also be extended to learning from the mass media and from "reference" groups. In any case, we may alter this proposition to read:

III. The principal part of the learning of criminal behavior occurs in those groups which comprise the individual's major source of reinforcements.

IV. **"When criminal behavior is learned, the learning includes (a) techniques of committing the crime, which are sometimes very complicated, sometimes very simple; (b) the specific direction of motives, drives, rationalizations, and attitudes."**

A study by Klaus and Glaser[30] as well as many other studies[31] indicate that reinforcement contingencies are of prime importance in learning various behavioral techniques. And, of course, many techniques, both simple and complicated, are specific to a particular deviant act such as jimmying, picking locks of buildings and cars, picking pockets, short- and big-con techniques, counterfeiting and safe-cracking. Other techniques in criminal behavior may be learned in conforming or neutral contexts, e.g., driving a car, signing checks, shooting a gun, etc. In any event, we need not alter the first part of this proposition.

The second part of this proposition does, however, deserve some additional comments. Sutherland's major focus here seems to be motivation. Much of what we have already discussed in this paper often goes under the general heading of motivation. The topic of motivation is as important as it is complex. This complexity is related to the fact that the same stimulus may have two functions: it may be both a reinforcing stimulus and a discriminative stimulus controlling the behavior which is followed by reinforcement.[32] Thus, motivation

---

[30] D. J. Klaus and R. Glaser, "Increasing Team Proficiency Through Training," Pittsburgh: American Institute of Research, 1960.

[31] See Robert L. Burgess, "Communication Networks and Behavioral Consequences," forthcoming.

[32] A central principle underlying this analysis is that reinforcing stimuli, both positive and negative, elicit certain respondents. Unconditioned reinforcers elicit these responses without training, conditioned reinforcers elicit such responses through respondent conditioning. Staats and Staats (*Complex Human Behavior*, New York: Holt, Rinehart and Winston, 1964) have characterized such respondents as "attitude" responses. Thus, a positive reinforcer elicits a positive attitude. Furthermore, these respondents have stimulus characteristics which may become discriminative stimuli setting the occasion for a certain class of operants called "striving" responses for

may be seen to be a function of the processes by which stimuli acquire conditioned reinforcing value and become discriminative stimuli. Reinforcers and discriminative stimuli here would become the dependent variables; the independent variables would be the conditioning procedures previously mentioned and the level of deprivation. For example, when a prisoner is deprived of contact with members of the opposite sex, such sex reinforcers will become much more powerful. Thus, those sexual reinforcers that are available, such as homosexual contact, would come to exert a great deal of influence and would shape behaviors that would be unlikely to occur without such deprivation. And, without going any further into this topic, some stimuli may be more reinforcing, under similar conditions of deprivation, for certain individuals or groups than for others. Furthermore, the satiation of one or more of these reinforcers would allow for an increase in the relative strength of others.

Much, therefore, can be learned about the distinctive characteristics of a group by knowing what the available and effective reinforcers are and the behaviors upon which they are contingent. Basically, we are contending that the nature of the reinforcer system and the reinforcement contingencies are crucial determinants of individual and group behavior. Consequently, a description of an individual's or group's reinforcers, and an understanding of the principles by which reinforcers affect behavior, would be expected to yield a great deal of knowledge about individual and group deviant behavior.

Finally, the rationalizations which Cressey identifies with regard to trust violators and the peculiar extensions of "defenses to crimes" or "techniques of neutralization" by which deviant behavior is justified, as identified by Sykes and Matza,[33] may be analyzed as operant behaviors of the escape or avoidance type which are maintained because they have the effect of avoiding or reducing the punishment that comes from social disapproval by oneself as well as by others. We may, therefore, rewrite this proposition to read:

    IV.   The learning of criminal behavior, including specific techniques, attitudes, and avoidance procedures, is a function of the

positive reinforcers and escape and/or avoidance behaviors for negative reinforcers. These respondents and their attendant stimuli may be generalized to other reinforcing stimuli. Thus, striving responses can be seen to generalize to new positive reinforcers since these also will elicit the respondent responses and their characteristic stimuli which have become S^D's for such behavior.

[33] Cressey, *Other People's Money, op. cit.,* pp. 93–138. G. M. Sykes and David Matza, "Techniques of Neutralization: A Theory of Delinquency," *American Sociological Review,* 22 (December, 1957), pp. 664–670.

effective and available reinforcers, and the existing reinforcement contingencies.

V. "The specific direction of motives and drives is learned from definitions of the legal codes as favorable or unfavorable."

In this proposition, Sutherland appears to be referring, at least in part, to the concept "norm" which may be defined as a statement made by a number of the members of a group, not necessarily all of them, prescribing or proscribing certain behaviors at certain times.[34] We often infer what the norms of a group are by observing reaction to behavior, i.e., the sanctions applied to, or reinforcement and punishment consequences of, such behavior. We may also learn what a group's norms are through verbal or written statements. The individual group member also learns what is and is not acceptable behavior on the basis of verbal statements made by others, as well as through the sanctions (i.e., the reinforcing or aversive stimuli) applied to his behavior (and other norm violators) by others.

Behavior theory specifies the place of normative statements and sanctions in the dynamics of acquiring "conforming" or "normative" behavior. Just as the behavior and even the physical characteristics of the individual may serve discriminative functions, verbal behavior, and this includes normative statements, can be analyzed as S^D's. A normative statement can be analyzed as an S^D indicating that the members of a group ought to behave in a certain way in certain circumstances. Such "normative" behavior would be developed and maintained by social reinforcement. As we observed in the Ayllon-Azrin study[35] of instructions and reinforcement contingencies, such verbal behavior would not maintain any particular class of behaviors if it were not at least occasionally backed by reinforcement consequences. Extending their analysis, an individual would not "conform" to a norm if he did not have a past history of reinforcement for such conforming behavior. This is important, for earlier we stated that we can learn a great deal about a group by knowing what the effective reinforcers are and the behaviors upon which they are contingent. We may now say that we can learn a great deal about an individual's or a group's behavior when we are able to specify, not only what the effective reinforcers are, but also what the rules or norms are by which these reinforcers are applied.[36]

[34] George C. Homans, *Social Behavior: Its Elementary Forms*, New York: Harcourt, Brace and World, 1961.

[35] Ayllon and Azrin, 1964, *op. cit.*

[36] Staats and Staats, *op. cit.*

For these two types of knowledge will tell us much about the types of behavior that the individual will develop or the types of behaviors that are dominant in a group.

For example, it has often been noted that most official criminal acts are committed by members of minority groups who live in slums. One distinguishing characteristic of a slum is the high level of deprivation of many important social reinforcers. Exacerbating this situation is the fact that these people, in contrast to other groups, lack the behavioral repertoires necessary to produce reinforcement in the prescribed ways. They have not been and are not now adequately reinforced for lawful or normative behavior. And as we know from the Law of Operant Reinforcement, a reinforcer will increase the rate of occurrence of any operant which produces it. Furthermore, we would predict that given a large number of individuals under similar conditions, they are likely to behave in similar ways. Within such groups, many forms of social reinforcement may become contingent upon classes of behaviors which are outside the larger society's normative requirements. Norms and legal codes, as discriminative stimuli, will only control the behavior of those who have experienced the appropriate learning history. If an individual has been, and is, reinforced for such "normative" behavior, that behavior will be maintained in strength. If he has not been, and is not now reinforced for such behaviors they would be weak, if they existed in his repertoire at all. And, importantly, the reinforcement system may shape and maintain another class of behaviors which do result in reinforcement and such behaviors may be considered deviant or criminal by other members of the group. Thus we may formulate this proposition to read:

V.   *The specific class of behaviors which are learned and their frequency of occurrence are a function of the reinforcers which are effective and available, and the rules or norms by which these reinforcers are applied.*

VI.   **"A person becomes delinquent because of an excess of definitions favorable to violation of law over definitions unfavorable to violation of law."**

This proposition is generally considered the heart of Sutherland's theory; it is the principle of differential association. It follows directly from proposition V, and we must now refer back to that proposition. In proposition V, the use of the preposition "from" in the phrase, "learned from definitions of the legal codes as favorable or unfavorable," is somewhat misleading. The meaning here is not so much that learning results *from* these definitions as it is that they form part of the *content* of one's learning, determining which direction one's behavior will go in relation to the law, i.e., lawabiding or lawbreaking.

These definitions of the law make lawbreaking seem either appropriate or inappropriate. Those definitions which place lawbreaking in a favorable light in a sense can be seen as essentially norms of evasion and/or norms directly conflicting with conventional norms. They are, as Sykes and Matza and Cressey note, "techniques of neutralization," "rationalizations," or "verbalizations" which make criminal behavior seem "all right" or justified, or which provide defenses against self-reproach and disapproval from others.[37] The principle of negative reinforcement would be of major significance in the acquisition and maintenance of such behaviors.

This analysis suggests that it may not be an "excess" of one kind of definition over another in the sense of a cumulative ratio, but rather in the sense of the relative amount of discriminative stimulus value of one set of verbalizations or normative statements over another. As we suggested in the last section, normative statements are, themselves, behaviors that are a function of reinforcement consequences. They, in turn, may serve as discriminative stimuli for other operant behaviors (verbal and nonverbal). But recall that reinforcement must be forthcoming, at least occasionally, before a verbal statement can continue as a discriminative stimulus. Bear in mind, also, that behavior may produce reinforcing consequences even in the absence of any accompanying verbal statements.

In other terms, a person will become delinquent if the official norms or laws do not perform a discriminative function and thereby control "normative" or conforming behavior. We know from the Law of Differential Reinforcement that that operant which produces the most reinforcement will become dominant if it results in reinforcement. Thus, if lawful behavior did not result in reinforcement, the strength of the behavior would be weakened, and a state of deprivation would result, which would, in turn, increase the probability that other behaviors would be emitted which are reinforced, and such behaviors would be strengthened. And, of course, these

---

[37] Sykes and Matza, *op. cit.,* Cressey, *Other People's Money, op. cit.,* pp. 93–138; Donald R. Cressey, "The Differential Association Theory and Compulsive Crimes," *Journal of Criminal Law, Criminology and Police Science,* 45 (May–June, 1954), pp. 29–40; Donald R. Cressey, "Social Psychological Foundations for Using Criminals in the Rehabilitation of Criminals," *Journal of Research in Crime and Delinquency,* 2 (July, 1965), pp. 45–59. See revised proposition IV.

behaviors, though common to one or more groups, may be labelled deviant by the larger society. And such behavior patterns, themselves, may acquire conditioned reinforcing value and, subsequently, be enforced by the members of a group by making various forms of social reinforcement, such as social approval, esteem, and status contingent upon that behavior.

The concept "excess" in the statement, "excess of definitions favorable to violation of law," has been particularly resistant to operationalization. A translation of this concept in terms of modern behavior theory would involve the "balance" of reinforcement consequences, positive and negative. The Law of Differential Reinforcement is crucial here. That is, a person would engage in those behaviors for which he had been reinforced most highly in the past. (The reader may recall that in the Ayllon-Azrin study with schizophrenics, it was found that the patients selected and performed those behaviors which provided the most reinforcers when reinforcement was available for more than one response.) Criminal behavior would, then, occur under those conditions where an individual has been most highly reinforced for such behavior, and the aversive consequences contingent upon the behavior have been of such a nature that they do not perform a "punishment function."[38] This leads us to a discussion of proposition VII. But, first, let us reformulate the sixth proposition to read:

VI. Criminal behavior is a function of norms which are discriminative for criminal behavior, the learning of which takes place when such behavior is more highly reinforced than noncriminal behavior.

VII. "Differential associations may vary in frequency, duration, priority, and intensity."

In terms of our analysis, the concepts frequency, duration, and priority are straightforward enough. The concept *intensity* could be operationalized to designate the number of the individual's positive and negative reinforcers another individual or group controls, as well

---

[38] This, then, is essentially differential reinforcement as Jeffery presents it. We have attempted to show how this is congruent with differential association. Further, while Jeffery ignores the key concepts of "definitions" and "excess" we have incorporated them into the reformulation. These definitions, viewed as verbalizations, become discriminative stimuli; and "excess" operates to produce criminal behavior in two related ways: (1) verbalizations conducive to law violation have greater discriminative stimulus value than other verbalizations, and (2) criminal behavior has been more highly reinforced and has produced fewer aversive outcomes than has law abiding behavior in the conditioning history of the individual.

as the reinforcement value of that individual or group. As previously suggested the group which can mediate the most positive reinforcers and which has the most reinforcement value, as well as access to a larger range of aversive stimuli, will exert the most control over an individual's behavior.

There is a good reason to suspect, however, that Sutherland was not so much referring to differential associations with other persons, as differential associations with criminal *patterns*. If this supposition is correct, then this proposition can be clarified by relating it to differential contingencies of reinforcement rather than differential social associations. From this perspective, the experimental evidence with regard to the various schedules of reinforcement is of major importance. There are three aspects of the schedules of reinforcement which are of particular importance here: (1) the *amount* of reinforcement: the greater the amount of reinforcement, the higher the response rate; (2) the *frequency* of reinforcement which refers to the number of reinforcements per given time period: the shorter the time period between reinforcements, the higher the response rate; and (3) the *probability* of reinforcement which is the reciprocal of responses per reinforcement: the lower the ratio of responses per reinforcement, the higher the rate of response.[39]

Priority, frequency, duration, and intensity of association with criminal persons and groups are important to the extent that they insure that deviant behavior will receive greater amounts of reinforcement at more frequent intervals or with a higher probability than conforming behavior. But the frequency, probability, and amount of reinforcement are the crucial elements. This means that it is the coming under the control of contingencies of reinforcement that selectively produces the criminal definitions and behavior. Consequently, let us rewrite this proposition to read:

VII.   *The strength of criminal behavior is a direct function of the amount, frequency, and probability of its reinforcement.*

IX.   "While criminal behavior is an expression of general needs and values, it is not explained by those general needs and values since noncriminal behavior is an expression of the same needs and values."

[39]R. T. Kelleher and L. R. Gollub, "A Review of Positive Conditioned Reinforcement," *Journal of the Experimental Analysis of Behavior* (October, 1962), pp. 543–597. Because the emission of a fixed ratio or variable ratio of responses requires a period of time, the rate of responding will indirectly determine the frequency of reinforcement.

In this proposition, Sutherland may have been reacting, at least in part, to the controversy regarding the concept "need." This controversy is now essentially resolved. For, we have finally come to the realization that "needs" are unobservable, hypothetical, fictional inner-causal agents which were usually invented on the spot to provide spurious explanations of some observable behavior. Furthermore, they were inferred from precisely the same behavior they were supposed to explain.

While we can ignore the reference to needs, we must discuss values. Values may be seen as reinforcers which have salience for a number of the members of a group or society. We agree with Sutherland to the extent that he means that the nature of these general reinforcers do not necessarily determine which behavior they will strengthen. Money, or something else of general value in society, will reinforce any behavior that produces it. This reinforcement may depend upon noncriminal behavior, but it also may become contingent upon a set of behaviors that are labelled as criminal. Thus, if Sutherland can be interpreted as meaning that criminal and noncriminal behavior cannot be maintained by the same set of reinforcers, we must disagree. However, it may be that there are certain reinforcing consequences which only criminal behavior will produce, for the behavior finally shaped will depend upon the reinforcer that is effective for the individual. Nevertheless, it is the reinforcement, not the specific nature of the reinforcer, which explains the rate and form of behavior. But since this issue revolves around contingencies of reinforcement which are handled elsewhere, we will eliminate this last proposition.

Concluding Remarks

The purpose of this paper has been the application of the principles of modern behavior theory to Sutherland's differential association theory. While Sutherland's theory has had an enduring effect upon the thinking of students of criminal behavior, it has, till now, undergone no major theoretical revision despite the fact that there has been a steady and cumulative growth in the experimental findings of the processes of learning.

There are three aspects of deviant behavior which we have attempted to deal with simultaneously, but which should be separated. First, how does an individual *become* delinquent, or how does he learn delinquent behavior? Second, what *sustains* this delinquent behavior? We have attempted to describe the ways in which the principles of modern behavior theory are relevant to the development and maintenance of criminal behavior. In the process, we have seen that the principle of differential reinforcement is of crucial importance. But we must also attend to a third question, namely, what sustains the pattern or *contingency* of reinforcement? We only have hinted at some of the possibly important variables. We have mentioned briefly, for example, structural factors such as the level of deprivation of a particular group with regard to important social reinforcers, and the lack of effective reinforcement of "lawful" behavior[40] and the concomitant failure to develop the appropriate behavioral repertoires to produce reinforcement legally.[41] We have also suggested that those behaviors which do result in reinforcement may, themselves, gain reinforcement value and be enforced by the members of the group through the manipulation of various forms of social reinforcement such as social approval and status, contingent upon such behaviors.[42] In short, new norms may develop and these may be termed delinquent by the larger society.

There are many other topics that are of direct relevance to the problem of deviant behavior which we have not been able to discuss given the requirements of space. For instance, no mention has been made of some outstanding research in the area of punishment. This topic is, of course, of prime importance in the area of crime prevention. To illustrate some of this research and its relevance, it has been found experimentally that the amount of behavior suppression produced by response-contingent aversive stimuli is a direct function of the intensity of the aversive stimulus, but that a mild aversive stimulus may produce a dramatic behavior-suppression if it is paired with reinforcement for an alternative and incompatible behavior. Furthermore, it has been discovered that if an aversive stimulus is repeatedly paired with positive reinforcement, and reinforcement is not available otherwise, the aversive stimulus may become a discriminative stimulus (S^D) for reinforcement and, consequently, not decrease the behavior's frequency of occurrence.

[40] Robert K. Merton, *Social Theory and Social Structure*, Glencoe, Ill.: The Free Press, pp. 161–195. For a more complete discussion of social structure in terms relevant to this paper, see Robert L. Burgess and Don Bushell, Jr., *Behavioral Sociology*, Parts IV and V, forthcoming, 1967.

[41] *Ibid.*, and Richard A. Cloward, "Illegitimate Means, Anomie, and Deviant Behavior," *American Sociological Review*, 24 (April, 1959), pp. 164–177.

[42] Albert K. Cohen, *Delinquent Boys: The Culture of the Gang*, Glencoe, Ill.: The Free Press, 1955.

There are, in conclusion, numerous criteria that have been used to evaluate theories. One such set is as follows:

1. The amount of empirical support for the theory's basic propositions.
2. The "power" of the theory, i.e., the amount of data that can be derived from the theory's higher-order propositions.
3. The controlling possibilities of the theory, including (a) whether the theory's propositions are, in fact, *causal* principles, and (b) whether the theory's propositions are stated in such a way that they suggest possible *practical* applications.

What dissatisfaction there has been with differential association can be attributed to its scoring low on these criteria, especially (1) and (3). We submit that the reformulated theory presented here answers some of these problems and better meets each of these criteria. It is our contention, moreover, that the reformulated theory not only specifies the conditions under which criminal behavior is learned, but also some of the conditions under which deviant behavior in general is acquired. Finally, while we have not stated our propositions in strictly axiomatic form, a close examination will reveal that each of the later propositions follow from, modify, or clarify earlier propositions.

Table 1

A Differential Association-Reinforcement Theory of Criminal Behavior

Sutherland's Statements	*Reformulated Statements*
1. "Criminal behavior is learned." 8. "The process of learning criminal behavior by association with criminal and anti-criminal patterns involves all of the mechanisms that are involved in any other learning."	1. Criminal behavior is learned according to the principles of operant conditioning.
2. "Criminal behavior is learned in interaction with other persons in a process of communication."	2. Criminal behavior is learned both in nonsocial situations that are reinforcing or discriminative and through that social interaction in which the behavior of other persons is reinforcing or discriminative for criminal behavior.

Table 1 (*continued*)

Sutherland's Statements	Reformulated Statements
3. "The principal part of the learning of criminal behavior occurs within intimate personal groups."	3. The principal part of the learning of criminal behavior occurs in those groups which comprise the individual's major source of reinforcements.
4. "When criminal behavior is learned, the learning includes (a) techniques of committing the crime, which are sometimes very complicated, sometimes very simple; (b) the specific direction of motives, drives, rationalizations, and attitudes."	4. The learning of criminal behavior, including specific techniques, attitudes, and avoidance procedures, is a function of the effective and available reinforcers, and the existing reinforcement contingencies.
5. "The specific direction of motives and drives is learned from definitions of the legal codes as favorable or unfavorable."	5. The specific class of behaviors which are learned and their frequency of occurrence are a function of the reinforcers which are effective and available, and the rules or norms by which these reinforcers are applied.
6. "A person becomes delinquent because of an excess of definitions favorable to violation of law over definitions unfavorable to violation of law."	6. Criminal behavior is a function of norms which are discriminative for criminal behavior, the learning of which takes place when such behavior is more highly reinforced than noncriminal behavior.
7. "Differential associations may vary in frequency, duration, priority, and intensity."	7. The strength of criminal behavior is a direct function of the amount, frequency, and probability of its reinforcement.
9. "While criminal behavior is an expression of general needs and values, it is not explained by those general needs and values since noncriminal behavior is an expression of the same needs and values."	9. (Omit from theory.)

Illegitimate
Means and
Delinquent Subcultures
Richard A. Cloward / Lloyd E. Ohlin

The Availability of Illegitimate Means

Social norms are two-sided. A prescription implies the existence of a prohibition, and *vice versa.* To advocate honesty is to demarcate and condemn a set of actions which are dishonest. In other words, norms that define legitimate practices also implicitly define illegitimate practices. One purpose of norms, in fact, is to delineate the boundary between legitimate and illegitimate practices. In setting this boundary, in segregating and classifying various types of behavior, they make us aware not only of behavior that is regarded as right and proper but also of behavior that is said to be wrong and improper. Thus the criminal who engages in theft or fraud does not invent a new way of life; the possibility of employing alternative means is acknowledged, tacitly at least, by the norms of the culture.

This tendency for proscribed alternatives to be implicit in every prescription, and *vice versa,* although widely recognized, is nevertheless a reef upon which many a theory of delinquency has foundered. Much of the criminological literature assumes, for example, that one may explain a criminal act simply by accounting for the individual's readiness to employ illegal alternatives of which his culture, through its norms, has already made him generally aware. Such explanations are quite unsatisfactory, however, for they ignore a host of questions regarding the *relative availability* of illegal alternatives to various potential criminals. The aspiration to be a physician is hardly enough to explain the fact of becoming a physician; there is much that transpires between the aspiration and the achievement. This is no less true of the person who wants to be a successful criminal. Having decided that he "can't make it legitimately," he cannot simply choose among an array of illegitimate means, all equally available to him . . . . It is assumed in the theory of anomie that access to conventional means is differentially distributed, that some individuals, because of their social class, enjoy certain advantages that are denied to those elsewhere in the class structure. For example, there are variations in the degree to which members of various classes are fully exposed to and thus acquire the values, knowledge, and skills that facilitate upward mobility. It should not be startling, therefore, to suggest that there are socially structured variations in the availability of illegitimate means as well. In connection with delinquent subcultures, we shall be concerned principally with differentials in access to illegitimate means within the lower class.

Many sociologists have alluded to differentials in access to illegitimate means without explicitly incorporating this variable into a theory of deviant behavior. This is particularly true of scholars in the "Chicago tradition" of criminology. Two closely related theoretical perspectives emerged from this school. The theory of "cultural transmission," advanced by Clifford R. Shaw and Henry D. McKay, focuses on the development in some urban neighborhoods of a criminal tradition that persists from one generation to another despite constant changes in population.[1] In the theory of "differential association," Edwin H. Sutherland described the processes by which criminal values are taken over by the individual.[2] He asserted that criminal behavior is learned, and that it is learned in interaction with others who have already incorporated criminal values. Thus the first theory stresses the value systems of different areas; the second, the systems of social relationships that facilitate or impede the acquisition of these values.

[1]See esp. C. R. Shaw, *The Jack-Roller* (Chicago: University of Chicago Press, 1930); Shaw, *The Natural History of a Delinquent Career* (Chicago: University of Chicago Press, 1931); Shaw *et al.*, *Delinquency Areas* (Chicago: University of Chicago Press, 1940); and Shaw and H. D. McKay, *Juvenile Delinquency and Urban Areas* (Chicago: University of Chicago Press, 1942).

[2]E. H. Sutherland, ed., *The Professional Thief* (Chicago: University of Chicago Press, 1937); and Sutherland, *Principles of Criminology*, 4th Ed. (Philadelphia: Lippincott, 1947).

Scholars in the Chicago tradition, who emphasized the processes involved in learning to be criminal, were actually pointing to differentials in the availability of illegal means—although they did not explicitly recognize this variable in their analysis. This can perhaps best by seen by examining Sutherland's classic work, *The Professional Thief.* "An inclination to steal," according to Sutherland, "is not a sufficient explanation of the genesis of the professional thief."[3] The "self-made" thief, lacking knowledge of the ways of securing immunity from prosecution and similar techniques of defense, "would quickly land in prison; . . . a person can be a professional thief only if he is recognized and received as such by other professional thieves." But recognition is not freely accorded: "Selection and tutelage are the two necessary elements in the process of acquiring recognition as a professional thief . . . . A person cannot acquire recognition as a professional thief until he has had tutelage in professional theft, *and tutelage is given only to a few persons selected from the total population.*" For one thing, "the person must be appreciated by the professional thieves. He must be appraised as having an adequate equipment of wits, front, talking-ability, honesty, reliability, nerve and determination." Furthermore, the aspirant is judged by high standards of performance, for only "a very small percentage of those who start on this process ever reach the stage of professional thief . . . . " Thus motivation and pressures toward deviance do not fully account for deviant behavior any more than motivation and pressures toward conformity account for conforming behavior. The individual must have access to a learning environment and, once having been trained, must be allowed to perform his role. Roles, whether conforming or deviant in content, are not necessarily freely available; access to them depends upon a variety of factors, such as one's socioeconomic position, age, sex, ethnic affiliation, personality characteristics, and the like. The potential thief, like the potential physician, finds that access to his goal is governed by many criteria other than merit and motivation.

What we are asserting is that access to illegitimate roles is not freely available to all, as is commonly assumed. Only those neighborhoods in which crime flourishes as a stable, indigenous institution are fertile criminal learning environments for the young. Because these environments afford integration of different age-levels of offender, selected young people are exposed to "differential association" through which tutelage is provided and criminal values

[3]All quotations on this page are from *The Professional Thief*, pp. 211–13. Emphasis added.

and skills are acquired. To be prepared for the role may not, however, ensure that the individual will ever discharge it. One important limitation is that more youngsters are recruited into these patterns of differential associations than the adult criminal structure can possibly absorb. Since there is a surplus of contenders for these elite positions, criteria and mechanisms of selection must be evolved. Hence a certain proportion of those who aspire may not be permitted to engage in the behavior for which they have prepared themselves.

Thus we conclude that access to illegitimate roles, no less than access to legitimate roles, is limited by both social and psychological factors. We shall here be concerned primarily with socially structured differentials in illegitimate opportunities. Such differentials, we contend, have much to do with the type of delinquent subculture that develops.

Learning and Performance Structures

Our use of the term "opportunities," legitimate or illegitimate, implies access to both learning and performance structures. That is, the individual must have access to appropriate environments for the acquisition of the values and skills associated with the performance of a particular role, and he must be supported in the performance of the role once he has learned it.

Tannenbaum, several decades ago, vividly expressed the point that criminal role performance, no less than conventional role performance, presupposes a patterned set of relationships through which the requisite values and skills are transmitted by established practitioners to aspiring youth:

> It takes a long time to make a good criminal, many years of specialized training and much preparation. But training is something that is given to people. People learn in a community where the materials and the knowledge are to be had. A craft needs an atmosphere saturated with purpose and promise. The community provides the attitudes, the point of view, the philosophy of life, the example, the motive, the contacts, the friendships, the incentives. No child brings those into the world. He finds them here and available for use and elaboration. The community gives the criminal his materials and habits, just as it gives the doctor, the lawyer, the teacher, and the candlestick-maker theirs.[4]

[4]Frank Tannenbaum, "The Professional Criminal," *The Century,* Vol. 110 (May-Oct. 1925); p. 577.

Sutherland systematized this general point of view, asserting that opportunity consists, at least in part, of learning structures. Thus "criminal behavior is learned" and, furthermore, it is learned "in interaction with other persons in a process of communication." However, he conceded that the differential-association theory does not constitute a full explanation of criminal behavior. In a paper circulated in 1944, he noted that "criminal behavior is partially a function of opportunities to commit [*i.e.*, to perform] specific classes of crime, such as embezzlement, bank burglary, or illicit heterosexual intercourse." Therefore, "while opportunity may be partially a function of association with criminal patterns and of the specialized techniques thus acquired, it is not determined entirely in that manner, and consequently differential association is not the sufficient cause of criminal behavior."[5]

To Sutherland, then, illegitimate opportunity included conditions favorable to the performance of a criminal role as well as conditions favorable to the learning of such a role (differential associations). These conditions, we suggest, depend upon certain features of the social structure of the community in which delinquency arises.

Differential Opportunity: A Hypothesis

We believe that each individual occupies a position in both legitimate and illegitimate opportunity structures. This is a new way of defining the situation. The theory of anomie views the individual primarily in terms of the legitimate opportunity structure. It poses questions regarding differentials in access to legitimate routes to success-goals; at the same time it assumes either that illegitimate avenues to success-goals are freely available or that differentials in their availability are of little significance. This tendency may be seen in the following statement by Merton:

Several researches have shown that specialized areas of vice and crime constitute a "normal" response to a situation where the cultural emphasis upon pecuniary success has been absorbed, but where there is little access to conventional and legitimate means for becoming successful. The occupational opportunities of people in these areas are largely confined to manual labor and the lesser white-collar jobs. Given the Ameri-

---

[5] See A. K. Cohen, Alfred Lindesmith, and Karl Schussler, eds., *The Sutherland Papers* (Bloomington, Ind.: Indiana University Press, 1956), pp. 31–35.

can stigmatization of manual labor *which has been found to hold rather uniformly for all social classes,* and the absence of realistic opportunities for advancement beyond this level, the result is a marked tendency toward deviant behavior. The status of unskilled labor and the consequent low income cannot readily compete *in terms of established standards of worth* with the promises of power and high income from organized vice, rackets and crime . . . . [Such a situation] leads toward the gradual attenuation of legitimate, but by and large ineffectual, strivings and the increasing use of illegitimate, but more or less effective, expedients.[6]

The cultural-transmission and differential-association tradition, on the other hand, assumes that access to illegitimate means is variable, but it does not recognize the significance of comparable differentials in access to legitimate means. Sutherland's "ninth proposition" in the theory of differential association states:

Though criminal behavior is an expression of general needs and values, it is not explained by those general needs and values since non-criminal behavior is an expression of the same needs and values. Thieves generally steal in order to secure money, but likewise honest laborers work in order to secure money. The attempts by many scholars to explain criminal behavior by general drives and values, such as the happiness principle, striving for social status, the money motive, or frustration, have been and must continue to be futile since they explain lawful behavior as completely as they explain criminal behavior.[7]

In this statement, Sutherland appears to assume that people have equal and free access to legitimate means regardless of their social position. At the very least, he does not treat access to legitimate means as variable. It is, of course, perfectly true that "striving for social status," "the money motive," and other socially approved drives do not fully account for either deviant or conforming behavior. But if goal-oriented behavior occurs under conditions in which there are socially structured obstacles to the satisfaction of these drives by legitimate means, the resulting pressures, we contend, might lead to deviance.

[6]R. K. Merton, *Social Theory and Social Structure,* Rev. and Enl. Ed. (Glencoe, Ill.: Free Press, 1957), pp. 145–46.

[7]*Principles of Criminology, op. cit.,* pp. 7–8.

The concept of differential opportunity structures permits us to unite the theory of anomie, which recognizes the concept of differentials in access to legitimate means, and the "Chicago tradition," in which the concept of differentials in access to illegitimate means is implicit. We can now look at the individual, not simply in relation to one or the other system of means, but in relation to both legitimate and illegitimate systems. This approach permits us to ask, for example, how the relative availability of illegitimate opportunities affects the resolution of adjustment problems leading to deviant behavior. We believe that the way in which these problems are resolved may depend upon the kind of support for one or another type of illegitimate activity that is given at different points in the social structure. If, in a given social location, illegal or criminal means are not readily available, then we should not expect a criminal subculture to develop among adolescents. By the same logic, we should expect the manipulation of violence to become a primary avenue to higher status only in areas where the means of violence are not denied to the young. To give a third example, drug addiction and participation in subcultures organized around the consumption of drugs presuppose that persons can secure access to drugs and knowledge about how to use them. In some parts of the social structure, this would be vary difficult; in others, very easy. In short, there are marked differences from one part of the social structure to another in the types of illegitimate adaptation that are availiable to persons in search of solutions to problems of adjustment arising from the restricted availability of legitimate means.[8] In this sense, then, we can think of individuals as being located in two opportunity structures—one legitimate, the other illegitimate. Given limited access to success-goals by legitimate means, the nature of the delinquent response that may result will vary according to the availability of various illegitimate means.[9]

[8]For an example of restrictions on access to illegitimate roles, note the impact of racial definitions in the following case: "I was greeted by two prisoners who were to be my cell buddies. Ernest was a first offender, charged with being a 'hold-up' man. Bill, the other buddy, was an old offender, going through the machinery of becoming a habitual criminal, in and out of jail. . . . The first thing they asked me was, 'What are you in for?' I said, 'Jack-rolling.' The hardened one (Bill) looked at me with a superior air and said, 'A hoodlum, eh? An ordinary sneak thief. Not willing to leave jack-rolling to the niggers, eh? That's all they're good for. Kid, jack-rolling's not a white man's job.' I could see that he was disgusted with me, and I was too scared to say anything" (Shaw, The Jack-Roller, op. cit., p. 101).

[9]For a discussion of the way in which the availability of illegitimate means influences the adaptations of inmates to prison life, see R. A. Cloward, "Social Control in the Prison," Theoretical Studies of the Social Organization of the Prison, Bulletin No. 15 (New York: Social Science Research Council, March 1960), pp. 20–48.

Techniques
of Neutralization
Gresham M. Sykes / David Matza

In attempting to uncover the roots of juvenile delinquency, the social scientist has long since ceased to search for devils in the mind or stigma of the body. It is now largely agreed that delinquent behavior, like most social behavior, is learned and that it is learned in the process of social interaction.

The classic statement of this position is found in Sutherland's theory of differential association, which asserts that criminal or delinquent behavior involves the learning of (a) techniques of committing crimes and (b) motives, drives, rationalizations, and attitudes favorable to the violation of law.[1] Unfortunately, the specific content of what is learned—as opposed to the process by which it is learned—has received relatively little attention in either theory or research. Perhaps the single strongest school of thought on the nature of this content has centered on the idea of a delinquent sub-culture. The basic characteristic of the delinquent sub-culture, it is argued, is a system of values that represents an inversion of the values held by respectable, law-abiding society. The world of the delinquent is the world of the law-abiding turned upside down and its norms constitute a countervailing force directed against the conforming social order. Cohen[2] sees the process of developing a delinquent sub-culture as a matter of building, maintaining, and reinforcing a code for behavior which

[1] E. H. Sutherland, *Principles of Criminology,* revised by D. R. Cressey, Chicago: Lippincott, 1955, pp. 77–80.

[2] Albert K. Cohen, *Delinquent Boys,* Glencoe, Ill.: The Free Press, 1955.

From "Techniques of Neutralization: A Theory of Delinquency" by Gresham M. Sykes and David Matza in *American Sociological Review*, Vol. 22, Dec. 1957, pp. 664–670. By permission of the authors and The American Sociological Association.

exists by opposition, which stands in point by point contradiction to dominant values, particularly those of the middle class. Cohen's portrayal of delinquency is executed with a good deal of sophistication, and he carefully avoids overly simple explanations such as those based on the principle of "follow the leader" or easy generalizations about "emotional disturbances." Furthermore, he does not accept the delinquent sub-culture as something given, but instead systematically examines the function of delinquent values as a viable solution to the lower-class, male child's problems in the area of social status. Yet in spite of its virtues, this image of juvenile delinquency as a form of behavior based on competing or countervailing values and norms appears to suffer from a number of serious defects. It is the nature of these defects and a possible alternative or modified explanation for a large portion of juvenile delinquency with which this paper is concerned.

The difficulties in viewing delinquent behavior as springing from a set of deviant values and norms—as arising, that is to say, from a situation in which the delinquent defines his delinquency as "right"—are both empirical and theoretical. In the first place, if there existed in fact a delinquent subculture such that the delinquent viewed his illegal behavior as morally correct, we could reasonably suppose that he would exhibit no feelings of guilt or shame at detection or confinement. Instead, the major reaction would tend in the direction of indignation or a sense of martyrdom.[3] It is true that some delinquents do react in the latter fashion, although the sense of martyrdom often seems to be based on the fact that others "get away with it" and indignation appears to be directed against the chance events or lack of skill that led to apprehension. More important, however, is the fact that there is a good deal of evidence suggesting that many delinquents *do* experience a sense of guilt or shame, and its outward expression is not to be dismissed as a purely manipulative gesture to appease those in authority. Much of this evidence is, to be sure, of a clinical nature or in the form of impressionistic judgments of those who must deal first hand with the youthful offender. Assigning a weight to such evidence calls for caution, but it cannot be ignored if we are to avoid the gross stereotype of the juvenile delinquent as a hardened gangster in miniature.

In the second place, observers have noted that the juvenile

[3]This form of reaction among the adherents of a deviant subculture who fully believe in the "rightfulness" of their behavior and who are captured and punished by the agencies of the dominant social order can be illustrated, perhaps, by groups such as Jehovah's Witnesses, early Christian sects, nationalist movements in colonial areas, and conscientious objectors during World Wars I and II.

delinquent frequently accords admiration and respect to law-abiding persons. The "really honest" person is often revered, and if the delinquent is sometimes overly keen to detect hypocrisy in those who conform, unquestioned probity is likely to win his approval. A fierce attachment to a humble, pious mother or a forgiving, upright priest (the former, according to many observers, is often encountered in both juvenile delinquents and adult criminals) might be dismissed as rank sentimentality, but at least it is clear that the delinquent does not necessarily regard those who abide by the legal rules as immoral. In a similar vein, it can be noted that the juvenile delinquent may exhibit great resentment if illegal behavior is imputed to "significant others" in his immediate social environment or to heroes in the world of sport and entertainment. In other words, if the delinquent does hold to a set of values and norms that stand in complete opposition to those of respectable society, his norm-holding is of a peculiar sort. While supposedly thoroughly committed to the deviant system of the delinquent sub-culture, he would appear to recognize the moral validity of the dominant normative system in many instances.[4]

In the third place, there is much evidence that juvenile delinquents often draw a sharp line between those who can be victimized and those who cannot. Certain social groups are not to be viewed as "fair game" in the performance of supposedly approved delinquent acts while others warrant a variety of attacks. In general, the potentiality for victimization would seem to be a function of the social distance between the juvenile delinquent and others and thus we find implicit maxims in the world of the delinquent such as "don't steal from friends" or "don't commit vandalism against a church of your own faith."[5] This is all rather obvious, but the implications have not received sufficient attention. The fact that supposedly valued behavior tends to be directed against disvalued social groups hints that the "wrongfulness" of such delinquent behavior is more widely recognized by delinquents than the literature has indicated. When the pool of victims is limited by considerations of kinship, friendship,

[4]As Weber has pointed out, a thief may recognize the legitimacy of legal rules without accepting their moral validity. Cf. Max Weber, *The Theory of Social and Economic Organization* (translated by A. M. Henderson and Talcott Parsons), New York: Oxford University Press, 1947, p. 125. We are arguing here, however, that the juvenile delinquent frequently recognizes *both* the legitimacy of the dominant social order and its moral "rightness."

[5]Thrasher's account of the "Itschkies"—a juvenile gang composed of Jewish boys—and the immunity from "rolling" enjoyed by Jewish drunkards is a good illustration. Cf. F. Thrasher, *The Gang*, Chicago: The University of Chicago Press, 1947, p. 315.

ethnic group, social class, age, sex, etc., we have reason to suspect that the virtue of delinquency is far from unquestioned.

In the fourth place, it is doubtful if many juvenile delinquents are totally immune from the demands for conformity made by the dominant social order. There is a strong likelihood that the family of the delinquent will agree with respectable society that delinquency is wrong, even though the family may be engaged in a variety of illegal activities. That is, the parental posture conducive to delinquency is not apt to be a positive prodding. Whatever may be the influence of parental example, what might be called the "Fagin" pattern of socialization into delinquency is probably rare. Furthermore, as Redl has indicated, the idea that certain neighborhoods are completely delinquent, offering the child a model for delinquent behavior without reservations, is simply not supported by the data.[6]

The fact that a child is punished by parents, school officials, and agencies of the legal system for his delinquency may, as a number of observers have cynically noted, suggest to the child that he should be more careful not to get caught. There is an equal or greater probability, however, that the child will internalize the demands for conformity. This is not to say that demands for conformity cannot be counteracted. In fact, as we shall see shortly, an understanding of how internal and external demands for conformity are neutralized may be crucial for understanding delinquent behavior. But it is to say that a complete denial of the validity of demands for conformity and the substitution of a new normative system is improbable, in light of the child's or adolescent's dependency on adults and encirclement by adults inherent in his status in the social structure. No matter how deeply enmeshed in patterns of delinquency he may be and no matter how much this involvement may outweigh his associations with the law-abiding, he cannot escape the condemnation of his deviance. Somehow the demands for conformity must be met and answered; they cannot be ignored as part of an alien system of values and norms.

In short, the theoretical viewpoint that sees juvenile delinquency as a form of behavior based on the values and norms of a deviant sub-culture in precisely the same way as law-abiding behavior is based on the values and norms of the larger society is open to serious doubt. The fact that the world of the delinquent is embedded in the larger world of those who conform cannot be overlooked nor

[6]Cf. Solomon Kobrin, "The Conflict of Values in Delinquency Areas," *American Sociological Review,* 16 (October, 1951), pp. 653–661.

can the delinquent be equated with an adult thoroughly socialized into an alternative way of life. Instead, the juvenile delinquent would appear to be at least partially committed to the dominant social order in that he frequently exhibits guilt or shame when he violates its proscriptions, accords approval to certain conforming figures, and distinguishes between appropriate and inappropriate targets for his deviance. It is to an explanation for the apparently paradoxical fact of his delinquency that we now turn.

As Morris Cohen once said, one of the most fascinating problems about human behavior is why men violate the laws in which they believe. This is the problem that confronts us when we attempt to explain why delinquency occurs despite a greater or lesser commitment to the usages of conformity. A basic clue is offered by the fact that social rules or norms calling for valued behavior seldom if ever take the form of categorical imperatives. Rather, values or norms appear as *qualified* guides for action, limited in their applicability in terms of time, place, persons, and social circumstances. The moral injunction against killing, for example, does not apply to the enemy during combat in time of war, although a captured enemy comes once again under the prohibition. Similarly, the taking and distributing of scarce goods in a time of acute social need is felt by many to be right, although under other circumstances private property is held inviolable. The normative system of a society, then, is marked by what Williams has termed *flexibility;* it does not consist of a body of rules held to be binding under all conditions.[7]

This flexibility is, in fact, an integral part of the criminal law in that measures for "defenses to crimes" are provided in pleas such as nonage, necessity, insanity, drunkenness, compulsion, self-defense, and so on. The individual can avoid moral culpability for his criminal action—and thus avoid the negative sanctions of society—if he can prove that criminal intent was lacking. *It is our argument that much delinquency is based on what is essentially an unrecognized extension of defenses to crimes, in the form of justifications for deviance that are seen as valid by the delinquent but not by the legal system or society at large.*

These justifications are commonly described as rationalizations. They are viewed as following deviant behavior and as protecting the individual from self-blame and the blame of others after the act. But there is also reason to believe that they precede deviant behavior and make deviant behavior possible. It is this possibility

[7]Cf. Robin Williams, Jr., *American Society,* New York: Knopf, 1951, p. 28.

that Sutherland mentioned only in passing and that other writers have failed to exploit from the viewpoint of sociological theory. Disapproval flowing from internalized norms and conforming others in the social environment is neutralized, turned back, or deflected in advance. Social controls that serve to check or inhibit deviant motivational patterns are rendered inoperative, and the individual is freed to engage in delinquency without serious damage to his self image. In this sense, the delinquent both has his cake and eats it too, for he remains committed to the dominant normative system and yet so qualifies its imperatives that violations are "acceptable" if not "right." Thus the delinquent represents not a radical opposition to law-abiding society but something more like an apologetic failure, often more sinned against than sinning in his own eyes. We call these justifications of deviant behavior techniques of neutralization; and we believe these techniques make up a crucial component of Sutherland's "definitions favorable to the violation of law." It is by learning these techniques that the juvenile becomes delinquent, rather than be learning moral imperatives, values or attitudes standing in direct contradiction to those of the dominant society. In analyzing these techniques, we have found it convenient to divide them into five major types.

The Denial of Responsibility

In so far as the delinquent can define himself as lacking responsibility for his deviant actions, the disapproval of self or others is sharply reduced in effectiveness as a restraining influence. As Justice Holmes has said, even a dog distinguishes between being stumbled over and being kicked, and modern society is no less careful to draw a line between injuries that are unintentional, i.e., where responsibility is lacking, and those that are intentional. As a technique of neutralization, however, the denial of responsibility extends much further than the claim that deviant acts are an "accident" or some similar negation of personal accountability. It may also be asserted that delinquent acts are due to forces outside of the individual and beyond his control such as unloving parents, bad companions, or a slum neighborhood. In effect, the delinquent approaches a "billiard ball" conception of himself in which he sees himself as helplessly propelled into new situations. From a psycho-dynamic viewpoint, this orientation toward one's own actions may represent a profound alienation from self, but it is important to stress the fact that interpretations of responsibility are cultural constructs and not merely idiosyncratic beliefs. The similarity between this mode of justifying illegal behavior assumed by the delinquent and the implications of a "sociological" frame of reference or a "humane" jurisprudence is readily apparent.[8] It is not the validity of this orientation that concerns us here, but its function of deflecting blame attached to violations of social norms and its relative independence of a particular personality structure.[9] By learning to view himself as more acted upon than acting, the delinquent prepares the way for deviance from the dominant normative system without the necessity of a frontal assault on the norms themselves.

The Denial of Injury

A second major technique of neutralization centers on the injury or harm involved in the delinquent act. The criminal law has long made a distinction between crimes which are *mala in se* and *mala prohibita*—that is between acts that are wrong in themselves and acts that are illegal but not immoral—and the delinquent can make the same kind of distinction in evaluating the wrongfulness of his behavior. For the delinquent, however, wrongfulness may turn on the question of whether or not anyone has clearly been hurt by his deviance, and this matter is open to a variety of interpretations. Vandalism, for example, may be defined by the delinquent simply as "mischief"—after all, it may be claimed, the persons whose property has been destroyed can well afford it. Similarly, auto theft may be viewed as "borrowing," and gang fighting may be seen as a private quarrel, an agreed upon duel between two willing parties, and thus of no concern to the community at large. We are not suggesting that this technique of neutralization, labelled the denial of injury, involves an explicit dialectic, rather, we are arguing that the delinquent frequently, and in a hazy fashion, feels that his behavior does not really cause any great harm despite the fact that it runs counter to law. Just as the link between the individual and his acts may be broken by the denial of responsibility, so may the link between acts and their consequences by broken by the denial of injury. Since society sometimes agrees with the delinquent, e.g., in matters such

[8]A number of observers have wryly noted that many delinquents seem to show a surprising awareness of sociological and psychological explanations for their behavior and are quick to point out the causal role of their poor environment.

[9]It is possible, of course, that certain personality structures can accept some techniques of neutralization more readily than others, but this question remains largely unexplored.

as truancy, "pranks," and so on, it merely reaffirms the idea that the delinquent's neutralization of social controls by means of qualifying the norms is an extension of common practice rather than a gesture of complete opposition.

The Denial of the Victim

Even if the delinquent accepts the responsibility for his deviant actions and is willing to admit that his deviant actions involve an injury or hurt, the moral indignation of self and others may be neutralized by an insistence that the injury is not wrong in light of the circumstances. The injury, it may be claimed, is not really an injury; rather, it is a form of rightful retaliation or punishment. By a subtle alchemy the delinquent moves himself into the position of an avenger and the victim is transformed into a wrong-doer. Assaults on homosexuals or suspected homosexuals, attacks on members of minority groups who are said to have gotten "out of place," vandalism as revenge on an unfair teacher or school official, thefts from a "crooked" store owner—all may be hurts inflicted on a transgressor, in the eyes of the delinquent. As Orwell has pointed out, the type of criminal admired by the general public has probably changed over the course of years and Raffles no longer serves as a hero;[10] but Robin Hood, and his latter day derivatives such as the tough detective seeking justice outside the law, still capture the popular imagination, and the delinquent may view his acts as part of a similar role.

To deny the existence of the victim, then, by transforming him into a person deserving injury is an extreme form of a phenomenon we have mentioned before, namely, the delinquent's recognition of appropriate and inappropriate targets for his delinquent acts. In addition, however, the existence of the victim may be denied for the delinquent, in a somewhat different sense, by the circumstances of the delinquent act itself. Insofar as the victim is physically absent, unknown, or a vague abstraction (as is often the case in delinquent acts committed against property), the awareness of the victim's existence is weakened. Internalized norms and anticipations of the reactions of others must somehow be activated, if they are to serve as guides for behavior; and it is possible that a diminished awareness of the victim plays an important part in determining whether or not this process is set in motion.

[10]George Orwell, *Dickens, Dali, and Others*, New York. Reynal, 1946

The Condemnation of the Condemners

A fourth technique of neutralization would appear to involve a condemnation of the condemners or, as McCorkle and Korn have phrased it, a rejection of the rejectors.[11] The delinquent shifts the focus of attention from his own deviant acts to the motives and behavior of those who disapprove of his violations. His condemners, he may claim, are hypocrites, deviants in disguise, or impelled by personal spite. This orientation toward the conforming world may be of particular importance when it hardens into a bitter cynicism directed against those assigned the task of enforcing or expressing the norms of the dominant society. Police, it may be said, are corrupt, stupid, and brutal. Teachers always show favoritism and parents always "take it out" on their children. By a slight extension, the rewards of conformity—such as material success—become a matter of pull or luck, thus decreasing still further the stature of those who stand on the side of the law-abiding. The validity of this jaundiced viewpoint is not so important as its function in turning back or deflecting the negative sanctions attached to violations of the norms. The delinquent, in effect, has changed the subject of the conversation in the dialogue between his own deviant impulses and the reactions of others; and by attacking others, the wrongfulness of his own behavior is more easily repressed or lost to view.

The Appeal to Higher Loyalties

Fifth, and last, internal and external social controls may be neutralized by sacrificing the demands of the larger society for the demands of the smaller social groups to which the delinquent belongs such as the sibling pair, the gang, or the friendship clique. It is important to note that the delinquent does not necessarily repudiate the imperatives of the dominant normative system, despite his failure to follow them. Rather, the delinquent may see himself as caught up in a dilemma that must be resolved, unfortunately, at the cost of violating the law. One aspect of this situation has been studied by Stouffer and Toby in their research on the conflict between particularistic and universalistic demands, between the claims of friendship and general social obligations, and their results suggest that "it is possible to classify people according to a predisposition to select one or the other horn of a dilemma in role

---

[11]Lloyd W. McCorkle and Richard Korn, "Resocialization Within Walls," *The Annals of the American Academy of Political and Social Science,* 293, (May, 1954), pp. 88–98.

conflict."[12] For our purposes, however, the most important point is that deviation from certain norms may occur not because the norms are rejected but because other norms, held to be more pressing or involving a higher loyalty, are accorded precedence. Indeed, it is the fact that both sets of norms are believed in that gives meaning to our concepts of dilemma and role conflict.

The conflict between the claims of friendship and the claims of law, or a similar dilemma, has of course long been recognized by the social scientist (and the novelist) as a common human problem. If the juvenile delinquent frequently resolves his dilemma by insisting that he must "always help a buddy" or "never squeal on a friend," even when it throws him into serious difficulties with the dominant social order, his choice remains familiar to the supposedly law-abiding. The delinquent is unusual, perhaps, in the extent to which he is able to see the fact that he acts in behalf of the smaller social groups to which he belongs as a justification for violations of society's norms, but it is a matter of degree rather than of kind.

"I didn't mean it." "I didn't really hurt anybody." "They had it coming to them." "Everybody's picking on me." "I didn't do it for myself." These slogans or their variants, we hypothesize, prepare the juvenile for delinquent acts. These "definitions of the situation" represent tangential or glancing blows at the dominant normative system rather than the creation of an opposing ideology; and they are extensions of patterns of thought prevalent in society rather than something created *de novo*.

Techniques of neutralization may not be powerful enough to fully shield the individual from the force of his own internalized values and the reactions of conforming others, for as we have pointed out, juvenile delinquents often appear to suffer from feelings of guilt and shame when called into account for their deviant behavior. And some delinquents may be so isolated from the world of conformity that techniques of neutralization need not be called into play. Nonetheless, we would argue that techniques of neutralization are critical in lessening the effectiveness of social controls and that they lie behind a large share of delinquent behavior. Empirical research in this area is scattered and fragmentary at the present time, but the work of Redl,[13] Cressey,[14] and others has supplied a body of

[12]See Samuel A. Stouffer and Jackson Toby, "Role Conflict and Personality," in *Toward a General Theory of Action,* edited by Talcott Parsons and Edward A. Shils, Cambridge: Harvard University Press, 1951, p. 494.

[13]See Fritz Redl and David Wineman, *Children Who Hate,* Glencoe: The Free Press, 1956.

[14]See D. R. Cressey, *Other People's Money,* Glencoe: The Free Press, 1953.

significant data that has done much to clarify the theoretical issues and enlarge the fund of supporting evidence. Two lines of investigation seem to be critical at this stage. First, there is need for more knowledge concerning the differential distribution of techniques of neutralization, as operative patterns of thought, by age, sex, social class, ethnic group, etc. On *a priori* grounds it might be assumed that these justifications for deviance will be more readily seized by segments of society for whom a discrepancy between common social ideals and social practice is most apparent. It is also possible however, that the habit of "bending" the dominant normative system—if not "breaking" it—cuts across our cruder social categories and is to be traced primarily to patterns of social interaction within the familial circle. Second, there is need for a greater understanding of the internal structure of techniques of neutralization, as a system of beliefs and attitudes, and its relationship to various types of delinquent behavior. Certain techniques of neutralization would appear to be better adapted to particular deviant acts than to others, as we have suggested, for example, in the case of offenses against property and the denial of the victim. But the issue remains far from clear and stands in need of more information.

In any case, techniques of neutralization appear to offer a promising line of research in enlarging and systematizing the theoretical grasp of juvenile delinquency. As more information is uncovered concerning techniques of neutralization, their origins, and their consequences, both juvenile delinquency in particular, and deviation from normative systems in general may be illuminated.

A Control Theory of Delinquency

Travis Hirschi

"The more weakened the groups to which [the individual] belongs, the less he depends on them, the more he consequently depends only on himself and recognizes no other rules of conduct than what are founded on his private interests."[1]

Control theories assume that delinquent acts result when an individual's bond to society is weak or broken. Since these theories embrace two highly complex concepts, the *bond* of the individual to *society*, it is not surprising that they have at one time or another formed the basis of explanations of most forms of aberrant or unusual behavior. It is also not surprising that control theories have described the elements of the bond to society in many ways, and that they have focused on a variety of units as the point of control. . . .

Elements of the Bond

Attachment

In explaining conforming behavior, sociologists justly emphasize sensitivity to the opinion of others.[2] Unfortunately, . . . they tend to suggest that

From *Causes of Delinquency* by Travis Hirschi. Berkeley, California: University of California Press, 1969, pp. 16–26.

[1] Emile Durkheim, *Suicide*, trans. John A. Spaulding and George Simpson (New York: The Free Press, 1951), p. 209.

[2] Books have been written on the increasing importance of interpersonal sensitivity in modern life. According to this view, controls from within have become less important than controls from without in *producing* conformity. Whether or not this observation is true as a description of historical trends, it is true that interpersonal sensitivity has become more important in *explain-*

man *is* sensitive to the opinion of others and thus exclude sensitivity from their explanations of deviant behavior. In explaining deviant behavior, psychologists, in contrast, emphasize insensitivity to the opinion of others.[3] Unfortunately, they too tend to ignore variation, and, in addition, they tend to tie sensitivity inextricably to other variables, to make it part of a syndrome or "type," and thus seriously to reduce its value as an explanatory concept. The psychopath is characterized only in part by "deficient attachment to or affection for others, a failure to respond to the ordinary motivations founded in respect or regard for one's fellows";[4] he is also characterized by such things as "excessive aggressiveness," "lack of superego control," and "an infantile level of response."[5] Unfortunately, too, the behavior that psychopathy is used to explain often becomes part of the *definition* of psychopathy. As a result, in Barbara Wootton's words: "[The psychopath] is . . . *par excellence*, and without shame or qualification, the model of the circular process by which mental abnormality is inferred from anti-social behavior while anti-social behavior is explained by mental abnormality."[6]

The problems of diagnosis, tautology, and name-calling are avoided if the dimensions of psychopathy are treated as causally and therefore problematically interrelated, rather than as logically and therefore necessarily bound to each other. In fact, it can be argued that all of the characteristics attributed to the psychopath follow from, are effects of, his lack of attachment to others. To say that to lack attachment to others is to be free from moral restraints is to use lack of attachment to explain the guiltlessness of the psy-

---

ing conformity. Although logically it should also have become more important in explaining nonconformity, the opposite has been the case, once again showing that Cohen's observation that an explanation of conformity should be an explanation of deviance cannot be translated as "an explanation of conformity has to be an explanation of deviance." For the view that interpersonal sensitivity currently plays a greater role than formerly in producing conformity, see William J. Goode, "Norm Commitment and Conformity to Role-Status Obligations," *American Journal of Sociology*, LXVI (1960), 246–258. And, of course, also see David Riesman, Nathan Glazer, and Reuel Denney, *The Lonely Crowd* (Garden City, New York: Doubleday, 1950), especially Part I.

[3] The literature on psychopathy is voluminous. See William McCord and Joan McCord, *The Psychopath* (Princeton: D. Van Nostrand, 1964).

[4] John M. Martin and Joseph P. Fitzpatrick, *Delinquent Behavior* (New York: Random House, 1964), p. 130.

[5] *Ibid.* For additional properties of the psychopath, see McCord and McCord, *The Psychopath*, pp. 1–22.

[6] Barbara Wootton, *Social Science and Social Pathology* (New York: Macmillan, 1959), p. 250.

chopath, the fact that he apparently has no conscience or superego. In this view, lack of attachment to others is not merely a symptom of psychopathy, it *is* psychopathy; lack of conscience is just another way of saying the same thing; and the violation of norms is (or may be) a consequence.

For that matter, given that man is an animal, "impulsivity" and "aggressiveness" can also be seen as natural consequences of freedom from moral restraints. However, since the view of man as endowed with natural propensities and capacities like other animals is peculiarly unpalatable to sociologists, we need not fall back on such a view to explain the amoral man's aggressiveness.[7] The process of becoming alienated from others often involves or is based on active interpersonal conflict. Such conflict could easily supply a reservoir of *socially derived* hostility sufficient to account for the aggressiveness of those whose attachments to others have been weakened.

Durkheim said it many years ago: "We are moral beings to the extent that we are social beings."[8] This may be interpreted to mean that we are moral beings to the extent that we have "internalized the norms" of society. But what does it mean to say that a person has internalized the norms of society? The norms of society are by definition shared by the members of society. To violate a norm is, therefore, to act contrary to the wishes and expectations of other people. If a person does not care about the wishes and expectations of other people—that is, if he is insensitive to the opinion of others—then he is to that extent not bound by the norms. He is free to deviate.

The essence of internalization of norms, conscience, or superego thus lies in the attachment of the individual to others.[9] This view has several advantages over the concept of internalization. For one, explanations of deviant behavior based on attachment do

[7] "The logical untenability [of the position that there are forces in man 'resistant to socialization'] was ably demonstrated by Parsons over 30 years ago, and it is widely recognized that the position is empirically unsound because it assumes [!] some universal biological drive system distinctly separate from socialization and social context—a basic and intransigent human nature" (Judith Blake and Kingsley Davis, "Norms, Values, and Sanctions," *Handbook of Modern Sociology*, ed. Robert E. L. Faris [Chicago: Rand McNally, 1964], p. 471).

[8] Emile Durkheim, *Moral Education*, trans. Everett K. Wilson and Herman Schnurer (New York: The Free Press, 1961), p. 64.

[9] Although attachment alone does not exhaust the meaning of internalization, attachments and beliefs combined would appear to leave only a small residue of "internal control" not susceptible in principle to direct measurement.

not beg the question, since the extent to which a person is attached to others can be measured independently of his deviant behavior. Furthermore, change or variation in behavior is explainable in a way that it is not when notions of internalization or superego are used. For example, the divorced man is more likely after divorce to commit a number of deviant acts, such as suicide or forgery. If we explain these acts by reference to the superego (or internal control), we are forced to say that the man "lost his conscience" when he got a divorce; and, of course, if he remarries, we have to conclude that he gets his conscience back. . . .

Commitment

"Of all passions, that which inclineth men least to break the laws, is fear. Nay, excepting some generous natures, it is the only thing, when there is the appearance of profit or pleasure by breaking the laws, that makes men keep them."[10] Few would deny that men on occasion obey the rules simply from fear of the consequences. This rational component in conformity we label commitment. What does it mean to say that a person is committed to conformity? In Howard S. Becker's formulation it means the following:

> First, the individual is in a position in which his decision with regard to some particular line of action has consequences for other interests and activities not necessarily [directly] related to it. Second, he has placed himself in that position by his own prior actions. A third element is present though so obvious as not to be apparent: the committed person must be aware [of these other interests] and must recognize that his decision in this case will have ramifications beyond it.[11]

The idea, then, is that the person invests time, energy, himself, in a certain line of activity — say, getting an education, building up a business, acquiring a reputation for virtue. When or whenever he considers deviant behavior, he must consider the costs of this deviant behavior, the risk he runs of losing the investment he has made in conventional behavior.

If attachment to others is the sociological counterpart of the superego or conscience, commitment is the counterpart of the ego or common sense. To the person committed to conventional lines

[10] Thomas Hobbes, *Leviathan* (Oxford: Basil Blackwell, 1957), p. 195.
[11] Howard S. Becker, "Notes on the Concept of Commitment," *American Journal of Sociology*, LXVI (1960), 35–36.

of action, risking one to ten years in prison for a ten-dollar holdup is stupidity, because to the committed person the costs and risks obviously exceed ten dollars in value. (To the psychoanalyst, such an act exhibits failure to be governed by the "reality-principle.") In the sociological control theory, it can be and is generally assumed that the decision to commit a criminal act may well be rationally determined — that the actor's decision was not irrational given the risks and costs he faces. Of course, as Becker points out, if the actor is capable of in some sense calculating the costs of a line of action, he is also capable of calculational errors: ignorance and error return, in the control theory, as possible explanations of deviant behavior.

The concept of commitment assumes that the organization of society is such that the interests of most persons would be endangered if they were to engage in criminal acts. Most people, simply by the process of living in an organized society, acquire goods, reputations, prospects that they do not want to risk losing. These accumulations are society's insurance that they will abide by the rules. Many hypotheses about the antecedents of delinquent behavior are based on this premise. For example, Arthur L. Stinchcombe's hypothesis that "high school rebellion . . . occurs when future status is not clearly related to present performance"[12] suggests that one is committed to conformity not only by what one has but also by what one hopes to obtain. Thus "ambition" and/or "aspiration" play an important role in producing conformity. The person becomes committed to a conventional line of action, and he is therefore committed to conformity.

Most lines of action in a society are of course conventional. The clearest examples are educational and occupational careers. Actions thought to jeopardize one's chances in these areas are presumably avoided. Interestingly enough, even nonconventional commitments may operate to produce conventional conformity. We are told, at least, that boys aspiring to careers in the rackets or professional thievery are judged by their "honesty" and "reliability" — traits traditionally in demand among seekers of office boys.[13]

[12] Arthur L. Stinchcombe, *Rebellion in a High School* (Chicago: Quadrangle, 1964), p. 5.

[13] Richard A. Cloward and Lloyd E. Ohlin, *Delinquency and Opportunity* (New York: The Free Press, 1960), p. 147, quoting Edwin H. Sutherland, ed., *The Professional Thief* (Chicago: University of Chicago Press, 1937), pp. 211–213.

Involvement

Many persons undoubtedly owe a life of virtue to a lack of opportunity to do otherwise. Time and energy are inherently limited: "Not that I would not, if I could, be both handsome and fat and well dressed, and a great athlete, and make a million a year, be a wit, a bon vivant, and a lady killer, as well as a philosopher, a philanthropist, a statesman, warrior, and African explorer, as well as a 'tone-poet' and saint. But the thing is simply impossible."[14] The things that William James here says he would like to be or do are all, I suppose, within the realm of conventionality, but if he were to include illicit actions he would still have to eliminate some of them as simply impossible.

Involvement or engrossment in conventional activities is thus often part of a control theory. The assumption, widely shared, is that a person may be simply too busy doing conventional things to find time to engage in deviant behavior. The person involved in conventional activities is tied to appointments, deadlines, working hours, plans, and the like, so the opportunity to commit deviant acts rarely arises. To the extent that he is engrossed in conventional activities, he cannot even think about deviant acts, let alone act out his inclinations.[15] . . .

Belief

Unlike the cultural deviance . . . [theories, both support and conflict,] . . . the control theory assumes the existence of a common value system within the society or group whose norms are being violated. If the deviant is committed to a value system different from that of conventional society, there is, within the context of the theory, nothing to explain. The question is, "Why does a man violate the rules in which he believes?" It is not, "Why do men differ in their beliefs about what constitutes good and desirable conduct?" The person is assumed to have been socialized (perhaps imperfectly) into the group whose rules he is violating; deviance is not a question of one group imposing its rules on the members of another group. In other words, we not only assume the deviant *has* believed the rules, we assume he believes the rules even as he violates them.

[14] William James, *Psychology* (Cleveland: World Publishing Co., 1948), p. 186.

[15] Few activities appear to be so engrossing that they rule out contemplation of alternative lines of behavior, at least if estimates of the amount of time men spend plotting sexual deviations have any validity.

How can a person believe it is wrong to steal at the same time he is stealing? In the strain [or anomie] theory, this is not a difficult problem. (In fact, . . . the strain theory was devised specifically to deal with this question.) The motivation to deviance adduced by the strain theorist is so strong that we can well understand the deviant act even assuming the deviator believes strongly that it is wrong.[16] However, given the control theory's assumptions about motivation, if both the deviant and the nondeviant believe the deviant act is wrong, how do we account for the fact that one commits it and the other does not?

Control theories have taken two approaches to this problem. In one approach, beliefs are treated as mere words that mean little or nothing if the other forms of control are missing. "Semantic dementia," the dissociation between rational faculties and emotional control which is said to be characteristic of the psychopath, illustrates this way of handling the problem.[17] In short, beliefs, at least insofar as they are expressed in words, drop out of the picture; since they do not differentiate between deviants and nondeviants, they are in the same class as "language" or any other characteristic common to all members of the group. Since they represent no real obstacle to the commission of delinquent acts, nothing need be said about how they are handled by those committing such acts. The control theories that do not mention beliefs (or values), and many do not, may be assumed to take this approach to the problem.

The second approach argues that the deviant rationalizes his behavior so that he can at once violate the rule and maintain his belief in it. Donald R. Cressey has advanced this argument with respect to embezzlement,[18] and Sykes and Matza have advanced it with respect to delinquency.[19] In both Cressey's and Sykes and Matza's treatments, these rationalizations (Cressey calls them "verbalizations," Sykes and Matza term them "techniques of neutralization") occur prior to the commission of the deviant act. If the neutralization is successful, the person is free to commit the act(s) in question. Both in Cressey and in Sykes and Matza, the

[16] The starving man stealing the loaf of bread is the image evoked by most strain theories. In this image, the starving man's belief in the wrongness of his act is clearly not something that must be explained away. It can be assumed to be present without causing embarrassment to the explanation.

[17] McCord and McCord, *The Psychopath*, pp. 12–15.

[18] Donald R. Cressey, *Other People's Money* (New York: The Free Press, 1953).

[19] Gresham M. Sykes and David Matza, "Techniques of Neutralization: A Theory of Delinquency," *American Sociological Review*, XXII (1957), 664–670.

strain that prompts the effort at neutralization also provides the motive force that results in the subsequent deviant act. Their theories are thus, in this sense, strain theories. Neutralization is difficult to handle within the context of a theory that adheres closely to control theory assumptions, because in the control theory there is no special motivational force to account for the neutralization. This difficulty is especially noticeable in Matza's later treatment of this topic, where the motivational component, the "will to delinquency" appears *after* the moral vacuum has been created by the techniques of neutralization.[20] The question thus becomes: Why neutralize?

In attempting to solve a strain theory problem with control theory tools, the control theorist is thus led into a trap. He cannot answer the crucial question. The concept of neutralization assumes the existence of moral obstacles to the commission of deviant acts. In order plausibly to account for a deviant act, it is necessary to generate motivation to deviance that is at least equivalent in force to the resistance provided by these moral obstacles. However, if the moral obstacles are removed, neutralization and special motivation are no longer required. We therefore follow the implicit logic of control theory and remove these moral obstacles by hypothesis. Many persons do not have an attitude of respect toward the rules of society; many persons feel no moral obligation to conform regardless of personal advantage. Insofar as the values and beliefs of these persons are consistent with their feelings, and there should be a tendency toward consistency, neutralization is unnecessary; it has already occurred.

Does this merely push the question back a step and at the same time produce conflict with the assumption of a common value system? I think not. In the first place, we do not assume, as does Cressey, that neutralization occurs in order to make a specific criminal act possible.[21] We do not assume, as do Sykes and Matza, that neutralization occurs to make many delinquent acts possible. We do not assume, in other words, that the person constructs a system of rationalizations in order to justify commission of acts he

[20] David Matza, *Delinquency and Drift* (New York: Wiley, 1964), pp. 181–191.

[21] In asserting that Cressey's assumption is invalid with respect to delinquency, I do not wish to suggest that it is invalid for the question of embezzlement, where the problem faced by the deviator is fairly specific and he can reasonably be assumed to be an upstanding citizen. (Although even here the fact that the embezzler's nonshareable financial problem often results from some sort of hanky-panky suggests that "verbalizations" may be less necessary than might otherwise be assumed.)

wants to commit. We assume, in contrast, that the beliefs that free a man to commit deviant acts are *unmotivated* in the sense that he does not construct or adopt them in order to facilitate the attainment of illicit ends. In the second place, we do not assume, as does Matza, that "delinquents concur in the conventional assessment of delinquency."[22] We assume, in contrast, that there is *variation* in the extent to which people believe they should obey the rules of society, and, furthermore, that the less a person believes he should obey the rules, the more likely he is to violate them.[23]

In chronological order, then, a person's beliefs in the moral validity of norms are, for no teleological reason, weakened. The probability that he will commit delinquent acts is therefore increased. When and if he commits a delinquent act, we may justifiably use the weakness of his beliefs in explaining it, but no special motivation is required to explain either the weakness of his beliefs or, perhaps, his delinquent act.

The keystone of this argument is of course the assumption that there is variation in belief in the moral validity of social rules. . . .

The idea of a common (or, perhaps better, a single) value system is consistent with the fact, or presumption, of variation in the strength of moral beliefs. We have not suggested that delinquency is based on beliefs counter to conventional morality; we have not suggested that delinquents do not believe delinquent acts are wrong. They may well believe these acts are wrong, but the meaning and efficacy of such beliefs are contingent upon other beliefs and, indeed, on the strength of other ties to the conventional order.[24]

---

[22] *Delinquency and Drift,* p. 43.

[23] This assumption is not, I think, contradicted by the evidence presented by Matza against the existence of a delinquent subculture. In comparing the attitudes and actions of delinquents with the picture painted by delinquent subculture theorists, Matza emphasizes—and perhaps exaggerates—the extent to which delinquents are tied to the conventional order. In implicitly comparing delinquents with a supermoral man, I emphasize—and perhaps exaggerate—the extent to which they are not tied to the conventional order.

[24] The position taken here is therefore somewhere between the "semantic dementia" and the "neutralization" positions. Assuming variation, the delinquent is, at the extremes, freer than the neutralization argument assumes. Although the possibility of wide discrepancy between what the delinquent professes and what he practices still exists, it is presumably much rarer than is suggested by studies of articulate "psychopaths."

part Six

Theories of Social and Cultural Conflict

The development of secondary deviance occurs in part through the processes of stereotyping, retrospective interpretation, role engulfment, and the emergence of deviance as a master status. These processes involve the transformation of the personal identity of the deviant, for persistent reaction on the part of significant others and isolation of the individual from interaction in legitimate relationships exert pressure on him to restructure his identity around the deviation. This transformation of identity is also a stress-producing phenomenon and results in movement toward some mode of adaptation. When this adaptation involves the selection of a new reference group sympathetic to the problems of the individual, the result is the emergence of a deviant subculture. The influence of the subculture on the individual was discussed by the social and cultural support theorists of the preceding section. As Edwin Sutherland suggested, for example, it is through the subculture that persons acquire the techniques, motives, drives, attitudes, and rationalizations for crime. In addition to these influences, and because of the isolating effects of the larger society's reaction to the deviation, the subculture also serves as a primary source of support for the individual. Therefore, there is a high level of commitment on the part of the members to its norms and expectations. This commitment to a subculture is an underlying assumption of the conflict theorists and their analysis of deviance in society.

Louis Wirth maintained that all conduct has reference to cultural codes. Within the boundaries of a larger, more inclusive social system, there exists a variety of specific groups and organizations with differing norms and expectations. Thus, "not only does each community have a culture differing from that of every other community, but each gang and each family has a culture of its own which is in competition with other cultures for the allegiance of the individuals." Adherence, then, to the norms of one group may involve violation of the norms of another. Wirth cites the dilemma of immigrants and the relationship they maintained between the old and the new cultures. The first-generation immigrants avoided potential conflict by maintaining isolation within ethnic enclaves. Their children, however, often came into contact with the larger culture through, for example, the educational institutions. In many cases this contact and subsequent internalization of the new culture resulted in *internal conflict* for the individual. According to Wirth, this internalization of the norms of conflicting culture groups eventually results in an attempt by the individual to resolve his social-psychological stress. If that attempt involves the utilization of socially unapproved methods, his action may be defined as deviant by the larger system.

Expanding upon Wirth's idea, Thorsten Sellin maintains that the internalization of diverse moral codes is not always necessary in the development of deviance. The fact that there exist separate cultures may be a sufficient cause in itself. Thus, while Wirth views culture conflict as an *internal mental state*, Sellin holds that it can also be studied as an *external conflict of culture codes*. Like Wirth, Sellin uses the example of the immigrant to illustrate his thesis. He cites the case of a Sicilian father who killed the sixteen-year-old seducer of his daughter, and expressed surprise at his arrest since he had merely defended his family honor in a traditional Sicilian way. Where such conflicts occur, violations of norms are not a result of mental conflict but occur merely because persons who have absorbed the norms of one cultural group migrate to another. Customs of the new culture, therefore, may be misunderstood, and the individual gets into trouble through sheer ignorance.

Walter Miller applies the notion of culture conflict in his discussion of lower class culture and delinquency. His analysis of the focal concerns of the lower class emphasizes that adherence to the demands of one culture may preclude conformity to another. That is to say that in an attempt to participate in the forms of behavior and standards of value as they are defined in the lower class situation, the lower class child may inadvertently violate middle class norms and values. Thus, according to Miller, "the dominant component of the motivation of 'delinquent' behavior engaged in by members of lower class corner groups involves a positive effort to achieve states, conditions, or qualities valued within the actor's most significant cultural milieu."

The role of conflict in group behavior is also the

focus of the work by George Vold. There is, says Vold, a "continuous struggle to maintain, or to defend, the place of one's own group in the interaction of groups, always with due attention to the possibility of improving its relative status position." Conflict occurs when the interests and purposes of these diverse groups "tend to overlap, encroach on one another, and become competitive." The significance of conflict is heightened by the fact of the social-psychological reality of group loyalty, a loyalty based on common experiences, troubles, and expectations. The delinquent gang, according to Vold, is in fact a minority group, isolated from legitimate roles and interaction, and forced to rely on non-conformative methods.

This perspective is developed further in Austin Turk's discussion of *normative-legal conflict*. He states that cultural differences alone are not sufficient causes of group conflict. Authority and subordination in a social system result in conflict only when accompanied by the interaction of certain other factors. Most important among these, he contends, are the level of organization and sophistication of the opposing groups and the extent to which their respective cultural and social norms are internally congruent, or reflect a high level of consensus. High conflict situations, says Turk, occur when both subordinates and superordinates are highly organized and unsophisticated, and strongly adhere to divergent sets of normative beliefs.

Steven Spitzer is primarily concerned with applying a Marxian analysis of social structure to deviant behavior. Deviants are part of the problem population that has emerged as a consequence of the contradictions inherent in the capitalist mode of production and of the disturbances that have emerged within the class system. Thus, the rise of surplus labor, while providing a "disposable industrial army," creates problems of management and cost. At the same time, expanded educational opportunities, intended originally to ensure the diffusion of norms and values appropriate to the capitalist-class economy, have become a medium through which system related exploitations are exposed. Furthermore, the growth of machine capital has meant a corresponding increase in the surplus of human labor. This population becomes more problematic as capitalism advances. This situation is a product of the increasing size of the expendable population and its growing insensitivity to economic controls. It is also a result of the cost required for converting this potentially dangerous segment of society into a nonthreatening one through deviance defining processes. Techniques which have emerged for dealing with the overproduction of deviants include: *normalization,* the decarceration of deviants through outpatient services, parole and probation, halfway houses, and the like; *conversion,* cooptation of deviants as control agents; *containment,* geographic segregation of problem populations into separate residential areas or ghettos; and *support of criminal enterprise,* the provision of a parallel opportunity structure within organized crime.

Using a similar approach, Chambliss and Seidman suggest a series of formal propositions concerning the nature of law and crime. Pluralistic societies give rise to diverse and sometimes conflicting normative systems which influence behavior. The norms of the most powerful groups in society become represented in the law while those of the poor and lower class are defined as criminal. Norm enforcement will also reflect the political interests of powerful groups. Laws prohibiting behaviors popular among the lower classes will more likely be enforced than laws proscribing middle class activities. Similarly, even those laws equally applicable across the several social strata will be differentially enforced, with the lower classes more likely selected for treatment and more severely sanctioned than their higher status counterparts.

In sum, conflict theorists point to the role of cultural pluralism in the creation of deviance. Behavior that is encouraged and rewarded in one social system may be proscribed in another. The contact of these different cultural systems thus results in normative conflict and problems of adjustment for group members. While early theorists emphasized the psychological dimension of this problem, more recent developments in the area have focused on the consequences of conflict for the *designation* of group behaviors as deviant. It is suggested that groups having preferred status in the social system are able to influence the larger society's normative and legal structures. In this situation, those behavior forms which oppose dominant interests or violate dominant beliefs are defined as deviant and proscribed through the major institutions of social control. Persons engaging in these behaviors encounter difficulties in social relations that are met with disapproval and the application of negative sanctions.

While not explicit in the theories presented here, it may be inferred that the conflict between subculture and social system reinforces the larger society's initial definitions and reactions relative to the particular deviation in question. The behavioral characteristics associated with deviance are perpetuated within the subculture. It is, after all, a collection of individuals who have been exposed to and have internalized the stereotypes of deviance that comprise many deviant groups. Performing the role associated with the stereotype of his deviance, the non-conformer fulfills the boundary-maintaining function discussed in the first section of the book dealing with the functionalist approach. In addition to maintaining boundaries, such actions on the part of the deviant reaffirm society's notion of the necessity of isolating the non-conformist from legitimate roles and eventual redefinition, and at the same time justify society's stereotypical definitions and subsequent application of negative sanctions. Thus, the interaction between conformist and non-conformist results in a persistent renewal of deviance-defining processes that in turn contribute to the persistence of deviant subcultures.

Culture
Conflict
and Misconduct
Louis Wirth

Whatever may be the physical, the psychological and the temperamental differences between various races and societies, one thing is certain, namely that their cultures are different. Their traditions, their modes of living and making a living, the values that they place upon various types of conduct are often so strikingly different that what is punished as a crime in one group is celebrated as heroic conduct in another. The obvious fact about the relativity of social values is so strikingly expressed in some of our earliest sociological literature, such as Sumner's *Folkways*, for instance, that one may indeed wonder why it has not furnished the starting-point for the sociologists' research into delinquency and crime.

The ethnological evidence, which we are not considering here, seems to indicate that where culture is homogeneous and class differences are negligible, societies without crime are possible. A small compact, isolated, and homogeneous group seems to have no difficulty in maintaining its group life intact, in passing on its institutions, practices, attitudes, and sentiments to successive generations and in controlling the behavior of its members. Punishment, at least in the formal sense, as we know it in our society, is unknown and unnecessary in such a community. The control of the group over the individuals is complete and informal, and hence spontaneous. The community secures the allegiance, participation and conformity of the members

From "Culture Conflict and Misconduct" by Louis Wirth, in *Social Forces,* June, 1931, pp. 484–492. By permission of The University of North Carolina Press.

not through edicts of law, through written ordinances, through police, courts and jails, but through the overwhelming force of community opinion, through the immediate, voluntary, and habitual approval of the social code by all. The individual in his conduct is supported and fortified by the group as a whole. Even in such a community personal rivalry and friction and the impulsive violation of the mores may perhaps never be ruled out entirely, but such a community can at least be relatively free from external and internal cultural schisms which are the source of much of our own social strife and personal and social disorganization. On the other hand, for example, one needs only to spend some time in Germany, especially if one knew that country before the war with its reverence for law and order, its thrift and its honesty, to realize what a disorganizing effect a mutation of cultural values may exert upon human conduct. Such mutations, however, may be produced not merely by social upheaval, but also by migration, by social contact, and, less abruptly, by the ordinary process of attempting to transfer a tradition from one generation to the next.

Most human beings, living in a civilization akin to our own, are exposed to experiences that carry back to varied cultural settings. To understand their problems of adjustment, therefore, it is necessary to view the personalities from the perspective of their cultural matrix and to note the contradictions, the inconsistencies, and the incongruities of the cultural influences that impinge upon them. The hypothesis may be set forth that the physical and psychic tensions which express themselves in attitudes and in overt conduct may be correlated with culture conflicts. This hypothesis may, to be sure, not always prove fitting. If a program of adjustment based upon such a theory does not prove fitting and effective, another explanation for the conduct in question must be sought. In singling out culture conflicts we are merely pointing to one variety of many causal explanations of human conduct and conduct disorders. . . . .

Whatever differences of opinion may exist between our contemporary schools of sociological thought, there is one proposition on which all would agree, viz., that human conduct presents a problem only when it involves a deviation from the dominant code or the generally prevailing definition in a given culture, i.e., when a given society regards it as a problem. Our traditional legal conceptions of crime in terms of guilt, involving the determination by means of rigidly stereotyped process whether the accused has violated the prescribed code or not, is in large measure responsible for the arbitrary way in which we have been accustomed to evaluate social behavior, moral conduct, delinquency, and crime. The fact that we distinguish between crime and delinquency and are beginning to make legal process broader and more elastic, as the development of the juvenile court indicates, is a striking recognition of the inadeqacy of our conventional method of viewing and treating misconduct, and of our determination to break away from iron-clad legalistic restrictions. Our refusal to see misconduct in the relative perspective of the cultural setting in which it occurs and which makes it into the peculiar problem that it is, has been fostered in no small measure by the official conception of crime in which the determination of the guilt of the offender and the appropriate punishment were the chief points around which the proceedings turned. Not until we appreciate that the law itself—even if in extremely arbitrary form—is an expression of the wishes of a social group, and that it is not infallibly and permanently in accord with the cultural needs and definitions of all the social groups whom it seeks to restrain, can we begin to understand why there should be crime at all. As Dr. L. K. Frank has put it:

The law, both statutory and common law, sets forth the socially sanctioned ways of carrying on life which the social scientists are busily engaged in studying. In doing so, the law, theoretically, provides patterns of behavior for all life situations which, if observed in the individual's conduct, would enable him to avoid any conflict, or at least would protect him if any conflict did arise. . . . Moreover it is clear that in so far as there are shifts and changes in the material and non-material culture of a group the very existence of rather fixed and established patterns, legally sanctioned and legally enforced, tends to increase the difficulties of the individual and to foster personality deviations, because the individual is being forced by the cultural movements into the use of new patterns of behavior which lack legal sanction and by so much create in his mind conflicts which may be resolved in frank disregard of the law, both criminally and civilly or a more or less serious mental disorder.

Dr. Frank points out how significant it is for those concerned with the offender and the mentally deranged

to begin to understand and consider more carefully the role of cultural tradition and institutional life in the patterning of human behavior and its modification.

> This is especially important at the present time since it is evident that no small part of the behavior deviations represent efforts to encompass adjustments where the cultural traditions and the institutional patterns are in process of change. This suggests that every major category of behavior deviation may be considered as an index of a social disturbance of which the social scientists as a group may not be sufficiently aware.[1]

The prevalence of culture conflict as a factor in delinquency strikes one most forcefully when one is dealing, as one so frequently is in American cities, with immigrant families. And it is quite natural that this should be so, for the most obvious distinguishing characteristic of the immigrant is not his physical organism but his foreign culture. Much of what is strange and baffling in the behavior of the immigrant and especially his children disappears if he is thought of as an individual living in a dual cultural milieu. The mysteries of behavior found in the life of the immigrant rarely are intelligible to us if we fail to reckon with the fact that in the immigrant family and community we find not a homogeneous body of sentiments, traditions and practices, but conflicting currents of culture and divergent social codes bidding for the participation and allegiance of its members.

If we examine the statistics of crime which take account of the existence of immigrants and their children we have an important clue to a neglected factor in delinquency which has wide bearings and many implications. Sutherland points out that:

> The "second generation" of immigrants generally come into contact with the courts as delinquents more frequently than the first generation. The Census report of 1910 which shows the opposite can be disregarded because of the lack of homogeneity in the groups compared. Laughlin's study of prisoners in 1921-22 resulted in criminality rates as follows:
>
> Native white, both parents native-born 81.84
> Native-born, both parents foreign-born 91.14
> Native-born, one parent native-born and one foreign-born 115.58
>
> In 1920 in Massachusetts per 100,000 population fifteen years of age and over the following numbers were committed to penal and reformatory institutions for adults: 120 native-born of native parents, 226 native-

[1]First Colloquium on Personality of the Amer. Psychiatric Association, p. 25.

born of foreign or mixed parents, and 143 foreign-born. This is in general the rating of the three groups: native-born whites of native parents have the smallest number of commitments, foreign-born whites rank second, and native-born of foreign parents or mixed parents (the second generation) rank highest.[2]

The fact that second-generation crime should be even more prevalent than first generation crime does not seem difficult to understand when we note that the immigrant himself, living, as he generally does, in an isolated immigrant colony, even though he has not assimilated New-World standards, is at least supported and controlled by Old-World traditions, which are, to a large extent, reproduced in the immigrant colony, be it Chinatown, Little Sicily or the Ghetto. Under these circumstances, whatever the differences between native and immigrant culture may be, personal morale and community control are maintained. But the second generation is differently situated. The immigrant child, especially if born in America, does not have the life-long and exclusive attachments to the folkways and mores of the Old-World group that the parents have, who have been reared in the customs and traditions of their people and in whom the memories of the Old World call forth a strong emotional response. The child, because of the relative weakness of his attachment to the Old-World culture, and because of his greater mobility, has greater opportunity of making intimate contacts with the American social world than the parent whose contacts are generally confined to the society of his own countrymen, often within the confines of the immigrant colony itself. What is of greatest significance, however, is the circumstance that the child soon becomes incorporated into a neighborhood—a play—and a schoolgroup, frequently into a gang, where he establishes primary relations with other foreign and native children. It is under conditions such as these—in the course of intimate and spontaneous contacts—that assimilation takes place. The Americanization of the immigrant parents takes place, if at all, through the medium of the children. In the immigrant family the child thus comes to play a role not unlike that of the missionary between cultures. The term "Americanization," as Park and Miller point out, is not used popularly among immigrants as we use it. They call a badly demoralized boy "completely Americanized."[3] This explains, in part,

[2]E. H. Sutherland, *Criminology*, pp. 100-101.
[3]Old World Traits Transplanted, p. 288.

the fact that the character of the second generation's crime should be different from that of the first generation, as is pointed out by the investigation of the United States Immigration Commission of 1910, in which it was found that the crime of the second generation resembled that of the natives much more nearly than that of the immigrants.[4]

My own studies, particularly in the Jewish group, have shown that those social agencies which deal primarily with immigrant families have a unique opportunity, through the attention which they might devote to the collection and interpretation of these cultural facts, to make a contribution not only to the understanding of delinquency in their own cultural group but to delinquency in general. For culture conflicts are by no means confined to immigrant families, but they occur in other families and communities as well, especially where, as is the case in city life, contacts are extended, heterogeneous groups mingle, neighborhoods disappear, and people, deprived of local and family ties, are forced to live under the loose, transient, and impersonal relations that are characteristic of cities. It would be false to suggest that through the extension of social contact under modern conditions of life we are invariably and indefinitely extending the range and depth of culture conflicts. On the contrary, we often find evidence of harmonious blending and fusion of diverse cultural heritages, in the course of which new cultural constructs emerge which are accepted as natural by successive generations, and which organize and give meaning to the conduct of the individual. But it is nevertheless always important to be alert to situations in which culture appears in a state of flux and to understand the processes of change and transition.

Our conduct, whatever it may consist of, or however it might be judged by the world at large, appears genuinely moral to us when we can get the people whom we regard as significant in our social world to accept and approve it. One of the most convincing bits of evidence for the importance of the role played by culture conflict in the cases that have come to my attention, is the frequence with which delinquents, far from exhibiting a sense of guilt, made the charge of hypocrisy toward official representatives of the social order such as teachers, judges, newspapers, and social workers with whom they came in contact. Whether this charge is correct is not as important as the fact that the delinquent believes that these guardians of the social order must be aware of the conflict which he feels. Miss Van Waters remarks pertinently:

[4]Report of the U. S. Immigration Commission, 1910, pp. 14-16.

When young people violate sacred family traditions and smile complacently, with no loss of self-
esteem, it is *not* because they have become anti-social;
it indicates probably that they dwell in some other
island of social culture which smiles upon their activities, and which is endorsed by some powerful group of
adults. Almost all delinquencies of youth are expressed
social standards of a part of the adult community which
is under no indictment, and which flourishes without
condemnation.[5]

We may be able to determine statistically that certain regions in
the city have more delinquency than others, but we will not be able
to interpret the localization of crime adequately until we see that in
each area we may be dealing with a different community and that in
each community we may find a different set of conflicting strains of
cultural influences and mutually antagonistic groups. For these
reasons the high delinquency rates in each part of a given con-
glomerate cultural zone may be widely different. There may even be
communities in which delinquency is part of the cultural tradition.
Not only does each community have a culture differing from that of
every other community, but each gang and each family has a culture
of its own which is in competition with other cultures for the
allegiance of the individuals. It is important, therefore, to determine
whether in our studies of delinquency in the aggregate we are
dealing with natural areas or with cultural areas, and within each
cultural area it is important to know to which cultural groups within
the area or outside of it, the delinquent expresses his primary loyalty.

When a community, a family or a gang acquires traditions of
delinquency they serve as codes for the individual just as religious or
political traditions exert a controlling influence. A person's loyalty to
his gang may account for his misbehavior in his family and his
delinquency in the community. The backing of a gang makes it
easier for the individual to meet culture conflict situations with a
delinquent form of behavior, for the gang is essentially a conflict
group and tends to sanction a delinquent mode of conduct as
contrasted with the standards of the society represented by the law
and the police. If we fail to see that a gang has a moral code of its
own—however immoral it may appear to the rest of us—we will not
be able to understand the solidarity, the courage and the self-
sacrifice of which gangsters are capable. We will not understand then
why the criminal with the longest criminal record is often in a
position of leadership, why certain crimes are regarded with greater

[5]Miriam Van Waters: *Youth in Conflict*, p. 128.

resentment by criminals than by non-criminals, nor why gang justice inflicts the heaviest penalties upon those who commit the greatest of all underworld crimes, namely betraying a member to the police.

This point of view may help also to understand more adequately the phenomenon of recidivism. Recidivism is not merely a matter of acquiring proficiency in a given type of offense, but may be regarded as a series of successively similar situations and as a symptom of a deepening culture conflict which takes on more definite form as the offense is repeated. The commission of the same offense on the part of the individual is not merely made possible by the continued presence of similar opportunities, it is not merely a matter of facility and convenience on his part, but it may also be symptomatic of the emergence of a characteristic set of attitudes toward the social norms and of persistent pressure from a social group such as a gang. As Burgess, in his study of parole violations, has shown, the number of violations has tended to increase with the number involved in the crime; regularly the lowest rate was found where a man had no associates in crime, to the highest rate where he had five or more associates.

The first prerequisite for the cultural approach to delinquency is, obviously, at least as thorough a knowledge of contemporary cultures, as we have of the cultures of primitive peoples. We should be able to have a more thorough understanding of Polish delinquents because of Thomas' *Polish Peasant*, just as we seem to have a more thorough understanding of all immigrants because of the Carnegie Americanization Studies. But we are far from even an elementary knowledge of the differences in emphasis of social values of the many cultural groups that make up our social life. The sociologist has developed a technique of community analysis as shown in recent studies which ought to furnish the background for the research into delinquency. The beginnings of similar analyses of family groups, of play-, school- and gang-groups have been made. We can no more dispense with such studies in a scientific study of crime than the farmer can carry on scientific agriculture without a thorough knowledge of the soils and the other media in which plants grow.

The sociological study of delinquency, however, does not end with a general description nor even a careful analysis of the cultural milieu of the individual. On the contrary, the study of the culture on the objective side must be complemented through a study of the personal meanings, which the cultural values have for the individual. The concept of culture and the concept of personality do not stand in opposition to one another. A culture has no psychological significance until it is referred to a personality, and vice versa, a personality is unthinkable without a cultural milieu. The sociologist, moreover, is not primarily interested in personality, but in culture. But culture is not some sort of substance that passes from one generation to the next, or from one individual to another, by means of a biological mechanism, or a simple process of transference. The culture of the group, that is to say the customs, are based on the habits of the individuals, grow out of changes in the habits of individuals and are broken down by the coming together of individuals with different habits. Ordinarily customs are passed from adults to children and in the process emotional elements appear, especially when contradictory impulses are involved. If the human personality is conceived of, as the sociologists propose, in terms of status or position in society, then it is evident that all of us being members of a number of social groups, each with a culture of its own, we are called upon to play a number of sometimes grossly conflicting roles. Upon the mutual compatibility of these cultures and consequently of these roles will depend in large measure the efficiency of our adjustments and the integration or disorganization of our personality. The study of the constitutional factors which may condition a person's capacity or tendency to react to these situations in one way or another cannot, of course, be left out of account; but it must be admitted that what the sociologist is particularly fitted to discover in a given case is not to which biological or psychological type the individual belongs, but the social type he represents.

If the conduct of the individual, as has just been suggested, is seen as a constellation of a number of roles either integrated or mutually conflicting, each of which is oriented with reference to a social group in which he has some sort of place, we can appreciate the significance of understanding these cultures for the control of the conduct of the individual. But the important features of each cultural situation are not immediately evident to the observer and do not constitute objectively determinable data. They must be seen in terms of the subjective experiences and attitudes of the individual, which, as our experience shows, can best be determined by means of autobiographical expressions and by naive utterances, especially those which reveal what he assumes to be obvious and generally taken for granted.

A culture conflict can not be objectively demonstrated by a comparison between two cultural codes. It can be said to be a factor in delinquency only, if the individual feels it, or acts as if it were present. This cannot usually, as I have found, be determined on the basis of interviews with him alone, nor on the basis, merely, of his subjective reactions as contained in autobiographical materials. Not until we collect and analyze the opinions and attitudes of different members of the same family or gang to which the individual belongs, do we see the culture conflict clearly revealed. Our attitudes represent for the most part the reflected judgments and conceptions of others, who do not necessarily live in the same culture in which we live, and who do not, therefore, have the same perspective and values that we have. These differences in attitudes and values are often the measure of the distance that separates us from others. In the immigrant family nothing is more startling than the gulf that separates the older generation from the younger. One of the most characteristic expressions of the awareness of this conflict, as I have found it in children, is the conviction that they belong to an out-cast group. This gnawing feeling of inferiority deprives the individual of the group sanction which is necessary to preserve personal morale. Such a culture conflict frequently eventuates in what Menninger has called the "isolation type of personality." He says:

> Seclusiveness, self-consciousness and other symptoms ordinarily regarded as typical of the "schizoid" personality may characterize a personality rendered incapable, rather than undesirous of social contacts, by childhood influences. That is to say that there may indeed be an inherited "constitutional" type of unsocial personality, but in addition an acquired type. This latter type is produced by artificial denial of the proper opportunities for social contacts, by such barriers as geographic isolation, religious and economic differences in the neighborhood, pathological parents, real physical defects and blemishes, and imagined physical or psychic inferiority.[6]

On the other hand, the same feeling of inferiority may express itself in compensatory behavior in the form of a flagrant violation of the social code.

We have already cautioned against the notion that all delinquency is caused by, or involves culture conflict. It is equally important to point out that not every case of culture conflict inevitably leads to delinquency. It is not the culture conflict that makes the individual a delinquent, but his inability to deal with it in a socially approved way. There are many avenues open to a person in such a situation.

[6]Karl A. Menninger, "The Isolation Type of Personality," *Abstract of Proceedings of 7th Meeting of the Orthopsychiatric Association.*

"It appears," as Professor Thomas has said, "that in a given critical situation one person may readjust on a higher level of efficiency, another may commit a crime and another go to a hospital for the insane."[7]

Delinquency represents merely one way in which the conflict may be expressed if not resolved. Other avenues, given a certain type and situation, may lie in the direction of rumination, phantasy, brooding, and suicide. A third form which this heightened self-consciousness might take is the effort on the part of the individual to secure the acceptance of his cultural values—no matter how delusional they may be—by others. Such a person, far from becoming a criminal, may develop into a prophet, a reformer or a political leader.

In general, culture conflict, as I have encountered it in my cases, may eventuate in delinquency under the following types of situations:

1. Where the culture of a group, to which the individual belongs, sanctions conduct, which violates the mores or the laws of another group, to whose code he is also subject.
2. Where the individual belongs to a group in which certain forms of conduct have a different meaning and where there is a difference of emphasis in values than in the dominant society.
3. Where the individual belongs to a group, whose very basis of organization is conflict with the larger society, from which the individual feels himself to be an outcast. This is obviously true in criminal gangs.
4. Where we have societies in which formal law is at variance with tradition, such as, for instance, where the use of alcohol is sanctioned by tradition but forbidden by law.
5. Where social life is very mobile and where culture is in a state of flux, such as in those areas of cities where there is no organized family or community life and where the social frame-work, that ordinarily supports the individual in his conduct, disintegrates or fails to function.
6. Where the individual belongs to a group, which is itself the product of the incomplete blending of different cultural strains, such as a family in which father and mother belong to different racial or religious groups.
7. Where an individual belongs to a group in which he finds himself dissatisfied and stigmatized, but from which he cannot readily escape into the group that he considers superior.

[7] W. I. Thomas, *Colloquium on Personality*, p. 8.

The Conflict of Conduct Norms

Thorsten Sellin

Culture Conflicts as Conflicts of Cultural Codes

. . . There are social groups on the surface of the earth which possess complexes of conduct norms which, due to differences in the mode of life and the social values evolved by these groups, appear to set them apart from other groups in many or most respects. We may expect conflicts of norms when the rural dweller moves to the city, but we assume that he has absorbed the basic norms of the culture which comprises both town and country. How much greater is not the conflict likely to be when Orient and Occident meet, or when the Corsican mountaineer is transplanted to the lower East Side of New York. Conflicts of cultures are inevitable when the norms of one cultural or subcultural area migrate to or come in contact with those of another . . . .

Conflicts between the norms of divergent cultural codes may arise

1. when these codes clash on the border of contiguous culture areas;
2. when, as may be the case with legal norms, the law of one cultural group is extended to cover the territory of another; or
3. when members of one cultural group migrate to another.[1]

[1]This is unfortunately not the whole story, for with the rapid growth of impersonal communication, the written (press, literature) and the spoken word (radio, talkie), knowledge concerning divergent conduct norms no longer grows solely out of direct personal contact with their carriers. And out of such conflicts grow some violations of custom and of law which would not have occurred without them.

From *Culture Conflict and Crime* by Thorsten Sellin. The Social Science Research Council Bulletin 41, pp. 63–70.

Speck, for instance, notes that "where the bands popularly known as Montagnais have come more and more into contact with Whites, their reputation has fallen lower among the traders who have known them through commercial relationships within that period. The accusation is made that they have become less honest in connection with their debts, less trustworthy with property, less truthful, and more inclined to alcoholism and sexual freedom as contacts with the frontier towns have become easier for them. Richard White reports in 1933 unusual instances of Naskapi breaking into traders' store houses."[2]

Similar illustrations abound in the works of the cultural anthropologists. We need only to recall the effect on the American Indian of the culture conflicts induced by our policy of acculturation by guile and force. In this instance, it was not merely contact with the white man's culture, his religion, his business methods, and his liquor, which weakened the tribal mores. In addition, the Indian became subject to the white man's law and this brought conflicts as well, as has always been the case when legal norms have been imposed upon a group previously ignorant of them. Maunier[3] in discussing the diffusion of French law in Algeria, recently stated: "In introducing the *Code Penal* in our colonies, as we do, we transform into offenses the ancient usages of the inhabitants which their customs permitted or imposed. Thus, among the Khabyles of Algeria, the killing of adulterous wives is ritual murder committed by the father or brother of the wife and not by her husband, as elsewhere. The woman having been sold by her family to her husband's family, the honor of her relatives is soiled by her infidelity. Her father or brother has the right and the duty to kill her in order to cleanse by her blood the honor of her relatives. Murder in revenge is also a duty, from family to family, in case of murder of or even in case of insults to a relative: the vendetta, called the *rekba* in Khabylian, is imposed by the law of honor. But these are crimes in French law! Murder for revenge, being premediatated and planned, is assassination, punishable by death! . . . What happens, then, often when our authorities pursue the criminal, guilty of an offense against public safety as well as against morality: public enemy of the French order, but who has acted in accord with a respected custom? The witnesses of the assassination, who are his relatives, or neighbors, fail to lay charges

[2]Speck, Frank G. "Ethical Attributes of the Labrador Indians." *American Anthropologist.* N. S. 35:559–94. October–December 1933. P. 559.

[3]Maunier, René. "La diffusion du droit francais en Algérie." Harvard Tercentenary Publications, *Independence, Convergence, and Borrowing in Institutions, Thought, and Art.* Cambridge: Harvard University Press. 1937. Pp. 84–85.

against the assassin; when they are questioned, they pretend to know nothing; and the pursuit is therefore useless. A French magistrate has been able to speak of the conspiracy of silence among the Algerians'; a conspiracy aiming to preserve traditions, always followed and obeyed, against their violation by our power. This is the tragic aspect of the conflict of laws. A recent decree forbids the husband among the Khabyles to profit arbitrarily by the power given him according to this law to repudiate his wife, demanding that her new husband pay an exorbitant price for her—this is the custom of the *lefdi*. Earlier, one who married a repudiated wife paid nothing to the former husband. It appears that the first who tried to avail himself of the new law was killed for violating the old custom. The abolition of the ancient law does not always occur without protest or opposition. That which is a crime was a duty; and the order which we cause to reign is sometimes established to the detriment of 'superstition'; it is the gods and the spirits, it is believed, that would punish any one who fails to revenge his honor."

When Soviet law was extended to Siberia, similar effects were observed. Anossow[4] and Wirschubski[5] both relate that women among the Siberian tribes, who in obedience to the law, laid aside their veils were killed by their relatives for violating one of the most sacred norms of their tribes.

We have noted that culture conflicts are the natural outgrowth of processes of social differentiation, which produce an infinity of social groupings, each with its own definitions of life situations, its own interpretations of social relationships, its own ignorance or misunderstanding of the social values of other groups. The transformation of a culture from a homogeneous and well-integrated type to a heterogeneous and disintegrated type is therefore accompanied by an increase of conflict situations. Conversely, the operation of integrating processes will reduce the number of conflict situations. Such conflicts within a changing culture may be distinguished from those created when different cultural systems come in contact with one another, regardless of the character or stage of development of these systems. In either case, the conduct of members of a group involved in the conflict of codes will in some respects be judged abnormal by the other group.

[4]Anossow, J. J. "Die volkstümlichen Verbrechen im Strafkodex der USSR." *Monatsschrift für Kriminalpsychologie und Strafrechtsreform.* 24: 534–37. September 1933.
[5]Wirschubski, Gregor. "Der Schutz der Sittlichkeit im Sowjetstrafrecht." *Zeitschrift für die gesamte Strafrechtswissenschaft.* 51: 317–28. 1931.

The Study of Culture Conflicts

In the study of culture conflicts, some scholars have been concerned with the effect of such conflicts on the conduct of specific persons, an approach which is naturally preferred by psychologists and psychiatrists and by sociologists who have used the life history technique. These scholars view the conflict as internal. Wirth[6] states categorically that a culture "conflict can be said to be a factor in delinquency only if the individual feels it or acts as if it were present." Culture conflict is mental conflict, but the character of this conflict is viewed differently by the various disciplines which use this term. Freudian psychiatrists[7] regard it as a struggle between deeply rooted biological urges which demand expression and the culturally created rules which give rise to inhibitive mechanisms which thwart this expression and drive them below the conscious level of the mind, whence they rise either by ruse in some socially acceptable disguise, as abnormal conduct when the inhibiting mechanism breaks down, or as neuroses when it works too well. The sociologist, on the other hand, thinks of mental conflict as being primarily the clash between antagonistic conduct norms incorporated in personality. "Mental conflict in the person," says Burgess in discussing the case presented by Shaw in *The Jack-Roller,* "may always be explained in terms of the conflict of divergent cultures."[8]

If this view is accepted, sociological research on culture conflict and its relationships to abnormal conduct would have to be strictly limited to a study of the personality of cultural hybrids. Significant studies could be conducted only by the life-history case technique applied to persons in whom the conflict is internalized, appropriate control groups being utilized, of course. . . .

The absence of mental conflict, in the sociological sense, may, however, be well studied in terms of culture conflict. An example may make this clear. A few years ago a Sicilian father in New Jersey killed the sixteen-year-old seducer of his daughter, expressing surprise at his arrest since he had merely defended his family honor

---

[6] Wirth, Louis. "Culture Conflict and Misconduct." *Social Forces.* 9: 484–92. June 1931. P. 490. Cf. Allport, Floyd H. "Culture Conflict versus the Individual as Factors in Delinquency." *Ibid.* Pp. 493–97.

[7] White, William A. *Crimes and Criminals.* New York: Farrar & Rinehart. 1933. Healy, William. *Mental Conflict and Misconduct.* Boston: Little, Brown & Co. 1917. Alexander, Franz and Healy, William. *Roots of Crime.* New York: Alfred A. Knopf. 1935.

[8] Burgess, Ernest W. in Clifford R. Shaw's *The Jack-Roller.* Chicago: University of Chicago Press. 1930. Pp. 184–197, p. 186.

in a traditional way. In this case a mental conflict in the sociological sense did not exist. The conflict was external and occurred between cultural codes or norms. We may assume that where such conflicts occur violations of norms will arise merely because persons who have absorbed the norms of one cultural group or area migrate to another and that such conflict will continue so long as the acculturation process has not been completed. . . . Only then may the violations be regarded in terms of mental conflict.

If culture conflict may be regarded as sometimes personalized, or mental, and sometimes as occurring entirely in an impersonal way solely as a conflict of group codes, it is obvious that research should not be confined to the investigation of mental conflicts and that contrary to Wirth's categorical statement that it is impossible to demonstrate the existence of a culture conflict "objectively . . . by a comparison between two cultural codes"[9] this procedure has not only a definite function, but may be carried out by researches employing techniques which are familiar to the sociologist.

The emphasis on the life history technique has grown out of the assumption that "the experiences of one person at the same time reveals the life activities of his group" and that "habit in the individual is an expression of custom in society."[10] This is undoubtedly one valid approach. Through it we may hope to discover generalizations of a scientific nature by studying persons who (1) have drawn their norms of conduct from a variety of groups with conflicting norms, or (2) who possess norms drawn from a group whose code is in conflict with that of the group which judges the conduct. In the former case alone can we speak of mental or internal culture conflict; in the latter, the conflict is external.

If the conduct norms of a group are, with reference to a given life situation, inconsistent, or if two groups possess inconsistent norms, we may assume that the members of these various groups will individually reflect such group attitudes. Paraphrasing Burgess, the experiences of a group will reveal the life activities of its members. While these norms can, no doubt, be best established by a study of a sufficient number of representative group members, they may for some groups at least be fixed with sufficient certainty to serve research purposes by a study of the social institutions, the administration of justice, the novel, the drama, the press, and other

[9]Wirth, Louis. *Op. cit.* P. 490. It should be noted that Wirth also states that culture should be studied "on the objective side" and that "the sociologist is not primarily interested in personality but in culture."

[10]Burgess, Ernest W. *Op. cit.* P. 186.

expressions of group attitudes. The identification of the groups in question having been made, it might be possible to determine to what extent such conflicts are reflected in the conduct of their members. Comparative studies based on the violation rates of the members of such groups, the trends of such rates, etc., would dominate this approach to the problem.

In conclusion, then, culture conflict may be studied either as mental conflict or as a conflict of cultural codes. The criminologist will naturally tend to concentrate on such conflicts between legal and nonlegal conduct norms. The concept of conflict fails to give him more than a general framework of reference for research. In practice, it has, however, become nearly synonymous with conflicts between the norms of cultural systems or areas. Most researches which have employed it have been done on immigrant or race groups in the United States, perhaps due to the ease with which such groups may be identified, the existence of more statistical data recognizing such groupings, and the conspicuous differences between some immigrant norms and our norms.

Lower Class Culture as a Generating Milieu for Gang Delinquency

Walter B. Miller

The etiology of delinquency has long been a controversial issue, and is particularly so at present. As new frames of reference for explaining human behavior have been added to traditional theories, some authors have adopted the practice of citing the major postulates of each school of thought as they pertain to delinquency, and going on to state that causality must be conceived in terms of the dynamic interaction of a complex combination of variables on many levels. The major sets of etiological factors currently adduced to explain delinquency are, in simplified terms, the physiological (delinquency results from organic pathology), the psychodynamic (delinquency is a "behavioral disorder" resulting primarily from emotional disturbance generated by a defective mother-child relationship), and the environmental (delinquency is the product of disruptive forces, "disorganization," in the actor's physical or social environment).

This paper selects one particular kind of "delinquency"[1]—law-violating acts committed by mem-

[1]The complex issues involved in deriving a definition of "delinquency" cannot be discussed here. The term "delinquent" is used in this paper to characterize behavior or acts committed by individuals within specified age limits which if known to official authorities could result in legal action. The concept of a "delinquent" individual has little or no utility in the approach used here; rather, specified types of *acts* which may be committed rarely or frequently by few or many individuals are characterized as "delinquent."

From "Lower Class Culture as a Generating Milieu for Gang Delinquency," by Walter B. Miller, in *The Journal of Social Issues,* Vol. 14, No.3 (1958), pp. 5–19. By permission of the author and The Society for the Psychological Study of Social Issues.

bers of adolescent street corner groups in lower class communities —and attempts to show that the dominant component of motivation underlying these acts consists in a directed attempt by the actor to adhere to forms of behavior, and to achieve standards of value as they are defined within that community. It takes as a premise that the motivation of behavior in this situation can be approached most productively by attempting to understand the nature of cultural forces impinging on the acting individual as they are perceived *by the actor himself*—although by no means only that segment of these forces of which the actor is consciously aware—rather than as they are perceived and evaluated from the reference position of another cultural system. In the case of "gang" delinquency, the cultural system which exerts the most direct influence on behavior is that of the lower class community itself—a long-established, distinctively patterned tradition with an integrity of its own—rather than a so-called "delinquent subculture" which has arisen through conflict with middle class culture and is oriented to the deliberate violation of middle class norms.

The bulk of the substantive data on which the following material is based was collected in connection with a service-research project in the control of gang delinquency. During the service aspect of the project, which lasted for three years, seven trained social workers maintained contact with twenty-one corner group units in a "slum" district of a large eastern city for periods of time ranging from ten to thirty months. Groups were Negro and white, male and female, and in early, middle, and late adolescence. Over eight thousand pages of direct observational data on behavior patterns of group members and other community residents were collected; almost daily contact was maintained for a total time period of about thirteen worker years. Data include workers' contact reports, participant observation reports by the writer—a cultural anthropologist— and direct tape recordings of group activities and discussions.[2]

[2]A three year research project is being financed under National Institutes of Health Grant M–1414, and administered through the Boston University School of Social Work. The primary research effort has subjected all collected material to a uniform data-coding process. All information bearing on some seventy areas of behavior (behavior in reference to school, police, theft, assault, sex, collective athletics, etc.) is extracted from the records, recorded on coded data cards, and filed under relevant categories. Analysis of these data aims to ascertain the actual nature of customary behavior in these areas, and the extent to which the social work effort was able to effect behavioral changes.

Focal Concerns of Lower Class Culture

There is a substantial segment of present-day American society whose way of life, values, and characteristic patterns of behavior are the product of a distinctive cultural system which may be termed "lower class." Evidence indicates that this cultural system is becoming increasingly distinctive, and that the size of the group which shares this tradition is increasing.[3] The lower class way of life, in common with that of all distinctive cultural groups, is characterized by a set of focal concerns—areas or issues which command widespread and persistent attention and a high degree of emotional involvement. The specific concerns cited here, while by no means confined to the American lower classes, constitute a distinctive *patterning* of concerns which differs significantly, both in rank order and weighting from that of American middle class culture. The following chart presents a highly schematic and simplified listing of six of the major concerns of lower class culture. Each is conceived as a "dimension" within which a fairly wide and varied range of alternative behavior patterns may be followed by different individuals under different situations. They are listed roughly in order of the degree of *explicit* attention accorded each, and, in this sense represent a weighted ranking of concerns. The "perceived alternatives" represent polar positions which define certain parameters within each dimension. As will be explained in more detail, it is necessary in relating the influence of these "concerns" to the motivation of delinquent behavior to specify *which* of its aspects is oriented to, whether orientation is *overt* or *covert, positive* (conforming to or seeking the aspect), or *negative* (rejecting or seeking to avoid the aspect).

The concept "focal concern" is used here in preference to the concept "value" for several interrelated reasons: (1) It is more readily derivable from direct field observation. (2) It is descriptively

---

[3] Between 40 and 60 per cent of all Americans are directly influenced by lower class culture, with about 15 per cent, or twenty-five million, comprising the "hard core" lower class group—defined primarily by its use of the "female-based" household as the basic form of child-rearing unit and of the "serial monogamy" mating pattern as the primary form of marriage. The term "lower class culture" as used here refers most specifically to the way of life of the "hard core" group; systematic research in this area would probably reveal at least four to six major subtypes of lower class culture, for some of which the "concerns" presented here would be differently weighted, especially for those subtypes in which "law-abiding" behavior has a high overt valuation. It is impossible within the compass of this short paper to make the finer intracultural distinctions which a more accurate presentation would require.

neutral—permitting independent consideration of positive and negative valences as varying under different conditions, whereas "value" carries a built-in positive valence. (3) It makes possible more refined analysis of subcultural differences, since it reflects actual behavior, whereas "value" tends to wash out intracultural differences since it is colored by notions of the "official" ideal.

Chart 1
Focal Concerns of Lower Class Culture

Area	Perceived Alternatives (state, quality, condition)	
1. Trouble:	law-abiding behavior	law-violating behavior
2. Toughness:	physical prowess, skill; "masculinity"; fearlessness, bravery, daring	weakness, ineptitude; effeminacy; timidity, cowardice, caution
3. Smartness:	ability to outsmart, dupe, "con"; gaining money by "wits"; shrewdness, adroitness in repartee	gullibility, "con-ability"; gaining money by hard work; slowness, dull-wittedness, verbal maladroitness
4. Excitement:	thrill; risk, danger; change, activity	boredom; "deadness," safeness; sameness, passivity
5. Fate:	favored by fortune, being "lucky"	ill-omened, being "unlucky"
6. Autonomy:	freedom from external constraint; freedom from superordinate authority; independence	presence of external constraint; presence of strong authority; dependency, being "cared for"

TROUBLE

Concern over "trouble" is a dominant feature of lower class culture. The concept has various shades of meaning; "trouble" in one of its aspects represents a situation or a kind of behavior which results in unwelcome or complicating involvement with official authorities or agencies of middle class society. "Getting into trouble" and "staying out of trouble" represent major issues for male and female, adults and children. For men, "trouble" frequently involves fighting or sexual adventures while drinking; for women, sexual involvement with disadvantageous consequences. Expressed desire to avoid behavior which violates moral or legal norms is often based less on an explicit commitment to "official" moral or legal standards than on a desire to avoid "getting into trouble," e.g., the complicating consequences of the action.

The dominant concern over "trouble" involves a distinction of critical importance for the lower class community—that between "law-abiding" and "non-law-abiding" behavior. There is a high degree of sensitivity as to where each person stands in relation to these two classes of activity. Whereas in the middle class community a major dimension for evaluating a person's status is "achievement" and its external symbols, in the lower class, personal status is very frequently gauged along the law-abiding-non-law-abiding dimension. A mother will evaluate the suitability of her daughter's boyfriend less on the basis of his achievement potential than on the basis of his innate "trouble" potential. This sensitive awareness of the opposition of "trouble-producing" and "non-trouble-producing" behavior represents both a major basis for deriving status distinctions, and an internalized conflict potential for the individual.

As in the case of other focal concerns, which of two perceived alternatives—"law-abiding" or "non-law-abiding"—is valued varies according to the individual and the circumstances; in many instances there is an overt commitment to the "law-abiding" alternative, but a covert commitment to the "non-law-abiding." In certain situations, "getting into trouble" is overtly recognized as prestige-conferring; for example, membership in certain adult and adolescent primary groupings ("gangs") is contingent on having demonstrated an explicit commitment to the law-violating alternative. It is most important to note that the choice between "law-abiding" and "non-law-abiding" behavior is still a choice *within* lower class culture; the distinction between the policeman and the criminal, the outlaw and the sheriff, involves primarily this one dimension; in other respects they have a high community of interests. Not infrequently brothers raised in an identical cultural milieu will become police and criminals respectively.

For a substantial segment of the lower class population "getting into trouble" is not in itself overtly defined as prestige-conferring, but is implicitly recognized as a means to other valued ends, e.g., the covertly valued desire to be "cared for" and subject to external constraint, or the overtly valued state of excitement or risk. Very frequently "getting into trouble" is multi-functional, and achieves several sets of valued ends.

TOUGHNESS

The concept of "toughness" in lower class culture represents a compound combination of qualities or states. Among its most important components are physical prowess, evidenced both by demonstrated possession of strength and endurance and athletic skill; "masculinity," symbolized by a distinctive complex of acts and avoidances (bodily tatooing; absence of sentimentality; non-concern with "art," "literature," conceptualization of women as conquest objects, etc.); and bravery in the face of physical threat. The model for the "tough guy"—hard, fearless, undemonstrative, skilled in physical combat—is represented by the movie gangster of the thirties, the "private eye," and the movie cowboy.

The genesis of the intense concern over "toughness" in lower class culture is probably related to the fact that a significant proportion of lower class males are reared in a predominantly female household, and lack a consistently present male figure with whom to identify and from whom to learn essential components of a "male" role. Since women serve as a primary object of identification during pre-adolescent years, the almost obsessive lower class concern with "masculinity" probably resembles a type of compulsive reaction-formation. A concern over homosexuality runs like a persistent thread through lower class culture. This is manifested by the institutionalized practice of baiting "queers," often accompanied by violent physical attacks, an expressed contempt for "softness" or frills, and the use of the local term for "homosexual" as a generalized pejorative epithet (e.g., higher class individuals or upwardly mobile peers are frequently characterized as "fags" or "queers"). The distinction between "overt" and "covert" orientation to aspects of an area of concern is especially important in regard to "toughness." A positive overt evaluation of behavior defined as "effeminate" would be out of the question for a lower class male; however, built into lower class culture is a range of devices which permit men to adopt behaviors and concerns which in other cultural milieux fall within the province of women, and at the same time to be defined as "tough" and manly. For example, lower class men can be professional short-order cooks in a diner and still be regarded as "tough." The highly intimate circumstances of the street corner gang involve the recurrent expression of strongly affectionate feelings towards other men. Such expressions, however, are disguised as their opposite, taking the form of ostensibly aggressive verbal and physical interaction (kidding, "ranking," roughhousing, etc.).

SMARTNESS

"Smartness," as conceptualized in lower class culture, involves the capacity to outsmart, outfox, outwit, dupe, "take," "con" another or others, and the concomitant capacity to avoid being outwitted, "taken," or duped oneself. In its essence, smartness involves the capacity to achieve a valued entity—material goods, personal status—through a maximum use of mental agility and a minimum use of physical effort. This capacity has an extremely long tradition in lower class culture, and is highly valued. Lower class culture can be characterized as "non-intellectual" only if intellectualism is defined specifically in terms of control over a particular body of formally learned knowledge involving "culture" (art, literature, "good" music, etc.), a generalized perspective on the past and present conditions of our own and other societies, and other areas of knowledge imparted by formal educational institutions. This particular type of mental attainment is, in general, overtly disvalued and frequently associated with effeminancy; "smartness" in the lower class sense, however, is highly valued.

The lower class child learns and practices the use of this skill in the street corner situation. Individuals continually practice duping and outwitting one another through recurrent card games and other forms of gambling, mutual exchanges of insults, and "testing" for mutual "conability." Those who demonstrate competence in this skill are accorded considerable prestige. Leadership roles in the corner group are frequently allocated according to demonstrated capacity in the two areas of "smartness" and "toughness"; the ideal leader combines both, but the "smart" leader is often accorded more prestige than the "tough" one—reflecting a general lower class respect for "brains" in the "smartness" sense.[4]

The model of the "smart" person is represented in popular media by the card shark, the professional gambler, the "con" artist, the promoter. A conceptual distinction is made between two kinds of people: "suckers," easy marks, "lushes," dupes, who work for their money and are legitimate targets of exploitation; and sharp operators, the "brainy" ones, who live by their wits and "getting" from the suckers by mental adroitness.

[4]The "brains-brawn" set of capacities are often paired in lower class folk lore or accounts of lower class life, e.g., "Brer Fox" and "Brer Bear" in the Uncle Remus stories, or George and Lennie in "Of Mice and Men."

Involved in the syndrome of capacities related to "smartness" is a dominant emphasis in lower class culture on ingenious aggressive repartee. This skill, learned and practiced in the contex⁺ of the corner group, ranges in form from the widely prevalent semi-ritualized teasing, kidding, razzing, "ranking," so characteristic of male peer group interaction, to the highly ritualized type of mutual insult interchange known as "the dirty dozens," "the dozens," "playing house," and other terms. This highly patterned cultural form is practiced on its most advanced level in adult male Negro society, but less polished variants are found throughout lower class culture—practiced, for example, by white children, male and female, as young as four or five. In essence, "doin' the dozens" involves two antagonists who vie with each other in the exchange of increasingly inflammatory insults, with incestuous and perverted sexual relations with the mother a dominant theme. In this form of insult interchange, as well as on other less ritualized occasions for joking, semi-serious, and serious mutual invective, a very high premium is placed on ingenuity, hair-trigger responsiveness, inventiveness, and the acute exercise of mental faculties.

EXCITEMENT

For many lower class individuals the rhythm of life fluctuates between periods of relatively routine or repetitive activity and sought situations of great emotional stimulation. Many of the most characteristic features of lower class life are related to the search for excitement or "thrill." Involved here are the highly prevalent use of alcohol by both sexes and the widespread use of gambling of all kinds—playing the numbers, betting on horse races, dice, cards. The quest for excitement finds what is perhaps its most vivid expression in the highly patterned practice of the recurrent "night on the town." This practice, designated by various terms in different areas ("honky-tonkin'"; "goin' out on the town"; "bar hoppin'"), involves a patterned set of activities in which alcohol, music, and sexual adventuring are major components. A group or individual sets out to "make the rounds" of various bars or night clubs. Drinking continues progressively throughout the evening. Men seek to "pick up" women, and women play the risky game of entertaining sexual advances. Fights between men involving women, gambling, and claims of physical prowess, in various combinations, are frequent consequences of a night of making the rounds. The explosive potential of this type of adventuring with sex and aggression, frequently leading to "trouble," is semi-explicitly sought by the individual. Since there is always a good likelihood that being out on the town will eventuate in fights, etc., the practice involves elements of sought risk and desired danger.

Counterbalancing the "flirting with danger" aspect of the "excitement" concern is the prevalance in lower class culture of other well established patterns of activity which involve long periods of relative inaction, or passivity. The term "hanging out" in lower class culture refers to extended periods of standing around, often with peer mates, doing what is defined as "nothing," "shooting the breeze," etc. A definite periodicity exists in the pattern of activity relating to the two aspects of the "excitement" dimension. For many lower class individuals the venture into the high risk world of alcohol, sex, and fighting occurs regularly once a week, with interim periods devoted to accommodating to possible consequences of these periods, along with recurrent resolves not to become so involved again.

FATE

Related to the quest for excitement is the concern with fate, fortune, or luck. Here also a distinction is made between two states—being "lucky" or "in luck," and being unlucky or jinxed. Many lower class individuals feel that their lives are subject to a set of forces over which they have relatively little control. These are not directly equated with the supernatural forces of formally organized religion, but relate more to a concept of "destiny," or man as a pawn of magical powers. Not infrequently this often implicit world view is associated with a conception of the ultimate futility of directed effort towards a goal: if the cards are right, or the dice good to you, or if your lucky number comes up, things will go your way; if luck is against you, it's not worth trying. The concept of performing semi-magical rituals so that one's "luck will change" is prevalent; one hopes that as a result he will move from the state of being "unlucky" to that of being "lucky." The element of fantasy plays an important part in this area. Related to and complementing the notion that "only suckers work" (Smartness) is the idea that once things start going your way, relatively independent of your own effort, all good things will come to you. Achieving great material rewards (big cars, big houses, a roll of cash to flash in a fancy night club), valued in lower class as well as in other parts of American culture, is a recurrent theme in lower class fantasy and folk lore; the cocaine dreams of Willie the Weeper or Minnie the Moocher present the components of this fantasy in vivid detail.

The prevalence in the lower class community of many forms of gambling, mentioned in connection with the "excitement" dimension, is also relevant here. Through cards and pool which involve skill, and thus both "toughness" and "smartness"; or through race horse betting, involving "smartness"; or through playing the numbers, involving predominantly "luck," one may make a big killing with a minimum of directed and persistent effort within conventional occupational channels. Gambling in its many forms illustrates the fact that many of the persistent features of lower class culture are multi-functional—serving a range of desired ends at the same time. Describing some of the incentives behind gambling has involved mention of all of the focal concerns cited so far—Toughness, Smartness, and Excitement, in addition to Fate.

AUTONOMY

The extent and nature of control over the behavior of the individual—an important concern in most cultures—has a special significance and is distinctively patterned in lower class culture. The discrepancy between what is overtly valued and what is covertly sought is particularly striking in this area. On the overt level there is a strong and frequently expressed resentment of the idea of external controls, restrictions on behavior, and unjust or coercive authority. "No one's gonna push *me* around," or "I'm gonna tell him he can take the job and shove it. . . ." are commonly expressed sentiments. Similar explicit attitudes are maintained to systems of behavior-restricting rules, insofar as these are perceived as representing the injunctions, and bearing the sanctions of superordinate authority. In addition, in lower class culture a close conceptual connection is made between "authority" and "nurturance." To be restrictively or firmly controlled is to be cared for. Thus the overtly negative evaluation of superordinate authority frequently extends as well to nurturance, care, or protection. The desire for personal independence is often expressed in such terms as "I don't need *nobody* to take care of me. I can take care of myself!" Actual patterns of behavior, however, reveal a marked discrepancy between expressed sentiment and what is covertly valued. Many lower class people appear to seek out highly restrictive social environments wherein stringent external controls are maintained over their behavior. Such institutions as the armed forces, the mental hospital, the disciplinary school, the prison or correctional institution, provide environments which incorporate a strict and detailed set of rules defining and limiting behavior, and enforced by an authority system which controls and applies coercive sanctions for deviance from these rules. While under the jurisdiction of such systems, the lower class person generally expresses to his peers continual resentment of the coercive, unjust, and arbitrary exercise of authority. Having been released, or having escaped from these milieux, however, he will often act in such a way as to insure recommitment, or choose recommitment voluntarily after a temporary period of "freedom."

Lower class patients in mental hospitals will exercise considerable ingenuity to insure continued commitment while voicing the desire to get out; delinquent boys will frequently "run" from a correctional institution to activate efforts to return them; to be caught and returned means that one is cared for. Since "being controlled" is equated with "being cared for," attempts are frequently made to "test" the severity or strictness of superordinate authority to see if it remains firm. If intended or executed rebellion produces swift and firm punitive sanctions, the individual is reassured, at the same time that he is complaining bitterly at the injustice of being caught and punished. Some environmental milieux, having been tested in this fashion for the "firmness" of their coercive sanctions, are rejected, ostensibly for being too strict, actually for not being strict enough. This is frequently so in the case of "problematic" behavior by lower class youngsters in the public schools, which generally cannot command the coercive controls implicitly sought by the individual.

A similar discrepancy between what is overtly and covertly desired is found in the area of dependence-independence. The pose of tough rebellious independence often assumed by the lower class person frequently conceals powerful dependency cravings. These are manifested primarily by obliquely expressed resentment when "care" is not forthcoming rather than by expressed satisfaction when it is. The concern over autonomy-dependency is related both to "trouble" and "fate." Insofar as the lower class individual feels that his behavior is controlled by forces which often propel him into "trouble" in the face of an explicit determination to avoid it, there is an implied appeal to "save me from myself." A solution appears to lie in arranging things so that his behavior will be coercively restricted by an externally imposed set of controls strong enough to forcibly restrain his inexplicable inclination to get in trouble. The periodicity observed in connection with the "excitement" dimension is also relevant here; after involvement in trouble-producing behavior (assault, sexual adventure, a "drunk"), the individual will actively seek a locus of imposed control (his wife, prison, a restrictive job);

after a given period of subjection to this control, resentment against it mounts, leading to a "break away" and a search for involvement in further "trouble."

Focal Concerns of the Lower Class Adolescent Street Corner Group

The one-sex peer group is a highly prevalent and significant structural form in the lower class community. There is a strong probability that the prevalence and stability of this type of unit is directly related to the prevalence of a stabilized type of lower class child-rearing unit—the "female-based" household. This is a nuclear kin unit in which a male parent is either absent from the household, present only sporadically, or, when present, only minimally or inconsistently involved in the support and rearing of children. This unit usually consists of one or more females of child-bearing age and their offspring. The females are frequently related to one another by blood or marriage ties, and the unit often includes two or more generations of women, e.g., the mother and/or aunt of the principal child-bearing female.

The nature of social groupings in the lower class community may be clarified if we make the assumption that it is the *one-sex peer unit* rather than the two-parent family unit which represents the most significant relational unit for both sexes in lower class communities. Lower class society may be pictured as comprising a set of age-graded one-sex groups which constitute the major psychic focus and reference group for those over twelve or thirteen. Men and women of mating age leave these groups periodically to form temporary marital alliances, but these lack stability, and after varying periods of "trying out" the two-sex family arrangement, gravitate back to the more "comfortable" one-sex grouping, whose members exert strong pressure on the individaul *not* to disrupt the group by adopting a two-sex household pattern of life.[5] Membership in a stable and solidary peer unit is vital to the lower class individual precisely to the extent to which a range of essential functions— psychological, educational, and others, are not provided by the "family" unit.

The adolescent street corner group represents the adolescent

[5]Further data on the female-based household unit (estimated as comprising about 15 per cent of all American "families") and the role of one-sex groupings in lower class culture are contained in Walter B. Miller, Implications of Urban Lower Class Culture for Social Work. *Social Service Review*, 1959, *33*, No. 3.

variant of this lower class structural form. What has been called the "delinquent gang" is one subtype of this form, defined on the basis of frequency of participation in law-violating activity; this subtype should not be considered a legitimate unit of study per se, but rather as one particular variant of the adolescent street corner group. The "hanging" peer group is a unit of particular importance for the adolescent male. In many cases it is the most stable and solidary primary group he has ever belonged to; for boys reared in female-based households the corner group provides the first real opportunity to learn essential aspects of the male role in the context of peers facing similar problems of sex-role identification.

The form and functions of the adolescent corner group operate as a selective mechanism in recruiting members. The activity patterns of the group require a high level of intra-group solidarity; individual members must possess a good capacity for subordinating individual desires to general group interests as well as the capacity for intimate and persisting interaction. Thus highly "disturbed" individuals, or those who cannot tolerate consistently imposed sanctions on "deviant" behavior cannot remain accepted members; the group itself will extrude those whose behavior exceeds limits defined as "normal." This selective process produces a type of group whose members possess to an unusually high degree both the *capacity* and *motivation* to conform to perceived cultural norms, so that the nature of the system of norms and values oriented to is a particularly influential component of motivation.

Focal concerns of the male adolescent corner group are those of the general cultural milieu in which it functions. As would be expected, the relative weighting and importance of these concerns pattern somewhat differently for adolescents than for adults. The nature of this patterning centers around two additional "concerns" of particular importance to this group—concern with "belonging," and with "status." These may be conceptualized as being on a higher level of abstraction than concerns previously cited, since "status" and "belonging" are achieved *via* cited concern areas of Toughness, etc.

BELONGING

Since the corner group fulfills essential functions for the individual, being a member in good standing of the group is of vital importance for its members. A continuing concern over who is "in" and who is not involves the citation and detailed discussion of highly refined criteria for "in-group" membership. The phrase "he hangs with us" means "he is accepted as a member in good standing by current consensus"; conversely, "he don't hang with us" means he is not so accepted. One achieves "belonging" primarily by demonstrating knowledge of and a determination to adhere to the system of standards and valued qualities defined by the group. One maintains membership by acting in conformity with valued aspects of Toughness, Smartness, Autonomy, etc. In those instances where conforming to norms of this reference group at the same time violates norms of other reference groups (e.g., middle class adults, institutional "officials"), immediate reference group norms are much more compelling since violation risks invoking the group's most powerful sanction: exclusion.

STATUS

In common with most adolescents in American society, the lower class corner group manifests a dominant concern with "status." What differentiates this type of group from others, however, is the particular set of criteria and weighting thereof by which "status" is defined. In general, status is achieved and maintained by demonstrated possession of the valued qualities of lower class culture—Toughness, Smartness, expressed resistance to authority, daring, etc. It is important to stress once more that the individual orients to these concerns *as they are defined within lower class society;* e.g., the status-conferring potential of "smartness" in the sense of scholastic achievement generally ranges from negligible to negative.

The concern with "status" is manifested in a variety of ways. Intragroup status is a continued concern, and is derived and tested constantly by means of a set of status-ranking activities; the intragroup "pecking order" is constantly at issue. One gains status within the group by demonstrated superiority in Toughness (physical prowess, bravery, skill in athletics and games such as pool and cards), Smartness (skill in repartee, capacity to "dupe" fellow group members), and the like. The term "ranking," used to refer to the pattern of intra-group aggressive repartee, indicates awareness of the fact that this is one device for establishing the intra-group status hierarchy.

The concern over status in the adolescent corner group involves in particular the component of "adultness," the intense desire to be seen as "grown up," and a corresponding aversion to "kid stuff." "Adult" status is defined less in terms of the assumption of "adult" responsibility than in terms of certain external symbols of adult status—a car, ready cash, and in particular, a perceived "freedom" to drink, smoke, and gamble as one wishes and to come and go without external restrictions. The desire to be seen as "adult" is often a more significant component of much involvement in illegal drinking, gambling, and automobile driving than the explicit enjoyment of these acts as such.

The intensity of the corner group member's desire to be seen as "adult" is sufficiently great that he feels called upon to demonstrate qualities associated with adultness (Toughness, Smartness, Autonomy) to a much greater degree than a lower class adult. This means that he will seek out and utilize those avenues to these qualities which he perceives as available with greater intensity than an adult and less regard for their "legitimacy." In this sense the adolescent variant of lower class culture represents a maximization or an intensified manifestation of many of its most characteristic features.

Concern over status is also manifested in reference to other street corner groups. The term "rep" used in this regard is especially significant, and has broad connotations. In its most frequent and explicit connotation, "rep" refers to the "toughness" of the corner group as a whole relative to that of other groups; a "pecking order" also exists among the several corner groups in a given interactional area, and there is a common perception that the safety or security of the group and all its members depends on maintaining a solid "rep" for toughness vis-a-vis other groups. This motive is most frequently advanced as a reason for involvement in gang fights: "We *can't* chicken out on this fight; our rep would be shot!"; this implies that the group would be relegated to the bottom of the status ladder and become a helpless and recurrent target of external attack.

On the other hand, there is implicit in the concept of "rep" the recognition that "rep" has or may have a dual basis—corresponding to the two aspects of the "trouble" dimension. It is recognized that group as well as individual status can be based on both "law-abiding" and "law-violating" behavior. The situational resolution of the persisting conflict between the "law-abiding" and "law-violating" bases of status comprises a vital set of dynamics in determining whether a "delinquent" mode of behavior will be adopted by a group, under what circumstances, and how persistently. The determinants of this choice are evidently highly complex and fluid, and rest on a range of factors including the presence and perceptual immediacy of different community reference-group loci (e.g., professional criminals, police, clergy, teachers, settlement house workers), the personality structures and "needs" of group members, the presence in the community of social work, recreation, or educational programs which can facilitate utilization of the "law-abiding" basis of status, and so on.

What remains constant is the critical importance of "status" both for the members of the group as individuals and for the group as a whole insofar as members perceive their individual destinies as linked to the destiny of the group, and the fact that action geared to attain status is much more acutely oriented to the fact of status itself than to the legality or illegality, morality or immorality of the means used to achieve it.

Lower Class Culture and the Motivation of Delinquent Behavior

The customary set of activities of the adolescent street corner group includes activities which are in violation of laws and ordinances of the legal code. Most of these center around assault and theft of various types (the gang fight; auto theft; assault on an individual; petty pilfering and shoplifting; "mugging"; pocketbook theft). Members of street corner gangs are well aware of the law-violating nature of these acts; they are not psychopaths, nor physically or mentally "defective"; in fact, since the corner group supports and enforces a rigorous set of standards which demand a high degree of fitness and personal competence, it tends to recruit from the most "able" members of the community.

Why, then, is the commission of crimes a customary feature of gang activity? The most general answer is that the commission of crimes by members of adolescent street corner groups is motivated primarily by the attempt to achieve ends, states, or conditions which are valued, and to avoid those that are disvalued within their most meaningful cultural milieu, through those culturally available avenues which appear as the most feasible means of attaining those ends.

The operation of these influences is well illustrated by the gang fight—a prevalent and characteristic type of corner group delinquency. This type of activity comprises a highly stylized and culturally patterned set of sequences. Although details vary under different circumstances, the following events are generally included. A member or several members of group A "trespass" on the claimed territory of group B. While there they commit an act or acts which group B defines as a violation of its rightful privileges, an affront to their honor, or a challenge to their "rep." Frequently this act involves advances to a girl associated with group B; it may occur at a dance or party; sometimes the mere act of "trespass" is seen as deliberate provocation. Members of group B then assault members of group A, if they are caught while still in B's territory. Assaulted members of group A return to their "home" territory and recount to members of their group details of the incident, stressing the insufficient nature of the provocation ("I just *looked* at her! Hardly even said anything!"), and the unfair circumstances of the assault ("About *twenty* guys jumped just the *two* of us!"). The highly colored account is acutely inflammatory; group A, perceiving its honor violated and its "rep" threatened, feels obligated to retaliate in force. Sessions of detailed planning now occur; allies are recruited if the size of group A and its potential allies appears to necessitate larger numbers; strategy is plotted, and messengers dispatched. Since the prospect of a gang fight is frightening to even the "toughest" group members, a constant rehearsal of the provocative incident or incidents and the essentially evil nature of the opponents accompanies the planning process to bolster possibly weakening motivation to fight. The excursion into "enemy" territory sometimes results in a full scale fight; more often group B cannot be found, or the police appear and stop the fight, "tipped off" by an anonymous informant. When this occurs, group members express disgust and disappointment; secretly there is much relief; their honor has been avenged without incurring injury; often the anonymous tipster is a member of one of the involved groups.

The basic elements of this type of delinquency are sufficiently stabilized and recurrent as to constitute an essentially ritualized pattern, resembling both in structure and expressed motives for action classic forms such as the European "duel," the American Indian tribal war, and the Celtic clan feud. Although the arousing and "acting out" of individual aggressive emotions are inevitably involved in the gang fight, neither its form nor motivatonal dynamics can be adequately handled within a predominantly personality-focused frame of reference.

It would be possible to develop in considerable detail the processes by which the commission of a range of illegal acts is either explicitly supported by, implicitly demanded by, or not materially inhibited by factors relating to the focal concerns of lower class culture. In place of such a development, the following three statements condense in general terms the operation of these processes:

1. Following cultural practices which comprise essential elements of the total life pattern of lower class culture automatically violates certain legal norms.

2. In instances where alternate avenues to similar objectives are available, the non-law-abiding avenue frequently provides a relatively greater and more immediate return for a relatively smaller investment of energy.

3. The "demanded" response to certain situations recurrently engendered within lower class culture involves the commission of illegal acts.

The primary thesis of this paper is that the dominant component of the motivation of "delinquent" behavior engaged in by members of lower class corner groups involves a positive effort to achieve states, conditions, or qualities valued within the actor's most significant cultural milieu. If "conformity to immediate reference group values" is the major component of motivation of "delinquent" behavior by gang members, why is such behavior frequently referred to as negativistic, malicious, or rebellious? Albert Cohen, for example, in *Delinquent Boys* (Glencoe: Free Press, 1955) describes behavior which violates school rules as comprising elements of "active spite and malice, contempt and ridicule, challenge and defiance." He ascribes to the gang "keen delight in terrorizing 'good' children, and in general making themselves obnoxious to the virtuous." A recent national conference on social work with "hard-to-reach" groups characterized lower class corner groups as "youth groups in conflict with the culture of their *(sic)* communities." Such characterizations are obviously the result of taking the middle class community and its institutions as an implicit point of reference.

A large body of systematically interrelated attitudes, practices, behaviors, and values characteristic of lower class culture are designed to support and maintain the basic features of the lower class way of life. In areas where these differ from features of middle class culture, action oriented to the achievement and maintenance of the lower class system may violate norms of middle class culture and be perceived as deliberately non-conforming or malicious by an observer strongly cathected to middle class norms. This does not mean, however, that violation of the middle class norm is the dominant component of motivation; it is a by-product of action primarily oriented to the lower class system. The standards of lower class culture cannot be seen merely as a reverse function of middle class culture—as middle class standards "turned upside down"; lower class culture is a distinctive tradition many centuries old with an integrity of its own.

From the viewpoint of the acting individual, functioning within a field of well-structured cultural forces, the relative impact of "conforming" and "rejective" elements in the motivation of gang delinquency is weighted preponderantly on the conforming side. Rejective or rebellious elements are inevitably involved, but their influence during the actual commission of delinquent acts is relatively small compared to the influence of pressures to achieve what is valued by the actor's most immediate reference groups. Expressed awareness by the actor of the element of rebellion often represents only that aspect of motivation of which he is explicitly conscious; the deepest and most compelling components of motivation—adherence to highly meaningful group standards of Toughness, Smartness, Excitement, etc.—are often unconsciously patterned. No cultural pattern as well-established as the practice of illegal acts by members of lower class corner groups could persist if buttressed primarily by negative, hostile, or rejective motives; its principal motivational support, as in the case of any persisting cultural tradition, derives from a positive effort to achieve what is valued within that tradition, and to conform to its explicit and implicit norms.

Group Conflict Theory as Explanation of Crime

George B. Vold

Basic Considerations in Conflict Theory

The social-psychological orientation for conflict theory rests on social interaction theories of personality formation and the 'social process' conception of collective behavior.[1] Implicit to this view is the assumption that man always is a group-involved being whose life is both a part of, and a product of his group associations. Implicit also is the view of society as a congerie of groups held together in a shifting but dynamic equilibrium of opposing group interests and efforts.[2]

This continuity of group interaction, the endless series of moves and counter-moves, of checks and cross checks, is the essential element in the concept of social process. It is this continuous ongoing of interchanging influence, in an immediate and dynamically maintained equilibrium, that gives special significance to the designation 'collective behavior,' as opposed to the idea of simultaneously behaving individuals.[3] It is this fluid flow of collec-

[1] Cf. Robert E. Park and Ernest W. Burgess, *Introduction to Science of Sociology,* University of Chicago Press, Chicago, 1924. 'Competition,' pp. 504–10; 'Conflict,' pp. 574–9; 'Collective Behavior,' pp. 865–74.

[2] Cf. Arthur F. Bentley, *The Process of Government,* University of Chicago Press, Chicago, 1908, 'Social Pressures,' pp. 258–96.

[3] R. E. Park and E. W. Burgess, op. cit. p. 865, also Muzafer Sherif, op. cit. ch. 5, 'Properties of Group Situations,' pp. 98–121.

tive action that provides opportunity for a continuous possibility of shifting positions, of gaining or losing status, with the consequent need to maintain an alert defense of one's position, and also always with the ever-present and appealing chance of improving on one's status relationship. The end result is a more or less continuous struggle to maintain, or to defend, the place of one's own group in the interaction of groups, always with due attention to the possibility of improving its relative status position. Conflict is viewed, therefore, as one of the principal and essential social processes upon which the continuing on-going of society depends.[4]

As social interaction processes grind their way through varying kinds of uneasy adjustment to a more or less stable equilibrium of balanced forces in opposition, the resulting condition of relative stability is what is usually called social order or social organization. But it is the adjustment, one to another, of the many groups of varying strengths and of different interests that is the essence of society as a functioning reality.

The normal principle of social organization is that groups are formed out of situations in which members have common interests and common needs that can be best furthered through collective action.[5] In other words, groups arise out of important needs of group members, and groups must serve the needs of the members or they soon wither away and disappear. New groups are therefore continuously being formed as new interests arise, and existing groups weaken and disappear when they no longer have a purpose to serve.[6]

Groups come into conflict with one another as the interests and purposes they serve tend to overlap, encroach on one another, and become competitive. In other words, conflicts between groups occur principally when the groups become competitive by attempting to operate in the same general field of interaction. There is never any serious conflict between groups whose operations can be channeled so that they perform satisfactorily without moving in on one another's territory of common interests and common purposes.[7]

The danger that any existing group must protect itself against, when in contact with any other group in the same area of interests

[4]For a discussion of the relation between the principal social processes and the resulting social order, see R. E. Park and E. W. Burgess, op. cit. pp. 506–10.

[5]Cf. Albion W. Small, *General Sociology,* University of Chicago Press, Chicago, 1905, pp. 495–500.

[6]Cf. Charles H. Cooley, *Social Organization,* Scribner, New York, 1924, 'Primary Aspects of Organization,' pp. 3–57.

[7]Charles H. Cooley, op. cit. 'Hostile Feelings between Classes,' pp. 301–9.

and needs, is the ever-present one of being taken over, of being replaced. A group must always be in a position to defend itself in order to maintain its place and position in the world of constantly changing adjustments. The principal goal, therefore, of one group in contact with another, is to keep from being replaced. Where there is no problem of competition and replacement, there is little likelihood of serious inter-group conflict, be it between nations, races, religions, economic systems, labor unions, or any other type of group organization.

Groups become effective action units through the direction and co-ordination of the activities of their members. For the members, the experience of participation in group activity and the sharing of troubles and satisfactions operate to make the individual a group-conscious person. It is out of this experience background that group identification and group loyalty become psychological realities. The loyalty of the group member to his group is one of the most profoundly significant facts of social psychology, though there is no assured explanation of *why* the loyalty and identification develop. Both loyalty and identification tend to be emotionally toned attachments not closely related to any rational understanding the individual may have of the place or significance of a particular group in the general scheme of things.[8]

It has long been realized that conflict between groups tends to develop and intensify the loyalty of the group members to their respective groups.[9] This is clearly one of the important elements in developing *esprit de corps* and 'group-mindedness' attitudes on the part of individual members. The individual is most loyal to the group for which he has had to fight the hardest, and to which he has had to give the greatest measure of self for the common end of group achievement.[10]

Nothing promotes harmony and self-sacrifice within the group quite as effectively as a serious struggle with another group for survival. Hence, patriotic feeling runs high in war time, and the more desperate the situation (short of collapse and the chaos of defeat and despair) in battle, the higher runs the feeling that nothing is too great a sacrifice for the national good. A group crisis, in which

[8]Muzafer Sherif, *An Outline of Social Psychology*, Harper, New York, 1948, ch. 13, 'Adolescent Attitudes and Identification,' pp. 314–38.

[9]Walter Bagehot, *Physics and Politics*, 1869, reprinted by Knopf, New York, 1948, 'The Use of Conflict,' pp. 44–84.

[10]Muzafer Sherif, op. cit. ch. 7, 'The Formation of Group Standards or Norms,' pp. 156–82.

the member must stand up and be counted, is an age-old device for separating the men from the boys. It needs to be remembered that groups have always paid tribute to 'service beyond the call of duty.' Thus it is that some of our finest ideals of character and manhood are the offshoots of group conflict where the individual has had opportunity to serve the common purpose and not merely to serve his own selfish ends.[11]

The logical outcome of group conflict should be either, on the one hand, conquest and victory for one side with the utter defeat and destruction or subjugation for the other side; or, on the other hand, something less conclusive and decisive, a stalemate of compromise and withdrawal to terminate the conflict with no final settlement of the issues involved. It should be noted that, generally speaking, there is never any compromise with a position of weakness—the weak, as a rule, are quickly overwhelmed, subjugated to and intergrated with the victors in some subordinate and inferior capacity. The group that will survive and avoid having to go down in defeat is the one strong enough to force some compromise settlement of the issues in conflict. This general pattern has been a commonplace occurrence in the conflicts between national groups and also between political factions within the nation.[12]

Crime and the Conflict Process

The foregoing brief sketch of some of the elements involved in the conflicts of groups should be sufficient to alert the thoughtful reader to further applications of these general group relationships to more specific situations. For example, politics, as it flourishes in a democracy, is primarily a matter of finding practical compromises between antagonistic groups in the community at large.[13] The prohibitionist wishes to outlaw the manufacture and sale of alcoholic beverages; the distillers and brewers wish unrestricted opportunity to make and sell a product for which there is a genuine economic demand (i.e. 'demand' in the sense of not only having a desire for the product but also having the ability to pay for it). The complicated collection of regulations that American communities know so well,

[11]Ibid. ch. 12, 'Ego-Involvement in Personal and Group Relationships,' pp. 282–313; also ch. 16, 'Men in Critical Situations,' pp. 401–424.

[12]Cf. Park and Burgess, op. cit., p. 575; also Hadley Cantril, *The Psychology of Social Movements*, Wiley, New York, 1941, chs. 8 and 9, 'The Nazi Party,' pp. 210–70.

[13]Walter Bagehot, op. cit. chs. 3 and 4, 'Nation-Making,' pp. 85–160.

including special taxes, special licensing fees and regulations, special inspections, and special rules for closing hours etc., are all part of the compromise settlement in the clash of these incompatible interests in the political organization of society.

As political groups line up against one another, they seek the assistance of the organized state to help them defend their 'rights' and protect their interests. Thus the familiar cry, 'there ought to be a law' (to suppress the undesirable) is understandable as the natural recourse of one side or the other in a conflict situation. Yet for exactly the same reason such action has a necessary logical opposition which resists the proposed legislation. Whichever group interest can marshal the greatest number of votes will determine whether or not there is to be a new law to hamper and curb the interests of some opposition group.[14]

Suppose, for purposes of illustration, that a new law has been enacted by a normal, legal, legislative majority. Those who opposed it and fought it before adoption are understandably not in sympathy with its provisions, and do not take kindly to efforts at law enforcement. In other words, the whole political process of law making, law breaking, and law enforcement becomes a direct reflection of deep-seated and fundamental conflicts between interest groups and their more general struggles for the control of the police power of the state. Those who produce legislative majorities win control over the police power and dominate the policies that decide who is likely to be involved in violation of the law.[15]

The struggle between those who support the law and those who violate it existed in the community before there was legislative action; it was the basis for the battle in the legislature; it is then continued through the judicial proceedings of prosecution and trial; and it culminates eventually in the prison treatment of the violators by those who wish to have the law enforced. The principle of compromise from positions of strength operates at every stage of this conflict process. Hence, there is bargaining in the legislature to get the law passed; there is bargaining between prosecution and defense in connection with the trial; between prison officials and inmates; and between parole agent and parolee. This is the background for Sutherland's famous 'sociological definition' of crime as a social

---

[14]E. H. Sutherland and Donald R. Cressey, *Principles of Criminology*, 5th ed., Lippincott, New York, 1955, ch. 1, 'Criminology and the Criminal Law,' pp. 3–22.

[15]E. H. Sutherland, 'Crime and the Conflict Process,' *Journal of Juvenile Research*, 13:38–48, 1929.

situation, as a set of relationships rather than as an act of behavior under specific legal definition.[16]

ᵒSutherlana ana Cressey, op. cit. p. ֿ1ɔ.

Normative-
Legal Conflict
Austin T. Turk

Cultural differences alone do not cause social conflicts. Men may fight over abstractions, but when they do, it is because the differences in abstractions have some connection with differences in behavior, differences which have to be resolved if interaction is to continue. Where people do not have to deal with one another they can either annihilate one another or separate. But within political communities men are severely limited in their ability to settle their differences by either violence or withdrawal. Generally, resolutions of conflict have to be worked out within the limits established by the facts that the roles of authority and of subordination take precedence over all other roles and that challenges to the norms by which these roles are hooked together supersede all other difficulties in human relations. The problem is when, given the inevitable and necessary difference between the perspectives of authorities and of subjects, will they clash overtly? To say that "in general, the greater the cultural difference between them, the greater the probability of conflict" does not help a great deal, because we know that sometimes men differing very much in their symbolizations fight very little and sometimes men differing very little in culture fight long and hard. A more specific idea of when they will fight is required. The distinction between cultural and social norms and the concept of the social norms of domination and of deference enable us to work out a more precise formulation of the conditions of conflict between authorities and subjects.

From Austin T. Turk, *Criminality and Legal Order.* © 1969 by Rand McNally and Company, Chicago, pp. 54–64. Reprinted by permission of Rand McNally College Publishing Company.

Assuming that some difference exists between authorities and subjects in their evaluation of some attribute (e.g., past membership in a radical political organization) or act (e.g., smoking a marijuana cigarette), the fact that cultural and social norms may or may not agree implies four situational possibilities with greater or lesser conflict potential.

1. There may be close agreement between the cultural norm announced by authorities and their actual behavior patterns, and similarly high congruence between the way in which subjects who possess the attribute or commit the act evaluate it and their social norms.
2. There may be little or no agreement between authorities' verbal and behavioral norms and between those of subjects.
3. Authorities' talk and behavior may be highly congruent, while there is little if any agreement between the words and actions of subjects.
4. The attribute or act as described in the announced norm may have considerable behavioral import for subjects, though the announced cultural norm has little foundation in the social norms of the authorities. The point, in short, is that we recognize at the outset that there may be considerable and independent variation in the behavioral significance of a cultural norm both for authorities and for subjects.

Now, granting that the cultural difference in question may be behaviorally significant to either authorities or subjects, or to both, or to neither, how are the four situational possibilities related to the probability of conflict?

To begin, it is plausible that the probability that a cultural difference between authorities and subjects in regard to a legal norm will be associated with a conflict between them will depend upon the extent to which the cultural difference corresponds to a difference in social norms.

More specifically conflict is *most* likely in the "high-high" situation where there is high congruence between cultural and social norms for both authorities and subjects because there is little leeway for compromising on some combination of their different symbolizations. The incompatibility is real instead of merely semantic. Neither side is likely to give in without a contest, as in each case they not only "talk that way" but come close to acting in accord with the way they talk.

Conflict is *least* likely where neither authorities nor subjects really act in agreement with the way they talk—the "low-low" situation—because there is a wide range of tolerable modification of symbols in which a compromise can be effected, and because neither party is very prone to fight over an essentially meaningless set of symbols.

Where agreement between cultural and social norms is high for one party and low for the other, conflict is more probable in the "high-low" situation (where agreement is high for authorities and low for subordinates) because authorities are less likely to tolerate cultural differences when their cultural norm is strongly supported by their social norms. If their symbolization is really important to them, they are likely to assume that those who see things differently are equally committed, and therefore to see a genuine threat in the different symbolization. One by-product of enforcement in this situation is likely to be an increase in the commitment of those with the different and outlawed view, as the conflict into which they are forced will tend to create resentment of unwarranted persecution and a readiness to justify themselves by defending their view. Thus, enforcement may actually strengthen the view to which the authorities are opposed. This suggests that authorities would be well advised to determine whether and to what extent the different symbolization actually implies a difference in behavior before they move against what seems to be deviance. For example, suppose that someone states that he sees nothing wrong with smoking marijuana. Before penalizing the speaker, it would be wise to learn whether he actually smokes marijuana, encourages others to do so, thinks it is all right for children. If in fact he is far from being a real user or advocate and that he has a number of reservations about "pot" when he thinks about it seriously, then there is little or nothing to be gained and a great deal to be lost by driving him into a corner as one of the "marijuana people," where he may well be inducted into the hard core of resisters and begin to take on the appropriate role.

While the abstract possibility exists that authorities and subordinates could become involved in conflict with each other because of a difference in actual behavior patterns without either party having articulated cultural norms regarding their behavior, it is extremely unlikely that such a conflict could continue, or even exist beyond the most haphazard collisions, without one and probably both parties interpreting the struggle. Human beings find some way of talking about whatever they are experiencing, and what comes out is always in some sense an explanation of the situation and a justification of their movements in the situation. In the event of normative-legal conflict, authorities tend as a matter of course to appeal to legal norms, by citing generally used interpretations, modifying old and creating new interpretations, or by announcing new legal norms, in explaining why they must do what they are doing to counter resistance. Members of the opposition, however, to the exent they have less control over the legal process, are forced to fall back on nonlegal, "higher" principles such as justice, natural law, and the right to be left alone. Because people vary in their ability to use symbols to state and justify cultural norms, both sides, particularly subordinates, who are less likely to have symbol-using skills than authorities, may resort to relatively unsophisticated excuses (rationalizations) for not acting in specific instances in accord with some cultural norm.[1] As far as subjects are concerned, the less powerful and the less organized they are into distinct groupings, subcultures, the less likely they are to have generated or learned from others a full-blown philosophy and language with which to defend themselves verbally, and therefore the more likely they are to use more or less weak excuses in attempts to verbalize the conflict.

The "real" reasons for conflict, in terms of empirically determined contradictions in behavior patterns, will never exactly coincide with the interpretations given by the parties to their conflict, for reasons mentioned earlier in discussing relations between cultural and social norms. It goes without saying that the investigator must not fall into the trap of accepting without independent corroboration what any participant in a social conflict says about the nature and extent of the conflict, not only because participants are often, not always, biased in their interpretations but because it is his job to find *independently* the patterns of conflict and to analyze these patterns in the neutral, testable language of science instead of the partisan, value-oriented language of involvement.

An individual who has group support for his behavior is going to be more stubborn in the face of efforts to make him change than is someone who has only himself as an ally. This implies that conflict is more probable, the more *organized* are those who have an illegal attribute or engage in an illegal act. Where an attribute or act has been integrated into a system of relationships, implying that it is a part of some role which the individual performs, then we can expect

---

[1]Examples of such excuses can be found in Gresham M. Sykes and David Matza. "Techniques of Neutralization: A Theory of Delinquency," *American Sociological Review*, 22 (December, 1957), pp. 664–670. Their interpretation is that such techniques are used to justify violation of norms actually shared with the authorities. However, it may be that "denial of the victim," etc. reflect more the lack of verbal skills and the immaturity of delinquent boys than normative consensus.

that some kind and degree of coercion will be required to break the behavior pattern or to eliminate the attribute. In this connection, it is noteworthy that efforts to reform or educate the stigmatized so that their stigma is removed have been characterized historically by the reluctance of reformers and educators to recognize that their work depends ultimately upon the application of force to break apart the social and cultural contexts in which undesired patterns originate and are maintained.

The fiction that an attribute can be dealt with as though it were not part of a configuration of attributes making up a single complex, that the attribute can be eliminated without fundamental changes in that structure, has underlain the kind of uncoordinated tinkering characteristic of official reform programs. These are indications that some authorities are beginning to understand that such norm violations as juvenile misconduct, family disorganization, indifference to hygiene, personality disorder, and lack of usable work skills constitute insoluble problems until and unless a total, determined attempt is made to destroy the structures of values and social relationships—the cultural and social structures—creating and perpetuating the unwanted patterns of language and behavior, and to force people (impolitic phrasing!) into the structures that lead to "good."

Another factor affecting the conflict probability is *sophistication* by which is meant knowledge of patterns in the behavior of others which is used in attempts to manipulate them. Sophisticated norm-resisters are more accurate in assessing the strengths and weaknesses of their position relative to authorities, and consequently better able to avoid open warfare with the superior enemy without making significant concessions (e.g., by giving in on semantics while merely decreasing the visibility of their illegal attribute or behavior, by taking advantage of opportunities for ignoring the spirit though conforming to the letter of the law, and by accepting some legal restraints in return for tacit or explicit permission to maintain illicit cultural and social patterns more vital to their way of life).

Thus, it seems that conflict is more probable, the less *sophisticated* are the subjects who find themselves on the wrong side of a cultural difference defined as illegal by the authorities.

If the two variables of *organization* and *sophistication* are considered simultaneously, four types of actual or potential norm-resisters emerge: (1) organized, unsophisticated; (2) unorganized, unsophisticated; (3) organized, sophisticated; (4) unorganized, sophisticated. Because lack of organization and ultra-sophistication are each likely to mean less chance of conflict between authorities and subjects, it is reasonable to expect that the category of unorganized sophisticates (e.g., professional con-men) is least likely to be pulled into an unequal test of strength and that the organized unsophisticates (e.g., delinquent gangs) are most likely to constitute a solid and not very subtle core of resistance to norm enforcement. But some decision must be made about whether or how to rank the two mixed categories in reference to probable conflict with authorities. The available evidence suggests that skill in avoiding head-on collisions in social interaction is more crucial than the degree of organization in affecting the chance of authorities-subjects conflict. Organized sophisticates (e.g., syndicate criminals) are by definition more skilled in diplomacy and maneuver, with individual variations in such skills more likely to be controlled by others so as not to endanger the group as a whole, while unorganized unsophisticates (e.g., skidrow habitués) often blunder into trouble with the law.

Therefore, we may tentatively conclude that conflict between authorities and subjects is *most* probable if the subjects are highly organized and relatively unsophisticated, *less* probable if they are unorganized and unsophisticated, *still less* probable if organized but sophisticated, and *least* probable if unorganized and sophisticated.

So far, the conceptual variables of organization and sophistication have been used only to characterize subjects who have an attribute or do something announced to be illegal by the authorities. However, the course of relations between subjects and authorities is also affected by the organization and sophistication of authorities.

Potential variability in organization is much less for authorities than for subjects, because the concept of an authority *structure* implies a relatively high degree of organization of the activities of individuals making up the more powerful sector of the population. Initially, in the course of the struggles out of which they come to occupy a dominant position, they must necessarily achieve considerable unity to win. For them to stay in power long enough for the dominance-subordination relationship to be legitimated—for power to become authority—their original organization for war must metamorphose into an organization for control. Thus a recognizable set of authorities is by definition an *organization* of authorities, even though there may be enormous variation in bureaucratization and other organizational features. Lest we seem to be postulating an overly organized world, it may be well at this point to recall that criminology is not coterminous with political sociology. Though all crime is a matter of political conflict in the largest sense (Quinney,

1964), and though law making and breaking as an adjunct of political rivalries is an important (though neglected) subject of criminological research, the study of political phenomena as such requires many additional conceptual tools and involves many additional variables. In brief, our concern is limited to events occurring in authority structures; we ignore the more general problems of political stability and change to deal more intensively and effectively with interaction between sets of people who do get along somehow inside the confines of relatively stable social orders. That authorities *are* organized, whatever the organizational details, becomes a "constant" for criminalization studies.

Turning to the sophistication variable, it has been suggested that authorities are forced to maintain a delicate balance of consensus and coercion if the authority relationship is to be preserved, and that they must have knowledge to do this, knowledge of when and how the balance is being lost, and of how to go about restoring it. Clearly, sophistication is a prerequisite for enduring authority; so it could be argued that just as authority implies organization, it also implies sophistication. However, control agencies demonstrably vary a great deal in the extent to which their policies and practices are affected by appreciation of the need for knowledge, by the existence of knowledge-seeking mechanisms, and by the knowledge that does become available. While the implications of such variations have not yet been adequately worked out in studies of control organizations, it does appear that the less sophisticated authorities are, the more they tend to rely upon their power to coerce and the more incapable they are of handling potential conflicts by alternative tactics of avoidance, persuasion, and compromise.[2] Therefore, the more probable is conflict, the less sophisticated are the authorities.

Finally, the nature of the bonds between authorities and subjects can be expected to affect the probability of conflict over an illegal cultural difference. Where subjects are strongly identified with the authorities and generally agree in moral evaluations, an announced norm may be accepted in a "Father knows best" spirit. But where subjects keep their places not so much because they really believe in the system as because they have become habituated to the

[2]Trebach's data from prisoner interviews in New Jersey and Pennsylvania clearly suggest—despite the methodological shortcomings of the research—that federal officers in the United States, especially the FBI, are far less prone to use violence than are state and local officers, who are typically far less adequately trained and have met far less rigorous educational and other recruitment standards. Arnold S. Trebach. *The Rationing of Justice: Constitutional Rights and the Criminal Process* (New Brunswick, N. J.: Rutgers University Press, 1964), pp. 42–46, 252–256.

setup, defining as criminal some characteristic of them and their way of life may spark them to awareness and challenges to authority. The less the importance of normative consensus and the greater the importance of the social norm of deference as the basis of social order, the less likely are subjects to accept the authority structure when they do think about it, in reference both to the right of authorities to announce norms and to the official status of the behavior of enforcers.

We propose, then, that the probability of conflict is greater, the greater the extent to which the basis of legitimacy is the social norm of deference rather than "norm internalization," or consensus.

The propositions offered so far about the conditions under which authorities and subjects are and are not likely to clash over a legal norm must be systematically related to one another before they can be used to explain and predict occurrences in empirical situations, where all the variables are operating simultaneously—balancing, cancelling, or outweighing one another. If we take it that the most fundamental conditions affecting the conflict probability are the degree of correspondence between the legal cultural norm and relevant social norms of the authorities, the degree of correspondence between the divergent cultural interpretation or norm and the relevant social norms of the affected subordinates, and whether and how the two degrees of correspondence are similar or dissimilar, then the variables of organization of the subordinates, sophistication of the subordinates, and sophistication of the authorities will determine variation in the conflict probability *within* but not *among* the four basic situations defined by the combinations of high and low congruences of cultural and social norms for the two parties. A summary of the conditions under which normative-legal conflict is most-to-least likely to occur upon the announcement of a legal norm can be seen in Figure 1.

The probabilities of conflict will be highest in the high-high quadrant of Figure 1, lower in the quadrant where congruence is high for authorities and low for subordinates, next to lowest in the low-authorities and high-subordinates quadrant, and lowest in the low-low quadrant—although the probabilities will vary from a maximum to a minimum within each quadrant. Values within each quadrant can be expected to vary just as suggested above with the added expectation that all the values will be higher where the authorities are unsophisticated than where they are sophisticated. In detail, the cell numbered *1* says that conflict is most probable—exactly how probable must await the insertion of specific values from

FIGURE 1

Expected Relative Probabilities of
Normative-Legal Conflict*

				Authorities			
				HC		LC	
				U	S	U	S
			U	1	5	17	21
		O					
			S	3	7	19	23
HC							
			U	2	6	18	22
	UO						
			S	4	8	20	24
Subjects							
			U	9	13	25	29
		O					
			S	11	15	27	31
LC							
			U	10	14	26	30
	UO						
			S	12	16	28	32

HC = High congruence of cultural and social norms
LC = Low congruence of cultural and social norms
 O = Organized
UO = Unorganized
 S = Sophisticated
 U = Unsophisticated
 * 1—32 = Highest-lowest probabilities

research—where there are (1) high-high congruences, (2) organized, unsophisticated subordinates, and (3) unsophisticated authorities. Cell 2 says the next lower conflict probability is expected where we find (1) high-high congruences, (2) unorganized, unsophisticated subordinates, and (3) unsophisticated authorities. And so on down to the lowest probability in cell 32, which we expect where there are (1) low-low congruences, (2) unorganized, sophisticated subordinates, and (3) sophisticated authorities. Again, however, we do not know just *how* unlikely is conflict in this minimum-chance situation until we can plug in an absolute probability estimate based upon research findings. All that can be postulated is that this will be the lowest value of the 32 possibilities and that the value will be somewhere above .00, because the authorities are, after all, on public record against an attribute actually found in some part of the population, or at least defined differently in some part. In sum, conflict is presumed to be more likely when a cultural difference exists and is brought out into the open by the announcement of a norm than when no difference exists or when definitions of right and wrong are not given legal status. We have indicated the conditions under which the probability is and is not likely to increase.

Toward a Marxian Theory of Deviance

Steven Spitzer

The Production of Deviance in Capitalist Society

The concept of deviance production offers a starting point for the analysis of both deviance and control. But for such a construct to serve as a critical tool it must be grounded in an historical and structural investigation of society. For Marx, the crucial unit of analysis is the mode of production that dominates a given historical period. If we are to have a Marxian theory of deviance, therefore, deviance production must be understood in relationship to specific forms of socio-economic organization. In our society, productive activity is organized capitalistically and it is ultimately defined by "the process that transforms on the one hand, the social means of subsistence and of production into capital, on the other hand the immediate producers into wage labourers" (Marx, 1967:714).

There are two features of the capitalist mode of production important for purposes of this discussion. First, as a mode of production it forms the foundation or infrastructure of our society. This means that the starting point of our analysis must be an understanding of the economic organization of capitalist societies and the impact of that organization on all aspects of social life. But the capitalist mode of production is an important starting point in another sense. It contains contradictions which reflect the internal tendencies of capitalism. These contradictions are important because they explain the changing character of the capitalist system and the nature of its impact on social, po-

"Toward a Marxian Theory of Deviance" by Steven Spitzer in *Social Problems* Vol. 22, No. 5, June, 1975, pp. 641–651.

litical and intellectual activity. The formulation of a Marxist perspective on deviance requires the interpretation of the process through which the contradictions of capitalism are expressed. In particular, the theory must illustrate the relationship between specific contradictions, the problems of capitalist development and the production of a deviant class.

The superstructure of society emerges from and reflects the ongoing development of economic forces (the infrastructure). In class societies this superstructure preserves the hegemony of the ruling class through a system of class controls. These controls, which are institutionalized in the family, church, private associations, media, schools and the state, provide a mechanism for coping with the contradictions and achieving the aims of capitalist development.

Among the most important functions served by the superstructure in capitalist societies is the regulation and management of problem populations. Because deviance processing is only one of the methods available for social control, these groups supply raw material for deviance production, but are by no means synonymous with deviant populations. Problem populations tend to share a number of social characteristics, but most important among these is the fact that their behavior, personal qualities and/or position threaten the *social relations of production* in capitalist societies. In other words, populations become generally eligible for management as deviant when they disturb, hinder or call into question any of the following:

1. capitalist modes of appropriating the product of human labor (e.g., when the poor "steal" from the rich)
2. the social conditions under which capitalist production takes place (e.g., those who refuse or are unable to perform wage labor)
3. patterns of distribution and consumption in capitalist society (e.g., those who use drugs for escape and transcendence rather than sociability and adjustment)
4. the process of socialization for productive and non-productive roles (e.g., youth who refuse to be schooled or those who deny the validity of "family life")[1]

[1] To the extent that a group (e.g., homosexuals) blatantly and systematically challenges the validity of the bourgeois family it is likely to become part of the problem population. The family is essential to capitalist society as a unit for consumption, socialization and the reproduction of the socially necessary labor force (cf. Frankford and Snitow, 1972; Secombe, 1973; Zaretsky, 1973).

5. the ideology which supports the functioning of capitalist society (e.g., proponents of alternative forms of social organization)

Although problem populations are defined in terms of the threat and costs that they present to the social relations of production in capitalist societies, these populations are far from isomorphic with a revolutionary class. It is certainly true that some members of the problem population, may under specific circumstances possess revolutionary potential. But this potential can only be realized if the problematic group is located in a position of functional indispensability within the capitalist system. Historically, capitalist societies have been quite successful in transforming those who are problematic and indispensable (the protorevolutionary class) into groups who are either problematic and dispensable (candidates for deviance processing), or indispensable but not problematic (supporters of the capitalist order). On the other hand, simply because a group is manageable does not mean that it ceases to be a problem for the capitalist class. Even though dispensable problem populations cannot overturn the capitalist system, they can represent a significant impediment to its maintenance and growth. It is in this sense that they become eligible for management as deviants.

Problem populations are created in two ways — either directly through the expression of fundamental contradictions in the capitalist mode of production or indirectly through disturbances in the system of class rule. An example of the first process is found in Marx's analysis of the "relative surplus-population."

Writing on the "General Law of Capitalist Accumulation" Marx explains how increased social redundance is inherent in the development of the capitalist mode of production:

With the extension of the scale of production, and the mass of the labourers set in motion, with the greater breadth and fullness of all sources of wealth, there is also an extension of the scale on which greater attraction of labourers by capital is accompanied by their greater repulsion . . . The labouring population therefore produces, along with the accumulation of capital produced by it, the means by which itself is made relatively superfluous, . . . and it does this to an always increasing extent (Marx, 1967:631).

In its most limited sense the production of a relative surplus-population involves the creation of a class which is economically redundant. But insofar as the conditions of economic existence determine social existence, this process helps explain the emergence of groups who become both threatening and vulnerable at the same time. The marginal status of these populations reduces their stake in the maintenance of the system while their powerlessness and dispensability renders them increasingly susceptible to the mechanisms of official control.

The paradox surrounding the production of the relative surplus-population is that this population is both useful and menacing to the accumulation of capital. Marx describes how the relative surplus-population "forms a disposable industrial army, that belongs to capital quite as absolutely as if the latter had bred it at its own cost," and how this army, "creates, for the changing needs of the self-expansion of capital, a mass of human material always ready for exploitation" (Marx, 1967:632).

On the other hand, it is apparent that an excessive increase in what Marx called the "lowest sediment" of the relative surplus-population might seriously impair the growth of capital. The social expenses and threat to social harmony created by a large and economically stagnant surplus-population could jeopardize the preconditions for accumulation by undermining the ideology of equality so essential to the legitimation of production relations in bourgeois democracies, diverting revenues away from capital investment toward control and support operations, and providing a basis for political organization of the dispossessed.[2] To the extent that the relative surplus-population confronts the capitalist class as a threat to the social relations of production it reflects an important contradiction in modern capitalist societies: a surplus-population is a necessary product of and condition for the accumulation of wealth on a capitalist basis, but it also creates a form of social expense which must be neutralized or controlled if production relations and conditions for increased accumulation are to remain unimpaired.

Problem populations are also generated through contradictions which develop in the system of class rule. The institutions which make up the superstructure of capitalist society originate and are maintained to guarantee the interests of the capitalist class. Yet these institutions necessarily reproduce, rather than resolve, the contradictions of the capitalist order. In a dialectical fashion, arrangements which arise in order to buttress capitalism are trans-

---

[2] O'Connor (1973) discusses this problem in terms of the crisis faced by the capitalist state in maintaining conditions for profitable accumulation and social harmony.

formed into their opposite—structures for the cultivation of internal threats. An instructive example of this process is found in
the emergence and transformation of educational institutions in
the United States.

The introduction of mass education in the United States can
be traced to the developing needs of corporate capitalism (cf.
Karier, 1973; Cohen and Lazerson, 1972; Bowles and Gintis, 1972;
Spring, 1972). Compulsory education provided a means of training,
testing and sorting, and assimilating wage-laborers, as well as
withholding certain populations from the labor market. The system was also intended to preserve the values of bourgeois society
and operate as an "inexpensive form of police" (Spring, 1973:31).
However, as Gintis (1973) and Bowles (1973) have suggested, the
internal contradictions of schooling can lead to effects opposite of
those intended. For the poor, early schooling can make explicit the
oppressiveness and alienating character of capitalist institutions,
while higher education can instill critical abilities which lead students to "bite the hand that feeds them." In both cases educational
institutions create troublesome populations (i.e., drop outs and
student radicals) and contribute to the very problems they were
designed to solve.

After understanding how and why specific groups become
generally bothersome in capitalist society, it is necessary to investigate the conditions under which these groups are transformed
into proper objects for social control. In other words, we must ask
what distinguishes the generally problematic from the specifically
deviant. The rate at which problem populations are converted into
deviants will reflect the relationship between these populations
and the control system. This rate is likely to be influenced by the:

1. *Extensiveness and Intensity of State Controls.* Deviance processing
   (as opposed to other control measures) is more likely to occur
   when problem management is monopolized by the state. As
   state controls are applied more generally the proportion of
   official deviants will increase.
2. *Size and Level of Threat Presented by the Problem Population.* The
   larger and more threatening the problem population, the
   greater the likelihood that this population will have to be controlled through deviance processing rather than other methods.
   As the threat created by these populations exceeds the capacities of informal restraints, their management requires a broad-
   ening of the reaction system and an increasing centralization
   and coordination of control activities.

3. *Level of Organization of the Problem Population.* When and if problem populations are able to organize and develop limited amounts of political power, deviance processing becomes increasingly less effective as a tool for social control. The attribution of deviant status is most likely to occur when a group is relatively impotent and atomized.

4. *Effectiveness of Control Structures Organized through Civil Society.* The greater the effectiveness of the organs of civil society (i.e., the family, church, media, schools, sports) in solving the problems of class control, the less the likelihood that deviance processing (a more explicitly political process) will be employed.

5. *Availability and Effectiveness of Alternative Types of Official Processing.* In some cases the state will be able effectively to incorporate certain segments of the problem population into specially created "pro-social" roles. In the modern era, for example, conscription and public works projects (Piven and Cloward, 1971) helped neutralize the problems posed by troublesome populations without creating new or expanding old deviant categories.

6. *Availability and Effectiveness of Parallel Control Structures.* In many instances the state can transfer its costs of deviance production by supporting or at least tolerating the activities of independent control networks which operate in its interests. For example, when the state is denied or is reluctant to assert a monopoly over the use of force it is frequently willing to encourage vigilante organizations and private police in the suppression of problem populations. Similarly, the state is often benefited by the policies and practices of organized crime, insofar as these activities help pacify, contain and enforce order among potentially disruptive groups (Schelling, 1967).

7. *Utility of Problem Populations.* While problem populations are defined in terms of their threat and costs to capitalist relations of production, they are not threatening in every respect. They can be supportive economically (as part of a surplus labor pool or dual labor market), politically (as evidence of the need for state intervention) and ideologically (as scapegoats for rising discontent). In other words, under certain conditions capitalist societies derive benefits from maintaining a number of visible and uncontrolled "troublemakers" in their midst. Such populations are distinguished by the fact that while they remain generally bothersome, the costs that they inflict are most immediately absorbed by other members of the problem population.

Policies evolve, not so much to eliminate or actively suppress these groups, but to deflect their threat away from targets which are sacred to the capitalist class. Victimization is permitted and even encouraged, as long as the victims are members of an expendable class.

Two more or less discrete groupings are established through the operations of official control. These groups are a product of different operating assumptions and administrative orientations toward the deviant population. On the one hand, there is *social junk* which, from the point of view of the dominant class, is a costly yet relatively harmless burden to society. The discreditability of social junk resides in the failure, inability or refusal of this group to participate in the roles supportive of capitalist society. Social junk is most likely to come to official attention when informal resources have been exhausted or when the magnitude of the problem becomes significant enough to create a basis for "public concern." Since the threat presented by social junk is passive, growing out of its inability to compete and its withdrawal from the prevailing social order, controls are usually designed to regulate and contain rather than eliminate and suppress the problem. Clear-cut examples of social junk in modern capitalist societies might include the officially administered aged, handicapped, mentally ill and mentally retarded.

In contrast to social junk, there is a category that can be roughly described as *social dynamite*. The essential quality of deviance managed as social dynamite is its potential actively to call into question established relationships, especially relations of production and domination. Generally, therefore, social dynamite tends to be more youthful, alienated and politically volatile than social junk. The control of social dynamite is usually premised on an assumption that the problem is acute in nature, requiring a rapid and focused expenditure of control resources. This is in contrast to the handling of social junk frequently based on a belief that the problem is chronic and best controlled through broad reactive, rather than intensive and selective measures. Correspondingly, social dynamite is normally processed through the legal system with its capacity for active intervention, while social junk is frequently (but not always)[3] administered by the agencies and agents of the therapeutic and welfare state.

[3] It has been estimated, for instance, that 1/3 of all arrests in America are for the offense of public drunkenness. Most of these apparently involve "sick" and destitute "skid row alcoholics" (Morris and Hawkins, 1969).

Many varieties of deviant populations are alternatively or simultaneously dealt with as either social junk and/or social dynamite. The welfare poor, homosexuals, alcoholics and "problem children" are among the categories reflecting the equivocal nature of the control process and its dependence on the political, economic and ideological priorities of deviance production. The changing nature of these priorities and their implications for the future may be best understood by examining some of the tendencies of modern capitalist systems.

Monopoly Capital and Deviance Production

Marx viewed capitalism as a system constantly transforming itself. He explained these changes in terms of certain tendencies and contradictions immanent within the capitalist mode of production. One of the most important processes identified by Marx was the tendency for the organic composition of capital to rise. Simply stated, capitalism requires increased productivity to survive, and increased productivity is only made possible by raising the ratio of machines (dead labor) to men (living labor). This tendency is self-reinforcing since, "the further machine production advances, the higher becomes the organic composition of capital needed for an entrepreneur to secure the average profit." (Mandel, 1968:163). This phenomenon helps us explain the course of capitalist development over the last century and the rise of monopoly capital (Baran and Sweezy, 1966).

For the purposes of this analysis there are at least two important consequences of this process. First, the growth of constant capital (machines and raw material) in the production process leads to an expansion in the overall size of the relative surplus-population. The reasons for this are obvious. The increasingly technological character of production removes more and more laborers from productive activity for longer periods of time. Thus, modern capitalist societies have been required progressively to reduce the number of productive years in a worker's life, defining both young and old as economically superfluous. Especially affected are the unskilled who become more and more expendable as capital expands.

In addition to affecting the general size of the relative surplus-population, the rise of the organic composition of capital leads to an increase in the relative stagnancy of that population. In Marx's original analysis he distinguished between forms of superfluous population that were floating and stagnant. The floating population consists of workers who are "sometimes repelled, sometimes attracted again in greater masses, the number of those employed increasing on the whole, although in a constantly decreasing proportion to the scale of production" (1967:641). From the point of view of capitalist accumulation the floating population offers the greatest economic flexibility and the fewest problems of social control because they are most effectively tied to capital by the "natural laws of production." Unfortunately (for the capitalists at least), these groups come to comprise a smaller and smaller proportion of the relative surplus-population. The increasing specialization of productive activity raises the cost of reproducing labor and heightens the demand for highly skilled and "internally controlled" forms of wage labor (Gorz, 1970). The process through which unskilled workers are alternatively absorbed and expelled from the labor force is thereby impaired, and the relative surplus-population comes to be made up of increasing numbers of persons who are more or less permanently redundant. The boundaries between the "useful" and the "useless" are more clearly delineated, while standards for social disqualification are more liberally defined.

With the growth of monopoly capital, therefore, the relative surplus-population begins to take on the character of a population which is more and more absolute. At the same time, the market becomes a less reliable means of disciplining these populations and the "invisible hand" is more frequently replaced by the "visible fist." The implications for deviance production are twofold: (1) problem populations become gradually more problematic — both in terms of their size and their insensitivity to economic controls, and (2) the resources of the state need to be applied in greater proportion to protect capitalist relations of production and insure the accumulation of capital.

State Capitalism and New Forms of Control

The major problems faced by monopoly capitalism are surplus population and surplus production. Attempts to solve these problems have led to the creation of the welfare/warfare state (Baran and Sweezy, 1966; Marcuse, 1964; O'Connor, 1973; Gross, 1970). The warfare state attacks the problem of overconsumption by providing "wasteful" consumption and protection for the expansion of foreign markets. The welfare state helps absorb and deflect social expenses engendered by a redundant domestic population. Accordingly, the economic development of capitalist societies has come to depend increasingly on the support of the state.

The emergence of state capitalism and the growing interpenetration of the political and economic spheres have had a number of implications for the organization and administration of class rule. The most important effect of these trends is that control functions are increasingly transferred from the organs of civil society to the organs of political society (the state). As the maintenance of social harmony becomes more difficult and the contradictions of civil society intensify, the state is forced to take a more direct and extensive role in the management of problem populations. This is especially true to the extent that the primary socializing institutions in capitalist societies (e.g., the family and the church) can no longer be counted on to produce obedient and "productive" citizens.

Growing state intervention, especially intervention in the process of socialization, is likely to produce an emphasis on general-preventive (integrative), rather than selective-reactive (segregative) controls. Instead of waiting for troublemakers to surface and managing them through segregative techniques, the state is likely to focus more and more on generally applied incentives and assimilative controls. This shift is consistent with the growth of state capitalism because, on the one hand, it provides mechanisms and policies to nip disruptive influences "in the bud," and, on the other, it paves the way toward a more rational exploitation of human capital. Regarding the latter point, it is clear that effective social engineering depends more on social investment and anticipatory planning than coercive control, and societies may more profitably manage populations by viewing them as human capital, than as human waste. An investment orientation has long been popular in state socialist societies (Rimlinger, 1961, 1966), and its value, not surprisingly, has been increasingly acknowledged by many capitalist states.[4]

In addition to the advantages of integrative controls, segregative measures are likely to fall into disfavor for a more immediate reason—they are relatively costly to formulate and apply. Because of its fiscal problems the state must search for means of economizing control operations without jeopardizing capitalist expansion.

[4] Despite the general tendencies of state capitalism, its internal ideological contradictions may actually frustrate the adoption of an investment approach. For example, in discussing social welfare policy Rimlinger (1966:571) concludes that "in a country like the United States, which has a strong individualistic heritage, the idea is still alive that any kind of social protection has adverse productivity effects. A country like the Soviet Union, with a centrally planned economy and a collectivist ideology, is likely to make an earlier and more deliberate use of health and welfare programs for purposes of influencing productivity and developing manpower."

Segregative handling, especially institutionalization, has been useful in manipulating and providing a receptacle for social junk and social dynamite. Nonetheless, the per capita cost of this type of management is typically quite high. Because of its continuing reliance on segregative controls the state is faced with a growing crisis — the overproduction of deviance. The magnitude of the problem and the inherent weaknesses of available approaches tend to limit the alternatives, but among those which are likely to be favored in the future are:

1. *Normalization.* Perhaps the most expedient response to the overproduction of deviance is the normalization of populations traditionally managed as deviant. Normalization occurs when deviance processing is reduced in scope without supplying specific alternatives, and certain segments of the problem population are "swept under the rug." To be successful this strategy requires the creation of invisible deviants who can be easily absorbed into society and disappear from view.

    A current example of this approach is found in the decarceration movement which has reduced the number of inmates in prisons (BOP, 1972) and mental hospitals (NIMH, 1970) over the last fifteen years. By curtailing commitments and increasing turn-over rates the state is able to limit the scale and increase the efficiency of institutionalization. If, however, direct release is likely to focus too much attention on the shortcomings of the state a number of intermediate solutions can be adopted. These include subsidies for private control arrangements (e.g., foster homes, old age homes) and decentralized control facilities (e.g., community treatment centers, halfway houses). In both cases, the fiscal burden of the state is reduced while the dangers of complete normalization are avoided.

2. *Conversion.* To a certain extent the expenses generated by problem and deviant populations can be offset by encouraging their direct participation in the process of control. Potential troublemakers can be recruited as policemen, social workers and attendants, while confirmed deviants can be "rehabilitated" by becoming counselors, psychiatric aides and parole officers. In other words, if a large number of the controlled can be converted into a first line of defense, threats to the system of class rule can be transformed into resources for its support.[5]

[5] In his analysis of the lumpenproletariat Marx (1964) clearly recognized how the underclass could be manipulated as a "bribed tool of reactionary intrigue."

3. *Containment*. One means of responding to threatening populations without individualized manipulation is through a policy of containment or compartmentalization. This policy involves the geographic segregation of large populations and the use of formal and informal sanctions to circumscribe the challenges that they present. Instead of classifying and handling problem populations in terms of the specific expenses that they create, these groups are loosely administered as a homogeneous class who can be ignored or managed passively as long as they remain in their place.

   Strategies of containment have always flourished where social segregation exists, but they have become especially favored in modern capitalist societies. One reason for this is their compatibility with patterns of residential segregation, ghettoization, and internal colonialism (Blauner, 1969).

4. *Support of Criminal Enterprise*. Another way the overproduction of deviance may be eased is by granting greater power and influence to organized crime. Although predatory criminal enterprise is assumed to stand in opposition to the goals of the state and the capitalist class, it performs valuable and unique functions in the service of class rule (McIntosh, 1973). By creating a parallel structure, organized crime provides a means of support for groups who might otherwise become a burden on the state. The activities of organized crime are also important in the pacification of problem populations. Organized crime provides goods and services which ease the hardships and deflect the energies of the underclass. In this role the "crime industry" performs a cooling-out function and offers a control resource which might otherwise not exist. Moreover, insofar as criminal enterprise attempts to reduce uncertainty and risk in its operations, it aids the state in the maintenance of public order. This is particularly true to the extent that the rationalization of criminal activity reduces the collateral costs (i.e., violence) associated with predatory crime (Schelling, 1967).

References

Baran, Paul, and Paul M. Sweezy
  1966 Monopoly Capital. New York: Monthly Review Press.
Blauner, Robert
  1969 "Internal colonialism and ghetto revolt." Social Problems 16 (Spring): 393–408.

Bowles, Samuel
1973 "Contradictions in United States higher education." Pp. 165–199 in James H. Weaver (ed.), Modern Political Economy: Radical Versus Orthodox Approaches. Boston: Allyn and Bacon.

Bowles, Samuel, and Herbert Gintis
1972 "I.Q. in the U.S. class structure." Social Policy 3 (November/December): 65–96.

Bureau of Prisons
1972 National Prisoner Statistics. Prisoners in State and Federal Institutions for Adult Felons. Washington, D.C.: Bureau of Prisons.

Cohen, David K., and Marvin Lazerson
1972 "Education and the corporate order." Socialist Revolution (March/April): 48–72.

Foucault, Michel
1965 Madness and Civilization. New York: Random House.

Frankford, Evelyn, and Ann Snitow
1972 "The trap of domesticity: notes on the family." Socialist Revolution (July/August): 83–94.

Gintis, Herbert
1973 "Alienation and power." Pp. 431–465 in James H. Weaver (ed.), Modern Political Economy: Radical Versus Orthodox Approaches. Boston: Allyn and Bacon.

Gorz, Andre
1970 "Capitalist relations of production and the socially necessary labor force." Pp. 155–171 in Arthur Lothstein (ed.), All We Are Saying . . . New York: G. P. Putnam.

Gross, Bertram M.
1970 "Friendly fascism: a model for America." Social Policy (November/December): 44–52.

Helmer, John, and Thomas Vietorisz
1973 "Drug use, the labor market and class conflict." Paper presented at Annual Meeting of the American Sociological Association.

Karier, Clarence J.
1973 "Business values and the educational state." Pp. 6–29 in Clarence J. Karier, Paul Violas, and Joel Spring (eds.), Roots of Crisis: American Education in the Twentieth Century. Chicago: Rand McNally.

Mandel, Ernest
1968 Marxist Economic Theory (Volume I). New York: Monthly Review Press.

Marcuse, Herbert
1964 One-Dimensional Man. Boston: Beacon Press.

Marx, Karl
1964 Class Struggles in France 1848–1850. New York: International Publishers.
1967 Capital (Volume I). New York: International Publishers.

McIntosh, Mary
1973 "The growth of racketeering." Economy and Society (February): 35–69.
Morris, Norval, and Gordon Hawkins
1969 The Honest Politician's Guide to Crime Control. Chicago: University of Chicago Press.
Musto, David F.
1973 The American Disease: Origins of Narcotic Control. New Haven: Yale University Press.
National Institute of Mental Health
1970 Trends in Resident Patients—State and County Mental Hospitals, 1950–1968. Biometry Branch, Office of Program Planning and Evaluation. Rockville, Maryland: National Institute of Mental Health.
O'Connor, James
1973 The Fiscal Crisis of the State. New York: St. Martin's Press.
Piven, Frances, and Richard A. Cloward
1971 Regulating the Poor: The Functions of Public Welfare. New York: Random House.
Rimlinger, Gaston V.
1961 "Social security, incentives, and controls in the U.S. and U.S.S.R." Comparative Studies in Society and History 4 (November): 104–124.
1966 "Welfare policy and economic development: a comparative historical perspective." Journal of Economic History (December): 556–571.
Schelling, Thomas
1967 "Economics and criminal enterprise." Public Interest (Spring): 61–78.
Secombe, Wally
1973 "The housewife and her labour under capitalism." New Left Review (January-February): 3–24.
Spring, Joel
1972 Education and the Rise of the Corporate State. Boston: Beacon Press.
1973 "Education as a form of social control." Pp. 30–39 in Clarence J. Karier, Paul Violas, and Joel Spring (eds.), Roots of Crisis: American Education in the Twentieth Century. Chicago: Rand McNally.
Turk, Austin T.
1969 Criminality and Legal Order. Chicago: Rand McNally and Company.
Zaretsky, Eli
1973 "Capitalism, the family and personal life: parts 1 & 2." Socialist Revolution (January-April/May-June): 69–126, 19–70.

Law, Order, and Power
William J. Chambliss and Robert B. Seidman

From the anthropological inquiries into primitive societies and the philosophical concerns with the law we have inherited a set of beliefs about legal systems that is best described as a myth. These beliefs take the form of "natural-law" (in various guises) perspectives in jurisprudence, of "value-consensus" perspectives in the social sciences, and "public-interest" assumptions in the culture at large. The popular view is that (1) the law represents the values of society; (2) if it does not represent the values of everyone, then it at least expresses the best common denominator of the society and operates through a value-neutral governmental structure, which is ultimately controlled by the choice of the people; and (3) in the long run the law serves the best interests of the society.

It is easy to maintain a myth like this provided that one does not look to see what in fact takes place in the day-to-day operations of the legal system. When everyday events that constitute the law in action are examined and brought together so as to represent the legal system as a dynamic, living institution, the mythical character of such claims becomes all too apparent. To suggest that the law represents the "value-consensus" in a pluralistic, stratified society is to assume that the only consensus that really matters is that of those whose views and interests are represented by the lawmakers. It is . . . patently absurd to argue that the law can ever represent everyone's views in strati-

From *Law, Order, and Power* by William J. Chambliss and Robert B. Seidman. Reading, Massachusetts: Addison-Wesley Publishing Company, 1971, pp. 502–504, 473–475.

fied societies, since the patterns of life of the different strata differ so markedly that the value-systems must differ correspondingly. Conflicting as well as competing value-systems cannot, by their very nature, coexist in a system of norms that strives to maintain some semblance of logical consistency.

It is logically possible, however, for the government, and the legal system as its principal norm-interpreter, to act as a value-neutral force working out reasoned solutions to conflict. But logic does not determine the shape of legal systems any more than it determines the shape of history. The reality of unequal power and control of resources, the selective process by which persons are moved from apprenticeship to decision-making, the criteria by which success is judged by those who have the power to make decisions — all these factors converge to influence the men who occupy the decision-making positions in the legal system and together they determine the output of the system. They make it inevitable that the legal system will *not* operate as a value-neutral arena in which conflicts are solved according to principles of justice and fairness. They create the conditions under which conflicts will be resolved in favor of those who control the resources of the system. If justice or fairness happen to be served, it is sheer coincidence.

[An] examination of the law in action also puts to rest the comfortable idea that the law represents the "public interest." One can of course define "public interest" as the maintenance of the existing system of power and privilege. In that case, it becomes a tautology that the law represents that interest. The law does . . . represent the interests of those in power. But if the interests of society are conceived more broadly (as they usually are, implicitly if not explicitly, by those who argue that the law serves the public interest), then they are not served by the law in practice. The interests of the disenfranchised in a stratified society are not served by a system in which adequate housing, medical care, and legal protection depend on being enfranchised.

In America it is frequently argued that to have "freedom" is to have a system which allows one group to make a profit over another. To maintain the existing legal system requires a choice. On this argument that choice is between maintaining a legal system that serves to support the existing economic system with its power structure and developing an equitable legal system accompanied by the loss of "personal freedom." But the old question comes back to plague us: Freedom for whom? Is the black man who provides such a ready source of cases for the welfare workers, the mental hospitals, and the prisons "free"? Are the slum dwellers who are arrested night after night for "loitering," "drunkenness," or being "suspicious" free? The freedom protected by the system of law is the freedom of those who can afford it. The law serves *their* interests, but they are not "society"; they are one element of society. They may in some complex societies even be a majority (though this is very rare), but the myth that the law serves the interests of "society" misrepresents the facts.

. . . Complex, stratified societies are inevitably pluralistic. As such, the law will always represent the interests of one group as against the interests of others. . . . Even the offenses on which there is a superficial consensus (such as murder, rape, theft) are not so unanimously viewed as wrongdoing if the surface of the abstract caricature is scratched.

. . . The . . . study of the law in action also makes it abundantly clear that the State is hardly a value-neutral arena in which conflicts are worked out for the "good of everyone." Rather, . . . the conflicting interests [are] such that law comes to represent the entrenched power groups.

The theory we . . . [propose] as an alternative to a value-consensus model is heavily influenced by the conflict model of society. . . . The basic notion derived from this model is that society is composed of groups that are in conflict with one another and that the law represents an institutionalized tool of those in power which functions to provide them with superior moral as well as coercive power in the conflict. . . . However, this general proposition is not sufficient to account for all aspects of the legal order. We . . . [supplement] this premise with a number of complementary propositions about the nature of the conflict in stratified societies and the relationship of the law to this conflict. We also [add] to this perspective the critically important element of the bureaucratic character of the legal system—an element which in and of itself guarantees that the legal order will take on a shape and character at variance with what it might have been if the law reflected the "public interest." . . .

Poverty and the Criminal Process

The shape and character of the legal system in complex societies can be understood as deriving from the conflicts inherent in the structure of these societies which are stratified economically and politically. Generally, the legal system in its normative strictures and organizational operations will exhibit those norms and those practices that maintain and enhance the position of entrenched power-holders. Those broad principles underlying the legal order are ramified in and attenuated by the organizational aims of complex societies. The logical structure and its . . . implications . . . may be set forth as a set of propositions. We begin with propositions about the relationship between a group's norms and the law:

Propositions

1. One's "web of life" or the conditions of one's life affect one's values and (internalized) norms.
2. Complex societies are composed of groups with widely different life conditions.
3. Therefore, complex societies are also composed of highly disparate conflicting sets of norms.
4. The probability of a group's having *its* particular normative system embodied in law is *not* distributed equally among the social groups but, rather, is closely related to the group's political and economic position.
5. The higher a group's political or economic position, the greater is the probability that its views will be reflected in the laws.

According to these first five propositions, then, the law will differentially reflect the perspectives, values, definitions of reality, and morality of the middle and upper classes while being in opposition to the morality and values of the poor and lower classes. Given this twist in the content of the law, we are not surprised that the poor should be criminal more often than the nonpoor. The systematically induced bias in a society against the poor goes considerably farther than simply having values incorporated within the legal system which are antithetical to their ways of life. Since, in complex societies, the decision to enforce the laws against certain persons and not against others will be determined primarily by criteria derived from the bureaucratic nature of the law-enforcement agencies, we have the following propositions which explain what takes place within these agencies and the kinds of decisions they are likely to make:

1. The legal system is organized through bureaucratically structured agencies, some of which are primarily norm-creating agencies and others of which are primarily norm-enforcing agencies.

2. The formal role-expectation for each official position in the bureaucracy is defined by authoritatively decreed rules issuing from officials in other positions who themselves operate under position-defining norms giving them the power to issue such rules.

3. Rules, whether defining norm-creating positions or norm-applying positions, necessarily require discretion in the role-occupant for their application.

4. In addition, the rules are for a variety of reasons frequently vague, ambiguous, contradictory, or weakly or inadequately sanctioned.

5. Therefore, each level of the bureaucracy possesses considerable discretion as to the performance of its duties.

6. The decision to create rules by rule-creating officials or to enforce rules by rule-enforcing officials will be determined primarily by criteria derived from the bureaucratic nature of the legal system.

7. Rule-creation and rule-enforcement will take place when such creation or enforcement increases the rewards for the agencies and their officials, and they will not take place when they are conducive to organizational strain.

8. The creation of the rules which define the roles of law-enforcing agencies has been primarily the task of the appellate courts, for which the principal rewards are in the form of approval of other judges, lawyers, and higher-status middle-class persons generally.

9. The explicit value-set of judges, lawyers, and higher-status middle-class persons generally is that which is embodied in the aims of legal-rational legitimacy.

10. Therefore, the rules created by appellate courts will tend to conform to the requirements of legal-rational legitimacy and to the specific administrative requirements of the court organization.

11. The enforcement of laws against persons who possess little or no political power will generally be rewarding to the enforcement agencies of the legal system, while the enforcement of laws against persons who possess political power will be conducive to strains for those agencies.

12. In complex societies, political power is closely tied to social position.

13. Therefore, those laws which prohibit certain types of behavior popular among lower-class persons are more likely to be en-

forced, while laws restricting the behavior of middle- or upper-class persons are not likely to be enforced.

14. Where laws are so stated that people of all classes are equally likely to violate them, the lower the social position of an offender, the greater is the likelihood that sanctions will be imposed on him.

15. When sanctions are imposed, the most severe sanctions will be imposed on persons in the lowest social class.

16. Legal-rational legitimacy requires that laws be stated in general terms equally applicable to all.

17. Therefore, the rules defining the roles of law-enforcement officials will require them to apply the law in an equitable manner.

18. Therefore, to the extent that the rules to be applied are potentially applicable to persons of different social classes, the role-performance of law-enforcement officials may be expected to differ from the role-expectation embodied in the norms defining their positions.

Taken as a unit, these propositions represent the basis of a theory of the legal process in complex societies. It is a theory derived essentially from the facts of the operation of criminal law—facts gathered by a large number of researchers into the criminal-law process at each level of the operation. .

part Seven

Integrative and Processual Theories of Deviance

The preceding sections of this book have been concerned with the major theoretical perspectives on deviance. At the same time an attempt has been made to suggest possible linkages among them. These linkages become even more apparent in the selections that follow. These may be regarded as integrative and processual theories, explicitly or implicitly built upon assumptions contained in the various perspectives presented in the earlier sections. Because these theorists have derived their models from many of the same general theories on deviance, their works share a common theme. The general concern of each is with the social creation of deviance as a behavioral category. As such, they deal with the structural origins of non-conforming behavior as well as with the process by which individuals come to be defined, and define themselves, as deviant. In two of the selections, those by Wilkins and by Farrell and Morrione, these structural and interactional variables are construed as reciprocal. Structural factors are viewed as effecting social interaction and subsequently having social psychological impact on individuals, individuals whose behavior, in turn, is seen as influencing the original social arrangements.

In addition to the integrative and processual aspects of these theories, they suggest that the factors that generate and support non-conformity are not unique to deviance. Factors such as social definition, interaction, adaptations to strain, and socialization all affect conformer and non-conformer alike. This kind of theoretical approach makes the study of deviant behavior a study of human behavior in general.

Richard Quinney utilizes this general approach in his discussion of the *social reality of crime*. According to Quinney, crime is the product of definitions of human behavior that are created by authorized political agents. His analysis, therefore, assumes the existence of conflict and power relations in determining the nature of criminal and non-criminal behavior. That conduct which somehow threatens or conflicts with the interests of the dominant group is designated as criminal. Reflecting Miller's description of the cultural foundations of delinquency, Quinney says that behavior characteristics are relative to specific segments of society: "behavior patterns are structured in segmentally organized society in relation to criminal definitions, and within this context persons engage in actions that have relative probabilities of being defined as criminal." Such modes of behavior are viewed as being culturally transmitted to members of various subgroups through the same processes by which more powerful members of society learn non-criminal behavior.

What Quinney calls *criminal conceptions* (or stereotypes) act to diffuse a common definition of particularly threatening behaviors throughout the social system. Such a definition is necessary if deviance is to be uniformly dealt with in that system. It is, in other words, of relatively great interest to the dominant group to ensure uniform reaction to certain behaviors, depending upon the perceived threat of those behaviors. Once political definitions of culturally learned behavior become stable, those defined as criminal begin to conceive of themselves as such and eventually come to play their role accordingly.

While Quinney's focus is on the *structural origins of deviance*, that is, on the conflict and dominance relations that enable some to define successfully the conduct of others, James Hackler emphasizes the *social psychological processes involved in deviance creation*. Like Quinney, he discusses the process of deviance creation by drawing assumptions from theoretical perspectives presented in earlier sections of the book. Hackler, however, focuses particularly on the impact of deviant definitions on individual self concept and behavior. He states that on the basis of definitions that exist in a society concerning certain categories of individuals, representatives of the conforming population anticipate failure on the part of members of these groups and withold opportunities from them. Such action has important consequences in terms of the identity and role formation of those experiencing this response. Applying this idea to the area of delinquency, Hackler proposes that lower-class children, for example, are expected to behave in predicted ways. These expectations when perceived by the child are important to the development of his self concept and behavior. In his words, "the *perceived* responses constantly indicate to the child the type of person he is and what is expected of him. This leads to self-categorizations and, along with the perceived expectations, influences the roles he will seek to play in an effort to behave in ways compatible with his imagined characteristics and capacities."

Hackler states that those who are treated differentially because of stable social anticipations may turn to one another for personal support. Within these groups the role expectations assigned to them by society become crystallized and are eventually reflected in their behavior. Subcultural norms then, according to Hackler, do not arise as negative reactions to middle-class norms and values, as Cohen had proposed earlier, but rather reflect the internalization of definitions assigned to the deviant by responsible authorities. Since these unfavorable definitions imply the withholding of legitimate opportunities, individuals also may be *prevented* from adopting the standards of comforming society. If such standards are not adopted, or are selectively adopted, a reintegration of the deviant into that society may be precluded.

Thus Hackler provides an analysis that further clarifies the relationship between structure and the individual by pointing to the social psychological impact that an excluding social structure has on the deviant's self concept and on the role that he subsequently adopts. From this model we gain an understanding of the process by which deviant careers become stable. Once excluded from the opportunity structure of legitimate society, and the normative standards which support these structures, the deviant cannot acquire or maintain the skills necessary for full participation in that society.

Focusing more on structural elements, Leslie Wilkins also proposes a model which addresses the persistence of deviant behavior over time. According to Wilkins, conforming behavior is made problematic by the unequal distribution of legitimate opportunities. Pressure to conform to normative standards without the appropriate means is likely to result in innovative methods of goal attainment. If these methods come to be defined as deviant, the consequence for the nonconformer is social isolation. Cut off from legitimate definitions and the norms and values of which they are an expression, the deviant is effectively prevented from returning to the conforming population. Groups of people, faced with similar problems of conformity and exclusion may, in turn, contribute to the development of subcultural systems which run counter to the normative definitions of legitimate society. Exclusion from legitimate definitions and opportunities, on the one hand, and adherence to subculturally derived deviant norms and values, on the other, has consequences for any further interaction that may occur between deviant and conforming others. Without the information necessary for smooth interaction, the previously defined deviant will elicit further negative responses, and the cycle of definitions and exclusion begins anew. Wilkins concludes, then, that the definitions intended to maintain conformity within social systems may, in fact, have the latently disfunctional consequence of producing and maintaining deviant behavior.

Farrell and Morrione advance a model which attempts to explain the homosexual career pattern of deviance-conformity. While the approach has application to other forms of deviance, homosexuality is thought to be most clearly representative of the general processes with which it deals. The model suggests that if an individual perceives others as identifying him as homosexual and reacting to him in accordance with the popular stereotype, his self definition may incorporate the stereotype. These responses and the accompanying feelings of stigma are likely to be experienced with frustration. Bitterness, withdrawal to a homosexual group, and enculturation to a deviant role may be the outcome.

Implicit in Farrell and Morrione's model is the notion that much of the behavior generally associated with homosexuality may be conforming rather than deviant behavior. It conforms to both society's and the subculture's definition of homosexuality. It is suggested that *society* demands this conformity in order to ensure consensus as to what a homosexual is. Without persons who could readily be identified as homosexual, the label might lack its otherwise salient meaning. Thus, contrary to Wilkins' suggestion that societal

375

definitions of deviance are latently disfunctional when they contribute to an intensification of such behavior, Farrell and Morrione conclude that *secondary deviance* is necessary to the maintenance of the social system. It is seen as serving a boundary-maintaining function which operates to produce conformity in a particular area of behavior among the larger population.

John DeLamater's integrative approach to the several deviance theories includes a reward-cost analysis. The origins of non-conformity are many. Its maintenance, however, depends upon the consequences of illegitimate behavior. For those originally socialized to deviant norms and values, the rewards of non-conformity are part of the early learning experiences. To the extent that the attitudes, values, and motivations supportive of deviance become part of the identity of individuals, they will develop strong commitments to their maintenance. Insofar as detection and sanction are avoided, rewards will regularly exceed deprivations.

Deviant behavior may also be a product of re-socialization. Initially exposed to conventional norms, individuals come to incorporate such standards as part of their self-concept. While any number of social or situational factors may produce the first instance of non-conformity, the consequences of such activities will determine subsequent behaviors. If the deviation remains covert, the individual may persist in light of the rewards of the behavior itself. On the other hand, threats of sanction from significant others or disenchantment with the illegitimate activities may produce their termination. Commitment to deviant norms, however, may follow the discovery and sanction of the individual by primary others or may be the result of pressure from co-deviants. In this case, the individual must not only have access to learning and opportunity structures but must acquire the techniques for neutralizing original ties to conventional society in order to achieve a satisfying reward-cost balance.

Finally, DeLamater points out that for those socialized to deviant behavior, formal labeling by social control agents will have little effect. A commitment to deviant values and norms effectively minimizes the costs of official sanction. Individuals whose early experiences were with conventional society, however, may find that efforts at social control act to sever primary ties and to preclude legitimate opportunities. While persons may wish to return to conventional behavior, given the increasing costs of non-conformity, they may be prevented from doing so. In this manner, the formal label becomes a self-fulfilling prophecy in the development of deviant careers.

Each of these theorists reaffirms the importance of the interactive relationship between deviant and conformer as a key to the stability of deviance over time. The persistence of deviance as a behavioral category occurs insofar as deviant definitions become stabilized in both society and the individual. When groups of people are viewed with the anticipation of failure and abrasive encounters between them and conformists reaffirm such definitions, deviance then becomes institutionalized. At the same time, since reaction to individuals on the basis of these stable definitions often means the exclusion of them from normal interaction, the deviant is effectively prevented from reassuming a conforming role. This occurs through both the atrophy of (or inability to obtain) necessary information and through an identification with a role of deviant as it has become defined for him by the larger society.

The Social Reality of Crime
Richard Quinney

Assumptions: Man and Society in a Theory of Crime

In studying any social phenomenon we must hold to some general perspective. Two of those used by sociologists, and by most social analysts for that matter, are the *static* and the *dynamic* interpretations of society. Either is equally plausible, though most sociologists take the static viewpoint.[1] This emphasis has relegated forces and events, such as deviance and crime, which do not appear to be conducive to stability and consensus, to the pathologies of society.

My theory of crime, however, is based on the dynamic perspective. The theory is based on these assumptions about man and society: (1) process, (2) conflict, (3) power, and (4) social action.

PROCESS

The dynamic aspect of social relations may be referred to as "social process." Though in analyzing society we use static descriptions, that is, we define the structure and function of social relations, we must be aware that social phenomena fluctuate continually.[2]

[1]See Robert A. Nisbet, *The Sociological Tradition* (New York: Basic Books, 1966); Reinhard Bendix and Bennett Berger, "Images of Society and Problems of Concept Formation in Sociology," in Gross, *Symposium on Sociological Theory*, pp. 92–118.

[2]Howard Becker, *Systematic Sociology on the Basis of the Beziehungslehre and Gebildelehre of Leopold von Wiess* (New York: John Wiley & Sons, 1932).

We apply this assumption to all social phenomena that have duration and undergo change, that is, all those which interest the sociologist. A social process is a continuous series of actions, taking place in time, and leading to a special kind of result: "a system of social change taking place within a defined situation and exhibiting a particular order of change through the operation of forces present from the first within the situation."[3] Any particular phenomenon, in turn, is viewed as contributing to the dynamics of the total process. As in the "modern systems approach," social phenomena are seen as generating out of an interrelated whole.[4] The methodological implication of the process assumption is that any social phenomenon may be viewed as part of a complex network of events, structures, and underlying processes.

CONFLICT

In any society conflicts between persons, social units, or cultural elements are inevitable, the normal consequences of social life. Conflict is especially prevalent in societies with diverse value systems and normative groups. Experience teaches that we cannot expect to find consensus on all or most values and norms in such societies.

Two models of society contrast sharply: one is regarded as "conflict" and the other, "consensus." With the consensus model we describe social structure as a functionally integrated system held together in equilibrium. In the conflict model, on the other hand, we find that societies and social organizations are shaped by diversity, coercion, and change. The differences between these contending but complementary conceptions of society have been best characterized by Dahrendorf.[5] According to his study, we assume in postulating the consensus (or integrative) model of society that: (1) society is a relatively persistent, stable structure, (2) it is well integrated, (3) every element has a function—it helps maintain the system, and (4) a functioning social structure is based on a consensus on values. For the conflict (or coercion) model of society, on the other hand, we assume that: (1) at every point society is subject to change, (2) it displays at every point dissensus and conflict, (3) every element contributes to change, and (4) it is based on the coercion of some of

[3]Robert MacIver, *Social Causation* (New York: Ginn, 1942), p. 130.

[4]Walter Buckley, "A Methodological Note," in Thomas J. Scheff, *Being Mentally Ill* (Chicago: Aldine, 1966), pp. 201–205.

[5]Ralf Dahrendorf, *Class and Class Conflict in Industrial Society* (Stanford: Stanford University Press, 1959), pp. 161–162.

its members by others. In other words, society is held together by force and constraint and is characterized by ubiquitous conflicts that result in continuous change: "values are ruling rather than common, enforced rather than accepted, at any given point of time."[6]

Although in society as a whole conflict may be general, according to the conflict model, it is still likely that we will find stability and consensus on values among subunits in the society. Groups with their own cultural elements are found in most societies, leading to social differentiation with conflict between the social units; nonetheless integration and stability may appear within specific social groups: "Although the total larger society may be diverse internally and may form only a loosely integrated system, within each subculture there may be high integration of institutions and close conformity of individuals to the patterns sanctioned by their own group."[7]

Conflict need not necessarily disrupt society. Some sociologists have been interested in the *functions* of social conflict, "that is to say, with those consequences of social conflict which make for an increase rather than a decrease in the adaptation or adjustment of particular social relationships or groups."[8] It seems that conflict can promote cooperation, establish group boundaries, and unite social factions. Furthermore, it may lead to new patterns that may in the long run be beneficial to the whole society or to parts of it.[9] Any doubts about its functional possibilities have been dispelled by Dahrendorf: "I would suggest . . . that all that is creativity, innovation, and development in the life of the individual, his group, and his society is due, to no small extent, to the operation of conflicts between group and group, individual and individual, emotion and emotion within one individual. This fundamental fact alone seems to me to justify the value judgment that conflict is essentially 'good' and 'desirable.'"[10] Conflict is not always the disruptive agent in a

[6]Ralf Dahrendorf, "Out of Utopia: Toward a Reorientation in Sociological Analysis," *American Journal of Sociology,* 67 (September, 1958), p. 127.

[7]Robin M. Williams, Jr., *American Society,* 2nd ed. (New York: Alfred A. Knopf, 1960), p. 375.

[8]Lewis A. Coser, *The Functions of Social Conflict* (New York: The Free Press, 1956), p. 8.

[9]Lewis A. Coser, "Social Conflict and the Theory of Social Change," *British Journal of Sociology,* 8 (September, 1957), pp. 197–207.

[10]Dahrendorf, *Class and Class Conflict in Industrial Society,* p. 208. The importance of conflict in society is also discussed in, among other works, George Simmel, *Conflict,* trans. Kurt H. Wolff (New York: The Free Press, 1955); Irving Louis Horowitz, "Consensus, Conflict and Cooperation: A Sociological Inventory," *Social Forces,* 41 (December, 1962), pp. 177–188; Raymond W. Mack, "The Components of Social Conflict," *Social Problems,* 12 (Spring, 1965), pp. 388–397.

society; at certain times it may be meaningful to see it as a cohesive force.

POWER

The conflict conception of society leads us to assume that coherence is assured in any social unit by coercion and constraint. In other words, *power* is the basic characteristic of social organization. "This means that in every social organization some positions are entrusted with a right to exercise control over other positions in order to ensure effective coercion; it means, in other words, that there is a differential distribution of power and authority."[11] Thus, conflict and power are inextricably linked in the conception of society presented here. The differential distribution of power produces conflict between competing groups, and conflict, in turn, is rooted in the competition for power. Wherever men live together conflict and a struggle for power will be found.

Power, then, is the ability of persons and groups to determine the conduct of other persons and groups.[12] It is utilized not for its own sake, but is the vehicle for the enforcement of scarce values in society, whether the values are material, moral, or otherwise. The use of power affects the distribution of values and values affect the distribution of power. The "authoritative allocation of values" is essential to any society.[13] In any society, institutional means are used to officially establish and enforce sets of values for the entire population.

Power and the allocation of values are basic in forming *public policy*. Groups with special *interests* become so well organized that they are able to influence the policies that are to affect all persons. These interest groups exert their influence at every level and branch of government in order to have their own values and interests represented in the policy decisions.[14] Any interest group's ability to

[11]Dahrendorf, *Class and Class Conflict in Industrial Society*, p. 165.

[12]Max Weber, *From Max Weber: Essays in Sociology*, trans. H. H. Gerth and C. Wright Mills (New York: Oxford University Press, 1946); Hans Gerth and C. Wright Mills, *Character and Social Structure* (New York: Harcourt, Brace, 1953), especially pp. 192–273; C. Wright Mills, *The Power Elite* (New York: Oxford University Press, 1956); George Simmel, *The Sociology of George Simmel*, trans. Kurt H. Wolff (New York: The Free Press, 1950), pp. 181–186; Robert Bierstedt, "An Analysis of Social Power," *American Sociological Review*, 15 (December, 1950), pp. 730–738.

[13]David Easton, *The Political System* (New York: Alfred A. Knopf, 1953), p. 137. Similar ideas are found in Harold D. Lasswell, *Politics: Who Gets What, When, How* (New York: McGraw-Hill, 1936); Harold D. Lasswell and Abraham Kaplan, *Power and Society* (New Haven: Yale University Press, 1950).

[14]Among the vast amount of literature on interest groups, see Donald C. Blaisdell, *American Democracy Under Pressure* (New York: Ronald Press, 1957); V. O. Key, Jr.,

influence public policy depends on the group's position in the political power structure. Furthermore, access to the formation of public policy is unequally distributed because of the structural arrangements of the political state. "Access is one of the advantages unequally distributed by such arrangements; that is, in consequence of the structural peculiarities of our government some groups have better and more varied opportunities to influence key points of decision than do others."[15] Groups that have the power to gain access to the decision-making process also inevitably control the lives of others.

A major assumption in my conception of society, therefore, is the importance of interest groups in shaping public policy. Public policy is formed so as to represent the interests and values of groups that are in positions of power. Rather than accept the pluralistic conception of the political process, which assumes that all groups make themselves heard in policy decision-making, I am relying upon a conception that assumes an unequal distribution of power in formulating and administering public policy.[16]

Politics, Parties, and Pressure Groups (New York: Thomas Y. Crowell, 1959); Earl Latham, *Group Basis of Politics* (Ithaca, N.Y.: Cornell University Press, 1952); David Truman, *The Governmental Process* (New York: Alfred A. Knopf, 1951); Henry W. Ehrmann (ed.), *Interest Groups on Four Continents* (Pittsburgh: University of Pittsburgh Press, 1958); Henry A. Turner, "How Pressure Groups Operate," *Annals of the American Academy of Political and Social Science,* 319 (September, 1958), pp. 63–72; Richard W. Gable, "Interest Groups as Policy Shapers," *Annals of the American Academy of Political and Social Science,* 319 (September, 1958), pp. 84–93; Murray S. Stedman, "Pressure Group and the American Tradition," *Annals of the American Academy of Political and Social Science,* 319 (September, 1958), pp. 123–219. For documentation on the influence of specific interest groups, see Robert Engler, *The Politics of Oil* (New York: Macmillan, 1961); Oliver Garceau, *The Political Life of the American Medical Association* (Cambridge: Harvard University Press, 1941); Charles M. Hardin, *The Politics of Agriculture: Soil Conservation and the Struggle for Power in Rural America* (New York: The Free Press of Glencoe, 1962); Grant McConnell, *Private Power and American Democracy* (New York: Alfred A. Knopf, 1966); Harry A. Millis and Royal E. Montgomery, *Organized Labor* (New York: McGraw-Hill, 1945); Warner Schilling, Paul Y. Hammond, and Glenn H. Snyder, *Strategy, Politics and Defense* (New York: Columbia University Press, 1962); William R. Willoughby, *The St. Lawrence Waterway: A Study in Politics and Diplomacy* (Madison: University of Wisconsin Press, 1961).

[15]Truman, *The Governmental Process*, p. 322.

[16]Evaluations of the pluralistic and power approaches are found in Peter Bachrach and Morton S. Baratz, "Two Faces of Power," *American Political Science Review,* 61 (December, 1962), pp. 947–952; Thomas I. Cook, "The Political System: The Stubborn Search for a Science of Politics," *Journal of Philosophy,* 51 (February, 1954), pp. 128–137; Charles S. Hyneman, *The Study of Politics* (Urbana: University of Illinois Press, 1959); William C. Mitchell, "Politics as the Allocation of Values: A Critique," *Ethics,* 71 (January, 1961), pp. 79–89; Talcott Parsons, "The Distribution of Power in American Society," *World Politics,* 10 (October, 1957), pp. 123–143; Charles Perrow, "The Sociological Perspective and Political Pluralism," *Social Research,* 31 (Winter, 1964), pp. 411–422.

SOCIAL ACTION

An assumption of man that is consistent with the conflict-power conception of society asserts that man's actions are purposive and meaningful, that man engages in voluntary behavior. This *humanistic* conception of man contrasts with the oversocialized conception of man. Man is, after all, capable of considering alternative actions, of breaking from the established social order.[17] Once he gains an awareness of self, by being a member of society, he is able to choose his actions. The extent to which he does conform depends in large measure upon his own self-control.[18] Nonconformity may also be part of the process of finding self-identity. It is thus *against* something that the self can emerge.[19]

By conceiving of man as able to reason and choose courses of action, we may see him as changing and becoming, rather than merely being.[20] The kind of culture that man develops shapes his ability to be creative. Through his culture he may develop the capacity to have greater freedom of action.[21] Not only is he shaped by his physical, social, and cultural experiences, he is able to select what he is to experience and develop. The belief in realizing unutilized human potential is growing and should be incorporated in a contemporary conception of human behavior.[22]

The *social action* frame of reference that serves as the basis of the humanistic conception of man is drawn from the work of such writers as Weber, Znaniecki, MacIver, Nadel, Parsons, and Becker.[23] It was originally suggested by Max Weber: "Action is social in

[17]For essentially this aspect of man see Peter Berger, *Invitation to Sociology: A Humanistic Perspective* (New York: Doubleday, 1963), chap. 6; Max Mark, "What Image of Man for Political Science?" *Western Political Quarterly*, 15 (December, 1962), pp. 593–604; Dennis Wrong, "The Oversocialized Conception of Man in Modern Sociology," *American Sociological Review*, 26 (April, 1961), pp. 183–193.

[18]Tamotsu Shibutani, *Society and Personality: An Interactionist Approach to Social Psychology* (Englewood Cliffs, N.J.: Prentice-Hall, 1961), especially pp. 60, 91–94, 276–278. Also see S. F. Nadel, "Social Control and Self-Regulation," *Social Forces*, 31 (March, 1953), pp. 265–273.

[19]Erving Goffman, *Asylums* (New York: Doubleday, 1961), pp. 318–320.

[20]Richard A. Schermerhorn, "Man the Unfinished," *Sociological Quarterly*, 4 (Winter, 1963), pp. 5–17; Gordon W. Allport, *Becoming: Basic Considerations for a Psychology of Personality* (New Haven: Yale University Press, 1955).

[21]Herbert J. Muller, *The Uses of the Past* (New York: Oxford University Press, 1952), especially pp. 40–42.

[22]Julian Huxley, *New Bottles for New Wines* (New York: Harper, 1957).

[23]Florian Znaniecki, *Social Actions* (New York: Farrar and Rinehart, 1936); MacIver, *Social Causation*; S. F. Nadel, *Foundations of Social Anthropology* (New York: The Free Press, 1951); Talcott Parsons, *The Structure of Social Action* (New York: The Free Press, 1949); Howard Becker, *Through Values to Social Interpretation* (Durham: Duke University Press, 1950).

so far as, by virtue of the subjective meaning attached to it by the acting individual (or individuals), it takes account of the behavior of others and is thereby oriented in its own course."[24] Hence, human behavior is *intentional,* has *meaning* for the actors, is *goal-oriented,* and takes place with an *awareness* of the consequences of behavior.

Because man engages in social action, a *social reality* is created. That is, man in interaction with others constructs a meaningful world of everyday life.

> It is the world of cultural objects and social institutions into which we are all born, within which we have to find our bearings, and with which we have to come to terms. From the outset, we, the actors on the social scene, experience the world we live in as a world both of nature and of culture, not as a private but as an intersubjective one, that is, as a world common to all of us, either actually given or potentially accessible to everyone; and this involves intercommunication and language.[25]

Social reality consists of both the social meanings and the products of the subjective world of persons. Man, accordingly, constructs activities and patterns of actions as he attaches meaning to his everyday existence.[26] Social reality is thus both a *conceptual reality* and a *phenomenal reality.* Having constructed social reality, man finds a world of meanings and events that is real to him as a conscious social being.

Theory: The Social Reality of Crime

The theory contains six propositions and a number of statements within the propositions. With the first proposition I define crime. The next four are the explanatory units. In the final proposition the other five are collected to form a composite describing the social reality of crime. The propositions and their integration into a theory of crime reflect the assumptions about explanation and about man and society outlined above.[27]

---

[24]Max Weber, *The Theory of Social and Economic Organization,* trans. A. M. Henderson and Talcott Parsons (New York: The Free Press), p. 88.

[25]Alfred Schutz, *The Problem of Social Reality: Collected Papers I* (The Hague: Martinus Nijhoff, 1962), p. 53.

[26]See Peter L. Berger and Thomas Luckmann, *The Social Construction of Reality* (Garden City, N.Y.: Doubleday, 1966).

[27]For earlier background material, see Richard Quinney, "A Conception of Man and Society for Criminology," *Sociological Quarterly,* 6 (Spring, 1965), pp. 119–127; Quinney, "Crime in Political Perspective," *American Behavioral Scientist,* 8 (Decem-

Proposition 1 (definition of crime)
Crime is a definition of human conduct that is created by authorized agents in a politically organized society.

This is the essential starting point in the theory—a definition of crime—which itself is based on the concept of definition. Crime is a *definition* of behavior that is conferred on some persons by others. Agents of the law (legislators, police, prosecutors, and judges), representing segments of a politically organized society, are responsible for formulating and administering criminal law. Persons and behaviors, therefore, become criminal because of the *formulation* and *application* of criminal definitions. Thus, *crime is created.*

By viewing crime as a definition, we are able to avoid the commonly used "clinical perspective," which leads one to concentrate on the quality of the act and to assume that criminal behavior is an individual pathology.[28] Crime is not inherent in behavior, but is a judgment made by some about the actions and characteristics of others.[29] This proposition allows us to focus on the formulation and administration of the criminal law as it touches upon the behaviors that become defined as criminal. Crime is seen as a result of a process which culminates in the defining of persons and behaviors as criminal. It follows, then, that *the greater the number of criminal definitions formulated and applied, the greater the amount of crime.*

Proposition 2 (formulation of criminal definitions)
Criminal definitions describe behaviors that conflict with the interests of the segments of society that have the power to shape public policy.

Criminal definitions are formulated according to the interests of those *segments* (types of social groupings) of society which have

---

ber, 1964), pp. 19–22; Quinney, "Is Criminal Behavior Deviant Behavior?" *British Journal of Criminology*, 5 (April, 1965), pp. 132–142.

[28]See Jane R. Mercer, "Social System Perspective and Clinical Perspective: Frames of Reference for Understanding Career Patterns of Persons Labelled as Mentally Retarded," *Social Problems*, 13 (Summer, 1966), pp. 18–34.

[29]This perspective in the study of social deviance has been developed in Becker, *Outsiders*; Kai T. Erikson, "Notes on the Sociology of Deviance," *Social Problems*, 9 (Spring, 1962), pp. 307–314; John I. Kitsuse, "Societal Reactions to Deviant Behavior: Problems of Theory and Method," *Social Problems*, 9 (Winter, 1962), pp. 247–256. Also see Ronald L. Akers, "Problems in the Sociology of Deviance: Social Definitions and Behavior," *Social Forces*, 46 (June, 1968), pp. 455–465; David J. Bordua, "Recent Trends: Deviant Behavior and Social Control," *Annals of the American Academy of Political and Social Science*, 369 (January, 1967), pp. 149–163; Jack P. Gibbs, "Conceptions of Deviant Behavior: The Old and the New," *Pacific Sociological Review*, 9 (Spring, 1966), pp. 9–14; Clarence R. Jeffrey, "The Structure of American Criminological Thinking," *Journal of Criminal Law, Criminology and Police Science*, 46 (January–February, 1956), pp. 658–672; Austin T. Turk, "Prospects for Theories of Criminal Behavior," *Journal of Criminal Law, Criminology and Police Science*, 55 (December, 1964), pp. 454–461.

the *power* to translate their interests into *public policy.* The interests—based on desires, values, and norms—which are ultimately incorporated into the criminal law are those which are treasured by the dominant interest groups in the society.[30] In other words, those who have the ability to have their interests represented in public policy regulate the formulation of criminal definitions.

That criminal definitions are formulated is one of the most obvious manifestations of *conflict* in society. By formulating criminal law (including legislative statutes, administrative rulings, and judicial decisions), some segments of society protect and perpetuate their own interests. Criminal definitions exist, therefore, because some segments of society are in conflict with others.[31] By formulating criminal definitions these segments are able to control the behavior of persons in other segments. It follows that *the greater the conflict in interests between the segments of a society, the greater the probability that the power segments will formulate criminal definitions.*

The interests of the power segments of society are reflected not only in the content of criminal definitions and the kinds of penal sanctions attached to them, but also in the *legal policies* stipulating how those who come to be defined as "criminal" are to be handled. Hence, procedural rules are created for enforcing and administering the criminal law. Policies are also established on programs for treating and punishing the criminally defined and for controlling and preventing crime. In the initial criminal definitions or the subsequent procedures, and in correctional and penal programs or policies of crime control and prevention, the segments of society that have power and interests to protect are instrumental in regulating the behavior of those who have conflicting interests and less power.[32]

---

[30]See Richard C. Fuller, "Morals and the Criminal Law," *Journal of Criminal Law, Criminology and Police Science,* 32 (March–April, 1942), pp. 624–630; Thorsten Sellin, *Culture Conflict and Crime* (New York: Social Science Research Council, 1938), pp. 21–25; Clarence R. Jeffery, "Crime, Law and Social Structure," *Journal of Criminal Law, Criminology and Police Science,* 47 (November–December, 1956), pp. 423–435; John J. Honigmann, "Value Conflict and Legislation," *Social Problems,* 7 (Summer, 1959), pp. 34–40; George Rusche and Otto Kirchheimer, *Punishment and Social Structure* (New York: Columbia University Press, 1939); Roscoe Pound, *An Introduction to the Philosophy of Law* (New Haven: Yale University Press, 1922).

[31]I am obviously indebted to the conflict formulation of George B. Vold, *Theoretical Criminology* (New York: Oxford University Press, 1958), especially pp. 203–242. A recent conflict approach to crime is found in Austin T. Turk, "Conflict and Criminality," *American Sociological Review,* 31 (June, 1966), pp. 338–352.

[32]Considerable support for this proposition is found in the following studies: William J. Chambliss, "A Sociological Analysis of the Law of Vagrancy," *Social Problems,* 12 (Summer, 1964), pp. 66–77; Kai T. Erikson, *Wayward Puritans* (New York: John Wiley, 1966); Jerome Hall, *Theft, Law and Society,* 2nd ed. (Indianapolis: Bobbs-

Finally, law changes with modifications in the interest structure. When the interests that underlie a criminal law are no longer relevant to groups in power, the law will be reinterpreted or altered to incorporate the dominant interests. Hence, *the probability that criminal definitions will be formulated is increased by such factors as (1) changing social conditions, (2) emerging interests, (3) increasing demands that political, economic, and religious interests be protected, and (4) changing conceptions of the public interest.* The social history of law reflects changes in the interest structure of society.

Proposition 3 (application of criminal definitions)

Criminal definitions are applied by the segments of society that have the power to shape the enforcement and administration of criminal law.

The powerful interests intervene in all stages in which criminal definitions are created. Since interests cannot be effectively protected by merely formulating criminal law, enforcement and administration of the law are required. The interests of the powerful, therefore, operate in *applying* criminal definitions. Consequently, crime is "political behavior and the criminal becomes in fact a member of a 'minority group' without sufficient public support to dominate the control of the police power of the state."[33] Those whose interests conflict with the interests represented in the law must either change their behavior or possibly find it defined as "criminal."

The probability that criminal definitions will be applied varies according to the extent to which the behaviors of the powerless conflict with the interests of the power segments. Law enforcement efforts and judicial activity are likely to be increased when the interests of the powerful are threatened by the opposition's behavior. Fluctuations and variations in the application of criminal definitions reflect shifts in the relations of the various segments in the power structure of society.

Merrill, 1952); Clarence R. Jeffery, "The Development of Crime in Early England," *Journal of Criminal Law, Criminology and Police Science,* 47 (March–April, 1957), pp. 647–666; Alfred R. Lindesmith, *The Addict and the Law* (Bloomington: Indiana University Press, 1965); Rusche and Kirchheimer, *Punishment and Social Structure;* Andrew Sinclair, *Era of Excess: A Social History of the Prohibition Movement* (New York: Harper & Row, 1964); Edwin H. Sutherland, "The Sexual Psychopath Law," *Journal of Criminal Law, Criminology and Police Science,* 40 (January–February, 1950), pp. 543–554.

[33]Vold, *Theoretical Criminology,* p. 202. Also see Irving Louis Horowitz and Martin Liebowitz, "Social Deviance and Political Marginality: Toward a Redefinition of the Relation Between Sociology and Politics," *Social Problems,* 15 (Winter, 1968), pp. 280–296.

Obviously, the criminal law is not applied directly by the powerful segments. They delegate enforcement and administration of the law to authorized *legal agents,* who, nevertheless, represent their interests. In fact, the security in office of legal agents depends on their ability to represent the society's dominant interests.

Because the interest groups responsible for creating criminal definitions are physically separated from the groups to which the authority to enforce and administer law is delegated, local conditions affect the manner in which criminal definitions are applied.[34] In particular, communities vary in the law enforcement and administration of justice they expect. Application is also affected by the visibility of acts in a community and by its norms about reporting possible offenses. Especially important are the occupational organization and ideology of the legal agents.[35] Thus, *the probability that criminal definitions will be applied is influenced by such community and organizational factors as (1) community expectations of law enforcement and administration, (2) the visibility and public reporting of offenses, and (3) the occupational organization, ideology, and actions of the legal agents to whom the authority to enforce and administer criminal law is delegated.* Such factors determine how the dominant interests of society are implemented in the application of criminal definitions.

The probability that criminal definitions will be applied in *specific situations* depends on the actions of the legal agents. In the final analysis, a criminal definition is applied according to an

[34]See Michael Banton, *The Policeman and the Community* (London: Tavistock, 1964); Egon Bittner, "The Police on Skid-Row: A Study of Peace Keeping," *American Sociological Review,* 32 (October, 1967), pp. 699–715; John P. Clark, "Isolation of the Police: A Comparison of the British and American Situations," *Journal of Criminal Law, Criminology and Police Science,* 56 (September, 1965), pp. 307–319; Nathan Goldman, *The Differential Selection of Juvenile Offenders for Court Appearance* (New York National Council on Crime and Delinquency, 1963); James Q. Wilson, *Varieties of Police Behavior* (Cambridge: Harvard University Press, 1968).

[35]Abraham S. Blumberg, *Criminal Justice* (Chicago: Quadrangle Books, 1967); David J. Bordua and Albert J. Reiss, Jr., "Command, Control and Charisma: Reflections on Police Bureaucracy," *American Journal of Sociology,* 72 (July, 1966), pp. 68–76; Aaron V. Cicourel, *The Social Organization of Juvenile Justice* (New York: John Wiley, 1968); Arthur Niederhoffer, *Behind the Shield: The Police in Urban Society* (Garden City, N.Y.: Doubleday, 1967); Jerome H. Skolnick, *Justice Without Trial: Law Enforcement in Democratic Society* (New York: John Wiley, 1966); Arthur L. Stinchcombe, "Institutions of Privacy in the Determination of Police Administrative Practice," *American Journal of Sociology,* 69 (September, 1963), pp. 150–160; David Sudnow, "Normal Crimes: Sociological Features of the Penal Code in a Public Defender Office," *Social Problems,* 12 (Winter, 1965), pp. 255–276; William A. Westley, "Violence and the Police," *American Journal of Sociology,* 59 (July, 1953), pp. 34–41; Arthur Lewis Wood, *Criminal Lawyer* (New Haven: College & University Press, 1967).

evaluation by someone charged with the authority to enforce and administer the law. In the course of "criminalization,"a criminal label may be affixed to a person because of real or fancied attributes: "Indeed, a person is evaluated, either favorably or unfavorably, not because he *does* something, or even because he *is* something, but because others react to their perceptions of him as offensive or inoffensive."[36] Evaluation by the definers is affected by the way in which the suspect handles the situation, but ultimately their evaluations and subsequent decisions determine the criminality of human acts. Hence, *the more legal agents evaluate behaviors and persons as worthy of criminal definition, the greater the probability that criminal definitions will be applied.*

Proposition 4 (development of behavior patterns in relation to criminal definitions)

Behavior patterns are structured in segmentally organized society in relation to criminal definitions, and within this context persons engage in actions that have relative probabilities of being defined as criminal.

Although behavior varies, all behaviors are similar in that they represent the *behavior patterns* of segments of society. Therefore, all persons—whether they create criminal definitions or are the objects of criminal definitions—act according to *normative systems* learned in relative social and cultural settings.[37] Since it is not the quality of the behavior but the action taken against the behavior that makes it criminal, that which is defined as criminal in any society is relative to the behavior patterns of the segments of society that formulate and apply criminal definitions. Consequently, *persons in the segments of society whose behavior patterns are not represented in formulating and applying criminal definitions are more likely to act in ways that will be defined as criminal than those in the segments that formulate and apply criminal definitions.*

Once behavior patterns are established with some regularity within the respective segments of society, individuals are provided

---

[36]Turk, "Conflict and Criminality," p. 340. For research on the evaluation of suspects by policemen, see Irving Piliavin and Scott Briar, "Police Encounters with Juveniles," *American Journal of Sociology,* 70 (September, 1964), pp. 206–214.

[37]Assumed within the theory of the social reality of crime is Sutherland's theory of differential association. See Edwin H. Sutherland, *Principles of Criminology,* 4th ed. (Philadelphia: J. B. Lippincott, 1947). An analysis of the differential association theory is found in Melvin L. De Fleur and Richard Quinney, "A Reformulation of Sutherland's Differential Association Theory and a Strategy for Empirical Verification," *Journal of Research in Crime and Delinquency,* 3 (January, 1966), pp. 1–22.

with a framework for developing *personal action patterns*. These patterns continually develop for each person as he moves from one experience to another. It is the development of these patterns that gives his behavior its own substance in relation to criminal definitions.

Man constructs his own patterns of action in participating with others. It follows, then, that *the probability that a person will develop action patterns that have a high potential of being defined as criminal depends on the relative substance of (1) structured opportunities, (2) learning experiences, (3) interpersonal associations and identifications, and (4) self-conceptions.* Throughout his experiences, each person creates a conception of himself as a social being. Thus prepared, he behaves according to the anticipated consequences of his actions.[38]

During experiences shared by the criminal definers and the criminally defined, personal action patterns develop among the criminally defined because they are so defined. After such persons have had continued experience in being criminally defined, they learn to manipulate the application of criminal definitions.[39]

Furthermore, those who have been defined as criminal begin to conceive of themselves as criminal; as they adjust to the definitions imposed upon them, they learn to play the role of the criminal.[40] Because of others' reactions, therefore, persons may develop personal action patterns that increase the likelihood of their being defined as criminal in the future. That is, *increased experience with criminal definitions increases the probability of developing actions that may be subsequently defined as criminal.*

Thus, both the criminal definers and the criminally defined are involved in reciprocal action patterns. The patterns of both the definers and the defined are shaped by their common, continued, and related experiences. The fate of each is bound to that of the other.

[38]On the operant nature of criminally defined behavior, see Robert L. Burgess and Ronald L. Akers, "A Differential Association-Reinforcement Theory of Criminal Behavior," *Social Problems,* 14 (Fall, 1966), pp. 128–147; C. R. Jeffery, "Criminal Behavior and Learning Theory," *Journal of Criminal Law, Criminology and Police Science,* 56 (September, 1965), pp. 294–300.

[39]A discussion of the part the person plays in manipulating the deviant defining situation is found in Judith Lorber, "Deviance as Performance: The Case of Illness," *Social Problems,* 14 (Winter, 1967), pp. 302–310.

[40]Edwin M. Lemert, *Human Deviance, Social Problems, and Social Control* (Englewood Cliffs, N.J.: Prentice-Hall, 1964), pp. 40–64; Edwin M. Lemert, *Social Pathology* (New York: McGraw-Hill, 1951), pp. 3–98. A related and earlier discussion is in Frank Tannenbaum, *Crime and the Community* (New York: Columbia University Press, 1938), pp. 3–81.

Proposition 5 (construction of criminal conceptions)

Conceptions of crime are constructed and diffused in the segments of society by various means of communication.

The "real world" is a social construction: man with the help of others creates the world in which he lives. Social reality is thus the world a group of people create and believe in as their own. This reality is constructed according to the kind of "knowledge" they develop, the ideas they are exposed to, the manner in which they select information to fit the world they are shaping, and the manner in which they interpret these conceptions.[41] Man behaves in reference to the *social meanings* he attaches to his experiences.

Among the constructions that develop in a society are those which determine what man regards as crime. Wherever we find the concept of crime, there we will find conceptions about the relevance of crime, the offender's characteristics, and the relation of crime to the social order.[42] These conceptions are constructed by communication. In fact, *the construction of criminal conceptions depends on the portrayal of crime in all personal and mass communications.* By such means, criminal conceptions are constructed and diffused in the segments of a society. The most critical conceptions are those held by the power segments of society. These are the conceptions that are certain of becoming incorporated into the social reality of crime. In general, then, *the more the power segments are concerned about crime, the greater the probability that criminal definitions will be created and that behavior patterns will develop in opposition to criminal definitions.* The formulation and application of criminal definitions and the development of behavior patterns related to criminal definitions are thus joined in full circle by the construction of criminal conceptions.

[41]See Berger and Luckmann, *The Social Construction of Reality.* Relevant research on the diffusion of information is discussed in Everett M. Rogers, *Diffusion of Innovations* (New York: The Free Press of Glencoe, 1962).

[42]Research on public conceptions of crime is only beginning. See Alexander L. Clark and Jack P. Gibbs, "Social Control: A Reformulation," *Social Problems,* 12 (Spring, 1965), pp. 398–415; Thomas E. Dow, Jr., "The Role of Identification in Conditioning Public Attitude Toward the Offender," *Journal of Criminal Law, Criminology and Police Science,* 58 (March, 1967), pp. 75–79; William P. Lentz, "Social Status and Attitudes Toward Delinquency Control," *Journal of Research in Crime and Delinquency,* 3 (July, 1966), pp. 147–154; Jennie McIntyre, "Public Attitudes Toward Crime and Law Enforcement," *Annals of the American Academy of Political and Social Science,* 374 (November, 1967), pp. 34–46; Anastassios D. Mylonas and Walter C. Reckless, "Prisoners' Attitudes Toward Law and Legal Institutions," *Journal of Criminal Law, Criminology and Police Science,* 54 (December, 1963), pp. 479–484; Elizabeth A. Rooney and Don C. Gibbons, "Social Reactions to 'Crimes Without Victims,'" *Social Problems,* 13 (Spring, 1966), pp. 400–410.

Proposition 6 (the social reality of crime)
The social reality of crime is constructed by the formulation and application of criminal definitions, the development of behavior patterns related to criminal definitions, and the construction of criminal conceptions.

These five propositions can be collected into a composite. The theory, accordingly, describes and explains phenomena that increase the probability of crime in society, resulting in the social reality of crime.

Since the first proposition is a definition and the sixth is a composite, the body of the theory consists of the four middle propositions. These form a model, as diagrammed in Figure 1, which relates the propositions into a theoretical system. Each proposition is related to the others forming a theoretical system of developmental propositions interacting with one another. The phenomena denoted in the propositions and their relationships culminate in what is regarded as the amount and character of crime in a society at any given time, that is, in the social reality of crime.

FIGURE 1
**Model of the
Social Reality of Crime**

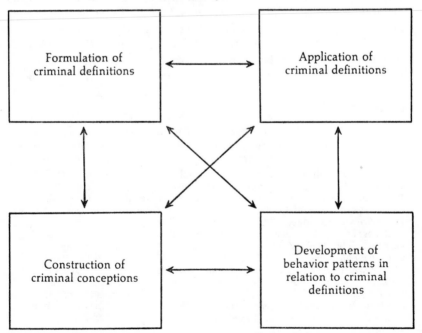

A Developmental Theory of Delinquency
James C. Hackler

Introduction

It is a long standing intellectual tradition in the social sciences to view socialization as a process of internalizing the norms and values of one's culture, community, or primary group. As a result of such internalization of norms and values, the socialized individual will behave in accord with the normative prescriptions prevailing among his associates. From this perspective, deviant behaviour is typically seen as resulting either from a failure to internalize conventional norms and values or from the internalization of norms and values that are themselves deviant.

An alternative perspective would suggest that norms or values may be the *product* of the interaction process which is part of all social situations. Rather than *causing* behaviour, the creation of norms and values and their internationalization may be the *result* of normal social processes. This perspective would claim that delinquent norms are the product of delinquent behaviour rather than the cause. One task, then, is to suggest other antecedent variables that would explain delinquency.

The writings of George Herbert Mead (1934) have been rather basic to the work of a number of sociologists who refer to themselves as "symbolic

From James C. Hackler, "A Developmental Theory of Delinquency." Reprinted from *The Canadian Review of Sociology and Anthropology*, 8:2 (1971), by permission of the author and the publisher.

interactionists." While this theoretical perspective has been used to explain the socialization process in general, it has not been applied specifically and explicitly to delinquency. The goal of this paper is not to propose original ideas but rather to utilize this relatively familiar knowledge:

(a) to apply this social psychological perspective directly to delinquent behaviour; (b) to state propositions explicitly rather than leave them implicit; [and] (c) to place these propositions in a developmental sequence . . . .

Briefly, the explanation presented here contends that children who are in a recognizable status (lower class, for example) are expected to behave in a predicted way. These predictions or anticipations on the part of the adult world are perceived by the child and are important to the development of his self-concept. The *perceived* responses constantly indicate to the child the type of person he is and what is expected of him. This leads to self-categorizations and, along with the perceived expectations, influences the roles he will seek to play in an effort to behave in ways compatible with his imagined characteristics and capacities.

The Distinction Between Normative Prescriptions and Behavioural Anticipations

Normative prescription will refer to the role requirements which are attached to a particular position in a social system. These requirements describe the way a person is supposed to behave according to the norms of the group. However, some persons may be unwilling or unable to fulfill these requirements or follow the prescriptions. Those who interact with someone else may *anticipate* performance which deviates from the prescribed standards. Anticipations regarding someone's performance, then, may or may not be identical to the prescriptions for that particular role. For example, teachers *prescribe* good manners and an eagerness to learn for all of their students. However, they do not *anticipate* good manners and an eagerness to learn from all of their students.

The distinction between prescriptions and anticipations is discussed and applied to a model of deviant behaviour by Lundberg, Schrag, Larsen, and Catton (1968: 558–60). In a sense, prescriptions have moral overtones, anticipations do not. In this paper we will use the terms prescriptions and norms interchangeably. On the other hand, behavioural anticipations for certain individuals or categories of individuals may deviate systematically from the accepted norms.

Some Processes in the Etiology of Delinquency

Our perspective will concentrate on the way a youngster views those who are important to him as significant others in primary groups or because they play roles which are particularly relevant to his success in the larger community. Peers and parents are illustrations of those who are significant others. Teachers may be thought of as persons playing roles which link a community institution, in this case the school, to the individual child.

The ensuing discussion can be summarized in the following propositions and assumptions.

General assumption

The socialization process can be described as selective involvement in activities that are compatible with a developing self-image and that are relevant to those roles which would help to validate a desired self-image.

1. Self-images and self-aspirations develop out of the responses of others and the perception by ego of those responses. That is, a person's self-image is at least partially determined by the actual anticipations of others and by ego's perception of those anticipations. (a) By others we include not only the significant others who stand in a primary relation to ego, but also (b) persons who represent community institutions that are crucial to role attainment. Representatives of community institutions who stand in a secondary relationship to ego identify him as a member of a category. On the basis of this identification, these representatives anticipate either poor or good performance from ego, and either deviation from or conformity to dominant community standards.

2. Such self-relevant responses, especially those indicating to ego what others think he is and what they expect of him, are perceived by ego and incorporated into his self-image. This conception of self influences the roles he will seek to play as he attempts to behave in ways compatible with his imagined characteristics and capacities. This will lead to involvement in activities he sees as appropriate for a person who plays such roles.

General assumption

Because representatives of community institutions anticipate behaviour appropriate to certain categorical memberships, they withhold or extend opportunities and facilities that would enhance ego's chances for success and thereby decrease or increase his stake in conformity (see Merton, 1938; Cloward and Ohlin, 1961).

3.   An individual from whom opportunities are withheld correctly perceives such lack of opportunity, and increasingly views accepted juvenile roles, such as "good student," etc., as being inconsistent with his developing self-image.

4.   Self-relevant responses from a "street group" or "street gang" (see Haskell, 1961: 222) indicating anticipations of deviant behaviour are further incorporated into the self-image, and ego views involvement in delinquent roles and activities as consistent with this image of self. Note: Ego could easily *misperceive* anticipations of peers and opt for a delinquent act for fear of being called "chicken," a label that would be quite threatening to the developing self-image.

5.   Involvement in activities deviant or variant from dominant community standards precludes the effective internalization of those standards because of the dissonance that such internalization would imply. Thus the selective involvement of ego in certain activities compatible with his self-image leads, through dissonance-reducing mechanisms, to the selective endorsement of normative prescriptions compatible with those activities and with that self-image.

The ideas expressed above are not new. In fact they are consistent with findings reported in the social psychological literature. But these findings have not been utilized to explain the evolution of deviant behaviour and to explicate the steps in that process.

This developmental sequence could be made still more explicit and systematic by linking specific variables in a causal chain as follows: (*a*) having low esteem leads to (*b*) the anticipation on the part of others that ego will act badly or at least not be able to act properly; this leads to (*c*) ego's *perception* that others anticipate improper behaviour if (i) opportunities to play conforming roles are perceived as blocked by those in dominant positions, such as teachers, and if (ii) ego views these self-relevant responses from primary and non-primary significant others as valid; this would lead to (*d*) the development of a delinquent self-concept; which leads to (*e*) the search for roles compatible with a delinquent self-concept; this leads to (*f*) delinquent behaviour; and finally leads to (*g*) the selective endorsement of delinquent norms through dissonance-reducing mechanisms. . . .

THE PERCEPTION OF LOW ESTEEM AND THE ANTICIPATION OF IMPROPER BEHAVIOUR

A child from some lower class background may not have parents who encourage the type of behaviour that would endear the child to the teacher, and the teacher, in turn, identifies such a child as a "problem" who will probably perform below par in other respects as well. It soon becomes clear to those stigmatized children that the teacher anticipates such substandard performance. This low esteem on the part of the teacher may be categorical attribution of inadequacy to specific groups such as ethnic or racial minorities, or it may be the result of certain characteristics exhibited by the child, such as sticking up for his rights and not letting anyone push him around, which the teacher has previously linked to poor academic performance. For a number of reasons, these representatives of an important socializing institution may respond to certain children in such a way as to make it clear to the child that he is not expected to succeed. It is anticipated that he will not meet the prescriptions which are relevant to school children.

The study by Jephcott and Carter (1954) illustrates the perception of low esteem nicely. The "rough" and "respectable" families that lived in a small mining town were not distinguishable by colour or obvious identifying characteristics, but teachers may have classified the children rather quickly and anticipated behaviour compatible with that classification.

In his book *Delinquent Boys*, Albert Cohen claims that a stress arises when lower-class children fail to make good when compared with the "middle-class measuring rod" (1955: 84–93). Essentially, he claims there is only one set of prescriptions and all children are judged accordingly. Some children fail to meet these prescriptions or norms—in fact, some children are stereotyped from the beginning, and the teacher clearly anticipates that the child will not perform according to the prescriptions.

THE WITHnOLDING OF OPPORTUNITIES

Once a child has been labelled incapable of benefitting from certain facilities, teachers may withhold opportunities for achievement that are made available to other children. While teaching junior high school in California, this writer had an experience which provides an excellent illustration. In the middle of a semester, a seventh grade girl with a Spanish accent appeared in a remedial arithmetic class. She arrived at the school neatly dressed and well-mannered, but lacking any records from a previous school and known to be the daughter of a migrant worker. The counselor assumed that she had some academic deficiencies and she was sent to the slowest section in the school. It soon became apparent that the little girl was very bright; but on the basis of a particular stereotyped image, it had been assumed that she should be placed with the slow learners. Teachers, like other representatives of community institutions, develop categorical stereotypes and a standardized *modus operandi* for dealing with such children.

Another excellent illustration comes from the study by Wax, Wax, and Dumont (1964: 104) in the United States where teachers in the federal schools on the Sioux Indian reservation managed to rationalize substandard teaching practices.

> Among the Pine Ridge educators an ideology has arisen which serves both to justify their current teaching practices and also to insulate themselves further from any contact with the Indian community. According to this ideology, the Sioux pupils are woefully lacking in knowledge, morals and manners because of an inadequate home life. Thus *the blunt facts of cultural difference and social isolation* between the Indian and the national society are converted into matters of cultural "lack." (*Italics* added.)

In other words, these teachers have developed an ideology that provides a clear set of anticipations for all Sioux children. Similar categorical anticipations develop with regard to other minority group children and with regard to children who exhibit characteristics identifying them as lower-class.

This author feels that children correctly perceive that the teachers anticipate poor performance and also that only limited opportunities to achieve conventional goals are extended to them.

There is some danger in placing so much emphasis on school and considering it the only opportunity structure available to children. In the United States the public schools clearly provide opportunity for upward mobility. It is also possible, in the U.S., that the "middle-class measuring rod" is applied to all with the result that many are bound to fail. But in other countries the school system may have a "lower-class measuring rod" as well. In Austria for example, and in other European countries, the goal of the school system is to train the child for his probable station in life rather than bring out his highest potential (Hackler, 1961). Similarly, in England the avenues that lead to the university are not seriously considered by the vast majority of working-class children.

In a more traditional society that has also developed a relatively well-integrated and viable "working-class," school is only one opportunity structure. Entering the work force as an apprentice is a satisfactory alternative to higher academic training for many boys. The Hauptschule and trade schools in Austria are frequently chosen by capable lower class youngsters in preference to struggles with Latin in the Gymnasium and other Mittelschulen.

There is also danger in assuming that a family which does not provide the background that would maximize success in school will automatically fail to provide adequately in other social situations. As Mack (1956: 12) stated rather well, "the family structure of the rough family is on the one hand ill-adapted to swim in the main stream of social progress, but it is not too badly adapted to some of the murky backwaters."

In attempting to emphasize the role of the anticipations of the teacher or other important adults, we should not assume that boys who have correctly perceived the anticipations of others are automatically frustrated. True, if self-worth is defined in terms of academic success in the eyes of the teacher, then many lower class children would be frustrated; but the lower class subculture may alleviate feelings of degradation. Boys may perceive the teacher correctly, but the gang and others who make up the social world of lower class youngsters may accept the delinquent role as a comfortable one rather than one of stress.

THE SELF-RELEVANCE OF COMMUNITY AGENTS OF SOCIALIZATION

The school system is but one of several community institutions which are important in the socialization of children; however, one can safely say it plays a major role and confine the discussion to the school. When we examine a child's perception of how the teacher sees him, we have a clue to the way he views the educational system and how it impinges on him. As far as the child is concerned the teacher may be viewed as an individual who is liked or disliked, but in addition, the teacher is seen as the valid representative of a particular community institution. As such, a teacher helps shape the self-concept of her students.

A major theme in the contributions of Mead and Cooley is the influence of the responses of others in moulding the self-image.

Although it is Mead's habit to speak of "the response of the other" as providing the key to the definition of the self, the phrase is somewhat ambiguous, for a distinction may be drawn between (a) the actual response of the other, and (b) the subject's perception of the response of the other. Mead often does not distinguish between the two; but it is consistent with his view that the perception of the other's response is the critical aspect. (Miyamoto and Dornbusch, 1956: 400.)

Miyamoto and Dornbusch provide data which support the claim that the *perceived* response of others has more impact on the self-concept than the *actual* response of others.

In order to modify his self-concept then, ego must recognize signals or responses from others. We can think of two types of responses relevant to the self-concept. First, there are the responses of "significant others." Such responses usually come from persons in a primary relationship to ego. In order to have much of an impact on ego's normative orientation and self-concept it is sometimes assumed that an effective tie of some strength is usually necessary (in most cases positive but possibly negative). Second, there are the responses of others who are important because of their *role* in a community institution rather than because of a primary relationship with ego. These responses have an impact on ego according to whether or not ego believes they emanate from valid representatives of the relevant community institutions whose reactions to performance are predictive of future success or failure. Normally, the responses of a teacher will be interpreted as having implications for future success or failure in school and for a job at a later time.

Some responses, then, are meaningful because of their credibility rather than because of affectivity. Teachers provide information to children concerning the chance of success which is not available otherwise. The lower-class child is particularly dependent on the teacher for information regarding his academic ability. The middle-class child may be able to get similar information, or at least responses which are interpreted as information, from his parents and neighbours. When a neighbour continues to mention college plans, the child may not be getting information about his capability, but assumptions about going to college influence his self-concept in the academic sphere.

Harvey, Kelley and Shapiro (1957) note the importance of the "authoritativeness" of the source of unfavourable evaluations regarding the self. Acquaintances had more impact than strangers, but if the acquaintance was not liked the subject tended to devalue the worth of that evaluation. This study utilized the traditional guinea pig of social psychologists, college students, and students generally have a range of acquaintances whom they regard as capable of evaluating them. If, however, the individual had only a single valid source of responses it would be difficult to discount the source or the responses even if the source was an individual who was much disliked. The teacher may be the only source of certain types of information available to children from deprived back-grounds. Dislike for the teacher may create more stress but it may not decrease the credibility of her responses on certain topics. This point is particularly relevant for those with limited sources of information and those who cannot discredit those sources which provide an unfavourable evaluation.

So far we have suggested that the advantaged child not only gets a larger number of favourable responses, but the fact that they come from a greater variety of sources permits him to discredit those which are unfavourable. Disregarding those responses which come from much-loved significant others in a primary relationship, it is clear that some children are better able to capitalize on responses which are primarily informational rather that having an affective content.

Our focus, then, is on those responses which influence that aspect of the self-concept concerned with ego's ability to get ahead in the world. This type of self-relevant response appeals to the instrumental aspects of ego's personality rather than the affective aspects. The concept of self-relevant response from those sources who are not significant others is well illustrated in the case of an actor. At a play, the audience gives self-relevant responses to the actor. His self-concept is moulded not only by the comments and facial expressions of other actors, whom he values as friends, but by the applause which comes from the often invisible mass on the other side of the floodlights. That applause represents a crucial element in telling the actor what he is like even though close affective ties are absent. The importance of this type of self-relevant response also varies depending on the particular role being played at the moment. The applause of the audience does not influence the professional actor's image of himself in his role as a loving father. Likewise, the moist kiss from his two-year-old daughter may contribute much to his self-esteem as a father but has little relevance to his self-concept as a competent actor. Similarly, a teacher would probably have little impact on a boy's self-concept as an athlete.

To summarize, then, a boy may neither like nor dislike his teacher, but her responses to him, particularly in the case of the lower-class boy, provide clues regarding his academic capability and how he is regarded by the world of adults—especially those adults who are in a position to influence his success. His mother and his friends provide self-relevant responses of the significant other type and may have a great impact on his self-image, but the boy may not consider them qualified judges in his role as a student. This perspective clearly has relevance for programmes of delinquency control; it is ordinarily easier to modify *representatives of systems* than to modify those who are in a more primary relationship with the individuals being treated.

BEHAVING ACCORDING TO AN IMAGE

The anticipations of others are expressed in responses which indicate to ego how others view him; hence, those anticipations are incorporated into the self-image. This in turn influences the anticipations that ego has for his own behaviour in the future. An unfavourable self-image, however, does not necessarily explain deviant activities or the endorsement of deviant norms. Representatives of socializing institutions may anticipate normative violations as well as low performance on the basis of the same stereotypes suggested above. These anticipations for normative violations would provide self-relevant responses that would lead to a self-image which is deviant as well as inadequate. From the standpoint of the youngster, merely thinking of oneself as a failure is not enough to create a motivation toward actual deviance. While it may provide stress and motivate action of some sort it does not indicate the form that action would take. We now turn to the importance of certain images that people would like to have of themselves as factors in determining behaviour. In emphasizing the importance of these sought-after images of self and the importance of the perceived anticipations of others, it is clear that we question certain assumptions concerning the role of norms as factors in guiding and instigating behaviour. Our perspective proposes that while norms are *recognized* at an early stage, they are not internalized at this stage, and they guide behaviour only after individuals have acted according to the anticipations of others and according to roles which fit one's self-image.

Much of our behaviour is motivated by a role or a position we covet. We may even be willing to act against conventional norms if by doing so we can reinforce a gratifying self-image. The beatnik, for example, openly flouts certain traditions in order to play a particular role. The overt rejection of conventional norms may be the price the beatnik must pay in order to obtain the real or imagined gratifications of this new role. Roles that are considered delinquent may be sought, not as a last resort, but because they offer a reward in terms of the self-concept. Stealing merchandise, selling it to junk men, spending the money on soda pop and movies may not be a reaction against middle-class norms. According to Cohen (1955) the delinquent subculture is "non-utilitarian, malicious and negativistic." Bordua (1961: 122) disagrees. "Boys who feed themselves by duplicating keys to bakery delivery boxes, creep out of their club rooms right after delivery, steal the pastry, pick up a quart of milk from a doorstep, and then have breakfast may not have a highly developed sense of nutritional values, but this is not non-utilitarian."

When discussing role-playing, we should keep in mind the dynamics of the situation preceding the delinquent act. In his reference group theory of delinquency, Haskell (1961: 222) points out that once a boy has chosen as a reference group a street group with some experience in delinquent behaviour, he will be sensitive to the approval of that group. We would add that a choice in favour of a delinquent act could easily be the result of *misperceiving* the anticipations of this street group. Individually, other boys in such a group might have misgivings about a specific act, but collectively they might present a facade of supporting a deviant act. The final impact of this sharing of pluralistic ignorance would be difficult to distinguish from the correct perception of delinquent values. For this reason, we have emphasized the *perception of anticipations* as being the crucial explanatory variable rather than internalized values.

Haskell also notes that boys holding jobs acted as a normative reference group for non-delinquent behaviour. However, this does not explain how the reference group influences the individual. The question as to "why" or "how" such reference groups influence individuals might be more effectively "explained" through their perception of the anticipations of others in the reference group.

Although Cohen (1955) has suggested that boys are reacting against middle-class norms, such behaviour might better be seen as playing roles that are encouraged by specific reference groups as a result of the perceived anticipations for those roles. The comments made by Mays (1954) about his shop-lifting boys suggest role-playing rather than reactions to middle-class norms. "It makes you sweat." "You had to keep going to prove you didn't have cold feet."

George Grosser (1952) would call this behaviour "role-expressive" since it fulfills the demands of a role. "It is an attempt to validate one's claim to being an authentic member of a given role, an attempt to bring one's self image into line with his notions of what one must be in order to be a proper member of the roles with which he identifies."

Grosser's point is particularly crucial in that it avoids defining delinquency as necessarily *against* something else, such as middle-class norms. It also brings the explanation of deviant behaviour in line with the explanation of behaviour in general. Most of us act so that others will believe we are a certain type of person. Building a particular façade is a common practice engaged in by all, essential to our self-concept, but often difficult to justify in terms of the norms we hold. The professor who smokes a pipe and wears elbow patches is engaging in role-expressive behaviour. "It commends itself, it is gratifying, because it seems so right—*not in a moral sense,* but in the sense that it fits so well with the image one would like to have of oneself." (Cohen, 1965; italics added.) We are constantly using the responses of others to check that image. If we are satisfied with the responses and we are content with the image, *then* the behaviour becomes good and correct and proper.

COGNITIVE DISSONANCE AND THE REDUCTION OF STRAIN BY ADOPTING DELINQUENT NORMS

Individuals who do not have much to gain by conformity or much to lose by non-conformity will not hesitate to play satisfying roles even if they lead to violations of conventional norms. Dissonance theory suggests that a rationale for such violations will then be adopted or created. When for example, students were asked to perform a tedious "experimental" task but afterwards were persuaded to tell another that the "experimental" task was an enjoyable one, they convinced themselves as well (Festinger and Carlsmith, 1959). Furthermore, the subjects who were paid only one dollar for telling another that the dull experiment was enjoyable subsequently rated it more enjoyable themselves than the subjects who received $20. Those who were paid $20 lied about the enjoyability of the task, but the reward they received enabled them to justify their actions. Little dissonance was present and attitude change was slight. Those who received only one dollar had to justify why they had lied for such a pittance. They had more dissonance to cope with, and they reduced it by modifying their attitudes more radically.

We can apply this principle to our previous discussion. If a boy receives $10,000 for his share in a robbery he could cling to conventional standards of morality more easily. Surely, such a prize is worth a breach of the norms, but stealing a bottle of soda pop is not such a prize. A youngster could not easily continue to endorse conventional norms and yet violate them for such inconsequential rewards. Dissonance would be high, and a norm more compatible with the behaviour or rationalizing the action would probably be endorsed.

The time sequence is of particular relevance here. In the Fastinger and Carlsmith experiment, the modification of attitudes *followed* certain acts. Our perspective proposes that behaviour which is contrary to conventional norms can be dictated by striving to play a coveted role. Further, the endorsement of deviant norms justifying one's own behaviour and reducing dissonance will follow the violation itself. The internalization of deviant norms will in the end, of course, contribute to a continuation of the deviant behaviour. In general, we suggest that norms may be *chosen* because of their utility and because they help us to realize goals rather than being followed simply because others in the society consider them the proper way to behave.

Summary

An explanation of delinquent behaviour following conventional social psychological thinking could be stated as a development process. Children from lower status backgrounds will be viewed as falling short of the standards imposed by the dominant society. Such children correctly perceive these anticipations both from parents and from those who are "authorities" on making judgments about children, namely teachers. Once viewed as not being capable of benefitting from educational and other opportunities, teachers, and other members of the dominant society, may withhold opportunities for achievement.

Attempts to play conforming roles may not be recognized by others, even though parents and others in a primary relationship to ego may actually punish a child when he deviates from conforming roles. The ability to recognize and reward conforming roles may be less prevalent in families that are held in low esteem. In addition, lower-class children are not in a good position to reject definitions of self that label them as inadequate and delinquency-prone.

Attempts to play deviant roles may be supported by the perceived anticipations of peer-groups made up of those children who find themselves in similar circumstances. The acting out of such anticipations confirms both the appropriateness of the role and the self-image with which it is consistent. Finally, through dissonance-reducing mechanisms, ego endorses the norms and values that are compatible with such behaviour.

References

Bordua, David J.
   1961 "Delinquent subcultures: sociological perspectives of gang delin-
   quency."
   Annals of the American Academy of Political and Social Science 338:119–
   136.
Cloward, Richard and Lloyd Ohlin
   1961 Delinquency and Opportunity.
   Glencoe, Illinois: Free Press.
Cohen, Albert K.
   1955 Delinquent Boys.
   Glencoe, Illinois: Free Press.
   1965 "The Sociology of the deviant act: anomie theory and beyond."
   American Sociological Review 30:5–14.
Festinger, Leon and J. M. Carlsmith
   1959 "Cognitive consequences of forced compliance."
   Journal of Abnormal and Social Psychology 58:203–210.
Grosser, George
   1952 "Juvenile delinquency and contemporary American sex roles."
   Harvard University, Cambridge, Massachusetts: unpublished Ph.D. dis-
   sertation. Quotation used here taken from A. K. Cohen and J. F. Short Jr.,
   "Juvenile delinquency," in R. K. Merton and R. A. Nisbet (eds.),
   Contemporary Social Problems.
   New York: Harcourt, Brace and World, 1961.
Hackler, James C.
   1961 "The Viennese school system: social mobility and its implications.'
   International Journal of Comparative Sociology 2:65–69.
Harvey, O. H., H. H. Kelley, and Martin M. Shapiro
   1957 "Reactions of unfavourable evaluations of the self made by other
   persons."
   Journal of Personality 25:393–411.
Haskell, Martin R.
   1961 "Toward a reference group theory of juvenile delinquency."
   Social Problems 8:220–230.
Jephcott, A. P. and M. P. Carter
   1954 The Social Background of Delinquency.
   Nottingham: University of Nottingham.
Lundberg, G. A., C. C. Schrag, O. N. Larson, and W. R. Catton Jr.
   1968 Sociology. 4th edition.
   New York: Harper and Row.
Mack, J. A.
   1956 "Delinquency and the changing social pattern."
   Glasgow· Fifth Charles Russel Memorial Lecture.

Mays, J. B.
  1954   Growing up in the City.
  Liverpool: Liverpool University Press.
Mead, G. H.
  1934   Mind, Self, and Society.
  Chicago: University of Chicago Press.
Merton, Robert K.
  1938   "Social structure and anomie."
  American Sociological Review 3:672–682.
Miyamoto, S. F., and S. M. Dornbusch
  1956   "A test of interactionist hypotheses of self-conception."
  American Journal of Sociology 61:399–403.
Wax, R. H., and R. V. Dumont Jr.
  1964   Formal Education in an American Indian Community. Supplement
  to Social Problems II.
  A Society for the Study of Social Problems Monograph.

The Deviance-
Amplifying System
Leslie T. Wilkins

It is possible that some societies, for some reason, find it necessary to treat deviance with extreme intolerance, and others are able to accommodate greater degrees of deviance, and, *as a result of such tolerance, experience less serious deviance.* It seems that it is possible for a society to operate in such a way that its social-sanctions systems become devalued. If such a feedback mechanism is in operation, the system within which it is applied tends towards instability. If a small initial stimulus generates a response, part of which response becomes a further stimulus, a highly critical and powerful servo-mechanism results. Such a feedback mechanism is at least implicit in the theoretical work of Kitsuse and Dietrick (1959:213). Re-examination of [Cohen's theory of the delinquency subculture] led Kitsuse and Dietrick to modify it in the following way . . . :

(i) The individual learns the values of the delinquent subculture through his participation in gangs which embody that subculture.

(ii) The motivations of individuals for participation in gangs are varied.

(iii) The malicious, non-utilitarian, and negativistic behaviour which is learned through participation in the subculture is met by formal negative sanctions, rejection, and limitation of access to prestigeful status within the middle-class system.

(iv) Thus, participation in the delinquent subculture creates similar problems for all its participants.

(v)   The participants' response to the barriers raised to exclude them from status in the middle-class system . . . is a hostile rejection of the standards of "respectable" society and an emphasis upon status within the delinquent gang.

(vi) The hostile rejection response reinforces the malicious, non-utilitarian, and negativistic norms of the subculture.

The links in this circular chain may be described as a 'positive feedback loop'. While such a loop continues the situation will continue to get further and further out of control. The point of entry into such a system which may result in modification of the loop does not have any significance in terms of the outcome. It may be easier to enter at one point rather than another, but ideally the modification required is to change the loop into a negative feedback so that the system tends towards a desirable stability. It will be noted that, like Cloward and Ohlin, Kitsuse and Dietrick limit their model to gang behaviour, though such restrictions seem to be unnecessary if their theory is extended to a general theory of deviance.

Progressions, Good and Bad

. . . The definitions of deviant behaviour relate to the information and cultural experiences of the individuals making the definitions. . . . Both communities of saints and communities of criminals would define certain behaviour as lying outside the limits of tolerance of that particular culture. If the definitions of deviance lead to the removal from the experience of 'normal' people of certain deviant persons, the future definitions of deviance will not include the experience relating to those so removed. Moreover, if the action against deviants is such that they are not retained within the general system of values and controls, the new group created by the definition, as well as the residual group, will tend to construct new values and controls. Not only will the parent population cease to include within its experience the information relevant to the deviant, but the deviants may cease to have information regarding normal behaviour. This mechanism relates to the loop proposed by Kitsuse and Dietrick.

In terms of a model based on the calculus of probabilities, the situation does not remain static. The sector which is cut off by the definition does not remain attached to the general distribution. The transition from one distribution to different distributions may be related to the theories of 'reference groups', and in terms of the present model is as illustrated in *Figure 1*.

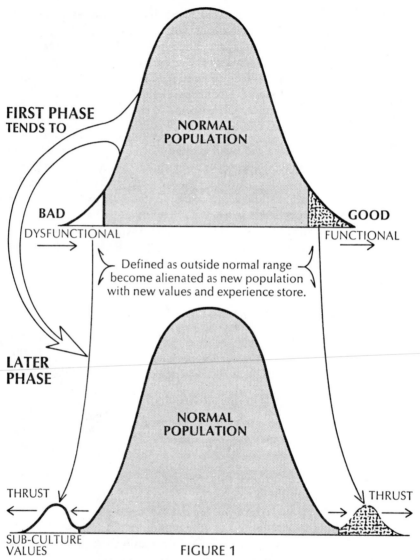

FIGURE 1
Evolution of sub-cultural and deviant social systems

Let us first consider deviations at the left-hand cut-off point which have been associated in these illustrations with the 'sinful' or 'criminal' end of the scales. It will be possible to show similar mechanisms which operate at the right-hand cut-off point, and to generalize the theory at a later stage.

The modification of the information available within the truncated sections of the distributions will generate forces which will force the two distributions apart. The norms of the distributions cut off will no longer be the same as the norms of the distributions from which identification has been severed (i.e. the parent distributions). That is to say, instead of a centripetal force towards the general (parent) norm of the culture, the norms of the truncated parts of the distribution will reveal characteristics of a centrifugal force. This is, of course, another way of expressing the effect of the 'positive feedback loop'.

Using Kitsuse and Dietrick's style of presentation as in the preceding section, the following feedback system may be proposed:

> Less tolerance leads to →
> > more acts being defined as crimes
> > leads to →
> > more action against criminals
> > leads to →
> > more alienation of deviants
> > leads to →
> > more crime by deviant groups
> > leads to →
> > less tolerance of deviants by conforming
> > > groups and round again⌐

The General Model

It is now possible to take some general postulates . . . and attempt to relate them together into a complex theory. The following postulates may be stated:

1. People tend to behave with respect to situations and things as they perceive them to be.
2. Distinctions between what is legitimate and what is illegitimate are made culturally.
3. Legitimate and illegitimate opportunities can be distinguished, and the *balance* between the two types of opportunity presents an important variable.
4. If the balance between legitimate and illegitimate opportunities remains constant, the amount of crime will tend to vary according to the total number of opportunities. Hence it follows that the disturbance of the balance will modify the crime rate, if the rate is considered in relation to the opportunity structure.
5. Since perceptions influence behaviour, the definitions (perceptions) of the culture have an influence upon the members of the

culture and the sub-cultures as perceived and defined by the culture itself.

6. Human decision-making skill (information processing) is influenced not only by the nature of the information, but by the 'channel' through which it is received.

7. Information which is perceived as irrelevant (orthogonal) to the dimension of action is treated as no information.

8. Systems in which information regarding the functioning of the system is fed back into the system present different characteristics from systems where such feedback information is lacking or is minimal.

9 People do not play 'expected values', thus actual odds do not explain behaviour; even perceived expected values may not provide a sufficient basis for prediction of behaviour since small probabilities are not treated in terms of pay-off maximization.

10. Norms are set for the culture, but different sections of a culture will experience greater or lesser difficulties in achieving success within the norms.

The above set of postulates cannot be related together in any simple unidirectional cause → effect model. The model proposed may be described as a deviation-amplifying system. The type of model proposed is well stated by Magoroh Maruyama (1962). As he says, 'The law of causality may now be revised to state A SMALL INITIAL DEVIATION WHICH IS WITHIN THE RANGE OF HIGH PROBABILITY MAY DEVELOP INTO A DEVIATION OF A VERY LOW PROBABILITY or (more precisely) into a deviation which is very improbable within the framework of probabilistic unidirectional causality.' Models based on deviation-amplifying systems have been found to be necessary to explain economic behaviour, and it is not surprising, nor does it represent a high degree of originality, to propose similar models for other forms of satisfaction-seeking human behaviour.

The implications of the deviation-amplifying system are far-reaching; as Maruyama says, 'these models are not in keeping with the sacred law of causality in the classical philosophy (which) stated that similar conditions produce similar effects'. It is now possible to demonstrate that in some cases similar conditions may result in dissimilar products.

Applying the general dynamic model and the postulates stated above to the particular problem of crime, the following system may be proposed:

(a) Certain types of information, in relation to certain systems, lead to more acts being defined as deviant. . . .

(b)   The individuals involved in the acts so defined are 'cut off' from the values of the parent system by the very process of definition.

(c)   The defining act provides an information set for the individuals concerned and they begin to perceive themselves as deviant. (Perhaps the main way in which any person gets to know what sort of person he is is through feedback from other persons.)

(d)   The action taken by society and the resulting self-perception of the individuals defined as deviant, lead to the isolation and alienation of the specified individuals.

(e)   This provides the first part of a deviation-amplifying system. The definition of society leads to the development of the self-perception as 'deviant' on the part of the 'outliers' (outlaws), and it is hardly to be expected that people who are excluded by a system will continue to regard themselves as part of it.

(f)   The deviant groups will tend to develop their own values which may run counter to the values of the parent system, the system which defined them as 'outliers'.

(g)   The increased deviance demonstrated by the deviant groups (resulting from the deviation-amplifying effect of the self-perception, which in turn may have derived from the defining acts of society) results in more forceful action by the conforming groups against the nonconformists.

(h)   Thus information about the behaviour of the nonconformists (i.e. as (f) above) received by the conforming groups leads to more acts being defined as deviant, or to more stringent action against the 'outliers';

and thus the whole system (a)-(g) can itself continue round and round again in an amplifying circuit.

This type of model need not be regarded as too surprising. A similar situation explains the relationship between confidence and prices on the Stock Market. If this type of model is a fair representation of the social system in relation to deviant behaviour, some interesting predictions can be made from the theory. In particular, if a model of this kind applies, it is not necessary to show that the individual parts have a large effect on any detail of the system; the important feature of this type of model is that it represents an unstable system. Small initial differences, perhaps even due to chance variations in the network, can build up into quite large forces. A number of mutual causal processes can be identified in other fields of science where the initial stimulus was extremely small, and possibly randomly generated, but where the final results were of very considerable importance.

It is possible to examine this model in relation to some differences in criminal behaviour which have not been satisfactorily explained by the simple unidirectional cause→effect model. The majority of students of the problem of drug addiction have expressed interest in the fact that Britain has no real problem in this area whereas it represents a very considerable problem in the United States and in some other countries.

Many observers from the United States have studied the system of drug addiction and narcotics control in England. Although different observers from America were in England at the same time and discussed with the same people, their views differ regarding what was observed. Some writers have reported that they could find no differences between the British and the United States systems of control, others have found what they believe to be major differences. It would appear that the perception of systems of control differs between observers who are, in fact, observing the same thing and taking similar evidence. Some have claimed that the different systems of control in the two countries could explain the difference in the incidence of addiction, others have claimed that since there are no differences, or none of any significance, the different patterns of addiction cannot be due to any differences in the systems of control. It may be that these conflicting views by experts are capable of resolution through the theory proposed. Perhaps the following summary statements indicate a satisfactory model for this problem:

(a)   the perception ('image') of the use of drugs in England differs from that in the United States;

(b)   the perception of the addict differs;

(c)   the perception of the police differs;

(d)   small differences in the control system, or even in the perception of the control system, could generate large differences in the perception of addiction, which could amplify the effects of the official controls;

(e)   less action is defined as 'crime' in Britain, and as a result, or in addition, fewer people are defined as 'criminal', whatever the objective differences may be;

(f)   the *balance* between legitimate and illegitimate means for obtaining drugs in the two countries differs;

(g)   the 'information set' (or folklore — it does not have to be true!) regarding the official control system and the function of drugs, both culturally and in the sub-cultures of the two countries, differs;

(h)   a different perception of a situation will give rise to behaviour which differs, since behaviour tends to be consistent with perception.

If this model is a sound one, it would be possible for the situation in England to change rapidly and radically owing only to minor changes in the balance of factors. Which factors are critical in an unstable (feedback) situation of this kind is not a particularly meaningful question — any change in the situation may change the outcome throughout the whole field. It is possible, or even probable, that any attempt to tighten up the British regulations with a view to making a minor problem even less of a problem may be a disturbance of the generating system of perceptions which could produce a more serious problem.

If complex models of this kind do in fact explain types of human behaviour which are disapproved of by society, social action to remedy a perceived 'evil' (dysfunctional behaviour) could take place at many points, but any action is likely to misfire and to result in the opposite effect to that which the action is desired to achieve.

If people are excluded by the system they are not likely to feel themselves to be part of it. This is the same argument as is made in theories of alienation and anomie. It would appear that the sanctions applied by a society to its sub-cultures may appear to them to be so extreme that they are alienated from the general values system of that society. The rejection of a . . . deviant . . . may act as an information set modifying his own tolerance . . . through his experience of the culture (that is his 'store'). If a society truncates its normal distribution at low values of standard deviations it will tend to reduce the cohesiveness of its own social order. Lack of tolerance for behaviour which is not completely *intolerable* may defeat its own ends, not only through the devaluation of sanctions, but by inducing a self-definition of deviance, where such a definition is not justified in terms of the social dysfunction of the behaviour.

References

Kitsuse, John I. and David C. Dietrick
   1959   "Delinquent Boys: A Critique." American Sociological Review 24
   (April): 208-215.
Maruyama, Magoroh
   1962   Mimeo paper circulated by Research Department of the Department of Corrections, Sacramento, California.

Conforming
to Deviance
Ronald A. Farrell /
Thomas J. Morrione

In this work we have attempted to explain the process by which societal reactions to primary deviance lead to increased deviation. Societal reactions refer to the perceived as well as the actual responses of others to deviance in recurrent and informal encounters. The focus is on the effects of these responses on the person's self definition and on the ways in which one adapts to rejection through involvement in deviant groups. Through these associations he may enculturate to the normative patterns and behavior of a subculture which bring him into increased conflict with society. Such conflict, while an apparent disadvantage for the individual, may be functional to the larger social system by serving to maintain its proscriptions of deviant behavior.

The approach developed here follows Becker's (1963: 22–25) suggestion of constructing a model that "takes into account the fact that patterns of behavior develop in an orderly sequence . . . Each step requires explanation, and what may operate as a cause at one step in the sequence may be of negligible importance at another step." Reiss (1970) has suggested that the objective of developing such a "career pattern" of deviance may be attained by linking together the labeling, anomie, and social and cultural support theories. Following along these lines, the intention of this work is to give precision to ideas contained in these and related theories by

Revision of a paper presented at the 43rd Annual Meeting of the Eastern Sociological Society, New York City, 1973.

bringing them together into a causal model of interrelated propositions.

Although the conceptual approach may be related to a number of different forms of deviance, the model deals with these processes as they pertain to homosexual behavior. Homosexuality was chosen because it represents behavior which is clearly, and with relatively little exception, defined as deviant (see Simmons, 1965). It also seems to exemplify in a lucid form the processes involved in this general theoretical approach. Whereas the *primary deviation* may have been caused by sexual preference or group influence in this instance, *secondary deviance* results from the reactions of others to the original behavior. If an individual perceives that others are identifying him as homosexual and reacting to him in accordance with the popular stereotype, his self definition may incorporate the stereotype. These responses, with the accompanied feelings of stigma, are likely to be experienced with frustration. Bitterness, withdrawal to a deviant group, and enculturation to a deviant role may be the outcome.[1]

Clearly we do not hold that homosexuality would not occur if persons did not perceive being reacted to as such. On the contrary, it would be our guess that *homosexual primary deviation* would exist on a larger scale in the absence of a negative definition and reaction. We do contend, however, that a relative absence of negative responses is likely to result in the homosexual's maintenance of a positive self definition, integration in the larger society, and a subsequent stabilization of his primary deviance. The major concern in this analysis, then, is not with the existence of the behavior, but with the form the behavior takes as a result of societal reactions.

General Assumption of the Model

Propositions related to the above processes are by no means new. They are developed in the sociological literature beginning with the work of Durkheim. In *The Rules of Sociological Method* (1904: 68–70) he suggested that deviance is not an intrinsic quality of acts but instead results from the definition which society gives them. If the *collective conscience* is strong, it will be sensitive and exacting and will react against the slightest deviations. Durkheim felt that as this public sentiment grows stronger, persons become more sensitive to their deviations, deviations which until then may have affected them only slightly. On becoming more self-conscious, they react more intensely, and their actions become the object of greater disgrace.

In his early work on crime and delinquency, Tannenbaum (1938: 16–21) likewise explained that as delinquent acts produce increased conflict between the individual and his community, there is a gradual shift from the definition of these specific acts as evil to a definition of the individual as evil, so that all his acts come to be looked upon with suspicion. The person's recognition of this ascription leads to the development of a criminal self concept, and to an identification and integration with a group which shares his activities.

If the processes described by Durkheim and Tannenbaum can be applied to homosexuality, it would follow that societal rejection of homosexuals results in their incorporation of a negative self definition, association in homosexual groups, and the subsequent enculturation to that subculture. It is this general assumption that lies at the basis of this work. What follows is an exposition and further clarification of this assumption.

THE LABELING PROCESS

The first concern is with the process of self definition. More specifically, this aspect of the model deals with the reasons why persons come to view themselves in terms of the societal stereotypes of their deviation. Systematic elaborations of the factors involved in this process are offered in the *interactionist perspective* (or *labeling theory*).[2] Through interaction the individual defines the attitudes of significant others toward him, thus giving their actions meaning. Subsequently internalizing these attitudes, he responds to his own behavior as he perceives others responding. There seem to be several distinct influences involved in this process as it applies to deviance and more particularly to the area of homosexuality.

Like other attributes, homosexual behavior may become a basis for social differentiation and the assignment of status. Because of the negative significance which society and subsequently the homosexual attach to such behavior however, this position often takes precedence over other positions and becomes the *major* source of identification. For this reason, there develops in the individual a heightened awareness of his deviation and a subsequent hypersensitivity to the responses of others. In this situation, otherwise routine interaction becomes problematic and the individual responds intensely to even the most subtle reactions, reactions that often occur in passing encounters and that others themselves are usually less (if at all) aware of. As these responses occur, it becomes increasingly difficult for the individual to maintain conceptions of self based on an integration of his more socially acceptable roles and a restructuring of the self around the deviant role may occur.

The individual's more general identity may also lose validity when others attempt to neutralize their "conflicting information" about him by reinterpreting other aspects of his situation and behavior in terms of his homosexuality. An important effect of this process is for the homosexual to find it increasingly difficult to maintain conceptions of self other than those based on his deviance. This is because such rereading involves a negative redefinition of the otherwise legitimate criteria on which he might base his self definition. As the alternative and more socially acceptable roles are diminished in this manner, the deviant identity comes to have precedence.

Another influence in this process is for the attribute of homosexual inclinations to have a generalized meaning. Thus, people assume that the individual possesses other traits thought to be associated with it. This constellation of negative traits is the cultural stereotype which serves to define the expectations of the homosexual role.[3] Such expectations are often communicated through the use of epithets like "queer," "fairy," and "faggot," as well as through non-verbal language such as winks, shrugs, nudges, and "giving the once-over." Serving as brief definitions of the situation, these responses are perceived by the individual in terms of rejection.

The major factors which appear to be operating in the process of self definition in the case of the homosexual, then, are: a highly salient position; a negative redefinition of other identities through retrospective interpretation; and attributing to homosexuality a distinct deviant role which is defined in terms of a negative stereotype. By employing these factors, a consistent definition of deviance is brought to the otherwise heterogeneous set of elements (i.e., statuses, roles, and behavior) that comprise the life of most homosexuals. In that these factors introduce normative consistency into the situation of the deviant, and ultimately into the interaction that occurs between him and non-deviants, the elements involved in the labeling process may be construed as means by which the members of society justify their proscriptions of homosexual conduct and thereby avoid and reduce cognitive conflict. For the homosexual, however, the labeling process serves to severely limit the roles that he might otherwise assume. Such a restricted role definition, in turn, further prescribes the nature and boundaries of his subsequent interaction. The social psychological impact of all this is for the individual to become engulfed in his deviant role, to define himself almost solely in terms of the cultural expectations attached to that role.

ADAPTING TO STIGMA

The process thus far discussed also has another outcome. That is for the homosexual label to operate as a stigma which produces frustration and a tendency toward some mode of adaptation. These adaptations are not usually rational and systematic processes, but might better be characterized as "semiconscious" attempts at reducing strain.

By drawing from *anomie theory* we can learn more about the causes of strain, as well as of the process of adapting to it.[4] This perspective regards deviance as an adaptation to strain which is brought about by ambivalence toward the normative patterns defining role expectations. This ambivalence occurs when conformity to these expectations is strongly motivated, but difficult to attain. Thus, the degree to which one has as his normative reference groups those who oppose his deviant tendencies is seen as a critical variable intervening between the reactions of others and the kinds of self feelings and behavior that he develops.

If the individual continually measures himself against persons from whom he perceives rejection and persistently looks to them for rewards, he is likely to conceive of himself negatively. Experiencing the subsequent frustration, he may seek out some mode of adaptation. These adaptations will be successful in reducing strain to the extent that they are acceptable in terms of his normative reference group identifications. Therefore, one's reference groups not only determine whether persons will experience strain in relations in which they perceive rejection, but they also determine the adequacy of particular means of adapting to such strain. If persons are to maintain deviant behavior in this situation, the likely mode of adaptation would be to break with former groups and develop new reference groups which accept and reward their deviance. In the case of the homosexual, the experience of strain is likely to result in the termination of relations with straight groups and the development of an intense social involvement with others who have experienced similar difficulty in their relations with this segment of society. Upon coming together they establish a normative system within which they are capable of conformity and the attainment of a more positive status (see Cohen, 1955: 66). Whereas their behavior previously resulted in negative responses, the same behavior is now reinterpreted to serve as a basis of the rewards and upward mobility unattainable in the larger society.

THE ENCULTURATION PROCESS

Since the homosexual community is the only place that homosexuality is fully accepted, the individual often becomes intensely involved with his group. As a result, he tends to readily accept its norms and adopt its behavior patterns. It is through interaction in these groups that he learns many important aspects of the homosexual career. This is an enculturation process similar to that described in *social and cultural support theory*.[5]

Asserting that deviance is learned in interaction with others who have already incorporated these patterns, this perspective focuses on the *systems of social relationships* that facilitate or impede the acquisition of such behavior. An important part of this process is the acquisition of rationalizations for one's deviance. This aspect of the learning serves to insulate the self against societal demands for conformity, enabling the individual to view his deviance in more positive terms and thus to engage in his behavior more freely.

Opportunities to enact the deviant role are also necessary. In other words, learning and justifying the role does not ensure that the individual will ever carry it out. For this he also must have access to appropriate social and cultural environments.

In the case of the homosexual, the "gay" bar provides the kind of social setting in which the individual may both learn and carry out his role. Once he has "come out," that is, identified himself as a homosexual by his presence in this situation, learning proceeds very rapidly. He soon acquires a knowledge of the various meeting places, special language, and social types of homosexuals. He learns the ways of making sexual contacts, the varieties of sexual acts, the methods of concealment, and, in some instances, the techniques of police evasion. As he restricts his social contacts to homosexual groups, he also internalizes the normative patterns of the subculture and subsequently becomes less restrained in his behavior. His preoccupation with homosexual activity may lead to "cruising for one-night stands," public solicitation of strangers, and engaging in narration of his sexual experiences and gossip of sexual exploits (see Leznoff and Westley, 1956 and Hooker, 1967 for a discussion of these and other aspects of the homosexual subculture). In many respects, his behavior begins to concur with the stereotype of the homosexual. This is because the normative system of the subculture partially defines its roles on the basis of the stereotype. Because the homosexual community is comprised largely of persons who have come to define themselves in terms of the stereotype, through their interaction, their conceptions of their roles feed into the normative patterns of the group and eventually come to manifest themselves in the behavior of group members.

As the individual enacts his deviant role, it becomes increasingly necessary for him to validate his behavior. The homosexual community also provides the "rationalizations" that enable him to accomplish this. The necessity of this part of the learning seems to be based in part on the person's inability to *fully* escape societal condemnation and demands for conformity, no matter how deep his involvement in the deviant group. This is because he must also participate in the larger society in order to satisfy his needs and attain many of his goals—goals which are encouraged not only through the general culture, but that are also a part of the normative patterns of the homosexual subculture. The needs for employment, education, and goods and services, and the attainment of a stable marriage relationship, occupational success, and community involvement, all necessitate a high extent of participation in the larger society. Only through "rationalizations" can the individual neutralize the societal definitions and reactions that he encounters in this situation. And only in this way can he continue in his deviant behavior without serious threat to his self concept.

Thus, while the labeling process may result in the development of a stereotypic self definition, the subsequent association in homosexual groups provides the social and cultural support necessary for the individual to become committed to his position and eventually to redefine his role in more positive terms. Not unlike the situation in any other group, then, the normative system of the homosexual community serves in part to validate the behavior of group members. While an important aspect of this collective support may be labeled "rationalizations," the basic process involved here is probably generically the same as that used to validate or justify action associated with any position that brings the individual into conflict with others.

Through interaction with other homosexuals, the individual soon learns the techniques and normative patterns and behavior of the "gay world." More generally, he learns a new way of viewing and dealing with the world around him, a way which is common to that of his associates. In sum, what is occurring in this process is a reevaluation and reinterpretation of his position in light of the new associations (this process is noted by many symbolic interactionists, especially Blumer, 1969). As he receives new input and attaches meaning to it, he is redefining his situation. The meaning given to the new input is influenced both externally from others through interaction and internally from the symbols he himself has acquired from the larger society and must rely on for interpretation. The net effect of this process is a form of action dependent upon his and other homosexuals' conceptions of his role. What is crucial here is that the individual does not enact a role which is not in some way contingent upon the process of interaction itself. While some of the support is derived from the stereotypic and secondary-like interaction within the larger society, the contention here is that a principal part of the learning occurs within the context of the primary group relations of the homosexual community.

This process is most apparent in the case of the individual who has just "come out" and whose role as homosexual is still unsupported by input from primary group associations. At this point in time, his identity and subsequent action are based largely on responses in more impersonal relations and on the internal consideration given to the role from the point of view of role-taking. Thus, rather than bringing to his interaction in homosexual groups a construct in the form of a declarative statement such as "I am a homosexual," he brings to it an interrogatory one such as "I am a homosexual, am I not?" His interaction with other homosexuals within the context of primary group associations, then, provides the external stimuli consistent with his otherwise tentative identification. If the exposure is sufficient, this experience reinforces his identity as a homosexual and gives rise to behavior which is common to other group members. Because the normative patterns of the homosexual subculture validate this identity and behavior, however, a more positive redefinition of the stereotypic role evolves. Thus actions that had previously been engaged in with apprehension and feelings of guilt are now reinterpreted as healthy expressions of one's homosexuality.[6]

If the individual does not perceive being defined and reacted to as deviant, he is not likely to feel a strong need for association in homosexual groups. By maintaining his integration in the larger society, his deviation is likely to stabilize at the primary level. In this instance he would not develop the feelings and behavior of a homosexual in a stereotypic sense. The perceived reactions of others based on the stereotype, on the other hand, result in the incorporation of a stereotypic self definition and the subsequent need for association in the deviant group. It is these associations which seem to be a major link between performing deviant acts (primary deviance) and systematically adopting deviant roles (secondary deviance). We are suggesting, then, that *homosexuals* become secondary deviants as a *result* of problem-solving action. Put another way, in the case of homosexuality, secondary deviance is an *outcome* for persons trying to adapt to the stigma that accompanies the homosexual label (rather than the adaptation itself, as may be the case for non-subcultural forms of deviance, and as is suggested by anomie theorists about deviance generally).

The problem with this kind of adaptation is that the behaviors that are learned in the homosexual community may bring the individual into further conflict with "straight" society. This is a form of external culture conflict, in that the violations of the straight society's norms occur because the homosexual has enculturated to the normative patterns and behavior of his deviant group, but must participate in the larger society to satisfy certain needs and attain certain goals (see Sellin, 1938: 63–70 for a discussion of external culture conflict). This conflict results in the individual's experiencing increased rejection and, at the same time, gives reinforcement to the negative stereotype. The process can continue in a circular manner with the cumulative effect of the negative definitions of deviance and the increased rejection resulting in individuals' becoming more involved in their deviant group and increasingly enculturating to its subculture.

Major Propositions of the Model

In the preceding pages we have attempted to explain the homosexual career pattern of deviance-conformity by bringing together ideas derived from labeling, anomie, and social and cultural support theories. We have dealt with the labeling process and the development of the self definition, anomie and the subsequent process of adapting to strain, and the process of enculturation to secondary deviance through the social and cultural support of the homosexual community.

More specifically, we have argued that the labeling process involves the creation of homosexuality as a salient and discrediting position prescribed in terms of a negative stereotype. Such a definition and the reactions that ensue restrict the alternative roles that the individual may assume, thereby limiting the nature and boundaries of his interaction. The effect is to become engulfed in the deviant role and to define one's self almost entirely in terms of its expectations.

Operating as a stigma, the societal reaction and self-definition then produce stress and the subsequent need for adaptation. In the case of the homosexual, a frequent adaptive outcome is to shift one's reference associations to other homosexuals, to a group whose members have experienced similar difficulties and wherein he is capable of conformity and the attainment of a more positive status.

As the individual receives input from the new associations and attaches meaning to it, he redefines his situation. The result is a form of behavior dependent upon his and other group members' conceptions of the homosexual role. Because those who form these associations are likely to be persons who have come to view themselves in terms of the stereotype, it is this role conception which serves as the basis for behavior. In that the group norms validate the homosexual role, a more positive personal identity is likely to evolve from the interaction.

Toward a Functionalist Interpretation

Implicit in the model is the suggestion that much of the behavior generally associated with homosexuality may be regarded as conforming, rather than deviant, behavior. It conforms both to society's and to the subculture's definition of homosexuality. A question which represents an extrapolation of the approach is "Why does *society* demand such conformity from the homosexual?" A possible answer to this query is offered by *functionalism* (see especially Durkheim, 1904: 65–73; Mead, 1918: 577–602; and Erikson, 1966: 8–19). The functionalist perspective suggests that society defines individuals or specific acts as deviant in order to insure the persistence of the social system. By achieving such a definition it sets up boundaries for the otherwise wide range of human behavior. This establishes a point of reference for non-deviants and facilitates the development of a rationale utilized by them to assert and to reinforce their perception of themselves as superior. The labeling process, then, becomes a way of intensifying the *collective conscience* regarding the behavior in question. As the negative feelings are experienced more vividly, the community gains increased control over its members in regard to this behavior. As Erikson (1966: 13) points out, "Each time the community moves to censure some act of deviation, . . . it sharpens the authority of the violated norm and restates where the boundaries of the group are located." Through such censure then, persons articulate and reassert the primacy of their norms, norms developed through prior interaction and transmitted through the socialization process.

Szasz (1970: 244) aiscusses this idea as it pertains to homosexuality. He asserts that ". . . the homosexual is considered not fully human because he is not heterosexual and therefore . . . undermines the beliefs and values of the dominant group. The male homosexual, by virtue of his homosexuality, refuses to authenticate women as the desirable sex object, and the heterosexual as the unquestionable embodiment of sexual normality." Thus he threatens many of the conventions of the social system. Subsequent action toward the homosexual, then, serves to define heterosexuality as a desired end. Once having taken action, society must then legitimize its position. This is accomplished through stereotyping and the related mechanisms of the labeling process. Such "stereotyping" becomes a way of validating societal action. As Szasz (1970: 256) points out, ". . . the oppressor declares the deviant dangerous or inferior to justify his aggression as self defense." While it is beyond the scope of this analysis, it could be argued that the stereotype and other mechanisms of the labeling process become institutionalized in religious, legal, medical, and other scientific approaches to homosexuality, approaches which in turn give reinforcement to the popular conceptions.

Implicit in the functionalist perspective is the notion that society is organized in such a way as to promote deviance as a resource, that is, to commit persons to long terms of service in deviant roles (see Erikson, 1966: 13–14). If this is in fact an "objective" of society, the informal means by which it is attained in the case of the homosexual may be through the processes discussed in the preceding pages. By defining the individual as homosexual and forcing him to seek refuge in the homosexual community, a self-fulfilling prophecy results in the form of his adoption of a role consistent with the societal definition. Manifesting such behavior, then, serves to insure consensus in the community as to what a homosexual is. Without such persons who could be readily identified as homosexual, the label of homosexual might lack its otherwise salient meaning. Thus the meaning of deviance is reaffirmed in the community as individuals go through this process and enact the deviant role. Accordingly, society sacrifices some of its members in order that the social system may be maintained.

Notes

1. *Secondary deviance,* as a descriptive concept for the deviant roles which result from societal reaction, was first used by Lemert (1951, 1967). According to Lemert (1967: 41) "the secondary

deviant. . . is a person whose life and identity are organized around the facts of deviance." "Deviations remain *primary* deviations or symptomatic and situational as long as they are rationalized or otherwise dealt with as functions of a socially acceptable role. . . [However,] when a person begins to employ his deviant behavior or a role based upon it as a means of defense, attack, or adjustment to the overt and covert problems created by the consequent societal reaction to him, his deviation is secondary" (Lemert, 1951: 75–76).

2. See Cooley (1902), Mead (1934), Thomas (1923), Lemert (1951, 1967), Garfinkel (1956), Kitsuse (1962), Goffman (1963), Becker (1963), Scheff (1966), Scott and Lyman (1968), and Schur (1971).

3. Stereotypic definitions seem to be perpetuated by the truncated form of interaction that results from stereotyping. Such interaction is lacking in interpretation and reinterpretation of symbols based on a continuing process of reciprocal role-taking. Instead, others define the deviant on the basis of the symbols which they bring into the situation. This limits and modifies feedback from the individual and thus renders his role consistent with the preestablished cultural definitions (see Farrell and Morrione, 1974).

4. See Merton (1938), Parsons (1951, Chapter 7); and Cohen (1955, 1959).

5. See particularly Sutherland (1947: 5–9), Glaser (1956), Sykes and Matza (1957) and Cloward and Ohlin (1960).

6. From a functionalist perspective, this process contributes to the continuity and persistence of the homosexual subculture.

References

Becker, Howard S.
   1963   Outsiders. New York: Free Press.
Blumer, Herbert.
   1969   Symbolic Interactionism: Perspective and Method. Englewood Cliffs: Prentice-Hall, Inc.
Cloward, Richard A. and Lloyd E. Ohlin.
   1960   Delinquency and Opportunity. New York: Free Press.
Cohen, Albert C.
   1955   Delinquent Boys. New York: Free Press.
   1959   "The Study of Social Disorganization and Deviant Behavior," in Robert K. Merton, Leonard Broom, and Leonard S. Cottrell (editors), Sociology Today. New York: Basic Books, Inc., 461–484.
Cooley, Charles Horton.
   1902   Human Nature and the Social Order. New York: Charles Scribner's Sons.

Durkheim, Emile.
  1904 The Rules of Sociological Method, trans. Sarah A. Solovay and
  John A. Mueller. New York: Free Press, 1938.
Erikson, Kai T.
  1966 Wayward Puritans: A Study in the Sociology of Deviance. New
  York: John Wiley & Sons, Inc.
Farrell, Ronald A. and Thomas J. Morrione.
  1974 "Social Interaction and Stereotypic Responses to Homosexuals,"
  Archives of Sexual Behavior. 3 (September): 425–442.
Garfinkel, Harold.
  1956 "Conditions of Successful Degradation Ceremonies." American
  Journal of Sociology 61(January): 420–424.
Glaser, Daniel.
  1956 "Criminality Theories and Behavioral Images." American Journal
  of Sociology. 61 (March): 433–444.
Goffman, Erving.
  1963 Stigma: Notes on the Management of Spoiled Identity. Englewood
  Cliffs, N.J.: Prentice-Hall, Inc.
Hooker, Evelyn.
  1967 "The Homosexual Community," in John H. Gagon and William
  Simon (editors), Sexual Deviance. New York: Harper & Row, 167–184.
Kitsuse, John.
  1962 "Societal Reaction to Deviant Behavior: Problems of Theory and
  Method." Social Problems 9 (Winter): 247–256.
Lemert, Edwin M.
  1951 Social Pathology: A Systematic Approach to the Theory of Sociopathic Behavior. New York: McGraw-Hill Book Company.
  1967 Human Deviance, Social Problems and Social Control. Englewood
  Cliffs, N.J.: Prentice-Hall, Inc.
Leznoff, Maurice and William Westley.
  1956 "The Homosexual Community." Social Problems 3 (April): 257–
  263.
Mead, George H.
  1918 "The Psychology of Punitive Justice." American Journal of Sociology 23: 577–602.
  1934 Mind, Self & Society. Chicago: The University of Chicago Press.
Merton, Robert K.
  1938 "Social Structure and Anomie." American Sociological Review 3
  (October): 672–682.
Parsons, Talcott.
  1951 The Social System. New York: Free Press.
Reiss, Ira L.
  1970 "Premarital Sex as Deviant Behavior: An Application of Current
  Approaches to Deviance." American Sociological Review 35 (February):
  78–87.

Scheff, Thomas J.
  1966   Being Mentally Ill. Chicago: Aldine Publishing Company.
Schur, Edwin M.
  1971   Labeling Deviant Behavior: Its Sociological Implications. New York: Harper & Row.
Scott, Marvin B. and Stanford M. Lyman.
  1968   "Paranoia, Homosexuality and Game Theory." Journal of Health and Social Behavior 9 (September): 179–187.
Sellin, Thorsten.
  1938   Culture Conflict and Crime. New York: Social Science Research Council.
Simmons, J. L.
  1965   "Public Stereotypes of Deviants." Social Problems 13 (Fall): 223–232.
Sutherland, Edwin.
  1947   Principles of Criminology. Chicago: J. B. Lippincott Company.
Sykes, Gresham M. and David Matza.
  1957   "Techniques of Neutralization: A Theory of Delinquency." American Sociological Review 22 (December): 664–670.
Szasz, Thomas.
  1970   The Manufacture of Madness. New York: Harper & Row.
Tannenbaum, Frank.
  1938   Crime and the Community. Boston: Ginn and Company.
Thomas, William I.
  1923   The Unadjusted Girl. Boston: Little, Brown and Company.

On the Nature of Deviance

John DeLamater

. . . Reward–cost, or "economic man," formulations of social behavior[1] are beset by a number of conceptual problems, such as the specification of what is rewarding to given persons. Typically, limited to broad generalizations, applicable to most people in the long run, these statements are more useful in *post hoc* applications than in predictive ones. At the same time, however, it seems clear that, unless forced to do so, most people will not repeatedly engage in behavior that has unpleasant consequences. It appears, therefore, that people do employ a dimension of anticipated pleasantness of consequences in selecting behavioral alternatives. Further, these alternatives are usually selected so as to optimize the reward–cost consequences of behavior (as opposed to the maximization of rewards independently of costs); this is a basic assumption in the analysis which follows.

It is also assumed that this principle is equally applicable to deviant and "normal" or socially-approved behavior. Many psychological and some sociological analyses of deviance seem to be trapped by its negative social and moral connotations. Since deviance is bad, disruptive, etc., it follows (in these conceptions) that it is caused by other abnormalities ("evil causes evil"). Thus . . . [drug] . . . addiction, alcoholism, and prostitution

"On the Nature of Deviance" by John DeLamater in *Social Forces* Vol. 46, No. 4, June, 1968, pp. 445–455.

[1] See, for example, John Thibaut and Harold Kelley, *The Social Psychology of Groups* (New York: John Wiley & Sons, 1959).

are attributed to abnormal personalities, and crime to the fact that "racketeers" (who are psychopathic) force others to commit crimes under threat of violence.

The analysts' values have interfered with objectivity in another way. To the extent that one wishes to reduce or eliminate deviance, it is difficult to recognize that such behavior may be highly rewarding. If the causes are also viewed as negative, one simply needs to focus on and remove these; the admission into conceptualization of rewards which can maintain deviant behavior complicates both the analysis and the solution. In any case, the potential rewards of deviance have, by and large, been neglected. What attention has been given them has been scattered and unsystematic. It is the purpose of this paper to indicate what these may be, and an approach to their analysis.

Following Erickson[2] a distinction will be made between behavior that violates norms and the labelling by society of the violator as "deviant." The former will be referred to as *deviance* or *deviant behavior*, and is the major concern of this paper. The *labelling* is taken as problematic; it may or may not occur, and an additional concern is the effects of labelling on the deviator's reward-cost balance. . . .

Deviant Socialization

If one analyzes the background of many deviants, it appears that they were *not originally* socialized into conventional society. In some cases, childhood socialization occurred in a deviant subculture, and was explicitly in terms of deviant (i.e., contraconventional) norms and values. . . .

More frequently, the potential deviant's socialization as a child was simply inadequate or lacking. Either the parents made no attempt to systematically train the child to any set of norms, or there were no parents or other adults available to serve as effective socializing agents (e.g., with children who are raised in institutions). . . . Here, there is simply a failure in socialization; the individual is not exposed to either conventional or deviant norms and values.

In either case, there is no initial commitment to conventional norms and values. As the individual's self-image or identity de-

[2] Kai Erickson, "Notes on the Sociology of Deviance," in Howard Becker (ed.), *The Other Side* (New York: The Free Press of Glencoe, 1964), pp. 9–22.

velops, therefore, it will not be in terms of these, but rather in terms of the standards of those around him.[3] In the first case, parents will be specifically reinforcing an identity based on deviant evaluative standards. In the second, the child's peers become of crucial importance, since they will be the primary determinants of both socialization and self-image. In both cases, as the child grows, peers become increasingly important in providing the child with behavioral alternatives and evaluative standards on which to base his identity. If the individual lives within a deviant subculture peer influences will, in all likelihood, be in the direction of deviance.

Therefore, many persons who become deviant appear to have learned contraconventional means and/or goals and supporting attitudes in their initial socialization. This occurs through the normal process of social learning, and, as suggested by the differential association theory,[4] probably includes the learning of attitudes, values and motivations supportive of deviance. To the extent that these become part of the individual's identity, he will have a fairly strong commitment to their maintenance. This type of learning and socialization prepares the individual for deviant behavior fairly directly; it removes the necessity for him to neutralize conventional norms or withdraw legitimacy attributions from them, eliminates the possibility of guilt feelings with which he would have to deal, etc. . . .

In short, considerable deviant behavior can probably be traced to the transmission, through early socialization, of such behavior and supporting attitudes, motivations, etc., in areas (or from parents) characterized by such patterns. There are few, if any informal reactive sanctions (i.e., those from peers, parents, etc.) in these cases for deviance, and such behavior is quite consistent with the individual's identity. The only potential negative sanction would be through action by formal agencies of social control. To the extent that the deviant can prevent detection and/or punishment by such agencies, or to the extent that they "overlook" the deviance, the rewards (whose specific nature is considered below) will regularly exceed the deprivations resulting from the deviance. Deviant behavior should thus be quite stable and difficult to change.

[3] Cf. Tamotsu Shibutani, "Reference Groups and Social Control," in Arnold Rose (ed.), *Human Behavior and Social Processes* (Boston: Houghton Mifflin Co., 1962), pp. 128–147.

[4] Donald Cressey, "Role Theory, Differential Association and Compulsive Crimes," in *ibid.*, pp. 443–467.

Deviant Resocialization

The deviant resocialization process is the one implied in most existing analyses. Here, the individual is assumed to be initially socialized into conventional or "middle-class" society. He learns socially-approved norms, values and motivations. (Whether he "internalizes" them or not is a moot question.) Similarly, his self-image or identity will be based on conventional standards and evaluations, since it is derived from the reactions of parents and peers who employ these in their evaluations of him.[5] On the basis of this socialization, he behaves more or less conventionally during the period prior to the deviance.

The process by which he becomes deviant begins with some event or experience which leads him to commit the initial deviant act or rule-breaking behavior. Any number of experiences may lead to this initial act. First, he may, in fact, be frustrated in attempts to achieve his goals by conventional means. . . . Similarly, the person may be incapable of meeting conventional standards due to personal or intellectual deficiency. . . . Third, the initial deviance may occur in a situation of intense role or value conflict;[6] by definition, such a conflict can only be resolved by deviating from one, or both set(s) of standards. Various psychological motivations may also lead to an initial deviant act. One such factor may be a strong desire to obtain status or acceptance in some group.[7] . . .

There are thus any number of conditions or experiences which can lead to the initial deviance. Some of these, such as role conflict or differential access to legitimate means, are a direct consequence of social structural arrangements. Others, however, such as the various psychological motivations, inability to meet role demands, etc., are primarily a function of the individual and his interaction with society. Although all of these might be characterized as "failure to achieve goals by conventional means" at one level of abstraction, this overlooks the fact that very different rewards will be involved in deviance due to the different sources.

Given some motivating condition, the deviant alternatives

---

[5] Shibutani, *op. cit.*

[6] Shibutani, *op. cit.*

[7] Albert Cohen and James Short, "Juvenile Delinquency," in Robert Merton and Robert Nisbet (eds.), *Contemporary Social Problems* (New York: Harcourt, Brace and World, 1961).

which are available are culturally determined.[8] Further, as Cloward[9] points out, not all possible alternatives are equally available; the individual's access to illegitimate means may be limited.

The initial deviant act is primarily an individual rather than a social occurrence [10] Due to some experience like those discussed above, the individual commits the deviance, either alone or in the presence of a very few others. During the period following the act, the deviance is often tentative and secret. The person is not committed to it, and if he engages in it again, he does so in such a way that those around him who represent conventional standards are unaware of it. During this period, therefore, he will not experience any negative sanctions from either his primary relations or control agencies. Thus, the rewards will far exceed the costs of the deviance. This is the period which Lemert[11] characterizes as "primary deviation," during which the deviant behavior has had relatively little impact on his identity or role organization. During this time, both the behavior and his interactions are very tentative;[12] each time he engages in the deviance he carefully gauges the reactions of those around him.

This initial phase may have one of at least three outcomes. First, the person may eschew further deviant behavior. This can occur if those with whom he has primary relations discover the deviance and threaten or induce strong sanctions, or if he finds the deviant behavior itself unrewarding. This is possible because he has not committed himself to the deviance; it has not affected his self-image.[13] Second, if he finds the deviance mildly rewarding, and can keep it secret, he may continue to perform it occasionally, when conditions enable him to do so without discovery.[14] This is probably the adaptation which occurs with many types of "individual" deviance, those which can be secretly engaged in by a single person — e.g., alcoholism, fetishism, when the deviant desires to maintain his primary ties with conventional society.

If, however, the deviance itself is very rewarding and/or diffi-

---

[8] Edwin Lemert, *Social Pathology* (New York: McGraw-Hill Book Co., 1951).

[9] Richard Cloward, "Illegitimate Means, Anomie and Deviant Behavior," *American Sociological Review*, 24 (April 1959), pp. 164–176.

[10] Howard Becker, *Outsiders* (New York: The Free Press of Glencoe, 1963).

[11] Lemert, *op. cit.*

[12] Albert Cohen, "The Sociology of the Deviant Act: Anomic Theory and Beyond," *American Sociological Review*, 30 (February 1965).

[13] Lemert, *op. cit.*; Becker, *op. cit.*

[14] Becker, *op. cit.*, describes this outcome in addicts.

cult to keep secret, the person may begin to commit himself to a deviant "career." This decision may be precipitated by either (1) discovery and negative sanctions from those persons with whom he has primary relations in society, or (2) strong pressure from those with whom he has been engaging in the deviance. (Note that this does not refer to formal labelling by society.) Thus, whether the deviance continues depends on the responses of others, both deviants and primary relations, and the reward-cost balance which the individual experiences. If the person decides to adopt the deviance on a regular basis, it then becomes necessary for him to neutralize or remove the control ties preventing it.[15]

An essential part of neutralization, as a number of authors have stressed,[16] is that of changing normative orientation. The individual must replace conventional norms with deviant ones, or develop justification for violating the conventional ones. This is necessary primarily to protect his self-image or identity. If he can justify his deviance, e.g., through "techniques of neutralization,"[17] he can prevent the negative self-evaluation which would occur if he applied conventional standards to his behavior. Similarly, he may adopt a set of deviant attitudes and standards by changing his "normative reference group."[18] Due to the new standards, his identity will change but remain a positive one even though he engages in the deviant behavior. Either of these adjustments will solve what Cohen[19] refers to as "the moral problem."

In one of these two ways, the person must neutralize the conventional norms and values at some point, nullify them as evaluative criteria for his behavior. The rationalization method is the easier of the two, since it is primarily a matter of cognitive learning. It provides (1) reasons why conventional norms and standards are inapplicable in the situation where the deviance occurs, and (2) justifications for the specific deviant behavior which does occur. The latter may include learning the motivations for that behavior[20]

---

[15] *Ibid.*

[16] Richard Cloward and Lloyd Ohlin, *Delinquency and Opportunity* (New York: The Free Press of Glencoe, 1960); and Albert Cohen, "The Study of Social Disorganization and Deviant Behavior," in Robert Merton, et al. (eds.), *Sociology Today* (New York: Basic Books, 1959), pp. 461–484.

[17] Gresham Sykes and David Matza, "Techniques of Neutralization," *American Sociological Review* 22 (December 1957), pp. 664–670.

[18] Shibutani, *op. cit.*

[19] Cohen, in Merton. *op. cit.*

[20] Cf. Cressey, *op. cit.*

as well as the nature of the rewards which can be obtained from it.[21] These learnings may be enough to allow the person to engage in the deviance without precipitating a negative evaluation. Note that this neutralization is highly selective, referring to specific situations and justifying only specific behaviors as acceptable in that situation. It is only through such specificity, perhaps, that either a reorganization of identity or internal conflicts can be prevented.

When such cognitive learning is not enough to solve the problem of negative self-evaluation due to the deviance, the person will have to change a number of his evaluative standards and withdraw his commitment to conventional norms in order to maintain the deviance. He must adopt a set of alternative norms and standards which will both justify the deviance and provide him with a positive self-evaluation. This is a much more extensive process, requiring a change in "normative reference groups,"[22] "status reference groups,"[23] and a reorganization of one's identity. The individual must also break his ties with those persons who represent conventional society in order for this process to occur.[24]

. . . If one of these two adjustments does not occur, the person will either relinquish the deviant behavior, retreat to conventional society and conform,[25] or evidence considerable ambivalence and vacillate back and forth. . . .

Thus, a strong force[26] in preventing deviance is the response or anticipated response of those with whom one has primary relationships. It is for this reason that deviant behavior is facilitated when it can be performed outside of their surveillance. Similarly, this perhaps accounts for the high proportion of "anomic" or "unattached" persons found in deviant subcultures. . . .

Another characteristic noted by several authors is that, between the initial deviant act and commitment to a deviant career, many individuals drift into the "grey areas" of society—such areas as the slums or central city where deviance is prevalent. . . . This geographical movement typically follows (or effects) the cutting of primary ties, and the withdrawal of legitimacy from conventional norms. This relocation provides the link between initial socializa-

---

[21] Cf. Becker, op. cit.

[22] Shibutani, op. cit.

[23] Cohen and Short, op. cit.

[24] Becker, op. cit.

[25] Cohen, in Merton, op. cit.

[26] Perhaps the only major one; cf. Becker, op. cit.

tion into conventional norms and values, and peer group support of deviance. A potential prostitute, drug addict, homosexual, etc., who comes from a "middle-class" background must move into a new environment if he is to obtain access to these illegitimate means and opportunities, to find support from others for such deviance, since it is only in these areas that learning structures and opportunities to play such roles exist.

One can speculate that this necessity of movement plays a part in reducing the number of those found in deviant subcultures who come from conventional backgrounds. Having committed the initial deviant act, and having at least neutralized conventional norms, such a person must still find access to the deviant role before he can commit himself to the behavior. Also, lacking peer support for the deviance in his conventional environment, any negative sanctions applied through primary relations will be more powerful; this itself may prevent further deviance. If it does not, the difficulties of movement to a grey area may serve as a further barrier to the continuation of the deviance, in that the person must know where to go and what to do when he gets there. Finally, once arriving there, he must gain access to the appropriate role structure. . . .

This analysis, therefore, argues that one reason why deviance rates are not as high among those with middle-class backgrounds is low access to deviant learning and opportunity structures. Again, we see that access to such structures is much higher in central city and slum areas. Those who are born and socialized into such areas have ready access to deviant roles; those who are not must move there. . . . This also suggests the hypothesis that conventionally-socialized persons are more likely to adopt individual types of deviance which can be maintained without peer support.

Most contemporary writers on deviance agree that peer support for deviant behavior is an important precondition.[27] A number of factors contribute to its importance. First, deviant behavior and supporting norms, attitudes and motivations are learned, just as conventional ones are.[28] In many cases, this learning occurs through contact with peers. Second, some deviant roles exist and can be played only in an organized role structure, with established and

---

[27] For example, Becker, op. cit.; Marshall Clinard, Sociology of Deviant Behavior (rev. ed.; New York: Holt, Rinehart and Winston, 1963).

[28] Edwin Sutherland and Donald Cressey, Principles of Criminology (6th ed.; New York: J. B. Lippincott Co., 1960).

controlled relations to other supporting roles. Thus, Becker[29] points out that an individual can become an addict only if he has a stable, dependable relation to a supplier of the drug. Similarly, a prostitute has to have a pimp, primarily to protect her from incursions by police and other criminals.[30] Third, peers provide primary relations (or replace broken ones) from which the individual can gain a positive identity and self-esteem. They accept him as a person and support his deviant behavior.[31] Peers are thus a powerful source of interpersonal rewards for the deviant, and, in addition, often provide him with the materials necessary to continue in his deviant role.

These considerations are particularly relevant to deviants who come from conventional backgrounds. They need new definitions, social support, and access to the deviant role structure, whereas those socialized into deviance initially may be able to maintain the role without such support. These comments are also more relevant to certain types of deviancy than others; some deviant behavior—e.g., sexual crimes, alcoholism—are more readily performed alone. Such individual deviance appears to be maintained by using other deviants as a reference group, although some studies indicate that such "loners" are more likely to be apprehended by formal control agencies.

Rewards in Deviance

As noted earlier, the rewards in deviance are only indirectly related to the factors which produce the initial deviance. Where initial socialization is deviant, deviant behavior occurs "naturally," so to speak. Many of the alternative behaviors which the individual has learned are deviant to a greater or lesser degree. It therefore requires no special rewards (or failures) to account for the occurrence of such behavior. However, it is maintained over time by several types of rewards which may accrue to the deviant.

Where original socialization is conventional, on the other hand, some positive or negative experience does appear to be necessary to explain the onset of the deviance. A number of possible ones were considered above. Thus, deviance may result from failure in or lack of access to conventional means of goal achievement,

[29] Becker, *op. cit.*
[30] Harold Greenwald, *The Call Girl* (New York: Ballantine Books, 1958).
[31] Cohen and Short, *op. cit.*

various kinds of role or value conflicts, or other social structural factors. The initial deviant act may also occur due to internal psychological conditions; thus, a desire for status and acceptance, the need to escape from role or other pressures with which the person cannot cope, or the "anomie" produced by the loss of one's ties to conventional society—through death, divorce, etc.—may all produce initial deviance. Given these precipitating events, it would seem that the person will try that deviant alternative(s) which is available *and* which he views as potentially providing an optimal reward-cost balance. Costs here include one's ability to neutralize conventional norms, the amount of "guilt" involved, time and effort necessary, etc.

Once committed to the deviance, through either of the processes described above, the principal rewards which serve to maintain the deviant behavior seem to be the same for both types. Which ones are of most importance in a given case depend on the reasons for the initial deviance, as well as on the type of deviance and the person himself. Thus, different persons may obtain different types of gratification through the same deviant behavior, or the same gratification from different types of deviance. In the discussion which follows, it is not assumed that the deviant himself is consciously aware of these obtained rewards . . .

In any type of group deviance, such as delinquent subcultures, criminal gangs, some . . . [drug] . . . addiction, etc., where the deviant associates with a number of others, one of the strongest rewards is the status and self-esteem which the deviant achieves.[32] The group typically develops a culture, a set of values, ideals and attitudes, which provide status to those engaged in the deviance.[33] With this status and associated positive evaluations from peers, the deviant can develop a positive identity and high self-esteem. He often has friendship if not close personal ties with the members of the group, and also finds these rewarding. Such achieved status and identity may be of primary importance where the initial deviance was caused by a failure to achieve status through conventional means. The deviant behavior itself is of only secondary importance in these cases; the direct rewards are from one's peers and associates rather than from the behavior itself. Any other behavioral route to status might be equally acceptable to the persons involved. These rewards can be self-provided where the initial socialization

[32] *Ibid.*

[33] *Ibid.;* see also Clinard, *op. cit.*

was deviant, since the individual's own (internalized?) standards provide him with esteem for the deviant behavior.

A related type of reward is derived from deviant behavior which allows the individual to resolve status or identity problems. Here, the behavior itself is of somewhat greater importance, since it bears a fairly direct relation to the status problem which initiated it. Thus, teenage drinking may be the result of adolescents' attempts to relate to the adult world. Similarly, sexual promiscuity, before or after marriage, may be due to the person's attempts to prove that he or she is a "man" or a "woman."[34] In these cases, the status rewards accrue as a result of the successful performance of the behavior. Such success is typically culturally defined as an attribute of the desired role or identity (e.g., adulthood or masculinity), as opposed to the first case where the attributes and ideals are defined by the deviant group itself.[35]

A third type of reward is the achievement of various material and success goals. These rewards are probably the principal ones in property crimes and delinquency. Thus, robbery, burglary, confidence games, gambling[36] and prostitution,[37] and some homosexual behavior[38] are all primarily oriented toward the material and monetary gains which can be derived from them. It is to this type of deviance that the failure or inability to attain such goals by legitimate means conception is most relevant. Here, the specific behavior is of intermediate importance, and is primarily determined by the differential in access to illegitimate means which the individual has. To the extent that the rewards sought by the deviant are solely material ones, this type of deviance can occur on an individualistic basis. Where the initial socialization is deviant, these may be the only means to material and success goals which the individual has learned.

A fourth class of rewards is the escape from role or value pressures which some types of deviance provide. This is probably the

[34] Cf. Greenwald, op. cit.

[35] Cf. Harold Finestone, "Cats, Kicks and Color," in Howard Becker (ed.), The Other Side (New York: The Free Press of Glencoe, 1964), pp. 281–297.

[36] Irving Zola, "Observations on Gambling in a Lower-Class Setting," in Becker, op. cit., pp. 247–260.

[37] Cf. Anonymous, Streetwalker (New York: Viking Press, 1960).

[38] Albert Reiss, "The Social Integration of Peers and Queers," in Becker, op. cit., pp. 181–210.

primary reward in most chronic alcoholism,[39] some . . . [drug] . . . addiction,[40] and the psychogenic mental illnesses. With regard to the latter, psychology and psychiatry have long recognized what are termed the "secondary gains" of mental illness.[41] The person who can lay claim to such a condition is excused for past misbehaviors, relieved of many or all role demands, and thus has a much less demanding environment with which to cope. . . .

These, then, appear to be the four primary classes of potential rewards in deviance. They vary as to whether they are derived from the deviance itself or relations with other deviants, and with the type of deviance involved. It is probable that a given person obtains more than one of these from his deviance, in varying combinations and to varying degrees. . . .

The Labelling of the Deviant

Just as the various types of rewards are of differential importance to the two types of deviant, labelling the individual as deviant has differential effects on the two types. Labelling as used here refers to action by a formal agency of social control; the effects of knowledge of the deviance by members of his primary group have been discussed above.

Labelling an individual whose initial socialization was into deviance, and who is thus committed to deviance as a way of life, probably has little effect on him other than to add more or less serious costs to his balance. These costs are primarily associated with deprivation of freedom and other unpleasant aspects of arrest and trial, or hospitalization, etc. The person's socialization has probably insulated him against any rehabilitative effects these costs might have; he will probably view society's reaction as unjustified, and maintain his commitment to the behavior.

With an individual whose initial socialization was conventional, however, the costs associated with labelling may be much higher. The labelling may end the secrecy of his deviance, and thus

[39] Earl Rubington, " 'Failure' as a Heavy Drinker; The Case of the Chronic-Drunkenness Offender on Skid Row," in David Pittman and Charles Snyder (eds.), *Society, Culture and Drinking Patterns* (New York: John Wiley and Sons, 1962), pp. 146–153.

[40] Finestone, *op. cit.*

[41] Ronald White, *The Abnormal Personality* (2d ed.; New York: The Ronald Press, 1956).

his primary relations may be disrupted by it.[42] Second, it may close conventional behavioral alternatives for him; e.g., once it is known that he is an addict, he may be unable to find employment. These two effects, the cutting of primary ties with conventional society and the closing of legitimate alternatives, may produce severe psychological effects for the deviant. In addition, they create a "self-fulfilling prophecy." Without primary relations as a deterrent (or a potential reward) and unable to achieve goals by conventional means, the person may be forced into a deviant career.[43] Also, if the person cannot neutralize conventional norms and standards, he may label himself as a deviant; as a result, he will incur a negative self-evaluation and may perceive his primary relations as being disrupted. Such self-labelling may produce as much of a self-fulfilling prophecy as does labelling by society's agents.

Particularly for the former "middle-class" person, these severe costs that occur when he is labelled may shift his overall balance to one of predominantly costs. The rewards achieved through the deviance may not be sufficient to balance the loss of friends and personal ties which occurs. (The latter may also reintegrate negative self-evaluations.) At the same time, however, the loss of these ties and access to legitimate alternatives can prevent him from relinquishing the deviance; he may be forced to remain in it in order to obtain the rewards of association with others, and perhaps access to money and material goods. To the degree that society refuses to allow him to "repent" and return to conventional life, he will be caught in a situation where the costs far outweigh the rewards. . . . Also, there may be explicit costs, in the form of norms and negative sanctions, associated with leaving the deviance when it is within a deviant subculture.

Thus, labelling seems to have the principal effect of forcing the person to remain deviant in order to obtain even minimal rewards. In some cases, it may cause the person to return (or enter) conventional society, but this can occur only when access to conventional alternatives and primary support for doing so are provided the former deviant. Interestingly, the major route out of prostitution and perhaps other types of deviance as well is the same as the route for the initially conventional person—geographic relocation, usually to another city.[44]

[42] Lemert, *op. cit.*

[43] Becker, *op. cit.*

[44] Greenwald, *op. cit.*

index

Index of Names

Note: Reference to names appearing in footnotes and reference sections is indicated by the letters f and r

Index of Subjects

Printer and Binder: Halliday Lithograph Corporation
81 82 10 9 8 7 6 5